Days of the Lord
THE LITURGICAL YEAR

Days of the Lord

THE LITURGICAL YEAR

Volume 7.

Solemnities and Feasts

 THE LITURGICAL PRESS
Collegeville, Minnesota

The English translation of Volume 7 of this series is by Madeleine Beaumont (pp. 1–172 and respective notes) and Mary Misrahi (pp. 173–317 and respective notes). The original French text of *Days of the Lord* (*Jours du Seigneur*, Brepols: Publications de Saint-André, 1988) was written by the authors of the *Missel dominical de l'assemblée* and *Missel de l'assemblée pour la semaine* under the direction of Robert Gantoy and Romain Swaeles, Benedictines of Saint-André de Clerlande.

ACKNOWLEDGMENTS

Excerpts from the English translation of *Lectionary for Mass* © 1969, 1981, International Committee on English in the Liturgy, Inc. (ICEL); excerpts from the English translation of *The Roman Missal* © 1973, ICEL. All rights reserved.

Scripture selections are taken from the New American Bible *Lectionary for Mass*, © 1970 by the Confraternity of Christian Doctrine, Washington, D.C., and are used by license of said copyright owner. All rights reserved. No part of the New American Bible *Lectionary for Mass* may be reproduced in any form without written permission from the copyright owner.

Scripture quotations are from the *New American Bible with Revised New Testament*, © 1986 Confraternity of Christian Doctrine. The text of the Old Testament in *The New American Bible with Revised New Testament* was published in *The New American Bible*, © 1970 Confraternity of Christian Doctrine. Other quotations, as indicated, are from *The Jerusalem Bible*, © 1966 by Darton, Longman & Todd, Ltd. and Doubleday & Company, Inc.

Cover design by Monica Bokinskie.

LIBRARY OF CONGRESS CATALOGING-IN-PUBLICATION DATA

(Revised for vol. 7)

Days of the Lord.

 Translation of: Jours du Seigneur.
 Includes bibliographical references.
 Contents: v. 1. Season of Advent. Season of Christmas/ Epiphany — v. 2. Lent — [etc.] — v. 7. Solemnities and feasts.
 1. Church year. 2. Catholic Church—Liturgy.
BX1970.J67313 1990   263'.9   90-22253
ISBN 0-8146-1899-5 (v. 1)   ISBN 0-8146-1903-7 (v. 5)
ISBN 0-8146-1900-2 (v. 2)   ISBN 0-8146-1904-5 (v. 6)
ISBN 0-8146-1901-0 (v. 3)   ISBN 0-8146-1905-3 (v. 7)
ISBN 0-8146-1902-9 (v. 4)

Contents

Introduction

The first six volumes of *Days of the Lord* are devoted to the various times of the Liturgical Year[1] and include the solemnities and feasts proper to the periods of Christmas-Epiphany, Lent, and the Easter season.[2] Ordinary Time includes, after Pentecost,[3] three "solemnities of the Lord": Trinity Sunday (Sunday after Pentecost), the Body and Blood of Christ (Sunday after Trinity Sunday), Sacred Heart (Friday after the Second Sunday after Pentecost). These can be considered separately[4] because their celebrations are not integrated, as are the others, into the organic sequence of the Sundays of Ordinary Time.[5]

Of the other twelve solemnities or feasts listed in the Sanctoral Cycle,[6] nine supersede the Sunday liturgy when their date, which is always the same in the calendar, falls on a Sunday: Presentation of the Lord (February 2), Birth of St. John the Baptist (June 24), feast of Saints Peter and Paul, Apostles (June 29), Transfiguration (August 6), Assumption (August 15), Triumph of the Cross (September 14), All Saints (November 1), All Souls (November 2), Dedication of St. John Lateran (November 9). The other three feasts, St. Joseph (March 19), Annunciation (March 25), and the Immaculate Conception (December 8)[7] do not supersede the Sunday liturgy. The first two always occur in Lent. If they fall on a Sunday, they are omitted. If a higher feast occurs on their day, they are moved. If the feast of the Immaculate Conception, which occurs in Advent, falls on a Sunday, it is moved to Monday.

The seventh and last volume of *Days of the Lord* is devoted to these fifteen celebrations to which the liturgy gives a particular importance. The privileged treatment they enjoy is due to the fact that they commemorate especially significant aspects of the mystery of God or Christ or else signal events of salvation history that the "sacrament of the liturgical year"[8] unfolds in the "today" of the Church and the world.

The
Three Solemnities
of Ordinary Time

Trinity Sunday

For many Christians, the Holy Trinity evokes a particularly lofty and impenetrable mystery of the faith, a most abstract dogma, completely apart from daily life, one among those dogmas that least count in their psychology and preoccupations. As a consequence, they find it difficult to grasp the object and interest of the solemnity of the Sunday after Pentecost. Throughout the year, the liturgy celebrates events of our salvation; and so they ask, "Why this exception, and what can be the meaning of this feast?"

In the fourth century, the Church underwent a serious crisis when Arius, a priest of Alexandria who died in 336, denied the divinity of Christ; as a consequence, faith in God, Father, Son, and Holy Spirit, together with the equality of the three divine Persons, was imperiled. The heresy, called Arianism, was successively condemned by the councils of Nicaea (325) and Constantinople (381), which affirmed and formulated the faith in a Creed, the one still recited today at Sunday Mass. But Arianism did not disappear after the two councils. It survived for a long time under various disguises, often more political than theological, but nevertheless endangering Catholic faith. Preaching strove to teach the faithful true doctrine. But liturgy was also pressed into service. Thus, in the middle of the fourth century, someone wrote the preface of the Trinity, which is still found today in the Roman Missal.[1] Around 800, a votive Mass of the Trinity was composed to be used on Sundays to give them a more Trinitarian emphasis.[2] Later on, even before 1000, Benedictine monasteries of Gaul and the Frankish regions celebrated the feast of the Trinity on the Sunday after Pentecost.[3] Therefore, this solemnity was born in a context of controversy. It was instituted as the liturgical expression of the faith in the unity and equality of the three Persons of the Holy Trinity.

> Father, all-powerful and ever-living God,
> we do well always and everywhere to give you thanks.
> We joyfully proclaim our faith
> in the mystery of your Godhead.

You have revealed your glory
as the glory of your Son
and of the Holy Spirit:
three Persons equal in majesty,
undivided in splendor,
yet one Lord, one God,
ever to be adored in your everlasting glory.[4]

For a long time, the Church of Rome was reluctant to adopt such a celebration. Finally, in 1334, it took its place in the calendar of the whole Church under John XXII, the second pope to reside in Avignon (1316–1334). The yearly feast of the Holy Trinity focuses the attention of the faithful on what must never be forgotten when one speaks of the Father, Son, and Holy Spirit and when one reflects on their specific part in the work of salvation: there are three divine Persons, but one God. This is what tradition and Church teaching have constantly proclaimed.

You were baptized in the name of the Trinity. We have respected the mystery of the Trinity in all we have done. Wherever we found the Father, the Son, and the Holy Spirit, we had one operation, one sanctifying action, albeit with some distinctive traits.

How is this possible? It is God who anointed you and the Lord who marked you with a seal and placed the Holy Spirit in your heart . . .

Then you found this particular thing: it is God who called you, while in baptism, it is with Christ that you were crucified in a special manner; afterwards, something special happened when you received the spiritual seal. You see that the Persons are distinct, but that the whole mystery of the Trinity follows from this distinction.[5]

The liturgy expresses in various ways and at every moment our faith in a unique God in three Persons, a fact to which we do not always advert. The prayers at Mass and the Office all end with an invocation—epiclesis—of the Father, Son, and Holy Spirit.[6] The psalmody of the Liturgy of the Hours and the recitation of the rosary are punctuated by "Glory be to the Father and to the Son and to the Holy Spirit." This doxology is developed in the hymn sung at the beginning of Mass to the glory of God the Father almighty, glory shared by Jesus Christ the Lord and the Holy Spirit. The Eucharistic Prayer unfolds according to a Trinitarian scheme and concludes with the great doxology

Through him [Christ],
with him,
in him,
in the unity of the Holy Spirit,

all glory and honor is yours,
almighty Father, for ever and ever.[7]

Thus, the liturgy, like the New Testament, like all the Greek and Latin Fathers before Augustine, has a very concrete and dynamic conception of the three Persons of the Trinity: everything comes from the Father and returns to him through the Son, in the Spirit.[8] Restored to this general and familiar liturgical context, now freed from the polemic and apologetic connotations it had at the time of its institution in the eighth and ninth centuries, the feast of the Holy Trinity acquires its full meaning.[9] Celebrated on the Sunday after Pentecost, it is a great doxology to the Father who raised his Son and brought him into the glory where he reigns with the Holy Spirit he has sent to us. When the sequence of the Sundays in Ordinary Time is about to begin, this feast sheds light on the face and true nature of Jesus, the Son of God, who, by his teaching and his acts, reveals the Father and leads humankind to himself in the Spirit.

> There is a holy and perfect Trinity, acknowledged as God in the Father and the Son and the Holy Spirit. . . . The Father does all things through the Word in the Holy Spirit. Thus the unity of the Holy Trinity is safeguarded and, in the Church, one God "who is above all and through all and in all" (Eph 4:6) is announced; "above all" as Father, principle and source, "through all" through the Word, "in all" in the Holy Spirit.[10]

The Christian assembly confesses this faith when, at the beginning of the liturgy, the priest addresses it saying "The grace of our Lord Jesus Christ and the love of God and the fellowship of the Holy Spirit be with you all."

This God Who Loves Us So

Yahweh, the Lord, God of Tenderness

What humankind knows about God it has learned from God himself and from the experience of the divine action in its midst. This is the fundamental teaching of the Bible. It does not seek to prove the existence of God by reasoning; it does not elaborate on his attributes: it relates how he made himself known, what he said about himself to confidants. These persons were, like all others, struggling with the ups and downs of common human history, whose true meaning and scope the Bible has revealed. "In the beginning," God created man and woman to inhabit the earth and enjoy its riches in order to live happily and forever in the friendship offered by the Creator. The experience of the Exodus was decisive for humankind to perceive the initial design of God and its realization after the entrance of sin into the world. Through the deliverance of the people from slavery, God solemnly and explicitly renewed the proposal of a covenant of which Moses was the unforgettable spokesman. In mysterious face-to-face encounters recorded in the Bible, God revealed to him what humans can understand about his mystery, full knowledge of which is beyond human capacities. Indeed, only God can adequately speak of God. This is what the liturgy of this Trinity Sunday rightly brings to mind by having us read the account of one of these encounters where God revealed himself to Moses (Exod 34:4-6, 8-9).

It is God who convoked Moses on "Mount Sinai," came "down in a cloud and stood with him there." These ways of speaking express in a picturesque and unambiguous manner God's transcendence: he takes the initiative to approach whomever he wants; no one can force the entrance of his abode or oblige him to manifest himself. "Thus the LORD passed before him, and cried out" his name that no one can know without this revelation: "The LORD, the LORD."

This is not the first time this name appears in the Bible: it occurs in particular in the narrative of the vision of the burning bush (Exod 3:13-15). Its primary meaning is difficult to determine with certainty.[1] God's liberation of his people from its slavery in Egypt showed that Yahweh is the one who saves. On the mountain, Moses learned the "why" of this conduct of a God who proclaims himself "a merciful and gracious God, slow to anger and rich in kindness and fidelity."[2] These are the very depths of his identity. The echo of this revelation is found throughout biblical tradition.[3] Numerous prophetic oracles and allegories are the expressive and often moving commentary on this statement of God to Moses.[4] The various currents of piety and mysticism born of the Bible are strongly marked by it. God is the All-Other. He remains the Unknowable whose mystery can never be totally penetrated and must be scrupulously respected. In order to avoid the risk of profanation (see Exod 20:7), Judaism will come to forbid anyone to pronounce the divine name. One will say, "Lord" instead of "Yahweh," and "Heaven," the "Holy," the "Most High," the "Father in Heaven," the Name," the "Place," the "Presence," the "Power," the "Word," instead of "God." Recalling what he himself said to Moses, people today still invoke him by naming the attributes or "measures"—*middot*—of his grace. Adonai [the Lord in Hebrew] is the eternal Being, all-powerful, forgiving, merciful, slow to anger, full of love and justice, "continuing his kindness for a thousand generations, and forgiving wickedness and crime and sin; yet not declaring the guilty guiltless, but punishing children and grandchildren to the third and fourth generation for their fathers' wickedness."[5] After sunset when Yom Kippur has begun, the whole assembly, after having confessed its sin, implores God's grace: "Our Father, our King, forgive us and listen to us. We do few good works, so give us your love, your kindness, and save us."[6] At the beginning of every Eucharist, the Christian assembly, confessing its sin, turns to God's mercy and love, God's most characteristic attributes. It is by creating and recreating humankind, by continually giving it a new heart, that God shows himself all-powerful. The prayer of Moses, who prostrated himself in adoration, will remain, on this earth, that of believers of all times. "If I find favor with you, O LORD, do come along in our company. This is indeed a stiff-necked people; yet pardon our wickedness and sins, and receive us as your own." When he took flesh, the Son of the God of mercy—Emmanuel "which means 'God with us' " (Matt 1:23)—received the name announced by the angel to Joseph: Jesus, which means "he will save his people from their sins" (Matt 1:21). Believers' expectations have been fulfilled beyond all hope, for he is, for us and forever, "the way and the truth and the life" (John 14:6). "The only Son, God, who is at the Father's side, has revealed him" (John 1:18), and taught us to pray to him saying, "Abba, Father."[7]

Nevertheless, God's secret name remains ineffable and his mystery impenetrable. Of course, we may—we must—speak of God, but always with extreme restraint and great humility, never forgetting that he is beyond our words.[8]

> O you, beyond everything,
>   is not this all we can sing about you?
> What hymn, what tongue will express you?
>   No word can speak of you.
> To what can the mind cling?
>   You surpass all intelligence.
> You are the only one who is unutterable,
>   because whatever is said comes from you.
> You are the only one who is unknowable,
>   because whatever is thought comes from you.
> O you, beyond everything,
>   is not this all we can sing about you?[9]

In the last analysis, the best words are those of worship and praise.

> *Glory and praise forever!*
>
> "Blessed are you, O Lord, the God of our fathers,
>   praiseworthy and exalted above all forever;
> And blessed is your holy and glorious name,
>   praiseworthy and exalted above all for all ages.
> Blessed are you in the temple of your holy glory,
>   praiseworthy and glorious above all forever.
> Blessed are you on the throne of your kingdom,
>   praiseworthy and exalted above all forever.
> Blessed are you who look into the depths
>   from your throne upon the cherubim,
>   praiseworthy and exalted above all forever.
> Blessed are you in the firmament of heaven,
>   praiseworthy and glorious forever."
> (Dan 3:52-56)[10]

Love of God, Grace of Christ, Fellowship of the Spirit

"The grace of our Lord Jesus Christ and the love of God and the fellowship of the Holy Spirit be with you all." This greeting, which the priest today addresses to the assembly gathered to celebrate the Eucharist, is taken from the Second Letter of Paul to the Corinthians.[11] But it is quite possible that Paul himself, as a conclusion for his letter, used a set expression already current in the Christian liturgy of his time and therefore familiar to his correspondents. Be that as it may, this precise formulation of the mystery of the Trinity attests the faith professed very early by the Church.[12] Besides, this way of speaking says in a few words how the mystery of the Trinity was revealed and what distinguishes each of the three divine Persons (2 Cor 13:11-13).

Nobody has ever seen God. He has revealed himself not by declarations—his name, Yahweh, remains mysterious—but by his action in the world and by his deeds in favor of humankind. Thus, people learned that he is the all-powerful Savior of those who trust in him and walk in his ways, the sovereign Master of the universe, the Most-High, "merciful and gracious, slow to anger and rich in kindness and fidelity" (Exod 34:6). The unimaginable depths of his love and mercy, the universal character of his saving design were manifested in "the fullness of times" (Eph 1:10) through the Lord Jesus Christ, in whom and by whom "grace and truth came" (John 1:17). He sent from the Father, with whom he is one (see John 10:30), the Spirit, who by its gifts causes believers to share in the very life of God.[13] The Father, the Son, and the Spirit, such are the names of the three Persons of the Trinity manifested by the different part each one plays in the work of salvation. At the heart of this revelation is Jesus Christ, the Word of God made flesh (see John 1:14), the "only Son, God, who is at the Father's side, [and] has revealed him" (John 1:18); he sent the Spirit "that proceeds from the Father" (John 15:26) and guides us "to all truth" (John 16:13).

> The Old Testament clearly proclaimed the Father, more obscurely the Son. The New Testament manifested the Son (see 1 Pet 1:20), and gave a glimpse of the divinity of the Spirit. Nowadays, the Spirit has gained recognition among us and reveals itself more clearly. For it was not prudent to openly proclaim the Son when one did not yet confess the Father's divinity and, when the Son's divinity was not yet recognized, to add the Holy Spirit as an extra burden—to use a somewhat bold expression. Otherwise, overwhelmed by too rich a food and turning to the light of the sun, eyes still too weak, humans would have risked to lose all their possibilities. On the contrary, through partial additions, through ascents according to David's word, through steps forward and progressions "from glory to glory" (2 Cor 3:18), the light of the Trinity will shine more brilliantly.[14]

God does not prove himself; he shows himself.[15] One believes in him; one has the certitude of his existence because one discovers his active presence in the world and in oneself, since one is touched by "the grace of our Lord Jesus Christ and the love of the Father and the fellowship of the Holy Spirit." This is a concrete and personal experience that happens in faith together with other believers.[16]

> Our human fate could be that we should be powerless to say anything, to know anything about you. That we should be impelled by an obscure need to uncertainly turn toward your Being, as plants unconsciously turn toward the light. That we should be incapable of understanding this need and explaining it. Our hunger for your absolute reality would stumble against the impossible and leave us the more destitute as it is the more irreducible. . . .
>
> But you looked at humankind. Not from far above as the powerful of this world do. You did not stoop toward humankind: you became human. On our dusty ways, with this body that everything threatens, with a human face, one of us was you, Jesus Christ.
>
> Some people knew it right away; not the learned persons who know everything about Scripture, not the Doctors who watch over the Law. But the Poor who do not think themselves enlightened: the prostitute, the adulterous woman, the publican, the sinners, and a few rich persons who did not rely on their wealth. Those saw, on a face, the mysterious and eternal Countenance of your love shine through the night in which we would still be if you had not decided to enter it.[17]

Lifting a corner of the veil covering his mystery, the One God revealed himself Father, Son, and Holy Spirit. He did this progressively at first, "in partial and various ways," and finally "in these last days . . . through a son . . . who is the refulgence of his glory / the very imprint of his being" (Heb 1:1-3). This revelation used very concrete ways. For it is by attracting its attention to his action in the world and in human lives that God brings humankind to discover who he is, his true nature, his transcendence, and his nearness. The article of the Creed that proclaims one God in three Persons must be placed on a plane altogether different from that of abstraction and metaphysical reflection. It follows that such a revelation determines, in an equally concrete manner, the relations that believers must have with one another. Created in God's image, humans must live with one another as the three divine Persons live in their unity: in joy, harmony, peace, in mutual encouragement—in order to seek perfection.[18] God himself is peace and joy because, in the communion of the three Persons, nothing is lacking in his fullness and perfection. Humankind inherits these goods with the salvation gained by the Pasch of Christ.[19] It shares in the very life of the God of love who creates among the faithful of the various Churches bonds of deep friendship that Paul urges his correspondents to express by greeting "one another with a holy kiss."[20]

In all cultures where it is a custom, the kiss expresses friendship: restores it, creates it when it is exchanged after a quarrel, a period of estrangement, even a war. Christians have kept this usage and given it an additional meaning and a new efficacy. The kiss exchanged between Christians expresses the charity that unites them in Christ and, at the same time, the shared gift of salvation: the peace that comes from the love of the Father, through the grace of the Lord Jesus, in the fellowship of the Spirit. This has become a liturgical gesture particularly pregnant with meaning, especially at the moment when those who exchange it are about to share the Bread of eternal life and drink the Cup of salvation. Even though they do not know one another, they proclaim themselves brothers and sisters in Christ; they impart to one another, inasmuch as lies in them, the gift of the peace received from the love of the Father, through the grace of Christ, in the fellowship of the Holy Spirit, thus conveying that they reject all that could separate them or even tarnish their mutual charity.[21]

Some of the Fathers of the Church have seen in the Holy Spirit the kiss of the Father and the Son.

> If we are right to think that the Father gives and the Son receives the kiss, we do not err in saying that the kiss itself is the Holy Spirit, that is to say, the one that, between the Father and the Son, is unalterable peace, the strong link, the undivided love, the unbreakable unity.[22]

The mystery of the Trinity reveals what can and must be between all those who have been created in God's image. Each one keeps his or her identity, without confusion, but exists and blossoms only in unity and communion with others, like the Father, the Son, and the Holy Spirit in the unity of the Trinity. The union of love to which believers know they are called has nothing in common with some sort of search for fusion in which the originality—the personality—of each one would be dissolved. On the contrary, the union of charity demands that each one remain unique, irreducibly distinct from the others. It appears most clearly in a diversified community: on the human level—men, women, children, of all ages and walks of life—and on the level of charisms, vocations, and functions. Uniformity is not unity.[23] The mystery of the Trinity, which could appear to express an abstract truth, without real impact on real life, proves to be the foundation of social and ecclesial life.

God So Loved the World That He Sent His Son

Through innumerable initiatives and interventions in the course of the history of the world and humankind, God revealed himself with increasing clarity, giving us intimations that he is at once transcendent and close, close because transcendent. First, people were struck by his omnipotence that nothing or no one could oppose. He rules the universe he created, determines the destiny of nations and peoples, pursues with a supreme freedom and efficacy the plan he has formed from all eternity. No historic vicissitude, no resistance on the part of sinful humanity succeeds in thwarting this plan. When everything seems jeopardized, the dawn of a new day rises: God can derive an unexpected and marvelous good from the worst situation, even from evil. This experience of God's disconcerting conduct awakened in humankind the consciousness of the fact that God's omnipotence is at the service of God's love, and not at the service of a will of tyrannical domination as is seen among the powerful of this world. By sending his Son, God showed that his love surpasses all we can imagine (John 3:16-18).[24]

By taking this inconceivable initiative, God willed to accomplish the salvation of all human beings and the world. To realize this design, ''he gave his only Son.'' ''Gave'' means ''delivered'' and not simply offered as a gift (see Rom 8:32).[25] Besides, when one hears ''only Son,'' one thinks of the episode of the sacrifice of Isaac (Gen 22:1-19).[26] God said to Abraham, ''Take your son Isaac, your only son, whom you love, and go to the land of Moriah. There you shall offer him up as a holocaust on a height that I will point out to you'' (Gen 22:2). Abraham obeyed. God saw that he had not ''withheld'' his son, his ''only son'' (Gen 22:12) and stopped the arm ready to immolate the boy. Very early, the Christian tradition, represented in particular by ancient iconography,[27] saw in this episode a prefiguration of Christ's sacrifice. God did not want Abraham to complete his action and immolate his ''only son.'' But God ''gave'' his own Son in order to save the world. Abraham's obedience and Isaac's self-denial were certainly very meritorious: ''in your descendants all the nations of the earth shall find blessing—all this because you obeyed my command'' (Gen 22:18). But in order to gain eternal life for every person, God had, so to speak, to incur personal risks. This is what he did when he ''gave'' his ''only Son.''

> In this prefiguration of the drama of redemption, it is of the utmost importance for us to see that God demands love, a proof of love in the obedience of the two heroes. We think that Jewish piety had thus understood this episode and that John echoes it when he unveils the act of love it foreshadows. ''God so loved the world that he gave his only Son'' (John 3:16). ''No one has greater love than this, to lay down one's life for one's friends'' (John 15:13). God did not want Isaac's physical suffering or Abraham's moral

suffering, but their love. Thus, John, by showing the open side of Christ, invites us to go beyond the visible sufferings and reach to the "heart" of our redemption, the divine Love incarnate.[28]

God "gave his only Son" so that he could take upon himself the sins of the world. Jesus' obedience to the Father reversed the meaning of death, a consequence of sin. From being a punishment, it became the Pasch of eternal life. For God did not send his Son "to condemn the world" but to show us, in a striking way, that in his love, he wants the salvation of the whole world. We know that true love, disinterested love, is a gift one offers but does not impose.[29] To overlook this offer, not to recognize it when it presents itself, always has serious consequences: one's future, one's life are gravely, sometimes irremediably, affected.[30] When the issue is the love of God, eternal salvation is at stake. Each one is responsible for what happens. It is not God who judges and condemns; it is the individual who, by welcoming Love or refusing it, enters life or withdraws from it.

> What shall we say? A God came here on earth, took on your nature, spoke your language, touched your hand, healed your wounds, raised your dead; what is more, a God delivered himself to bonds and insults of treason, allowed himself to be stripped in public between thieves, to be tied to a post, to be lacerated by blows, to be crowned with thorns; finally he died for you on a cross, and after all this, you think yourselves at liberty to blaspheme and laugh and fearlessly indulge all your sensual cravings. O, cease to be deluded: love is not a game; one is not loved by a God with impunity, one is not loved to the gallows with impunity. It is not justice that is merciless, it is love. We know all too well that love is life or death, and when God's love is at issue, it is eternal life or eternal death.[31]

When God proclaimed his name—Yahweh, the Lord—a long time ago, he enumerated the qualities by which we can always recognize him and to which we can incessantly appeal: "merciful and gracious . . . slow to anger and rich in kindness and fidelity" (First Reading).

This people bound to God by a covenant was, in the course of time, the privileged beneficiary of this conduct on God's part who, faithful to himself and his promises, revealed by his actions and initiatives boundless love and tenderness. When his people turned away from him, he seemed to turn away from them only to help them become aware of their aberration and of the misery resulting from their unfaithfulness. Slow to anger, he never ceased to exhort them to come back to him and accept anew his friendship always offered, his love quick to forgive.

"But when the fullness of time had come,"[32] God put the finishing touch to the revelation of his immense love: he "gave his only Son . . . that the world might be saved through him" (Gospel).

From now on, the "grace of our Lord Jesus Christ and the love of God and the fellowship of the Holy Spirit" remains with those who believe "in the name of God's only Son" (Second Reading).

Such is the mystery of the Holy Trinity, which was revealed to us and which we celebrate with thanksgiving. Already now, it is given us to participate through faith in the life of the Father, the Son, and the Holy Spirit, one God in three Persons. If we live today in peace, harmony, and friendship with all our brothers and sisters, we have the assurance of entering eternal life one day.

> Mystery of the living God
> and of his love for humankind:
> the Most High sends his Son to us
> and reveals himself as our Father;
> Christ exalted in glory
> gives us his Spirit in whom we praise you,
> God who is, who was and who comes![33]

This God Who Gathers Us

God in the Heavens Above and on the Earth Below

Particularly since Vatican II, people willingly speak of the "signs of the times" that one must examine closely and interpret.[1] Biblical authors never used such an expression; however, they perceived the signs of God's presence and action in the events of their history unceasingly reread and meditated. Deuteronomy is a collection of these kinds of reflections, concerning chiefly—as today's text shows—the manifestations of divine power at the time of the Exodus (Deut 4:32-34, 39-40).[2]

In the Bible, questions about the origin of the world are not the first questions. The reflection on the genesis of the universe was elaborated after a rather long experience of God's conduct toward his people.[3] Outstanding persons—Abraham, Jacob, and especially Moses—received extraordinary revelations. But the whole people was able to experience its singular destiny under the leadership of its God. Thus Yahweh appeared not only as a God above others—those invoked by the nations—but as the unique God, the only one who really exists, whereas the others are nothing,[4] or "silver and gold / the handiwork of men" (Ps 115:4).

> They have mouths but speak not;
>   they have eyes but see not;
> They have ears but hear not;
>   they have noses but smell not;
> They have hands but feel not;
>   they have feet but walk not;
>   they utter no sound from their throat.
> (Ps 115:5-7)[5]

"Ask now of the days of old, before your time, ever since God created man upon the earth; ask from one end of the sky to the other: Did anything so great ever happen before? Was it ever heard of? Did a people ever hear the voice of God, and live?" (Deut 4:32-33). At the time of the great manifestation on Sinai, the entire people had this unheard of and stupendous experience of the familiarity and nearness of the Most High (Deut 5:24). Coming as it did after the events of the coming out of Egypt, this theophany confirmed in a striking way the sovereign freedom of God and the gratuitousness of his choice. "Did any god venture to go and take a nation for himself from the midst of another nation, by testings, by signs and wonders, by war, with his strong hand and outstretched arm, and by great terrors . . . ?" (Deut 4:34). The memory of that time remains even today the foundation of faith and hope. What we call the Old Testament belongs to our history. "This is why you must now know, and fix in your heart, that the LORD is God in the heavens above and on earth below, and that there is no other" (Deut 4:39).

Facts often seem to give the lie to God's power and solicitude. In the psalms, there are numerous echoes of the doubt that threatens to work its way into the believers' minds. In order to rout the temptation, we must turn to God and make so bold as to say to him, like Jesus on the cross, "My God, my God, why have you forsaken me?" (Ps 22:1). By appealing to the Lord's promises and faithfulness, by recalling his former interventions—in particular those at the time of the Exodus—those heart-rending cries, which are still today our prayer, end with a new surge of hope and an affirmation of attachment to God, whose faithfulness cannot be doubted.[6] For the recognition of God implies a lifelong commitment on the believer's part. "You must keep his statutes and commandments which I enjoin on you today, that you and your children after you may prosper, and that you may have long life on the land which the LORD, your God, is giving you forever" (Deut 4:40). To remain, whatever the cost, on this way of obedience to God is often the last resource of humans about to be broken by trials, "Not my will but yours be done" (Luke 22:42). The meaning of events will be manifested only little by little, for it is always in the depths of history that God reveals himself and that we must discern his presence.

> The Church has always had the duty of scrutinizing the signs of the times and of interpreting them in the light of the gospel. Thus, in language intelligible to each generation, she can respond to the perennial questions which men [and women] ask about the present life and the life to come, and about the relationship of the one to the other. . . .
>
> The people of God believes that it is led by the Spirit of the Lord, who fills the earth. Motivated by this faith, it labors to decipher authentic signs of God's presence and purpose in the happenings, needs, and desires in which this people has a part along with other men [and women] of our age.[7]

Likewise, by his acts and words, Jesus of Nazareth revealed the mystery of his person as Son of God. In the same way, by what it accomplished,

believers recognized the coming of the Spirit which the Lord had promised
to send from the Father: "You who are Jews, indeed all of you staying
in Jerusalem. Let this be known to you, and listen to my words. . . .
This is what was spoken through the prophet Joel: 'It will come to pass
in the last days,' God says, / 'that I will pour out a portion of my spirit
upon all flesh' " (Acts 2:14, 16-17).

Happy the people the Lord has chosen to be his own.

Upright is the word of the LORD,
  and all his works are trustworthy.
He loves justice and right;
  of the kindness of the LORD the earth is full.
By the word of the LORD the heavens were made;
  by the breath of his mouth all their host.

———————

For he spoke, and it was made;
  he commanded, and it stood forth.

———————

But see, the eyes of the LORD are upon those who fear him,
  upon those who hope for his kindness,
To deliver them from death
  and preserve them in spite of famine.
Our soul waits for the LORD,
  who is our help and our shield.

———————

May your kindness, O LORD, be upon us
  who have put our hope in you.
(Ps 33:4-6, 9, 18-20, 22)

Children of God in the Spirit, Heirs with Christ

Among the three Persons of the Trinity, the Spirit is the most mysterious, almost by definition. It does not have any face, it does not use words
but an ineffable language.[8] It acts in secret in the depths of the human
heart and in the most hidden center of the realities of the world. But paradoxically, the Holy Spirit is the one Person of the Trinity with whom we
are—whether or not we attend to the fact—most frequently and most concretely in contact, and this in spite of its elusive nature that defies all
representation. Indeed, nothing happens in the world, in the Church,
in the liturgy, for the good and salvation of every believer, without the
Spirit's acting in a necessary, direct, and decisive way.[9] We are often able
to detect its invisible presence and action, sometimes even clearly, in the

most ordinary circumstances of daily life. But even though they may be striking, the gifts and fruits of the Spirit can be discovered only in faith. This is even truer when we speak of the radical transformation that its action produces in believers, which is the first and most fundamental of its missions in their regard (Rom 8:14-17).

In the same way God revealed himself by acting in the world, the Holy Spirit manifested itself by what it worked in Jesus, beginning with the solemn investiture of the Son of God at his baptism on the banks of the Jordan.[10] It was with him throughout his ministry.[11] However, it is at the time of Easter that the role of the Holy Spirit appears in full light to believers. For God "raised the Lord" (1 Cor 6:14) by the Spirit's power (see Rom 8:11). Through baptism, "the bath of rebirth / and renewal by the holy Spirit" (Titus 3:5), we "were indeed buried with him through baptism into death, so that, just as Christ was raised from the dead by the glory of the Father, we too might live in newness of life" (Rom 6:4). The Spirit has made us children; it leads us.

> When the Spirit comes in human beings, it frees them, renews them, and familiarly dwells in them. The entire interior life of these persons is transformed, and they experience this radical reversal of forces. The flesh ceases to dominate in every instance, despite the heartrending call of their enslaved minds; it is vanquished in its turn. Another force, another life shows itself by its inner fruits of a divine taste. They feel in themselves a steady certitude, lights, calls, desires full of fervor, pain and tenderness, an orientation and an urge at once habitual and deep. *They have the obscure experience of the Spirit.* Experience of the Spirit not in itself, but in these effects and signs that reveal it because they mold humans in its image. Let us say, in a word, that they experience the Spirit in the immense aspiration that it arouses in the soul. For the soul walking from faith to faith and from glory to glory becomes more and more sensitive to these light motions of the Spirit that themselves become deeper and deeper and more and more revealing. The Spirit of the perfect Son, divine filiation, becomes familiar to Christians, and, having been patiently taught, they finally enter in possession of "the sense and the instinct of the Holy Spirit."[12]

The certitude of really being children of God (see 1 John 3:1) is based on the witness that the Spirit bears "with our spirit." In other words, it is a certitude of faith. This is shown in the way we address God in prayer inspired by the Spirit. We say "Abba," a term that expresses respect and familiarity. This is what Jesus called his Father (and ours) in Gethsemane (Mark 14:36).[13]

> In this perspective, we can say that Christian prayer is, so to speak, God's tongue, which he patiently teaches us in the course of our lives. True, when

we pray, we are doing the talking. But who has formed this word on our lips and still more in our hearts? It is God who teaches us his language. Likewise the newborn cannot speak. It is its mother who awakens it to speech by speaking to it. She calls the infant and her call forms a word in it, the word which is its response. And the infant answers in its mother's tongue, in its mother tongue. The same is true of God and humans newly born to grace, reborn of God's Holy Spirit. God acted first, God spoke first and, under the action of his Word heard at last, the soul understood that it was adopted, that God was alive and was listening, and it spoke in its turn. But this word, which is prayer, was at bottom the very language of God that the soul was haltingly speaking when it pronounced the sacred Name: Abba, Father. And it is in this way that God, through the prayer he calls forth in our hearts, teaches us his language all our lives.[14]

The fact that we are adopted children makes us ''heirs of God and joint heirs with Christ,'' called to share eternal life with him in the glory to which he has been raised after his Pasch. Adoption results from a free and gratuitous choice on the part of the person who confers on a stranger the title and rights of a child. Being an heir entails the possession of goods to which the adopted person could otherwise claim no right. By speaking in this way, Paul stressed the absolute gratuitousness of the salvation granted by God, a fact of which Christian converts from paganism had to have been especially conscious, a point of doctrine on which Paul particularly insisted in the Letter to the Romans.[15]

Having become children of God by grace, called to be glorified with Christ, the Lord's disciples are, by the very fact of their election, involved in the completion of the ongoing work of Christ in the world. Such a responsibility, which no one can shirk without unfaithfulness, cannot be assumed without exposing oneself to persecution. All those sent by God have known this fate (Matt 23:34-37). Jesus died for having been uncompromisingly faithful to the mission entrusted to him by the Father and for having freely accepted and fulfilled it to the end. To ''suffer with him'' is not a mere condition—imposed, as it were, from the outside—in order to some day share in the glory of his resurrection. It is, in truth, a demand inseparable from discipleship. Jesus went so far as to declare blessed those who are insulted, persecuted, slandered on his account (see Matt 5:12); all this means that they really are his disciples. Christians do not accept suffering because they are masochists or desirous of paying the price of future bliss. They bear in their bodies ''the marks of Jesus'' (Gal 6:17). They say with Paul, ''In my flesh I am filling up what is lacking in the afflictions of Christ on behalf of his body, which is the church'' (Col 1:24). The Lord did not leave his work unfinished, but he entrusted it to his disciples so that through their preaching and their witness, all people might receive its benefits.

At the same time, one cannot live in a manner becoming God's children without putting to death the evil passions that lead to sin (see Rom 8:13). This daily struggle costs us suffering and all sorts of heartbreaks. It also obliges us to make choices, to embrace ways of life opposed to those of the world. The world, which poorly tolerates this form of contestation, retaliates by casting doubts on the honesty of behaviors it deems abnormal and dangerous; it attempts by every means possible, including violence, to bring the delinquents back to a conduct in accord with its norms.[16] The Holy Spirit enables Christians and the Church to fearlessly confront these contradictions, and its presence affords overflowing encouragement (see 2 Cor 1:5) to those the world rejects; it even grants them to love their enemies and pray for their persecutors (see Matt 5:44).

> Therefore, hasten to receive the Spirit
> that comes from God, the divine Spirit,
> in order to become such
> as I have explained,
> heavenly and divine,
> you of whom the Master spoke,
> in order to become also
> heirs of the kingdom of heaven forever. . . .
> Therefore run with ardor, run, all of you,
> in order to be judged worthy
> to reside within the kingdom of heaven
> and to reign with Christ,
> the master of all,
> to whom is due all glory,
> with the Father and the Spirit,
> forever and ever. Amen.[17]

In the Name of the Father, and of the Son, and of the Holy Spirit

To the assembly gathered on this Sunday to celebrate the feast of the Holy Trinity, the liturgy presents the majestic and solemn scene that, icon-like, concludes Matthew's Gospel (Matt 28:16-20).[18]

At Easter time, "the eleven disciples went to Galilee, to the mountain to which Jesus had ordered them." At first sight, this sentence seems banal; however, it is full of meaning. In the Bible, the "mountain" evokes one of the privileged places where revelation happens. It was on "the mountain" that, according to Matthew, Jesus promulgated the charter of the kingdom (Matt 5:1); on "a high mountain" that he was transfigured in front of Peter, James, and John (Matt 17:1). And now, for the last time, he convokes them on a mountain: there, he shows himself in his risen state[19] and solemnly installs them as his messengers.

It is equally worthy of attention that this last rendezvous happened in Galilee. It is in Galilee that Jesus began to preach the kingdom of God (Matt 4:12-17), that he called his first disciples to make them "fishers of men" (Matt 4:18-22), that he walked the ways and byways leading his disciples (Matt 4:23-24) and gathered around himself large crowds that had come not only from the region but also from "the Decapolis, Jerusalem, and Judea, and from beyond the Jordan" (Matt 4:25).

Seeing the Lord, the disciples silently worshiped him. In Matthew's Gospel, this prostration is the proper way to show one's respect toward Christ whom one has approached.[20] The gesture always has a definite liturgical connotation, particularly emphasized here. To silently worship the Lord is to behave as before the God one adores. It is a gesture of faith that overcomes all doubts: "Lord, you know everything; you know that I believe, help my unbelief" (see Mark 9:24; Luke 17:5; John 21:17). Then Jesus came near his disciples and told them, "All power in heaven and on earth has been given to me." As he had foretold during his trial (Matt 26:64), the risen Christ, already enthroned at the right hand of the Most High, manifested himself to his disciples as the Son of Man foreseen by the prophet Daniel (Dan 7:13).

> God greatly exalted him
> and bestowed on him the name
> that is above every name,
>   that at the name of Jesus[21]
> every knee should bend,
> of those in heaven and on earth and under the earth,
>   and every tongue confess that
> Jesus Christ is Lord,
> to the glory of the Father.
> (Phil 2:9-11)

The apostles' mission has a triple object. "Go, therefore, and make disciples of all the nations." Jesus is "the way and the truth and the life" (John 14:6). One must follow him, become his disciple, in order to share in his Pasch. This is what the apostles proclaim in Jerusalem immediately after Pentecost, "God has made him both Lord and Messiah" (Acts 2:36). And when questioned about the miracles the apostles work, Peter declares, "There is no salvation through anyone else, nor is there any other name under heaven given to the human race by which we are to be saved" (Acts 4:12). From now on,[22] through Christ and thanks to the universal mission entrusted to the apostles and the Church,[23] access to salvation is open to all peoples and nations, truly and without restriction. All begins with this announcement of universal salvation by Christ.

Baptize "them in the name of the Father, and of the Son, and of the holy Spirit." From the very beginning of the Church, baptism has been conferred on those who, welcoming the Word, recognize in Jesus the Lord and the Christ dead and risen for the salvation of all humans. Paul's letters in particular attest to an already well-developed reflection on this sacrament of faith—its meaning, effects, demands.[24] The rite is far from being Christian in its origins. The symbolism of water as a sign of life and purification is self-evident. Ritual baths, cleansing ablutions are found in all religions before and after Christianity.[25] Immediately before Jesus, John preached and gave "a baptism of repentance."[26] The baptism given by the apostles and disciples was from the beginning distinct from it.[27] For, being a "baptism of faith," it establishes new believers in a close relationship, a personal relationship, with the Name of Jesus, that is to say, with his person,[28] through participation in his paschal mystery. "You were buried with him in baptism, in which you were also raised with him through faith in the power of God, who raised him from the dead" (Col 2:12). Through him, with him, and in him, baptized persons are born to a new life, that of the three Persons of the Trinity. This is the reason baptism is conferred "in the name of the Father, and of the Son, and of the Holy Spirit." This profession of Trinitarian faith, explicitly formulated for the first time in Matthew's Gospel, rapidly imposed itself in the Church for the administration of baptism. What can appear today as a rather abstract expression must, on the contrary, be understood in a very concrete sense: "the life and work of Jesus are the life and work of the Father in the Spirit"[29] and we have a share in it. The ancient baptismal rite was very expressive from this point of view. Three questions were asked of those about to be baptized: "Do you believe in God the Father?" "Do you believe in Jesus Christ his Son?" "Do you believe in the Holy Spirit?" And at each response, the catechumens were plunged into the baptismal water.[30] The apostles are sent to give the "baptism of rebirth" to those who welcome the good news and are converted to the Lord.

Teach "them to observe all that I have commanded you." This is the third responsibility assigned to the apostles. The converts must not be left to themselves after their baptism. The apostles have the responsibility to help them progress in faith throughout their lives. This aspect of the mission constitutes a strict duty for missionaries of the Gospel and a right for new Christians. Paul's journeys and the apostolic writings prove that from the beginning of the Church, those who have been sent by the Lord have thus understood and assumed their responsibilities toward the faithful and the Christian communities. The object of this teaching is not limited to what is called "the truths of faith." It is also the education of believers in the duties of daily life. Baptized persons must learn to live as Christians, behave as children of the heavenly Father, and allow themselves to be led by the Spirit. Matthew particularly insisted on this point: we cannot rest content with welcoming in faith Jesus' teaching; we must put it into practice.[31] Likewise, Paul's letters underscore the same teaching in a striking way. They frequently remind the addressees of both the good news, which was the cause of their conversion to Christ, and of the baptism they have received; they contain doctrinal developments whose aim is always to show Christians how they must live. To believe in the gospel entails a new way of life that is based on what Christ taught and is a consequence of the transformation effected in believers at baptism. Jesus himself said, "Not everyone who says to me, 'Lord, Lord,' will enter the kingdom of heaven, but only the one who does the will of my Father in heaven" (Matt 7:21). The various New Testament writings reiterate, each one in its own way, this solemn warning: "Be doers of the word and not hearers only, deluding yourselves" (Jas 1:22); "faith without works is dead" (Jas 2:26). "Behold, I am coming soon. I bring with me the recompense I will give to each according to his deeds" (Rev 22:12).

The manifestation of the risen One on the mountain in Galilee ends with a promise, "And behold, I am with you always, until the end of the age." This word brings into relief the ecclesial significance of the narrative and, beyond, of the whole of Matthew's Gospel that it concludes.

Jesus came into the world and gave his life "to gather into one the dispersed children of God" (John 11:52). After his resurrection, he gathered the Eleven in order to charge them with the mission of realizing this plan. The first announcement of the good news calls people to a conversion that, after a first initiation, is ratified by baptism and the gift of the Spirit. Finally comes the catechesis that must be permanent.[32]

> The Church announces the good tidings of salvation to those who do not believe, so that all men [and women] may know the true God and Jesus Christ whom he has sent, and may repent and mend their ways. To believers also, the Church must ever preach faith and repentance. She must

prepare them for the sacraments, teach them to observe all that Christ has commanded, and win them to all the works of charity, piety, and the apostolate. For all these activities make it clear that Christ's faithful, though not of this world, are the light of the world and give glory to the Father in the sight of men [and women].[33]

Such is the triple dimension of the mission entrusted to the apostles and the Church by the risen Christ. None of these three elements may be neglected. Each one is linked to the other two, not as three phases to go through in succession, but as the three parts of an indivisible whole. In order to enable his own to accomplish this task in spite of their weakness and lack of faith, the Lord is "always" with them "until the end of the age." "But we hold this treasure in earthen vessels, that the surpassing power may be of God and not from us" (2 Cor 4:7). "Until the end of the age," the Church, "coming forth from the eternal Father's love, founded in time by Christ the Redeemer, and made one in the Holy Spirit,"[34] is the image of the Holy Trinity and the place where the three divine Persons work as one for the salvation of the whole world.

The fact that the mystery of the Holy Trinity is celebrated could lead us, in the liturgy of this Sunday, to remember only the Trinitarian formula recorded in the Gospel along with the order to baptize all nations given by Jesus to the apostles. However, it is not unimportant for today's Christians to recall the stages through which faith in a unique God passed (First Reading).

Israel progressively acceded to this faith by reflecting on its own history and by becoming increasingly conscious of the relationship that united it to its God. Such a journey still keeps all its value, for God continues to reveal himself by the way he acts in the world, particularly in the community of believers. But it is necessary to be attentive to the signs of his presence and to the testimony of the Spirit that "bears witness with our spirit that we are children of God" (Second Reading).

To announce the good news to all humans, to call them to conversion and baptism "in the name of the Father, and of the Son, and of the Holy Spirit," to teach them to observe the commandments given by the Lord, such is the mission of the Church and of each Christian according to each one's vocation and charisms (Gospel).

Blessed be God, the eternal Father,
Watching from his doorstep,
And extending his arms to his children, lost and found.
He has committed the whole universe
To the Son and the Spirit,

And his two hands have only one immense task:
To carry us to the secret of his face.

Praise to the Son, light of truth,
In him the love of God gives itself,
Open space, boundless land,
But always with the cross at the entrance.
His whole desire, in self-forgetfulness,
Is to be only
The source of the Spirit and the reflection of the Father
For all those who perceive his mystery.

Let us sing the Spirit, fountain of freedom,
In our hearts, it is a murmur
Of water that washes and transfigures
Those who, one day, will live a risen life.
Its whole desire, in self-forgetfulness,
Is to be only
Total transparency to the Father in his glory,
And presence of Jesus in his victory.[35]

This God
We Constantly Await

Wisdom Who Is with God Before All Ages

The Old Testament texts that speak of wisdom evoke now a quality humans acquire through education, experience, reflection, or as a gift from heaven, now an attribute of God.[1] Divine wisdom appears to be so transcendent to those who describe it that they often identify it with God himself or personify it without, however, compromising the strict monotheism of biblical faith.[2] This is the case with the passage from the Book of Proverbs we read today; a text especially well-written, in rhymes, and with a warmth that makes it a vibrant though restrained praise presenting Wisdom in a truly seductive way (Prov 8:22-31).[3]

As a great lady, Wisdom herself describes her high origin with this admirable blend of a natural simplicity and a pride devoid of ostentation that manifests an exquisite and rare nobility of soul. What she is comes from the Lord. It is he who made her before anything else: ''his prodigies of long ago,'' ''the earth,'' the ''fountains or springs of water,'' ''the mountains,'' ''the hills,'' ''the fields,'' ''the first clods of the world.'' It is he who brought her forth ''from of old,'' ''when there were no depths.'' But what is the origin of Wisdom? Was she ''brought forth'' from all eternity by God or ''created'' by him before other creatures? The vocabulary employed in this text does not allow a precise answer,[4] and this sort of question is not on the author's mind. For the Semitic mentality is not philosophical in our terms: ''it thinks of eternity in terms of time. This divine time in some way exists before the historical time that the Bible sees as beginning with the creative act.''[5] To situate the origin of Wisdom before this beginning, to present her as the first fruit of the divine activity, before the work of creation, is to strongly suggest her absolute preeminence over everything and to emphasize that she owes her existence to the sole initiative of God. The ''Song of Moses'' speaks in similar terms of the chosen people when Moses calls to the people, saying, ''Is he not your father who created you? / Has he not made you and es-

tablished you?'' (Deut 32:6). We must not require of this text answers
to questions that are totally outside its purview. On the other hand, we
may profitably reread it because it is remarkably apt in expressing other
realities.[6]

Speaking not only according to the conceptions of the time—the earth
seen as a solid platform surrounded by the ocean and holding the vault
of heaven that contains water in reserve for rain[7]—but also in the time-
less language of poetry, the Bible describes the work of creation as that
of an architect who builds a house in a vast barren domain that he begins
to mark out and clear. Now while God was doing all these things, Wisdom was ''beside him.'' In order to express this proximity and intimacy,
the author of Proverbs juxtaposed two images equally evocative.[8] The
author first depicted wisdom as God's artisan at his side, that is, as an
associate of the Creator, his co-worker and inspirer—in sum, as a signa-
tory party to the completed work. But Wisdom also says, ''I was his delight day by day, / Playing before him all the while.'' Wisdom paints
herself here as a child happy and proud to be with its parent at work;
for children, it is a marvelous game, for they have the impression of being part of what is taking shape before their eyes. This bright image suggests a great and affectionate nearness between Wisdom and the Creator.
Finally, Wisdom shares in the joy and admiration of humankind as it discovers in its turn the wonders of the creation that came out of the hands
of God who, for his part, delights in the joy his work causes.

> I danced in the morning when the world was begun,
> And I danced in the moon and the stars and the sun,
> And I came down from heaven and I danced on the earth;
> At Bethlehem I had my birth.
>
> Dance then wherever you may be;
> I am the Lord of the Dance, said he,
> And I'll lead you all, wherever you may be,
> And I'll lead you all in the dance, said he.[9]

The contemplation of the universe reveals to believers' eyes the wisdom
with which God created all things as if in play and invites them to share
in the joy that he himself felt at the sight of the work of his hands: ''God
looked at everything he had made, and he found it very good'' (Gen 1:31).
When designing and organizing this great domain—this immense
garden—with admirable harmony, he was thinking, in his wisdom, of
humankind to whom he intended to entrust it for its delight. God knew,
however, what would happen: the plan of salvation he conceived to re-

store what sin ruined is not a plan elaborated because of the failure of his initial design. When creating the universe, he already had in view the Savior he would some day send; what is more, he had him beside him "from of old . . . at the first." The author of the Book of Proverbs did not see so far: the meaning, the scope, the depth of the revelation gradually became clearer with the succession of God's admirable and surprising initiatives. The first of these was the creation that forcefully manifested a transcendent Wisdom whose true name will be learned only in the future.

> O Lord, our God,
> how wonderful is your name in all the earth!

> When I behold your heavens, the work of your fingers,
>   the moon and the stars which you set in place—
> What is man that you should be mindful of him,
>   or the son of man that you should care for him?
> You have made him little less than the angels,
>   and crowned him with glory and honor.
> You have given him rule over the works of your hands,
>   putting all things under his feet:
> All sheep and oxen,
>   yes, and the beasts of the field,
> The birds of the air, the fishes of the sea,
>   and whatever swims the paths of the seas.
> (Ps 8:4-9)

Just Persons in Peace with God, Through Christ, in the Spirit

For Paul, human history was divided into two clearly distinct periods: before and after Christ. During the first, human beings were slaves of sin, from whose bondage they hoped to be liberated. With the coming and the Pasch of the Lord, a new era began: salvation gained for all and open to all through faith, a faith that radically changes believers' condition and gives a completely new meaning to their lives (Rom 5:1-5).[10]

"We have been justified by faith." This affirmation is central in Paul's thought, preaching, and theology. Justice does not come from good works but from an absolutely gratuitous gift; it takes its source in the initiative of God, who alone can make us just. Paul learned this from experience. "Circumcised on the eighth day, of the race of Israel, of the tribe of Benjamin, a Hebrew of Hebrew parentage, in observance of the law a Pharisee" (Phil 3:5).[11] He was thrown down on the way to Damascus as he was going to that city in order to cast into prison the Lord's disciples.[12] It was not for having sought Christ that he encountered him! Obviously, he owed everything to the free divine initiative: "God, who from my mother's womb had set me apart and called me through his grace, was pleased to reveal his Son to me" (Gal 1:15-16). Whatever our personal histories, we all can attest to a similar experience. To be born in a Christian family and in Christian surroundings, to receive a religious education, to persevere in that way in spite of crises and contrary to so many others who leave it, to come back to it after straying for a time, be it short or long, to be converted . . . are as many graces manifestly not acquired through personal merits. A certain number of specific occasions may be recalled that have influenced or determined this itinerary. But on reflection, we see that it is God's grace which is the last and true explanation of everything.[13]

Faith in Christ establishes us in God's peace, that is, in relationships of friendship and trust that are shown by all sorts of benefactions, culminating in participation in "the glory of God." However, we possess this ultimate gift only in hope. Nevertheless, it is our "boast." Such an expression may surprise us, but it does not contradict in the least what Paul just said—on the contrary. What we are already now—in "peace with God"—we owe solely to divine grace and not to any personal merit whatsoever.[14] Likewise, our hope rests on God alone. Our situation is indeed paradoxical. We are already "children of God, and if children, then heirs, heirs of God and joint heirs with Christ. . . . " It is the Spirit itself that bears witness to this (Rom 8:14-17). But this is to be revealed in the future when, by the resurrection of our bodies, we shall be transfigured. To "boast" of what one already is and of what one hopes to become is to give glory to God to whom we owe everything. As a consequence, whatever joys, pleasures, and immediate advantages the world can offer are of no account. "I even consider everything as a loss because of the supreme good of knowing Christ Jesus my Lord" (Phil 3:8).

> The true and even the only peace of souls in this world consists in being filled with divine love and moved by the hope of heaven, to the point of regarding as trifles the successes or failures of this world, of rejecting earthly desires, of renouncing the greed of this age, and of rejoicing in insults and persecutions suffered for Christ. Then we will be able to say with Paul, "We boast in hope of the glory of God" (Rom 5:2).[15]

"Not only that, but we even boast of our afflictions, knowing that affliction produces endurance, and endurance produces proven character, and proven character, hope." It is a fact that well-off people tend to withdraw within themselves, to rely on nobody else, to expect nothing; the way we face trials tests the mettle of our hope, for hope is another name for faith. Without hope, suffering crushes, kills.[16] On the other hand, suffering is courageously confronted when we have the assurance that it leads to Christ and "the glory of God." We know then that what we are enduring is the labor of bringing to birth a new world in which we shall have a part.[17]

This certitude is something more than a hope to which we cling at any cost in order to survive as long as possible. "Hope does not disappoint, because the love of God has been poured out into our hearts through the holy Spirit that has been given to us" (Rom 5:5). Faith assures us that God loves us, that he loved us first,[18] that nothing "will be able to separate us from the love of God in Christ Jesus our Lord" (Rom 8:39). All of us have experienced this in many circumstances of our lives and in our own particular ways.

> Nothing more sublime and more joyful can be sung in heaven or on earth than to love God, and others in view of God, because of God, and in God. The art and the science of this song are given by the Holy Spirit.
>
> Christ, our cantor and singing master, sang from the beginning and will eternally intone the canticle of faithfulness and endless love. Then, all of us with all our might shall sing after him, here below as well as in the midst of the choir of God's glory.
>
> Thus, true and guileless love is the common chant that we all must know in order to join the choir of angels and saints in the kingdom of God; for love is the root and the cause of all virtues inside and the ornament and true decoration of good works outside. It lives by itself and is its own reward. In its action, it cannot err because Christ has gone before us on the way; he has taught us love, he has lived love, he with all those who belong to him. Therefore, we must imitate him if we want to live in bliss with him and possess salvation.[19]

Guided by the Spirit of Truth into All Truth

John's Gospel was written at the end of the first century by a witness who, before setting down his teaching, preached and pondered at length the words of Jesus and the "signs" he accomplished.[20] John wrote down his testimony and reflection in order to help Christians deepen their faith in "Jesus [who] is the Messiah, the Son of God, and . . . through this belief have life in his name,"[21] and develop their communion with God. This work of reflection undertaken very early in the Church must not surprise us.[22] Indeed, when "the hour had come" for Jesus "to pass from this world to the Father" (John 13:1), he had said to his disciples that

they still had a long way to go before understanding his teaching and
fathom all its implications (John 16:12-15).

"I have much more to tell you, but you cannot bear it now." In saying
this, Jesus does not speak like a teacher who deplores not having been
able to complete the planned teaching program. On the other hand, the
disciples have often proved their difficulty, incapacity even, of understanding at first what Jesus was saying or doing. In all fairness, this was
the result not so much of their narrow-mindedness, as of the fact that
the meaning of these words and actions was to be fully unveiled only
by the events to come and, in particular, by the Lord's Pasch.[23] But Jesus
adds, "When he comes, the Spirit of truth, he will guide you to all truth."
The understanding, as well as the revelation of the mystery, depends on
a particular intervention from above, concretely on the action of the Holy
Spirit, and not on the effort of human intellectual activity. However, it
is not a supplement, still less a new revelation, that the Spirit brings. "For,
in giving us, as He did, His Son, which is His Word—and He has no
other—He spake to us all together, once and for all, in this single Word,
and He has no occasion to speak further."[24] "The Spirit of truth" adds
nothing to the revelation sealed by Jesus but is given us to "guide [us]
to all truth." "He will not speak on his own, but he will speak what he
hears, and will declare to you the things that are coming." It bears witness to the Lord—it "glorifies" him—for it will "take from" what is the
Lord's and "declare" it to the disciples in order to open to them an increasingly deeper understanding welling up from within.

Like God's, Jesus' words are "spirit and life" (John 6:63). It is not sufficient to indefinitely repeat them as if they were written in texts that could
be the object of only a literal exegesis.[25] At any rate, the gospel, which
was first preached, was transmitted to us in writing in a language that
Jesus himself did not use.[26] This passage from one language to another,
which demands a work of comprehension not always appreciated,[27] was
led by the Holy Spirit: this is why one speaks of "inspired" writings.
On the basis of these writings, and in line with them, the work of reflection has never ceased in the Church in order to scrutinize the meaning
of the Gospels and Scriptures in general and of the events of salvation.
This is the task and mission of preachers and theologians who are indispensable to the Church and to individual Christians.[28] For what is at
stake is the vital encounter with God and his Christ, the understanding
of the good news by which everyone must live. All those who have
received the charism of opening, for their brothers and sisters in the faith,

the inexhaustible treasures of revelation must willingly listen to the Holy Spirit, under whose guidance this work is done.

> If you naturally hesitate before the too deep mysteries of faith, say without fear, not in a spirit of contradiction but with the desire to obey, "How can this be?" (Luke 1:34). May your question be prayer, love, piety, desire. Let it not haughtily scrutinize the divine majesty, but seek salvation by the means offered to us by the God of our deliverance. Then, the Angel of the great Counsel will answer you, "When the Advocate comes whom I will send from the Father, the Spirit of truth that proceeds from the Father, he will testify to me" (John 15:26). "He will teach you everything" (John 14:26).
>
> Therefore hasten to become a sharer of the Holy Spirit. It is present as soon as it is invoked, and it is invoked only if it is already present. And when it comes upon being invoked, it comes with the abundance of divine blessings. It is the impetuous stream that gladdens the city of God (Ps 46:5). And if, at its coming, it finds you humble and peaceful and full of holy fear at God's word, it will rest on you and will reveal to you what God the Father hides from the wise and the learned of this world. Then you will begin to see the radiance of all these truths which Wisdom, when she was on earth, could reveal to the disciples, but which they, for their part, could not bear before the coming of the Spirit, this Spirit of truth that would guide them to all truth.[29]

This role attributed to the Holy Spirit and which it assumes in the Church toward disciples, "corresponds to its place in the Trinitarian life": it is "the One that completes."[30] In the same way as it insures communion between the three divine Persons, it unites believers to the Father and to his Son by guiding them "to all truth." What Jesus had said and taught did not come from him but from the Father who sent him.[31] Likewise, the Spirit "will not speak on his own, but he will speak what he hears"; it makes known, by forcefully repeating it, the teaching proclaimed by the Lord who said, "Everything that the Father has is mine." Through the Holy Spirit, the Son continues—"completes"—until the end of time, the mission received from the Father: to lead humankind to eternal life, with the Father, in the communion of the Holy Spirit.[32]

> When Christ withdrew his bodily presence, not only the Holy Spirit but also the Father and the Son assisted the disciples in a spiritual manner. For if Christ left them in such a way that the Holy Spirit was in their midst in his place and not with him, then what happens to his promise, "I am with you always, until the end of the age" (Matt 28:20)? And this other promise, "We will come to him, and make our dwelling with him" (John 14:23), since he had promised to them to send the Holy Spirit while remaining also with them forever? . . .

> For we must not believe that the Father is in anyone without the Son and the Holy Spirit, or the Father and the Son without the Holy Spirit, or the Son without the Father and the Holy Spirit, or the Father and the Holy Spirit without the Son: wherever one of them is, the Trinity is, one God.[33]

One of the first images that come to religious persons' minds when thinking of God, whom nobody has ever seen, since he has no face, is that of wisdom. This divine wisdom is so transcendent that we are not content with regarding it as an attribute of the Most High. God does not only possess wisdom; he is Wisdom in person (First Reading).

By his teaching, his actions, his life, and his death, Jesus has shed a decisive light on the mystery of a faceless God: God is love. In faith, we experience this: by his Son, he makes us just persons established in a relationship with him, a relationship not only friendly but filial, to the point of promising us a share in his own glory one day. As a consequence, our life, animated by this hope that "does not disappoint," takes on a completely new meaning; for the love of God is not only announced to us but "poured out into our hearts through the Holy Spirit that has been given us" (Second Reading).

It is the Spirit that helps us to progressively discover God's mystery. "Spirit of truth," it guides the Church and believers "to all truth" by incessantly recalling and increasing their understanding of what Christ said and taught. Thus it bears witness to the intimate communion that unites the three divine Persons and of which we are sharers (Gospel).

> Immensity that desires us,
> Joy that gives itself lavishly,
> Source of life that liberates us,
> God embraces us in his love
> and calls us to unity.
>
> *Holy God, strong God,*
> *We are your dwelling forever!*
>
> If you keep my word,
> my Father will love you
> and we shall come into your home.
>
> I knock at your door,
> open to me,
> I am coming to share the meal.
>
> Welcome the Spirit of truth
> that the Father sends you
> to be with you forever.[34]

"In the name of the Father, and of the Son, and of the Holy Spirit"; "The grace of our Lord Jesus Christ and the fellowship of the Holy Spirit be with you all"; "Through our Lord Jesus Christ, your Son, who lives and reigns with you and the Holy Spirit, one God for ever and ever." These formulas recur so often in Christian prayer and liturgy that we risk pronouncing or hearing them without paying them much attention. The yearly solemnity of the Holy Trinity invites us to regularly renew our awareness of the content and the import of this faith in one God, Father, Son, and Holy Spirit.

Surveys prove that for many Christians, to speak of God, Father, Son, and Holy Spirit, matters very little. Probably, they fail to see what the mystery of the Trinity can concretely evoke. They believe in God, period, like so many others who belong to diverse religions or even, without belonging to any particular religion, profess the existence of a God above them.[35] By the same token, Jesus Christ is only an unusual person, an outstanding prophet. He lived among us doing good; he admirably spoke about God and taught a particularly lofty way of living as religious human beings. Others do not see very clearly what the Trinity adds to faith in Jesus. They do not realize that "if there is no Trinity, Jesus would no longer be Jesus; in any event, he would no longer be the one in whom we can *believe.*"[36]

He is "Jesus Christ the Lord" because he is "eternally begotten of the Father, / God from God, Light from Light, / true God from true God, / begotten, not made, one in Being with the Father."[37] Christians "believe" in him because he is personally "the" Word of God, and not merely a prophet, even a most prestigious one, who spoke as he did by virtue of an exceptional delegation of authority. "No one has ever seen God. The only Son, God, who is at the Father's side, has revealed him" (John 1:18).

Besides, he spoke to his disciples of Another, coming also from the Father (John 15:26), the Spirit of truth sent to guide them "to all truth." On Pentecost, it manifested itself publicly by transforming the withdrawn and fearful apostles into ardent missionaries of the faith and making them bold witnesses of Jesus Christ, the Son of God, dead and risen, seated at the right of the Father. In a less spectacular but no less real way, it has continued since then to guide the Church and to uphold Christians' hope by assuring them that God loves them.

Created in the image of God, human beings will be fully realized inasmuch as they live, in communion with others, a life similar to that of the

Father, and the Son, and the Holy Spirit, one God in three Persons. Each one of us has his or her own existence, his or her personal existence, being distinct from all others. However, we become more and more ourselves by living in communion with others, intimately united, not in spite but because of our diversity. Failing to do this, we shut ourselves up in the narrowest of prisons, that of our egos, where our personalities soon disintegrate. The Holy Trinity is thus the loftiest, the most concrete, the most ennobling model of life in the human community.[38]

> Unknown God, O you who are
> A presence in the nights of our history,
> Through you, in our darkness
> Hope dawns;
> Break the forces of death:
> With our eyes we shall see you,
> O unknown God!
>
> Jesus Lord, you who were
> With the Father before the ages,
> Your coming uncovers for us
> The Mystery;
> Open a trail in our life:
> We shall walk in your footsteps,
> Jesus Lord!
>
> Spirit of fire, O you who come,
> Take humankind in your breath,
> You show forth in its weakness
> Your power;
> Burn with love the children of God:
> We shall enter into your joy,
> Spirit of fire![39]

The Body and Blood of Christ

The sacrament of the Body and Blood of Christ has always been the object of a great veneration expressed especially at the moment of Communion. "No one eats this flesh without first adoring it," Augustine says. He does not speak thus in a sermon on the Eucharist but in a commentary on a psalm.[2] This means that prostration was already part of the Communion rite in his time. Besides, as soon as Christians were able to build places of worship, they made provisions for a place where, after the celebration, the Eucharistic species were taken with respect and even with a certain solemnity regarding Communion for the sick.[3] However, there was not yet what could be called a true worship of the Eucharist outside of Mass. This sort of worship developed from the ninth, but especially from the eleventh century on, as a consequence of controversies about what is called "the Real Presence" of Christ in the sacrament.[4] These controversies helped to develop the doctrine and understanding of the mystery: the Eucharist is *really* the Body and Blood of Christ, but *under the sign*—the sacrament—of bread and wine. The Council of Trent clearly defined this doctrine at its thirteenth session on October 11, 1551.[5] The controversies also stimulated Eucharistic devotion.

Male and female recluses were the first to become more aware of what the Eucharistic presence in the churches really meant. The walls of their cells, built against the church walls, had holes, called "hagioscopes," bored through them,[6] to allow them to see the altar on which Mass was celebrated and to receive Communion. They became accustomed to spending their daytime hours kneeling before this little window in order to adore the Blessed Sacrament.[7] Lanfranc, who became archbishop of Canterbury in 1070, instituted the custom of carrying consecrated bread during the procession with palms in order to express the presence of the Lord among his people. However, it was in the thirteenth century that Eucharistic devotion really blossomed. A nun, Saint Juliana (1192–1258), the first abbess of the Augustinian Sisters of the Assumption of Mont-Cornillon, near Liège in Belgium, campaigned in favor of the institution of a feast of the Blessed Sacrament. This request provoked mixed reactions on the part of theologians and bishops, but it was well received by Robert, bishop of Liège, who celebrated the feast for the first time in 1246. Pope Urban IV (1261–1264) published, on August 11, 1264, a bull that extended the feast to the universal Church, but his death on October 2 left this decree without effect. Pope Clement V, the first pope of Avignon (1305–1314), promulgated the feast anew, and his successor, John XXII (1316–1334), inserted the feast into the collection called *Clementines.* The new celebration then spread rapidly.[8]

None of these three popes mentions a procession of the Blessed Sacrament. This appears for the first time in Cologne between 1274 and 1279. It did not take long for the procession to spread into most countries and become the most characteristic and popular rite of this new solemnity. Even in the tiniest villages, people were at pains to give to this procession, according to their means, a fitting splendor. In the cities of Europe, the long cortège that went through the main streets adorned with draperies and banners was often impressive. The monstrance, in which a large host had been placed, was carried under a festive canopy, preceded by all the clergy and followed by the civil authorities. Religious, confraternities with their banners, and various other groups had their assigned places according to a strict etiquette. The procession paused at repositories that vied with one another in magnificence and where the Blessed Sacrament was set down while people sang a hymn; then the blessing with the monstrance was given. The greatest number of the faithful stood in the streets to see the procession pass by. They knelt as the Blessed Sacrament approached, or else they thronged around the repositories in order to receive the blessing. This Corpus Christi triumph publicly expressed the faith of an entire people acclaiming the Lord present in the host.[9]

But a time came when this demonstration did not rally the majority of the population. Gradually the practice took place amidst an increasingly indifferent crowd of people and even aroused hostility from certain quarters: these persons did not accept the demonstration of a faith they did not share or the constraints it imposed on them.[10] Then, Christians had to ask themselves whether they should maintain at any cost a procession perceived by a certain number of persons—or the greatest number—as a display of inopportune and intolerable power. They wondered whether an objectionable procession—not a rite obligatorily attached to the feast[11]—was still, in a world that had become pluralistic, a good way of honoring the Eucharist, "sacrament of faith."[12] Thus, it happened that in the years preceding Vatican II, Eucharistic processions in the streets were gradually replaced in many cities with other forms of celebration designed to enable Christians to pay homage to the Blessed Sacrament.[13]

Since Vatican II, this feast has been called the Body and Blood of Christ. This change of name is significant. The emphasis is no longer on devotion to the Blessed Sacrament reserved in the tabernacle and presented for the adoration of the faithful. The emphasis is on the celebration of the Eucharist. This is why the preface of Holy Thursday is used.

> Father, all-powerful and ever-living God,
> we do well always and everywhere to give you thanks
> through Jesus Christ our Lord.
> He is the true and eternal priest
> who established this unending sacrifice.
> He offered himself as a victim for our deliverance
> and taught us to make this offering in his memory.
> As we eat his body which he gave for us,
> we grow in strength.
> As we drink his blood which he poured out for us,
> we are washed clean.
> Now, with angels and archangels,
> and the whole company of heaven,
> we sing the unending hymn of your praise.[14]

Body and Blood of Christ for Eternal Life

A New Food That Makes Us Hungry for God

The Book of Exodus, with the various events that happened during the long walk in the desert, has never ceased to be commented upon and meditated. People have seen in it a sort of paradigm, a parable full of teachings to be carefully kept in mind. For certain biblical authors, the coming out of Egypt was a triumphal march under God's guidance; they delighted in evoking it because, in their eyes, it prefigured and announced a new intervention of the Almighty, another Exodus still more marvelous than the first. This Exodus transformed ''a handful'' of immigrants into a numerous people ''stronger than their foes'' (Ps 105:12, 24). The next Exodus would gather the whole people in order to lead them into the definitive Promised Land.[1] But, for other people, who in no way belittled the marvels accomplished by God, the Exodus was chiefly a time of testing. The text from Deuteronomy we read today expresses the latter interpretation (Deut 8:2-3, 14b-16a).[2]

''Remember how for forty years now the LORD, your God, has directed all your journeying in the desert, so as to test you by affliction and find out whether or not it was your intention to keep his commandments.'' This way of speaking is truly admirable. The event spoken of belongs to a distant past. However, one must remember it as one remembers a personal experience. No better and simpler way could have been found to say that in one way or another the trial of the desert remains always present. This reliving in the present of a particularly significant event of the past is not a kind of retrospective make-believe, as if we had participated in the actual Exodus.[3] On the contrary, it is objectively founded on the fact that God always acts in the same way, whether today or yesterday. The trials God sends—and of which the Exodus remains the prime example—always aim at making us aware of our total destitution when we stray from him, from his commandments. On the other hand, human beings are so made that they need to know the poverty in which their

41

unfaithfulness toward God places them, before being finally able to recognize their radical dependence on the Lord. In this sense, the trial, the Exodus, is a grace despite its painful character. It is a cause of salutary conversion. But we must also remember the Exodus as a way of warding off the temptation to live one's life without God. In whatever situation we find ourselves, we are poor before God, who alone can satisfy our needs; to forget this is a sure path to catastrophe.

Food is the primordial human need. In the desert, when the people did not find anything to eat, God himself provided for them by sending manna from heaven, a food hitherto unknown,[4] in order to answer the needs of each person.[5] But at the same time, the gift of the manna had another meaning. It was meant to make the people hungry for God, without whom they could not survive, to make them aware "that not by bread alone does man live, but by every word that comes from the mouth of the LORD," that is to say, his Word, his Law. To look for other foods, to fear that he will fail to give the one food we need most and he alone can provide is tantamount to doubting God (Matt 4:3-4). To no longer be content with this heavenly manna, worse, to be disgusted with it, is a sign of apostasy. In sum, by giving the manna, God tested every day the faithfulness of his people, the dispositions of their hearts.[6] The same goes for water, without which every land becomes a desert of death. Now, only God gives the water that really quenches thirst, because it becomes "a spring of water welling up to eternal life" (John 4:13-15). In any case, wells dug by human hands sooner or later "hold no water" (Jer 2:13; 14:3) or contain only muddy water. To find the wells in that condition when one is thirsty is terrible (Jer 38:6). "Remember how for forty years now the LORD, your God, has directed all your journeying in the desert."

> Your chosen and holy troop,
> You led like a flock;
> You guided them into the desert
> By the fire of light and the pillar of cloud.
>
> You gave them a heavenly bread
> And the angelic manna,
> Prefiguring your Body
> Come down from heaven.
>
> You struck the rock and the water gushed forth;
> They drank from the twelve rivulets,
> As a figure of the source of your side
> And of the preaching of the apostles.[7]

The experience of the march through the desert, in want and hunger, with the daily manna and the water from the rock as their only viaticum, belongs to the whole community of believers and asks of them the same questions: What is in your hearts? Are you going to keep the Lord's commandments or not? Did you understand that without him you are in a state of destitution that nothing or nobody can fill? Why remain far from him when, left to your own strength, you are unable to overcome the innumerable dangers of the crossing of "the vast and terrible desert with its saraph serpents and scorpions, its parched and waterless ground"? To think of the Exodus, that of former days, that of every believer and the Church of today, must not arouse terror, but on the contrary lead us to renew our trust in God and to give thanks to him for all he has done for us and for what he allows us to do with him.

> *Praise the Lord, Jerusalem.*
>
> Glorify the LORD, O Jerusalem;
>   praise your God, O Zion.
> For he has strengthened the bars of your gates;
>   he has blessed your children within you.
> He has granted peace in your borders;
>   with the best of wheat he fills you.
> He sends forth his command to the earth;
>   swiftly runs his word!
>
> ———————————
>
> He has proclaimed his word to Jacob,
>   his statutes and his ordinances to Israel.
> He has not done thus for any other nation;
>   his ordinances he has not made known to them.
> Alleluia.
> (Ps 147:12-15,19-20)

One Bread, One Body

It is in Paul's First Letter to the Corinthians, in chapters 10 and 11, that we find the most explicit testimonies in the New Testament concerning the Eucharistic faith of the primitive Church. They are the more important and precious because Paul evoked the Eucharist not for itself but in order to illustrate or corroborate what he said to the Christian community about other questions. This means that the doctrine and practice to which he incidentally alluded were familiar to his correspondents. It is very interesting to see on what occasion Paul spoke. However, what he said about the Eucharist is more important than the context in which he placed his teaching and his testimony, from which we read a brief excerpt today (1 Cor 10:16-17).[8]

"The cup of blessing that we bless, is it not a participation in the blood of Christ? The bread that we break, is it not a participation in the body of Christ?" This way of speaking—in the interrogative form—means that Paul's correspondents had no doubt whatever on this point. What we have here is a simple reminder of what they knew in faith. And, in our turn, we receive Paul's message in the same spirit. Like him and the Christians at Corinth, we understand the term "communion" in the strongest sense: this "food unknown to [our] fathers" (Deut 8:16) establishes between the believer and Christ dead and risen an intimate, a "real" union.[9] For we know "that the Lord Jesus, on the night he was handed over, took bread, and after he had given thanks, broke it and said, 'This is my body that is for you. Do this in remembrance of me.' In the same way also the cup, after supper, saying, 'This cup is the new covenant in my blood. Do this, as often as you drink it, in remembrance of me' " (1 Cor 11:23-25).

At the same time, Communion in the Body and Blood of Christ creates, between believers, a new union, a vital one, eminently superior to that which results from the community of faith and hope. "Because the loaf of bread is one, we, though many, are one body, for we all partake of the one loaf." Here again, through baptism, believers become members of the Body of Christ.[10] God has reestablished his Covenant by the sacrifice of his Son. Fed by the Body and Blood of Christ, we are "brought together in unity by the Holy Spirit."[11] The Eucharist makes the Church whose Head is Christ. The Eucharist insures and expresses its unity and charity. Source of all virtue, the Eucharist gives it life and unceasing growth.[12] The Christian tradition of the first centuries loved to express the cohesion of the faithful in the Church and their common union with Christ by speaking of the Eucharistic bread as the symbol of their faith spoken of by Paul.

> As this broken bread, scattered on the mountains,
> was gathered to be one,
> may your Church be assembled in the same way
> from the ends of the earth into your kingdom.
> For to you belong
> glory and power
> through Jesus Christ forever![13]

Communion in the Body and Blood of Christ establishes between all the faithful and the Lord a mysterious exchange. Day by day, it impels us toward his Pasch.

> Lord Jesus, we offer you to your Father,
> the world looks on and does not understand.

> What would this offering mean for ourselves
> if you were not in our midst as you promised?

> If you were not in us the one who offers himself to the Father,
> if we were not the body he takes along?

> Your blood flows back to the heart where you dwell
> and it comes back into us in your Eucharist.

> Then, this movement which impels us
> finds us offered because we offer you.[14]

Jesus, Living Bread That Gives Us Life

The long "Bread of Life Discourse," which fills all of chapter 6 in John's Gospel, has a definite Eucharistic tone overall, especially in its last part, from which we read an excerpt today. The liturgical context of the feast of the Body and Blood of Christ in no way distorts the sense of this passage. On the contrary, this reading casts light on the meaning and scope of the celebration (John 6:51-58).[15]

It was after feeding the multitude with "five barley loaves and two fish" that Jesus gave this discourse. This whole crowd—"about five thousand in number"—followed Jesus "across the Sea of Galilee" because of the "signs" and cures worked before their eyes. As evening came, they realized their poverty: nothing to eat and, in this desert, not the slightest possibility of finding bread for such a mob. For their part, the disciples were unable to cope with this situation. "Andrew, the brother of Simon Peter" noticed "a boy here who has five loaves and two fish." But this discovery only made their plight more evident: "What good are these for so many?" It was with this nothing that Jesus fed the crowd. All ate to their hearts' content and the leftovers filled twelve baskets (6:1-15).[16]

We are not surprised to see that such a miracle aroused the enthusiasm of the crowd. But Jesus knew why and escaped. The next day he said, "You are looking for me not because you saw signs but because you ate the loaves and were filled." He then undertook to teach them why they had to seek him. The "food that perishes" is not worth all the trouble of crossing the lake and looking for it on the other side. One thing alone counts: to "work . . . for the food that endures for eternal life, which the Son of Man will give you. For on him the Father, God, has set his seal." Concretely, what is needed is to believe in the one sent by the Father (6:22-29). It is Jesus, "the bread of God . . . which comes down from heaven and gives life to the world." "I am the bread of life; whoever comes to me will never hunger, and whoever believes in me will never thirst" (6:33-35). "I am the bread of life . . . . I am the living bread . . . whoever eats this bread will live forever" (6:48-52).

This insistence, this repetition of the words "I am," concentrates attention more and more on Jesus, on his person. The bread he speaks of is not like the bread God, through the mediation of Moses, provided for his people during their march through the wilderness: "Your ancestors ate the manna in the desert, but they died" (6:49). "I am the living bread . . . whoever eats this bread will live forever; and the bread that I will give is my flesh for the life of the world." This solemn affirmation, toward which the whole discourse leads, is nonetheless surprising. Jesus is personally the bread, the "living bread." Whoever eats it "will live forever." It is impossible not to understand these words and locutions in an immediately realistic sense. John made this clear by reporting the hearers' reactions: "How can this man give us [his] flesh to eat?" Echoes of this question still resound in the hearts of all believers, and with a special force in the assembly celebrating the feast of the Body and Blood of Christ. Yes, it is "this man," Jesus of Nazareth, who gives us his flesh to eat as he has "given" his life "for" the salvation of the world.[17] "This man" is indeed the Son of God, who "came down from heaven," who "became flesh / and made his dwelling among us" (John 1:14). Faith in the Eucharist goes hand in hand with faith in the incarnation; Jesus is really the bread "for the life of the world" because he is true God and true human being. The reality of his humanity—"this man"—founds the realism of the Eucharist, true Body of Christ, dead and now living at the right hand of the Father, true food.

The statements that follow, and in which Jesus invests all his authority, forcefully insist: "Amen, amen, I say to you, unless you eat the flesh of the Son of Man and drink his blood, you do not have life within you. Whoever eats my flesh and drinks my blood has eternal life, and I will raise him on the last day. For my flesh is true food and my blood is true drink. Whoever eats my flesh and drinks my blood remains in me and I in him." The repetition of the same words, whose meaning is very realistic—"to eat," "to drink," "flesh," "blood," "food"—nips in the bud any interpretation that would see in these affirmations a metaphorical or allegorical way of speaking. The Lord gives his body, "given for us," to eat, his blood, "shed for us," to drink.[18]

In the Eucharist, we receive, under the "signs"—the sacrament—of bread and wine, the Body and Blood of the risen Christ, eternally living with the Father. It is by virtue of this new condition that he can be our food under this form. It is also because of this new condition that when eating this bread and drinking this wine transformed by the Spirit into the Body and Blood of Christ, we participate already now in the life that the Son shares with his Father: this same life circulates in us.[19] "Whoever eats my flesh and drinks my blood remains in me and I in him. Just as the living Father sent me and I have life because of the Father, so also the one who feeds on me will have life because of me." The Eucharist establishes with Christ and through him with the Father such a close bond that it is comparable to the one that unites the Persons of the Trinity.[20] This life already communicated here on earth must grow into eternal life. The Eucharist, "remedy of immortality, antidote against death, but for eternal life in Jesus Christ,"[21] is the paschal sacrament par excellence. To participate in the Eucharist—"mystery of faith"—is to proclaim the resurrection of Christ and to receive the pledge of it.

> In the same way the bread that comes from the earth, after having received the invocation, is no longer ordinary bread, but Eucharist, made up of two things, one earthly, the other heavenly, so our bodies which participate in the Eucharist are no longer corruptible, since they have the hope of the resurrection.[22]

> Christ has died,
> Christ is risen,
> Christ will come again.[23]

During the forty years of the march in the wilderness after the Exodus, God fed his people with manna, "a food unknown to [their] fathers," and gave them water sprung from the rock. Thanks to this food falling from heaven and to this providential drink,[24] the people survived until their entrance into the Promised Land. The miraculous character of these events remained vivid in the collective memory of the believers, as the Bible attests. But by meditating on God's guidance, people understood better and better that the lesson to be learned was that they must gain an increased awareness of an infinitely more vital need than that for earthly food. "Not by bread alone does man live, but by every word that comes forth from the mouth of the LORD." From him and him alone can we expect the life that does not inexorably end in death (First Reading).

As a new Moses, Jesus also fed the crowds who, seeing "the signs he was performing on the sick," followed him into the desert where there was nothing to eat (John 6:2). They would have willingly made a king of this man who saw to their needs. Jesus eluded them by leaving the place where the miracle took place, but they ferreted him out. The discourse that he then addressed to them reveals to us the meaning of the "sign" he worked. He was sent by "the living Father" in order to be the food that makes us live forever. Yes, he is the true bread "that came down from heaven." We must eat his flesh and drink his blood given "for the life of the world" (Gospel).

"The Lord Jesus, on the night he was handed over, took bread, and after he had given thanks, broke it and said, 'This is my body that is for you. Do this in remembrance of me.' In the same way also the cup, after supper, saying, 'This cup is the new covenant in my blood. Do this, as often as you drink it, in remembrance of me.' For as often as you eat this bread and drink the cup, you proclaim the death of the Lord until he comes" (1 Cor 11:23-26). The bread we break and the cup we share are a communion in the Body and Blood of Christ dead and risen (Second Reading).

> All the ways of the living God
> Lead to Easter,
> All human ways to a dead end:
> Do not miss at the crossroads
> The inn with its low table;
> For the Lord is waiting for you there.
>
> Do not wait for your flesh
> To be already dead,
> Do not hesitate, open the door,
> Ask for God, he is the servant,
> Ask everything, he will bring it to you:
> He is board and lodging.
>
> Here eat to your heart's content,
> And drink also
> To quench your thirst, the cup is full;
> Do not wander on the roads
> Going to God without God coming:
> Be people of tomorrow.
>
> Take his body right now,
> He invites you
> To become Eucharist;
> And you will see that God takes you,
> That he hosts you in his life
> And makes of you blood relations.[25]

Body and Blood of Christ for the New Covenant

Covenantal Liturgy in the Sinai Desert

The history of salvation is identical with that of the Covenant, this friendly relation, source of life and endless happiness, offered by God to humankind.[1] Promised to Noah and his descendants after the flood,[2] it was explicitly concluded with Abraham and his descendants.[3] But it was at Sinai that the whole people, freed from slavery, solemnly accepted the Covenant by promising to honor the clauses stipulated in the divine Law transmitted by Moses. The Book of Exodus records the liturgy during which the commitment of the people to the Covenant proposed to them took place (Exod 24:3-8).[4]

Moses, the presider at this celebration, began by relating "all the words and ordinances of the LORD," that is to say, the Ten Commandments (Exod 20:1-17) and the detailed laws concerning their application (Exod 20:22–23:33).[5] The people "answered with one voice, 'We will do everything that the LORD has told us.' " This is the traditional pattern of every "liturgy of the assembly": proclamation of the Word of God with the reminder of the obligations implied and the promise to be faithful to them.[6] Here, however, Moses set down in writing "all the words of the LORD"—the Ten Commandments—as one takes care to do in order to avoid any contestation or discussion later on about the terms of a contract and its stipulated obligations.[7]

"Rising early the next day, he erected at the foot of the mountain an altar and twelve pillars for the twelve tribes of Israel." The erection of stones in commemoration of an event is found in all cultures and is still practiced today. "Jacob took a stone and set it up as a memorial stone" when he concluded a treaty with Laban (Gen 31:45). At the assembly in Shechem, where the people also proclaimed their attachment to God, Joshua "took a large stone and set it up . . . [and] . . . said to all the people, 'This stone shall be our witness, for it has heard all the words which the LORD spoke to us. It shall be a witness against you, should you wish to deny your God' '' (Josh 24:27).[8] At Sinai, Moses also built an altar on which he had holocausts offered and young bulls immolated as peace sacrifices. The holocaust was the sacrifice of worship par excellence. The immolated victim was entirely burned so that nothing was left, signifying that one totally belonged to God (Lev 3:1-17). In a peace offering, on the contrary, the victim was ritually divided between God and the person who offered it and then ate part of it. This was a rite performed in particular to seal a treaty or a covenant (Lev 3:1-17). The offering of these two sacrifices expressed well, on that day, the meaning and importance of the commitment of the people: to put into practice ''the words and ordinances of the LORD,'' was, as the holocaust signified, to recognize the absolute sovereignty of the Lord, but it was also, as the peace offering—sacrifice of communion—expressed it, to live in union with him.[9]

Afterwards, Moses took part of the blood of the victims and splashed it on the altar and sprinkled it on the people, saying, ''This is the blood of the covenant which the LORD has made with you.'' This rite seems strange if not somewhat repulsive, and we do not see its significance very clearly. We must remember that especially in the past but even today, blood is the symbol of life, is identified with it.[10] The mixing of a few drops of each other's blood initiates and signifies the community of destiny between two persons, the faithfulness that unites them in life and death. The rite of aspersion symbolically expresses God's response. The life offered him—the blood of the sacrifices—and which comes from him, the Living One, he bestows on those who enter into covenant with him. Therefore, there is nothing sanguinary in these sacrifices and rites, as if God thirsted for the blood of his creatures. God gives back and transforms the life sacrificed to him. He makes into a new life the death of his own, in which he takes no delight. The offered life is not lost but saved.

> The aspect of mortification is accidental in the sacrifice: in essence, to sacrifice oneself is not to deprive oneself of life but to offer oneself to a higher life. It is the resistance to passing into God that must die, not the sinner. Now this resistance does not come from God, nor does the suffering resulting from the struggle against it. Strictly speaking, God does not punish the sinners, even with a view to atonement, but he gives them the strength to assume, through love of life, the multifaceted death that ''entered the world'' ''by the envy of the devil'' (Wis 2:24), the fortitude to fight evil and change their defeat into victory.[11]

Such a struggle is a daily one. The certitude of obtaining God's help, for which we ask incessantly with trust allied to thanksgiving for his past graces, allows us to continue the fight without flagging.

I will take the cup of salvation,
and call on the name of the Lord.

How shall I make a return to the LORD
   for all the good he has done for me?
The cup of salvation I will take up,
   and I will call upon the name of the LORD.

Precious in the eyes of the LORD
   is the death of his faithful ones. . . .
I am your servant, the son of your handmaid;
   you have loosed my bonds.
To you will I offer sacrifice of thanksgiving,
   and I will call upon the name of the LORD.
My vows to the LORD I will pay
   in the presence of all his people.
(Ps 115:12-13, 15, 16b-18)

A New and Eternal Covenant Through Christ's Own Blood

The Letter to the Hebrews is the only writing of the New Testament that applies to Christ the titles of priest and high priest. It thus shows the connections between the Christian faith and one of the main currents of the preceding biblical tradition, the one that concerns worship: rites and sacrifices, priesthood, sanctuary of God in the midst of his people. We must therefore constantly refer to this cultic and priestly tradition when we read the Letter to the Hebrews. The effort this requires is rewarded. We soon begin to discern, with wonderment, how much the mystery of salvation worked by Christ is illuminated by the sophisticated teaching developed in the Letter to the Hebrews.[12] This is true of the passage that the liturgy gives us to read today after the excerpt from the Book of Exodus (Heb 9:11-15).

"Christ came as the high priest of the good things that have come to be": he opens access to the goods, the realities of the world to come.[13] In order to express the way in which Christ exercises this ministry and its efficacy, the author compared them to what the Jewish high priest did on the Day of Atonement, Yom Kippur.[14] This solemn celebration took place in the Temple. A bull and a goat were offered in sacrifice. The high priest then entered behind the veil—on that day only—into the holy of holies. With the blood of the animals that had been immolated, he purified the sanctuary and performed the cleansing rite on himself and the whole people.[15] The comparison with this solemn yearly liturgy highlights the eminent superiority and peerless efficacy of Christ's priesthood. By his body, "not made by hands, that is, not belonging to this creation," he himself is the temple, "greater and more perfect," of the new worship. "He entered once for all into the sanctuary, not with the blood of goats and calves but with his own blood, thus obtaining eternal redemption." The offering Christ made of himself fully realized, beyond all hope, what all the previous sacrifices signified.

To tell the truth, the comparison with past sacrifices here betrays its limits. The Blood of Christ, offered "through the eternal spirit," "unblemished," acquires a purification that is not merely ritual but interior. Through him, we are now enabled "to worship the living God." A new covenant is made, "since a death has taken place for deliverance from transgressions under the first covenant," whose expiatory sacrifices do not have to be repeated. Finally, having "entered once for all into the sanctuary," he is eternally, with the Father, the Mediator who intercedes efficaciously for those who one day must receive the eternal heritage already promised.[16] Besides, we must not forget that from the first instant of his entrance into the world, the Son of God made of his whole life an offering to the Father.[17]

> In fact, hardly had the Word become flesh when he manifested himself to the world in his priestly function, by making to the eternal Father an act of submission that was to last all throughout his life: "When he came into the world, he said, 'Behold, I come to do your will, O God'" (Heb 10:5-6). He was to bring this act to its perfection in a marvelous manner in the bloody sacrifice of the cross: "By this 'will,' we have been consecrated through the offering of the body of Jesus Christ once for all" (Heb 10:10).[18]

On the First Day of the Feast of Unleavened Bread

Matthew, Mark, and Luke report in equivalent terms the last paschal meal Jesus took with his disciples.[19] Today we read Mark's narrative (14:12-16, 22-26).

"Where do you want us to go and prepare for you to eat the Passover?" Answering this question put by his disciples on "the first day of the Feast of the Unleavened Bread,"[20] Jesus sent two of his disciples into the city, saying, "A man will meet you, carrying a jar of water.[21] Follow him. Wherever he enters, say to the master of the house, 'The Teacher says, "Where is my guest room where I may eat the Passover with my disciples?"'"[22] The disciples did as they were told "and found it just as he had told them."[23] They were shown "a large upper room furnished and ready," where they made the preparations for the celebration of the Passover. Jesus seems not to have wanted it known in advance where the paschal meal was to take place. Was it as a precaution against those who had decided to arrest him (14:2) and had already made a deal with Judas (14:10-11)? Or was it simply a way of making sure that nobody would come to disrupt the intimacy of this last paschal meal he desired to share with the little group of disciples chosen ''that they might be with him and he might send them forth to preach'' (3:14)? In any case, it is clear that this Pasch, prelude to his passion, meant a great deal to Jesus and that he himself carefully organized its celebration to the last detail.

In contrast with this beginning full of concrete and vivid touches, the rest of the narrative is extremely spare. The ritual gestures made by Jesus are those of any head of a household at a festive meal: a blessing coupled with a thanksgiving when taking the bread, then the cup as an acknowledgment that all these gifts come from God. To give a morsel of bread and to send the cup around were also usual practices in such a meal. But the words pronounced by Jesus when accomplishing these familiar gestures are extraordinary: ''this is my body . . . this is my blood.'' The evocation of his death close at hand is obvious. Still more, his blood is the ''blood of the covenant, which will be shed for many.'' Jesus did not merely make a prophetic gesture in order to announce that he was about to die.[24] He proclaimed that he was giving his life to seal the Covenant so that all might drink at the source of this life.[25]

Mark—like Matthew (26:26-29)—stylized the account. There is no mention of the meal prepared with so much care and attention: one would think that nothing but these gestures and these words happened.[26] It is the pattern of the Christian Eucharist, given without any explanation but filled with all that Jesus did and taught.

> The extreme simplicity of these words and of the gesture that accompanies them mirrors the incomprehensible simplicity of God. What he had first unfolded, in the announcement of the Good News, embracing the multiple aspects of human complexity, Jesus now encloses at the Last Supper, without excluding anything, in a rite that borders on insignificance. For only a sort of insignificance can signify the Abyss of the humility of the Glory. Anything resembling explanation or feeling would obscure God instead of revealing him. At the hour he had most ardently desired, Jesus rigorously refrained from doing. ''Body given . . . blood of the Covenant shed for many . . . take . . . eat . . . drink''; nothing more, whatever the differences between the four accounts. There is only the essential. When the essential has the aspect of insignificance, it risks to go unnoticed. Then there is a drift toward banality. But there are risks also when one claims to highlight the essential by having recourse to pedagogies in which the eminently significant value of the form of insignificance would disappear.[27]

During the last paschal meal eaten with his disciples, Jesus solemnly repeated the promise of his return, "Amen, I say to you, I shall not drink again the fruit of the vine until the day when I drink it new in the kingdom of God." The visible presence of Jesus ceased on earth the day of his death, but he is nevertheless present. The sacrament of his Body and Blood is the pledge of his presence. The Lord continues to invite us to his table until his return. The Eucharistic bread and wine have been given to believers to be their viaticum on the road of the exodus that leads to the definitive Pasch.

> Let us enter the upper room
> To celebrate Passover with him
> The table has the diameter of the world
>   as in the painting of da Vinci
> It is the span of the arms of the cross
> And his heart has the table ready
>
> The first to arrive share in the symbol
> And put their hands into the dish with God
> Those people who break bread together
> Become almost able to love
> Despite themselves they happened to fall into his arms
> Where all acquire their larger measure.[28]

God has taken the initiative to offer his Covenant to humankind and, at the same time, he has shown them how they can live, all the days of their lives, in this relation of proximity and friendship that it establishes. To welcome this gift is to freely and without second thought commit oneself to put into practice "the words and ordinances of the LORD" (First Reading).

Christ, the high priest of a covenant sealed in his blood, has entered, by his life and resurrection, into the heavenly sanctuary. In him, we have the mediator thanks to whom we can "worship the living God" (Second Reading).

Indeed, his Pasch has inaugurated the kingdom of the last times, which his return will establish. Then, the intimate feast of the Eucharist will yield to the eternal and solemn thanksgiving of the elect celebrating the wedding of the Lamb (Rev 19:5-10). "Blessed are those who have been called" to the Lord's Supper. By communicating here below with the Body and Blood of Christ, under the signs of bread and wine, believers receive the pledge of the promised heritage and prepare themselves to welcome the Lord on the day on which he will drink a new wine in the kingdom of God (Gospel).

Bend,
My Christ, bend
Toward your body, since already
It is from it that our hymns ascend.
We took it at your meal,
It took us, and here we are
Among your intimate guests,
Those whom you see when you look at them
And feed with yourself in you,
Those who must carry your voice
Because your love animates them.

You took flesh and blood from our own
in order to be flesh and blood for all;
From the Supper with your apostles
Until this sharing with us
The adorable Pasch is transmitted
through the course of ages till today.
For now you are the table
on which everything becomes Eucharist.

Now,
My Christ, now,
Recognize also your blood;
If it is not in our hearts, may it come to them!
More strongly urge their beating
So that they may draw the song
From the bottom of our human throats;
You who bathe them inside
As well as outside, so tenderly,
Toward your friends bend so low
that they may reflect you as themselves.

In the coming of your Kingdom,
We followed you on the way
Passing through what makes humans live,
Bringing tomorrow's life
To the darkest place of this cleft
Where death hides its secret:
Lo, its germ trembles,
Lo, here is the Pasch and everything is reborn.[29]

Body and Blood of Christ for the Time of the Church

Melchizedek, Priest of God Most High, Figure of Christ, Perfect Priest

Melchizedek is a most mysterious personage. He appears only once in the Old Testament, and in a fleeting manner. Nothing is known about him except that he was "king of Salem" and "priest of God Most High." These terse phrases do not even allow us to say with any certainty what his origin was.[1] But the vagueness that surrounds him has been exploited by the Letter to the Hebrews[2] and by patristic exegesis. Besides, the Roman Canon—Eucharistic Prayer I—joins the memory of the offering of Melchizedek to that of Abel, God's servant, and to that of "Abraham, our father in faith."[3] Therefore, it comes as no surprise that we read on this Sunday of the solemnity of the Body and Blood of Christ the passage from the Book of Genesis that describes the encounter between the father of believers and the "king of Salem," "priest of God most High." (Gen 14:18-20)

The Book of Genesis devotes nearly fourteen chapters to the story of Abraham: from his calling to his death (12:1–25:11). This ensemble poses a host of questions for historians and exegetes.[4] The fact that the redaction of this long story integrated elements of different times, including some relatively recent, attests to the importance that biblical traditions accorded Abraham, the first of the patriarchs.[5] In the second millennium before our era, the Fertile Crescent was the theater of various movements of populations, accompanied by strife between different groups, raids, and other such contentious events inherent to nomadic life. The long journey that took Abraham from Ur of the Chaldeans in southern Mesopotamia to Hebron, where he pitched his tent near the oaks of Mamre, by way of Canaan and Egypt, can be visualized within this general context (Gen 12:1–14:11). But suddenly, Genesis inserts the story of Abraham within universal history (Gen 14:12).[6] With his clan, he organized an expedition to deliver Lot, his nephew, and overcame "four kings" (Gen 14:1-16). At this juncture, the appearance of the mysterious Melchizedek took place.

A "king" who sought to gain the favor of the victorious leader of a coalition by welcoming him and by seeing to the needs of his troops, this was nothing out of the ordinary: it is better to make the first move rather than watch a stronger adversary indulge in pillage. However, the story suggests something quite other. This "king of Salem" was also a "priest of God Most High." The blessing pronounced by Melchizedek was a far cry from a word of politeness and allegiance inspired by ulterior motives. What we have here is a ritual formula accompanying the offering of the bread and wine brought by the king-priest, an efficacious and irrevocable word that does what is said,[7] since it is God who blesses.[8] But at the same time, the human being "blesses" God and gives thanks for his greatness and kindness[9] by asking him to continue to be favorable to the one God is blessing. In biblical worship, the two blessings go hand in hand,[10] and it will be the same in the New Testament.[11] Abraham recognized that he owed his victory over the four allied kings to divine protection and saw in this manifestation of God's favor the promise that God would remain by his side throughout his life. In response, Abraham expressed this: to Melchizedek, the "priest of God Most High,"[12] he gave in homage "a tenth of everything."

This cultic climate indicates the meaning of the episode. Abraham did not go to war in order to gain wealth or revenge. He solemnly declared that he did not want to receive anything from the "king of Sodom." "I have sworn to the LORD, God Most High, the creator of heaven and earth, that I would not take so much as a thread or a sandal strap from anything that is yours, lest you should say, 'I made Abraham rich.' Nothing for me except what my servants have used up and the share that is due to the men who joined me—Aner, Eshcol and Mamre; let them take their share" (Gen 14:22-24). The narrative places the first of the patriarchs on a plane different from that of others, even his allies. They could observe the laws of war and claim their rightful share of the booty from the "king of Sodom." For his part, Abraham was dealing with the "priest of God Most High" because his vocation concerned "all the communities of the earth" (Gen 12:3). Abraham, the father of believers, rendered homage to the person who, whatever his origin, spoke in the name of the one God who created "heaven and earth" and whom all humans must acknowledge because only he is the author of all blessing. The memory of this episode would come back when some later writer would evoke the person of the Messiah.

> The LORD has sworn, and he will not repent:
> "You are a priest forever, according to the order of Melchizedek."
> (Ps 110:4)

After the Letter to the Hebrews,[13] the Church Fathers would delight in saying that Christ's priesthood transcends every human institution: it has its mysterious origin in God, in the manner of that of Melchizedek, who blessed Abraham.

> The whole of the work contained in the holy books announces by words, reveals by facts, and establishes by examples the coming of our Lord Jesus Christ who, sent by the Father, was made human by being born of a virgin through the operation of the Holy Spirit. It is he who, all through the duration of this age and by the aid of true and manifest prefigurations, engenders, washes, sanctifies, chooses, separates, or redeems the Church in the Patriarchs: by Adam's sleep, by Noah's flood, by Melchizedek's blessing, by Abraham's justification, by Isaac's birth, by Jacob's servitude.[14]

It is thus that the person of Melchizedek has found a place, first in the biblical tradition, then in the tradition of the Church and even in the Roman Canon. This mysterious "priest of God Most High" is the distant figure of the one the Scriptures announced: Jesus, the Son of the Most High, born of our flesh, Mediator of a new Covenant for all humankind.[15] He is the only true priest by virtue of his twofold nature, divine and human, and not by virtue of his belonging to a human priestly lineage.

> For in him all the fullness was pleased to dwell,
> and through him to reconcile all things for him,
> making peace by the blood of his cross
> [through him], whether those on earth or those in heaven.
> (Col 1:19-20)

You are a priest for ever,
in the line of Melchizedek.

The LORD said to my Lord: "Sit at my right hand
  till I make your enemies your footstool."
The scepter of your power the LORD will stretch forth from Zion:
  "Rule in the midst of your enemies.
Yours is princely power in the day of your birth, in holy splendor;
  before the daystar, like the dew, I have begotten you."
The LORD has sworn, and he will not repent:

"You are a priest forever, according to the order of Melchizedek."
(Ps 110:1-4)

The Sign of Bread and Wine in Memory of the Lord

The way Paul spoke of the Eucharist in his First Letter to the Corinthians attests a practice already familiar to the Christians of his time.[16] It was enough for him to evoke the liturgical experience of his correspondents; there was no need to repeat each time a detailed account of the Last Supper: they knew it. Consequently, Paul recalled only the essentials that the rite of the Church commemorated. And since the same is true of our celebrations, it is fitting that this text be read on the feast of the Body and Blood of Christ (1 Cor 11:23-26).

"On the night he was handed over": this action, transmitted by tradition,[17] places what Jesus did and what we do in explicit and direct relation to the Pasch of Jesus' death and resurrection. Under the sign of the bread, it is his "body that is for [us]"; the cup of blessing "is the new covenant in [his] blood." The evocation of the sacrificial value of the Pasch of Christ and the Eucharist, offered to reestablish all humankind—alienated by sin—in God's friendship, could not be clearer. We are reminded of the song of the Suffering Servant:

> Because of his affliction . . .
> Through his suffering, my servant shall justify many,
>   and their guilt he shall bear. . . .
> Because he surrendered himself to death
>   and was counted among the wicked . . .
> he shall take away the sins of many,
>   and win pardon for their offenses.
> (Isa 53:11-12)[18]

But the Eucharist is much more than a mere commemoration of the past event of the death and resurrection of Christ, whose memory a rite would preserve. The celebration of the Jewish Pasch has another significance. The father of the family explains to the youngest son the reason and the meaning of the feast, saying, "This is because of what the LORD did for me when I came out of Egypt" (Exod 13:8). And in the first centuries of our era, Jewish commentary on this verse said, "In each generation, one must look at oneself as having left Egypt."[19] The Eucharistic "memorial" goes far beyond this actualization, as powerful as it may be. Under the signs of bread and wine, the Eucharist is truly—really—the Body of Christ given for us and his Blood shed for the multitude.[20] As a consequence, this is not a question of behaving "as if" we were participating in Christ's supper; we truly and really participate, here and now, in what he did "on the night he was handed over."

"For as often as you eat this bread and drink the cup, you proclaim the death of the Lord until he comes." The Eucharist establishes a bond of indissoluble continuity between the today of salvation, in which we already share, and its full manifestation, object of our hope, that will take place at Christ's return. This is one and the same mystery. The Eucharist announces what is still to come, and it gives us the pledge of it. It is the sacrament of faith and hope.

> If we leave this world after having participated in that sacrament, we shall enter with complete confidence into the heavenly sanctuary as if a golden armor made us invulnerable. And why speak of the life to come? The very earth, here below, becomes heaven through this mystery. Open therefore, open the doors of heaven, look: it is not enough to say of heaven but of the highest place of heaven, and you will see what I announced to you. I am going to show you what the treasures of highest heaven have that is most precious, treasures lying on the earth. For, if it is true that in a royal palace what is most august is neither the walls nor the gold paneling but the king on his throne, likewise in heaven itself, it is the king. Now you can see him, today, on the earth. I am not showing you angels or archangels or heaven or the heaven of heavens: I am showing you the master and Lord of all this. Do you understand that what is most precious you see on earth? And not only do you see it but you touch it; but you do even more, you feed on it, you receive it, you take it away into your home![21]

Multiplying the Bread to Feed the Crowds

The multiplication of the loaves worked by Jesus to feed the crowd that had followed him into the wilderness is recorded by all four evangelists.[22] The extraordinary character of this miracle and the apologetic intention of the evangelists do not suffice to explain such an insistent unanimity.[23] This spectacular miracle, done for the benefit of several thousand people, certainly shows Jesus as a peerless wonder-worker.[24] But the crowd did not comprehend the true meaning of the miracle worked by Jesus. Neither did the disciples.[25] Only later did they see a "sign" in the miracle of the multiplication of the loaves. Its meaning is particularly revealed when read in the context of the solemnity of the Body and Blood of Christ (Luke 9:11b-17).

"He . . . spoke to them about the kingdom of God, and he healed those who needed to be cured." This remark, which says nothing about the circumstances in which the miracle occurred, could appear insignificant being so general: Did Jesus ever do anything else but preach the good news of the kingdom and relieve the afflictions of those who came to him? However, the remark takes on a particular meaning within the framework of the liturgical celebration. It begins with the prayer addressed to the Lord to ask him for salvation, the cure for sin—the gravest of diseases, the source of all other evils—and the grace that our destitution needs; it continues with the proclamation of the Word that speaks of the kingdom of God[26] and urges us to enter into his mystery. We have here an invitation to hear this Gospel in the immediate context of today's liturgy.[27]

"The day was drawing to a close": as we hear this, many reminiscences come to mind. It was in the evening—"on the night he was handed over"—that Jesus gathered his own for the meal during which he instituted the Eucharist. The two disciples who were walking "downcast" on the road to Emmaus detained the stranger who had joined them, saying to him, "Stay with us, for it is nearly evening and the day is almost over." "And it happened that, while he was with them at table, he took bread, said the blessing, broke it, and gave it to them" (Luke 24:28-31).[28] Finally, how can we not notice that Jesus did the same ritual gestures at the multiplication of the loaves, the Last Supper, and Emmaus? It is only at the Last Supper that Jesus gave his flesh to eat and his blood to drink. Therefore, we must not mix up these three narratives. But the Gospel of the multiplication of the loaves as well as that of Emmaus have, in Luke, an unmistakable Eucharistic connotation.[29] We cannot hear it proclaimed, especially on this feast day, without confessing that Jesus is the one who, each day, breaks for us the Eucharistic bread.

"Dismiss the crowd so they can go to the surrounding villages and farms and find lodging and provisions; for we are in a deserted place here." After the apostles's return from their mission, Jesus had wanted to withdraw to a place apart. But the crowds "learned of this and followed him." Far from showing displeasure at this eagerness that ruined his plan, Jesus "received them" (Luke 9:10-11). At the end of the day, the apostles were intent on dispersing the crowd, and they pressed Jesus to give the order for departure. It is time, they say, to send these people away "to the surrounding villages and farms [to] find lodging and provisions; for we are in a deserted place here." "Give them some food yourselves." Jesus' response is, to say the least, unexpected. "Five loaves and two fish are all we have"—very little for the Twelve and Jesus[30]—"unless we ourselves go and buy food for all these people." To go and buy groceries for several thousand people[31] is a proposition whose absurdity is obvious: Jesus knew it and did not even react to this preposterous suggestion. He was telling his apostles that they had a part to play in relieving the needs of the crowd.

"Have them sit down in groups of [about] fifty."[32] The Twelve execute the order without hesitation and, it seems, against all expectation, without a hitch, even quickly. Truly, there was no longer an unorganized mob, but a well-structured assembly;[33] one is no longer in a wilderness, but in the immense hall of a solemn banquet presided over by Jesus.[34] "Then taking the five loaves and the two fish, and looking up to heaven, he said the blessing over them, broke them, and gave them to the disciples to set before the crowd." These ritual gestures correspond exactly to the attitude and actions of the Lord at the Last Supper, to those of the presider at the Eucharistic assembly as it has been established since the beginnings of the Church.

> On the day called the day of the sun, all, whether they dwell in the cities or the country, gather in one place. The memoirs of the apostles as well as the writings of the prophets are read as long as time permits.
>
> After the reading, the presider speaks to warn the hearers and exhort them to imitate these beautiful teachings. Then we stand up and pray aloud all together. Then, as we have already said, bread with wine and water are brought.
>
> The presider raises to heaven prayers and thanksgiving according to his strength, and the whole people answers with the acclamation "Amen."
>
> Then come the distribution and apportioning of the food, and those absent receive their share through the deacons' ministry.
>
> Those who are wealthy and freely desire to give, give what they want, each one ad libitum. What is collected is given to the presider, and he assists the orphans, the widows, the sick, the poor, the prisoners, the foreign guests, in a word, he helps all those in want.[35]

"They all ate and were satisfied. And when the leftover fragments were picked up, they filled twelve wicker baskets." Christian tradition has always seen a lesson in the insistence of the evangelists on this abundance and the care with which the remainders were gathered.[36] The Eucharist is the bread reserved by Christ to feed the multitudes of all times.[37] It is the "sign" par excellence prefigured in the miracle worked in the past: "Once we receive Christ's food, we shall not be hungry any more; and the service rendered by the apostles foreshadows the distribution of the Body and Blood of the Lord."[38] But when we reread the beginning of this Gospel passage, we can see in it a prefiguration of the whole Eucharistic celebration. Jesus began by teaching the crowds before giving them bread in abundance in this desert transformed into a banquet hall. In the Eucharist also, the bread of the Word is broken to be shared among all before the bread that has become the Body of Christ is distributed.

> This bread that Jesus breaks is, as far as the mystery is concerned, the word of God and the discourse about Christ: distributed, it increases; for, with a few discourses, he supplied all the peoples with an overabundant nourishment; he gave us discourses like bread, and, as we taste it, it multiplies in our mouths. Similarly, in a visible and incredible way, this bread, when broken, when distributed, when eaten, heaps up without undergoing any diminishment.
>
> And do not doubt that this food increases either in the hands that distribute it or in the mouths that eat it, since in all this the testimony of our activity is invoked in order to strengthen our faith.[39]

The Eucharist has a cosmic meaning and scope that the extreme simplicity of the rites only partially reveals. Today's liturgy gives us an opportunity to become aware, perhaps more aware, of this cosmic dimension.

The Book of Genesis preserves the memory of an encounter between Abraham and Melchizedek, a mysterious "priest of God Most High." No one knows where he came from. He made an offering of bread and wine before blessing God and the father of believers, then he was gone. He would have been forgotten had not the Christian tradition and the Roman Canon evoked Christ as priest "according to the order of Melchizedek," that is, beyond any human institution. It has also been noted that Melchizedek, the first person to which the Bible gives the name of priest, pronounced a blessing on Abraham while offering him bread and wine, somewhat akin to the blessing of the offerings that would be done later during the paschal meal. Jesus, too, pronounces a blessing at the Last Supper, a blessing that was endowed with new meaning (First Reading).

The bread that the Lord, "on the night he was handed over" took in his hands and broke to give to his disciples is his Body "for [us]." The cup of blessing is "the new covenant in [his] blood." Every time we eat this bread and drink this cup, we proclaim "the death of the Lord until he comes." Of the rite born in the remotest times and transmitted by the tradition of the Jewish Passover, Jesus made the perfect offering to "God Most High," the sacrament of his presence in our midst, the efficacious "sign" of our participation even now in the life he received from the Father, the pledge of eternal life to come and of the entrance into the kingdom on the day of his parousia. To participate in the Eucharist causes us to enter into the dynamics of salvation that have been unfolding since the beginning and is constantly expanding, a salvation to which all are called (Second Reading).

It was on the night of his passion that the Lord gave his disciples the sacrament of the new Covenant, saying to them, "Do this in remembrance of me." However, in order to fully understand the words and actions of that evening, we must see them by the light of what the Lord said and did throughout his ministry, the numerous "signs" he accomplished, in particular the multiplication of the loaves. Only Jesus can provide the food the crowds need, the food able to satisfy their hunger. The abundance of bread endlessly broken is such that down the ages there will always be enough left to allow the disciples to distribute it lavishly for all those who gather in order to commemorate the Lord by announcing, and calling for, his coming (Gospel).

> How beyond measure to celebrate Mass! We are snatched into the doings of God. The memory of the past is present, but "the memory must not enervate hope." We must not passively wait, either. In effect, we remember what will be. We are venturing into the magnetic field of the divine future. The Eucharistic gathering is a stopping place for nomads, a pause on the way of Exodus; when celebrating this sacrifice, we sing Easter songs. The manna we offer here is nothing else but God himself. He satiates and he makes hungry. He sets back on their way men and women haunted by the promise and impatient to begin building today and tomorrow the luminous city of humankind and God.[40]

The solemnity of the Body and Blood of Christ is not a kind of repeat performance of Holy Thursday. Of course, the same Eucharistic mystery is celebrated. But the liturgy of the Last Supper is the first phase of the great celebration that unfolds within the unity of the Easter Triduum.[41]

By turning our eyes toward the immolation of the Lamb, whose sacrifice redeems the sins of the world, and the passion of the Lord celebrated on the following day, the liturgy of Holy Thursday places the emphasis on the Eucharist as a sign of charity.[42]

The solemnity of the Body and Blood of Christ dwells rather on the Eucharist celebrated and received in the ordinary time of the Church, the Christian communities, each believer. Whoever eats the flesh and drinks the blood of Christ already possesses eternal life and receives the pledge of resurrection on the last day. By commemorating the Pasch of the Lord, one renews one's involvement in the Covenant his Pasch definitively sealed. By participating today in the meal of the Lord, one is getting ready to enter with him into the banquet hall on the day when he will come back to gather, in joy and thanksgiving, the immense multitude of those who hunger for God and have at last reached the end of their exodus.

A little bread, a little wine: in the sacrament of the Body and the Blood, we participate in the whole mystery of faith and salvation.

> When you approach, do not advance with extended palms or fingers held apart; with your left hand make a throne for your right hand since the latter is to receive your King, and, in your cupped hand, receive the Body of Christ, saying, "Amen." With care, sanctify your eyes through contact with the holy Body, then eat it, careful to lose nothing. For what you should lose would be like losing one of your own members. Tell me, if you were given specks of gold, would you not keep them with utmost care, taking pains not to lose any and suffer a loss? Are you not going to watch with greater care over this object more precious than gold and gems, so that you do not lose any crumb?
>
> Afterwards, having received the Body of Christ, approach also the chalice of his Blood. Do not extend your hands but, bowing, and in an attitude of adoration and respect, saying, "Amen," sanctify yourself by taking also the Blood of Christ. And while your lips are still damp, touch them lightly with your hands and sanctify your eyes, your forehead and your other senses. Then, while waiting for the prayer, give thanks to God who has judged you worthy of such great mysteries.[43]

Sacred Heart of Jesus

"On the last and greatest day of the feast, Jesus stood up and exclaimed, 'Let anyone who thirsts come to me and drink. Whoever believes in me, as scripture says: "Rivers of living water will flow from within him" ' " (John 7:37-38). "One soldier thrust his lance into his side, and immediately blood and water flowed out. . . . For this happened so that the scripture passage might be fulfilled: 'Not a bone of it will be broken.' And again another passage says: 'They will look upon him whom they have pierced' " (John 19:34, 36-37).

These words of Jesus, and the insistence with which John invites us to contemplate the pierced side of the Lord, very early directed Christians' piety and devotion toward the heart of Jesus, the source of all grace. But it was in the Middle Ages, especially in the thirteenth and fourteenth centuries, that the devotion to the Sacred Heart fully developed under the impulse of mystics like St. Mechthild of Magdeburg (ca. 1210–ca. 1280), first a Beguine, then, at the end of her life, a Cistercian nun at Helfta near Eisleben in Germany; St. Gertrude of Helfta (1256–ca. 1302), called the Great;[1] Bl. Henry Suso (ca. 1295–1366), a German Dominican and mystical theologian, to name only those who exerted the most decisive influence.

In the fourteenth century, the veneration of the Sacred Heart spread in connection with the movement called the "Modern Devotion."[2] In the sixteenth century, the Jesuits gave it a new impetus, and it reached a peak in the seventeenth century, thanks to the French Oratorians of Fr. de Bérulle (1575–1629) and to St. John Eudes (1601–1680) who, having been excluded from the Oratory (1643), founded the Congregation of Jesus and Mary (Eudists). It was he who on October 20, 1672, celebrated for the first time a feast in honor of the Sacred Heart of Jesus. Shortly afterwards, between 1673 and 1675, St. Margaret Mary Alacoque (1647–1690), a Visitandine of Paray-le-Monial in France, received apparitions of Christ, who asked her in particular to have a feast of the Sacred Heart of Jesus instituted on the Friday after the octave of Corpus Christi.[3] Rome delayed to act upon these insistent requests for nearly one hundred years. Only in 1765 did Pope Clement XII (1758–1769) allow the Polish bishops and the Roman Confraternity of the Heart of Jesus to celebrate this feast. Pius IX (1846–1878) extended it to the whole Church. His successor, Leo XIII (1878–1903), bestowed on it a higher rank and, on the occasion of the turn of the century, prescribed the consecration of the world to the Sacred Heart of Jesus.[4] Pius XI (1922–1939) endowed it with an octave and modified its liturgy in order to emphasize the reparation owed to the Heart of Jesus.[5] Finally, a few years before Vatican II, Pius XII (1939–1958), in his turn, published an encyclical on the occasion of the centenary of the extension of the feast of the Sacred Heart to the whole Church (1856–1956); its aim was to dissipate misunderstandings and respond to those who expressed reservations about this sort of worship.[6] We must indeed recognize that devotion to the Sacred Heart developed as an effect of various currents of piety that did not proceed from the same inspiration and that, as a consequence, we can hesitate on the exact object of the feast of the Sacred Heart. Between 1672 and 1840, there were more than thirty formularies granted to the French dioceses and to some religious congregations. Four were successively approved by Rome from 1765 to 1929.[7]

The Missal published after Vatican II (decree of March 26, 1970) brought significant modifications to the formulary of 1929.

> Father,
> we rejoice in the gifts of love we have received
>   from the heart of Jesus your Son.
> Open our hearts to share his life
> and continue to bless us with his love.
> (Opening Prayer)

> Father,
> may this sacrament fill us with love.
> Draw us closer to Christ your Son
> and help us to recognize him in others.
> (Prayer after Communion)

The emphasis is no longer on reparation. Only the prayer over the gifts, taken from the earlier formulary, still mentions it.[8] But, at this place in the Mass it is quite normal.

> Lord,
> look on the heart of Christ your Son

filled with love for us.
Because of his love
accept our eucharist and forgive our sins.

Even the preface was modified in a perspective more theological than devotional. From the contemplation of Christ "lifted high" on the cross—and not "hanging" as in the previous preface—the praise and thanksgiving of the celebrating Church well up.

Father, all-powerful and ever-living God,
we do well always and everywhere to give you thanks
through Jesus Christ our Lord.
Lifted high on the cross,
Christ gave his life for us,
so much did he love us.
From his wounded side flowed blood and water,
the fountain of sacramental life in the Church.
To his open heart the Savior invites all [people],
to draw water from the springs of salvation.

We do not forget that we are sinners, but forgiven sinners because of the offering Christ made of himself out of love.

This orientation of the feast of the Sacred Heart is in perfect harmony with the teaching of Scripture on God's love manifested in his Son, "meek and humble of heart," (Matt 11:29), who said, "Rejoice with me because I have found my lost sheep" (Luke 15:6).[9] This orientation is also definitely more in the line of patristic tradition anterior to the development of a more affective piety.

Jesus, Meek and Humble of Heart, Reveals the Love of God

Between God and His People, a Love Story

By meditating on the events that marked the sealing of the Covenant, the author of Deuteronomy asked himself: What are the reasons that led God to act the way he did? The importance of both the question and the answer we give it is essential. What is at stake is indeed the nature of the relations between God and his people and, correlatively, the deep meaning of the resulting obligations (Deut 7:6-11).

It is enough to recall how events transpired to reveal the obvious: everything comes from God's initiative. In Moses' discourse, Israel is "a people sacred to the LORD" because "he has chosen you from all the nations on the face of the earth to be a people peculiarly his own [and] . . . set his heart on you." This vocabulary is of itself very significant. The chosen people have become the sacred, and therefore inviolable, property acquired by God.[1] He has for his people an attachment which evokes that of a spouse toward the person[2] chosen from among all. But what does this people have that they should be chosen "from all the nations on the face of the earth?" This people had a very modest origin: "My father was a wandering Aramean who went down to Egypt with a small household and lived there as an alien." If they delight in recalling that they "became a nation great, strong and numerous" (Deut 26:5), it is because they owe it to God. The author of Deuteronomy exhorted his readers never to forget this. In order to emphasize this fact more clearly, the writer insisted on the paltriness of the beginnings and, repeating the terms of the promise made to Abraham (Gen 15:5), invited the readers to reflect on what happened: "Your ancestors went down to Egypt seventy strong, and now the LORD, your God, has made you as numerous as the stars of the sky" (Deut 10:22). It is true that the increase of the handful of immigrants was extraordinary. However, they are not to entertain illusions: "It was not because you are the largest of all nations that the LORD set his heart on you and chose you, for you are really the smallest of all nations." Then why? "It was because the Lord loved you and because of his fidelity to the oath he had sworn to your fathers, that he brought you out with his strong hand from the place of slavery, and ransomed you from the hand of Pharaoh, king of Egypt." It was through love and fidelity to his word—love and fidelity forever—that God freely chose as his own "a peculiar people" that, for its part, will never be able to boast of any title that would merit this signal privilege. "Understand, then, that the Lord, your God, is God indeed, the faithful God who keeps his merciful covenant down to the thousandth generation toward those who love him and keep his commandments."

To keep the commandments, that is to say, the clauses of the covenant agreed to, is the response of love to the love that God has first manifested to his own. We are diametrically opposed to a religion of fear; we are not facing a God who imposes his law through the terror his power inspires. To say that he "repays with destruction the person who hates him" is a way of stressing the seriousness, the depth of God's love by comparing him to a jealous lover who cannot tolerate seeing his or her immense love despised.[3] The great mystics of all religions have sensed, and often admirably expressed, the idea that between God and humankind there is indeed a wonderful love story.

> From the beginning until the end of times,
> Love is between you and me.
> How could such a love be extinguished?
> As the river enters the ocean,
> so my heart enters into you.[4]

To "carefully observe the commandments, the statutes and the decrees" of God, to practice them, is to say that one remains attached to God in complete trust. God multiplies his benefactions toward humans because he loves them. To obey him is the way humans can respond to his love that precedes theirs. Deuteronomy never ceases to proclaim this: "You shall love the Lord, your God, with all your heart, and with all your soul, and with all your strength. Take to heart these words which I enjoin on you today" (6:5-6). One and the same word—*agapē* in the New Testament—designates the infinite love of God for humankind and human love for God, to whose level no one ever approaches. But Jesus came. True God, he divinely loved humans with his heart of flesh; perfect human being, he infinitely loved God, his Father, and expressed it to him by "becoming obedient to death, / even death on a cross" (Phil 2:8). In him and through him, it is given us to love God and our brothers and sisters with a divine love—*agapē*—which the Spirit, sent by the Lord, pours out into our hearts.

> *The Lord's kindness is everlasting to those who fear him.*

Bless the LORD, O my soul;
  and all my being, bless his holy name.
Bless the LORD, O my soul,
  and forget not all his benefits;
He pardons all your iniquities,
  he heals all your ills.
He redeems your life from destruction,
  he crowns you with kindness and compassion.

———————

Merciful and gracious is the LORD,
  slow to anger and abounding in kindness.

———————

Not according to our sins does he deal with us,
  nor does he requite us according to our crimes.
(Ps 103:1-4, 8, 10)

God Is Love, the Source of Love

John is the New Testament writer who most frequently uses the verb "love" and the noun "love" when speaking either of God, Christ, or the Holy Spirit or of Christians in their relationships with the divine Persons or among themselves.[5] This is a significant indication—even if we limit ourselves to just the vocabulary—of the central place held by love in John's thought. But it is important to correctly understand what he meant. Indeed, agape,[6] love of charity, is distinct from human love because of its origin, its motives, its effects: it is a supernatural love.[7] The theology, spirituality, and mysticism that John developed are specifically Christian. The main lines of his teaching are found in every passage where, in one way or another, he dealt with the subject: thus, in today's text (1 John 4:7-16).

"Let us love one another." Whether in reference to the gospel message or not, this call to universal love can only be well received by all persons of good will, even though the sight of what is happening in the world causes them to doubt the realism of such a doubt. John addressed believers "Beloved," and appealed to their faith. They must make of this precept their rule of life because "love is of God," because "God is love." The vigor of this affirmation, repeated twice in a few lines, must attract attention. But we cannot take this statement as a definition of God, because it is illusory to claim to really define anybody.[8] We can describe a person by enumerating his or her qualities[9]—physical, moral, intellectual, psychological, and others—that appear most characteristic. We must immediately admit that the person is not reducible to the sum of the qualities listed, and still less to any one of them, no matter how typical, rare, or extreme. If such is true of us, it is a fortiori true of God. This is why the Bible, like all great religious traditions,[10] gives God numerous names, all the while knowing that he is infinitely beyond what we can say of him. John himself also named him "light" (1 John 1:5), "life" (1 John 5:11-20), and the "true" one (1 John 5:20), without claiming to give a complete list of God's names and attributes, which remains and always will remain impossible to establish. However, nothing is more exact than saying "God is love." He manifests himself as love in the most concrete, the most daily, and, we could say, the most obvious ways. Prophets and psalmists have taken pleasure in stressing this with wonderment: mercy and tenderness characterize all the initiatives, all the interventions, all the actions of the Lord God.[11] He added the finishing touch to his work of love on the day he "sent his only Son into the world . . . as expiation for our sins . . . so that we might have life through him." This deed, beyond imagination, manifests most clearly that truly "God is love," for "he first loved us" because that is the way he is. For our part, we had nothing, nothing at all, to render us lovable, since we were sinners. But by coming to us, God transformed us. His love made us his relatives, his friends.

> What were we when he loved us, except ugly and disfigured? He did not love us, however, to leave us to our ugliness, but to change us and to make us beautiful instead of disfigured. How shall we become beautiful? By loving him who is eternally beautiful. The more love grows in you, the more your beauty increases; for charity is the soul's beauty.[12]

To know God, to recognize his love for us, is completely different from an intellectual reasoning that says, "Yes, it is true, God loves us." In John's vocabulary, "to know" has a very strong, an almost technical meaning that expresses the intimate union which faith and received grace bring about between God and the believer.[13] Those who "have come to know and to believe in the love God has for us"—that "God is love"— are "begotten by God": to know is to be born to the divine life, to enter into communion with God, "to remain" in him who "remains" in us.[14] Birth into this divine life confers on believers the power to love God and to love like him. The very exercise of this aptitude is a good indicator of the vitality of the communion of life with God, and at the same time is a means of developing it. "If God so loved us, we also must love one another," John wrote. The duty of universal charity thus corresponds to a law of life and not to an obligation imposed from outside. "The law of love is to allow those who have no feet to walk."[15] The love for brothers and sisters is the decisive test of faith and of vital union with God: "Whoever is without love does not know God"; "whoever does not love a brother whom he sees cannot love God whom he has not seen" (1 John 4:20); he "is still in the darkness" (1 John 2:9). We are already now, and we shall be on the last day, judged on love—"not in word or speech but in deed and truth"—toward God and neighbor.[16]

Jesus Reveals His Father's Love

Some of Jesus' words are like invaluable precious stones, so brilliant that we discover again and again new glints in them; wherever they are placed, their splendor is a cause for wonder. This is the case for the hymn of jubilation that Jesus addressed to his Father, followed by the vibrant call of the Lord inviting everyone to become a disciple (Matt 11:25-30).[17]

"I give praise to you, Father, Lord of heaven and earth, for although you have hidden these things from the wise and the learned you have revealed them to the childlike."[18] God is a Father supremely admirable in his plans and conduct. He manifests his power by reserving his predilection for the most dispossessed, those unable to make advanced studies, overwhelmed by the explanations and discussions to which the learned persons devote themselves in their school teaching. Exegetes and theologians—"wise and learned"—no doubt exercise an indispensable mission in the service of the Church and believers. But their work cannot be "reduced to a pure intellectual game accessible only to specialists." They must refrain from imposing on simple souls "questions to which the latter are incapable of giving an answer." Well discharged in this spirit of service to their brothers and sisters, the task they assume is "an authentic spiritual work accomplished in humble and trustful listening" to the Lord.[19] In the last analysis, everyone must receive what none can see with their own eyes or hear with their own ears, "what has not entered the human heart," what only the Spirit of God can unveil (1 Cor 2:9-10). But, to reach this goal, the "wise and learned" must rid themselves of their riches, overcome the temptation to believe that they are the masters of truth and capable of acceding to heights unreachable by others. Not threatened by this risk, the "childlike"—the simple—are more inclined to count on God, their sole recourse. When they turn to him, they see themselves fulfilled beyond all expectation. Paradoxically, their poverty puts them in a privileged situation: "Blessed are the poor," Jesus can assure them, for he knows the Father's heart and "gracious will," his thoughts and ways of acting. He was sent to witness to them by his words and acts: "The words that I speak to you I do not speak on my own" (John 14:10); "I say to you, a son cannot do anything on his own, but only what he sees his father doing; for what he does, his son will do also" (John 5:19). God, whom nobody has ever seen (John 1:18), has no secret from his Son, and he sent him in order to have us enter into their inaccessible intimacy: "All things have been handed over to me by my Father. No one knows the Son except the Father, and no one knows the Father except the Son and anyone to whom the Son wishes to reveal him."

Having lifted his eyes to heaven to praise his Father, Jesus turned them again toward those who surround him, a crowd of simple folks marveling at finally hearing a rabbi say sublime things in a language they could understand: "Come to me, all you who labor and are burdened, and I will give you rest. Take my yoke upon you and learn from me, for I am meek and humble of heart; and you will find rest for yourselves. For my yoke is easy, and my burden light." Jesus spoke in the way of a master of wisdom who invites the passers-by to become his followers. This sort of public appeal always entails, if not a touch of polemics, at least an invitation to compare what is proposed with what others have to offer. There is some of this in Jesus' call.[20] But his words have a wider scope. The gospel certainly implies serious demands that may lead to radical choices and denials and, as a consequence, cause the timorous and weak disciples we are to hesitate. He tells us, "Become aware of the cost and nature of what is asked of you. What counts is to love. This involves sacrifices and self-denial. But we cannot say that love is a burden which is painful to bear and of which we must rid ourselves. On the contrary, to love, especially to love God and his Son, relaxes, dilates the soul, liberates, allows for growth by urging us to go beyond ourselves more and more." To be a disciple consists in becoming, with Jesus and like him, "meek and humble of heart."

> Why do you fear, he says, to be diminished if you are humble? Look at me and everything about me; come to my school, and you will clearly learn the greatness of the good. Do you see how in many ways he brings them to humility? By his own conduct: "Learn from me, for I am meek and humble"; by the advantages they will gain: "You will find rest for your-

selves"; by the light burden he has prepared for them: "My yoke is easy, and my burden light." Paul does the same thing, saying, "For this momentary light affliction is producing for us an eternal weight of glory beyond all comparison" (2 Cor 4:17).

But, you will object, how is the burden light since he said, "If anyone comes to me without hating his father and mother" and "Whoever does not carry his own cross and come after me cannot be my disciple" and "Everyone of you who does not renounce all his possessions cannot be my disciple," and when he enjoins to hate even our own souls (Luke 14:26-27, 33)? Let Paul instruct us, saying, "What will separate us from the love of Christ? Will anguish, or distress, or persecution, or famine, or nakedness, or peril, or the sword?" (Rom 8:35) and "The sufferings of this present time are as nothing compared with the glory to be revealed for us" (Rom 8:18). Let them instruct you, those who, after receiving one thousand blows [sic], came out of the Sanhedrin "rejoicing that they had been found worthy to suffer dishonor for the sake of the name" (Acts 5:41).[21]

The history of salvation began with the initiative of God, who chose a people in order to make of them the privileged recipients of his revelation and to realize through them his plan of universal redemption. Now, when we reflect on this choice, the conduct of God appears strange; it was with a small clan of nomadic Arameans—and not with a powerful people—that he made a covenant in order to achieve his grand undertaking. This historical experience reveals a God motivated by love only and imposing nothing in return except a response of faithful and eager love (First Reading).

The Lord gave incessant proofs of his tenderness and mercy throughout the history of salvation: by renewing declarations of his indefectible faithfulness, he kept offering his pardon to the people who were forgetful of their commitments; and he always granted it to them at the first sign of repentance, reestablishing them in his friendship and sealing with them a new covenant. Then came the day when "God sent his only Son into the world . . . as expiation for our sins . . . so that we might have life through him." Then we were able to recognize that "love is of God," that "God is love" (Second Reading).

Jesus, who alone knows the Father, came to reveal him to the "childlike," who understand that this knowledge is unattainable by human wisdom and intelligence. By responding to his call and by learning from this master, "meek and humble of heart," who does not crush them under burdens too heavy, they discover the way of love on which they start walking with joy and generosity, assured of finding, near the Lord, rest and peace (Gospel).

For humans to be children in his image,
God worked on them through the breath of the Spirit:
When we had neither form nor face,
His love was seeing us as free as he.

We had received from God the grace of life,
We held it captive to sin:
Hatred and death joined for injustice
And the law of all love was abandoned.

When the favorable day and hour came,
God gave us Jesus, the Beloved:
The tree of the cross shows the way
Toward a world in which everything is consecrated.

Who will set out on a journey toward these great spaces?
Who will take Jesus for a master and a friend?
The humble servant has the best place!
To serve God makes us free as he is.[22]

Jesus Reveals God's Tenderness Through His Pierced Heart

Infinite Mercy of the Holy God

Hosea is one of the earliest writer-prophets.[1] His book exerted a great influence on the way the Covenant between God and his people[2] was understood. He saw it in particular as a stormy conjugal life, full of crises, breaks, and reconciliations, over and over again. The people whom God chose behaved like a woman who regularly abandons her husband to give herself to prostitution. But God, like a passionately loving husband, kept exhorting her to come back to him, promising to forget the recurrent outrage of her scandalous infidelities.[3] It would be impossible to express more forcefully the incredible tenderness of God, a tenderness that nothing can diminish. But images crowd one another in Hosea's writing.[4] Thus, he showed how God, rightly incensed by the ingratitude of his people, was, as it were, unable to yield to anger and resentment: his heart always ended up dictating the sort of action to take (Hos 11:1, 3-4, 8c-9).[5]

"When Israel was a child I loved him, / out of Egypt I called my son." Hosea delighted in recalling that one must always go back to the Exodus, the founding event of God's people, the date of their election, the time of their first education.[6] What went before was a preparation; what followed resulted from it.[7] In the course of his meditation on the behavior of the sadly ungrateful people, Hosea tarried especially on the solicitude of God pursuing, with tenderness, the education of the one he calls "my son."

> Yet it was I who taught Ephraim to walk,
>   who took them in my arms;
> I drew them with human cords,
>   with bands of love;
> I fostered them like one
>   who raises an infant to his cheeks;
>   . . . I stooped to feed my child.

One thinks of a mother who recalls with emotion her nearness to and care of the child she raised. She does not regret in the least so much effort and all those years of daily self-sacrifice. She does not even complain; but she is deeply saddened to see that her son has not understood that she labored for his good and that he, after leaving her, stubbornly remains away and ignores her: he "did not know that I was [his] healer." God is wounded in the depths of his fatherly heart by the sin and ingratitude of his children. Such an image of a God so close to us is moving. And it antedates Christ by seven centuries.

> O my torn heart
> O my tearing heart
> Is there a greater love
> Is there a more resplendent forehead
> Is there a single love that is not wounded
>
> Is there a vaster reign
> Over wave or furrow
> Is there a more auspicious day
> In the shade where we shine
> Is there a single love that does not lack a link
>
> Is there a memory
> On the dark altar of the nights
> Is there another story
> In which yesterday be today
> Is there a single love that is its own fruit
>
> Is there another haven
> Where the ocean is decked with flags
> Is there another fate
> Is there another measure
> Is there a single love where death does not sing
>
> Is there a purer morning
> In the hours of the sea
> A more furtive finger
> On our bitter mouths
> Is there a single love that is not its own destiny
>
> Is there a higher tower
> From which to throw ornaments
> Is there a higher court
> In which to judge perjurers
> Is there a single love that does not need love
>
> Is there a more assured conqueror
> Of our human death
> A more friendly rigor
> A more powerful pain
> Than this boundless love treasured in my heart.[8]

The comparison does not stop here: Hosea pushed it further with a fine boldness, to its tenable limit. Painfully wounded, God asks himself, "How could I give you up?" These ungrateful people deserve a severe lesson: it might lead them to reflect and at least to realize the cruel and unfair wound they have inflicted on their father's affection. But hardly has this idea come to his mind than God rejects it and even reproaches himself with having had it:

> My heart is overwhelmed,
>   my pity is stirred.
> I will not give vent to my blazing anger,
>   I will not destroy Ephraim again.

As unlikely as it may be, here is now the affronted father being ashamed of a feeling of anger that nobody would find out of place, much to the contrary. In some way, it is he who feels the necessity for conversion to better sentiments. Is this a lack of awareness of the real situation? . . . weakness? Not at all:

> For I am God and not man,
>   the Holy One present among you;
> I will not let the flames consume you.

If God loves this much, with a disconcerting love similar to human love yet so different, it is because of his holiness, his transcendence. In spite of all analogies with human love, God's love is of another order, and is not to be compared with the love the best among us may know. We can express something of God's mystery, starting from human experience and from what we are. But at the same time, we must say that God is not so. For in him, none of his qualities has a reverse side, none can be mentioned with any sort of reservation. Moreover, we must add that everything, with him, reaches a degree of infinite perfection.[9] Humans are in the image of God and not the reverse. Knowing this, we may, like Hosea, have recourse to daring anthropomorphisms without, for all that, making a God in our own measure. The one whom we know because he took the initiative to reveal himself surpasses in all ways all the intimations we may have of him.

> *You will draw water joyfully from the springs of salvation.*

> God indeed is my savior;
>   I am confident and unafraid.
> My strength and my courage is the LORD,
>   and he has been my savior.

With joy you will draw water
  at the fountain of salvation . . .
Give thanks to the LORD, acclaim his name;
  among the nations make known his deeds,
  proclaim how exalted is his name.
Sing praise to the LORD for his glorious achievement;
  let this be known through all the earth.
Shout with exultation, O city of Zion,
  for great in your midst
  is the Holy One of Israel!
(Isa 12:2-6)

Toward the Fullness of God Through the Love of Christ

The Letter to the Ephesians is an exposition of Christian faith followed by an exhortation that reminds Christians of their incorporation into the body of Christ through baptism.[10] This magnificent plan of God unfolds in the Church. Paul evoked it with lyricism, in a style liturgical in character.[11] The excerpt read today is to be placed within this context that fits well with that of the feast of the Sacred Heart of Jesus (Eph 3:8-12, 14-19).

Conscious of his unworthiness, the apostle—"[I], the very least of all the holy ones"—received the mission and the "grace . . . to preach to the Gentiles the inscrutable riches of Christ and to bring to light [for all] what is the plan of the mystery hidden from ages past in God who created all things." What a sustained vigor, what an enthusiasm, what a breadth in this sentence! "The manifold wisdom of God . . . [is] made known through the church" to the whole universe: to those to whom the announcement of the good news is addressed on earth, but also to "the principalities and authorities in the heavens." They too discover "the eternal purpose that [God] accomplished in Christ Jesus our Lord." "God who created all things" knew from the beginning to what his initiatives were tending; and when he created humankind, he already saw in it the image of Christ.[12] But he did not unveil in advance what he was to do: no creatures, not even angelic ones, would have been able to comprehend such an unforeseeable plan. Therefore, God limited himself to preparing humans for his revelation by sending prophets to announce it "in partial and various ways" (Heb 1:1). Finally, the hour arrived when "the grace of God has appeared, saving all" (Titus 2:11). Those who welcomed the Lord's word recognized that the times were accomplished, and that God's "eternal purpose" was at last "accomplished in Christ Jesus our Lord." In the strength of this certitude faith gives us, "we have boldness of speech and confidence of access through faith in him"; and in spite of our weakness, we can fearlessly announce to all nations "the manifold wisdom of God."

Upon hearing of this mystery, we can only "kneel before the Father, from whom every family in heaven and on earth is named." Adoration is the fundamental attitude of believers before God, but it is always accompanied by thanksgiving. To worship God, even by prostration with face on the earth, is a gesture made by humans who recognize God's grandeur, but are not crushed by it. For to proclaim that only God possesses being in fullness is to say at the same time that we receive from him existence and being.[13] This awareness and its expression already have, by themselves, the value of thanksgiving. Similarly, to evoke divine blessings and give thanks for them is also an act of adoration. Finally, adoration and thanksgiving—acknowledgement of God's power and memory of the wonders he accomplished—have their "natural" prolongation in the invocation of God, to whom one addresses requests for the forgiveness of sins and fresh graces for oneself or others. This is what Paul did here.[14]

"That [God] may grant you to be strengthened with power through his Spirit in the inner self, and that Christ may dwell in your hearts through faith." This prayer lifts the veil and allows us a glimpse of Paul's spirituality and mystical life, the basis and constant object of his preaching, and the theological dimension of moral life to which he incessantly exhorted the addressees of his letters. Everything comes from the contemplation of the mystery of God—Father, Son, and Holy Spirit—which is absolutely central. The strength of the Father communicated through the Spirit makes humans interiorly unshakable. Paul experienced this personally: "We are not discouraged, rather although our outer self is wasting away, our inner self is being renewed day by day" (2 Cor 4:16). Through faith and baptism, Christians, united to Christ dead and risen, are one with him.[15] They become in him a new creature.[16] The whole of Christian life consists in persevering in faith in order that Christ, who took possession of us at baptism, may continue to "dwell in [our] hearts" and that we may continue to be "rooted and grounded in love."

Thus, we will be able "to comprehend with all the holy ones what is the breadth and length and height and depth, and to know the love of Christ that surpasses knowledge." The unfathomable mystery evoked by the apostle is that of salvation—God's "eternal purpose"—realized by Christ, who delivered himself for us through love. It was given us "to comprehend" it, "to know" it. This comprehension and knowledge comes from faith and not from an effort of intellect. They are based on spiritual experience guided by the Holy Spirit, and not on intellectual speculation. This is the reason the simple are not at a disadvantage. For it is with the heart that one must comprehend and know.[17] The love of Christ is and will remain always for us an abyss whose breadth, length, height, depth no one can ever measure. But those who live "rooted and grounded in love" are led by the Holy Spirit from height to height in the contemplation of the infinite riches of God, the way to which Christ opens us "so that [we] may be filled with all the fullness of God."

> Adorable Father,
> If my heart belonged entirely to your Adorer,
> The Spirit you send down on the world
>   so that the tremulous song of souls might answer you,
> Adorable Father,
> Your Grace in which all things human rest,
> Which holds them up and brings them back to you,
> Adorable Father,
> If I had welcomed your Son in spirit,
> As he became flesh on earth in the past,
> In order to take everything in his passion,
>   and translate it into light,
> Adorable Father,
> I would sing your ineffable Trinity,
> Not I, but your ineffable Adorer,
> Not I, but ineffably Our Lord,
> Adorable Father![18]

Blood and Water Flowed from the Open Side of Jesus

Being a direct and privileged witness of the passion and death of Jesus,[19] John carefully set down in writing the events and details that struck him most particularly. But he did so only after protracted meditation and years of preaching. His Gospel has transmitted to us a condensed narrative of these events.[20] "The one whom Jesus loved," John, called the "theologian" by tradition, thus opened spacious roads to the reflection of Christians desirous of scrutinizing, under the guidance of a witness and peerless spiritual master, the unfathomable mysteries of the faith.[21] John devoted special care to the story of the Lord's passion,[22] dwelling at greater length on a few episodes that appeared to him particularly significant. This is, indeed, the case for the one we read about today (19:31-37).

However, this account might seem at first sight a simple and detailed record of what happened after Jesus died, on a Friday before the beginning of the sabbath, "for the sabbath of that week was a solemn one," the feast of Passover.[23] In reality, this first detail points to the significance of the episode. In fact, several times, John placed the passion and its principal events in relation to this great feast day. The last week of Jesus' life began "six days before Passover," with the meal given at Bethany in his honor, in the house of Lazarus and his sisters. Seeing the "large crowd of the Jews [that] . . . came, not only because of Jesus, but also to see Lazarus, whom he had raised from the dead . . . the chief priests plotted to kill Lazarus too, because many of the Jews were turning away and believing in Jesus because of him" (12:1-11). Jesus took a last meal with his disciples "before the feast of Passover," knowing "that his hour had come to pass from this world to the Father" (13:1). "It was preparation day for Passover, and it was about noon" when Pilate pronounced the death sentence (19:14), and Jesus died a few hours later. A burial place was found in haste in a grave close to the spot of execution "because of the Jewish preparation day" (19:41-42). Concern about chronological exactitude is not sufficient to explain such an insistence. Manifestly, the evangelist wanted to suggest we read the passion of Jesus in reference to the paschal celebration that illuminates its meaning and allows us to perceive its place in God's design.[24]

To hasten the death of the condemned persons, "in order that the bodies might not remain on the cross on the sabbath, for the sabbath day of that week was a solemn one,[25] the Jews asked Pilate that their legs be broken and they be taken down." This the soldiers did to the first and then the second of those who had been crucified with Jesus. "But when they came to Jesus and saw he was already dead, they did not break his legs, but one soldier thrust his lance into his side, and immediately blood and water flowed out." Again, we could see here the statement of an eyewitness recorded simply for the sake of objectivity. But the evangelist said, "For this happened so that the scripture passage might be fulfilled: 'Not a bone of it will be broken.'" We read in one of the psalms:

Many are the troubles of the just man,
   but out of them all the LORD delivers him;
He watches over all his bones;
   not one of them shall be broken.
(Ps 34:20-21)

To be truthful, we do not see clearly how this word, taken by itself, can apply here to Jesus delivered to death. But we then recall that it was prescribed that the bones of the paschal lamb were not to be broken (Exod

12:46). In combination, these two biblical texts clarify the meaning of what
happened after the death of Jesus. Not one of his bones was broken because his death, at this precise hour, was that of the Lamb of the new
passover. The word of the psalm is perfectly realized in Jesus, the Just
One par excellence, who suffered the supreme punishment. God, it is
true, did not save him from death in the way suggested by those who
cruelly mocked him at Calvary: "He saved others; he cannot save himself. So he is the king of Israel! Let him come down from the cross now,
and we will believe in him. He trusted in God; let him deliver him now
if he wants him. For he said, 'I am the Son of God' " (Matt 27:42-43).[26]
But God did not abandon him and did not disappoint him in his expectation: "In the days when he was in the flesh, he offered prayers and
supplications with loud cries and tears to the one who was able to save
him from death, and he was heard because of his reverence. Son though
he was, he learned obedience from what he suffered; and when he was
made perfect, he became the source of eternal salvation for all who obey
him" (Heb 5:7-9).[27] In fact, Jesus died expressing at once his obedience
to and trust in God: "He said, 'It is finished.' And bowing his head, he
handed over the spirit" (John 19:30).

The Fourth Gospel begins with the testimony of John the Baptist, who,
seeing Jesus coming to him, recognized him as the Son of God and "the
Lamb of God, who takes away the sin of the world" (John 1:29).[28] The
Baptist designated him in the same terms to John and Andrew, the brother
of Simon Peter, both of whom "followed Jesus" upon hearing those
words (John 1:36-37).[29] This title evokes the prophetic oracle proclaimed
at the liturgy of Good Friday:

> Though he was harshly treated, he submitted
>   and opened not his mouth;
> Like a lamb led to the slaughter
>   or a sheep before the shearers,
>   he was silent and opened not his mouth.
> Oppressed and condemned, he was taken away,
>   and who would have thought any more of his destiny?
> When he was cut off from the land of the living,
>   and smitten for the sin of his people,
> A grave was assigned him among the wicked
>   and burial place with evildoers,
> Though he had done no wrong
>   nor spoken any falsehood.
> [But the Lord was pleased
>   to crush him in infirmity.]

If he gives his life as an offering for sin,
    he shall see his descendants in a long life,
    and the will of the LORD shall be accomplished through him.
    (Isa 53:7-10)[30]

The Acts of the Apostles relates that an Ethiopian, a high functionary at the court of Queen Candace, was reading this text when he was joined by the deacon Philip who, starting from this oracle, announced to him the good news of Jesus (Acts 8:26-40). The First Letter of Peter also reminds us that we have been liberated from sin "with the precious blood of Christ as of a spotless unblemished lamb. He was known before the foundation of the world but revealed in the final time for you" (1 Pet 1:19-20).[31] This image, to which we are accustomed and which has such a rich content,[32] was commonly used in early catechesis to describe the redeeming sacrifice of the Lord. But in the Book of Revelation, John gave the name of Lamb to the victorious Christ, who is enthroned in heaven near God and to whom the elect render solemn worship.[33] The founding event of the people of God found its perfect accomplishment in the sacrifice of Jesus, the Lamb of God. "Our paschal lamb, Christ, has been sacrificed" (1 Cor 5:7). The great exodus has begun on the road on which the Lord leads all believers.[34]

"One soldier thrust his lance into his side." It is useless to ask questions about the reason for this action, since Jesus was undoubtedly dead.[35] On the other hand, we must keep our eyes lifted up to "him whom they have pierced," to his open side from which "blood and water flowed out." The evangelist insisted: he testified to what he had seen "so that [we] also may [come to] believe." In other terms, we have here a mystery of faith. To perceive it and discover its meaning, we must have recourse to several texts written by John. He reported that "on the last and greatest day of the feast, Jesus stood up and exclaimed, 'Let anyone who thirsts come to me and drink. Whoever believes in me, as scripture says: "Rivers of living water will flow from within him." ' " He said this in reference to the Spirit that those who came to believe in him were to receive" (John 7:37-39).[36] John the Baptist testified that the Spirit had come down on Jesus at his baptism in the waters of the Jordan, and he designated him as "the one who will baptize with the Holy Spirit" (John 1:32-34).[37] Finally, in his conversation with the Samaritan woman at the well of Jacob, Jesus also spoke of a source of water springing up to quench all thirst (John 4:10-14).[38] For John, there exists a definite link between water and the Spirit, this supreme good that Jesus promised to send to his disciples when he would return to his Father and that would testify in Jesus' favor (John 1:5-15). But the blood is associated with water and the Spirit: "This is the one who came through water and blood, Jesus Christ, not by water alone, but by water and blood. The Spirit is the one that testifies, and the Spirit is truth. So there are three that testify, the Spirit, the water and the blood, and the three are of one accord" (1 John 5:6-8).[39]

Each one of these texts opens infinite perspectives on the mystery of the salvation gained for us by Christ, who leads us to the Father, thanks to the Spirit he has sent us from God. The converging lights of these texts illuminate the mystery of the pierced heart of Jesus whence life wells up like a source.

> Open my mouth to the rivulet
> Of the sacred blood flowing from your side,
> As the nursing infant
> Pulls its mother's breast to itself,
>
> So that I may drink joy
> And may exult in the Holy Spirit,
> So that the taste of the Cup may grow delicious,
> The unsullied love of the unmixed Wine.
>
> At your death, O You the Immortal,
> By the death you suffered in your body,
> You transported me into immortality,
> You broke the last nerves of death.[40]

At the end of this brief but concentrated meditation, a prophetic word came to John's memory, "They shall look on him whom they have thrust through" (Zech 12:10). Through what association of ideas did this text come to occupy the evangelist's mind? Why suddenly turn toward those who pierced Jesus' side, and what reaction can we hope to see on their part? When he was speaking to Christians during his lifetime, the evangelist probably explained his thought. If he did not do the same thing here, he nonetheless did not leave us in complete uncertainty about what we must understand. We can go back to the Book of Zechariah to see the context that sheds light on the meaning and scope of this quotation. At the same time, we must remember what John said elsewhere concerning the "elevation" of Jesus on the cross.

The prophet who wrote the second part of Zechariah[41] announced the coming of a humble and peaceful savior.[42] This Messiah-King embodies the ideal of the "poor of Yahweh" to whom he is close;[43] the good shepherd who leads his people[44] knows a tragic destiny, like the Suffering Servant announced by Isaiah.[45] Personally affected by the death of his emissary, God will make of this passion of the servant rejected by his people the beginning of a new era: "I will pour out on the house of David and on the inhabitants of Jerusalem a spirit of grace and petition; and they shall look on him whom they have thrust through" (Zech 12:10). "On that day there shall be open to the house of David and to the inhabitants of Jerusalem, a fountain to purify from sin and uncleanness" (Zech 13:1).[46] Such is the prophecy that finds its realization in Jesus and allows us to understand the mystery of his pierced heart from which springs a source where everyone may come and drink, as in the desert[47] of old, to avoid dying from thirst.

Besides, we remember this word of Jesus recorded by John: "And when I am lifted up from the earth, I will draw everyone to myself. He said this indicating the kind of death he would die" (12:32-33). It is for this "hour" that Jesus came. It marks the full realization of the eternal plan of God, accomplished by the death and resurrection of his Son. Then the Lord sees himself glorified. At last, it is for everyone the hour of the decisive choice.[48] Christ on the cross is the ultimate "sign"; prepared by all the others that mark Jesus' ministry, it unveils their deep meaning. To believe is, by contemplating the Lord's heart pierced by the soldier's lance, to repent one's sins in order to welcome the life won by his sacrifice. Christ's Pasch is a mystery of water and blood in which believers share by receiving baptism and partaking of the Cup of salvation.

> I have seen the living water
> welling up from the heart of Christ, alleluia!
> All those washed in this water
> will be saved and will sing: alleluia!
>
> I have seen the source
> become an immense river, alleluia!
> The children of God gathered
> sang their joy at being saved, alleluia!
>
> I have seen the Temple
> open to all from now on, alleluia!
> Christ returns victorious,
> showing the wound in his side, alleluia!
>
> I have seen the Word
> giving us God's peace, alleluia!
> All those who believe in his name
> will be saved and will sing: alleluia![49]

God has a fatherly heart that, even when outraged by the ingratitude of his children, cannot bring itself to chastise them as they deserve. His tenderness always wins the day. Sacred history is the succession of pardons that he never ceases to grant to his people in order to lead them to understand that outside of him, "the Holy God," they will find neither peace, nor safety, nor joy (First Reading).

But how could we have ever imagined that God can still go farther in the manifestation of his love? He held in reserve the project of an unprecedented intervention that aroused the admiration of even "the principalities and authorities in the heavens" when they learned of it at the same time as did humankind. This "eternal purpose" God realized "in Christ Jesus our Lord." By him who "dwell[s] in [our] hearts through faith," we are enabled to remain "rooted and grounded in love" and to know, thanks to the Church, "the manifold wisdom of God" "from whom every family in heaven and on earth is named," before whom we kneel, but with "confidence of access through faith in him." Such are "the breadth and length and height and depth" of the mystery which has been revealed to us and which we celebrate (Second Reading).

"Lamb of God who takes away the sin of the world," victim of the new Pasch, Jesus, on the cross, shows us his open side from which "blood and water flowed out" into a source of eternal life in which we share in the sacraments. The human heart of the Son of God is there until the end of time as the revelation of the boundless love and tenderness of his Father and our Father (Gospel).

Jesus' Death on the Cross Reveals God's Forgiveness

The Solicitude of God, Shepherd of His People

Among peoples with a deep-seated memory of their nomadic origins, the image of the shepherd is very potent. Whoever exercises a responsible function toward others whose lives are affected to a significant degree by the way he or she discharges this function is called "shepherd," "pastor." This is the case for the Bible, which is rooted in a pastoral culture.[1] As a consequence, it willingly evokes the head of the family or clan, the king, and, in a particular fashion, God himself by giving them the name of shepherd.[2] In the Old Testament, the longest development on the theme of God as shepherd is found in the Book of Ezekiel.[3] Today's first reading is an excerpt from it (Ezek 34:11-16).[4]

"For thus says the LORD God: I myself will look after and tend my sheep." Those who raised sheep on a modest scale cared personally for their flocks[5] or entrusted them to a relative.[6] The wealthy sheep raisers hired shepherds whose services were paid in money or in kind.[7] These shepherds had a heavy responsibility[8] and had to be trustworthy. From now on, God is going to take all matters in hand. The most demanding task consists in gathering the scattered flock "when it is cloudy and dark." This is no easy undertaking, because the sheep can wander quite far. The shepherd must then cover great distances and even go into "foreign lands." In any case, the search for "good pastures" and watering places also necessitates long and exhausting marches. To this is added the need for an unflagging watchfulness to avoid the danger of predators and the raids of pillagers. In sum, this is nomadic life with all its attendant hardships, toil, and hazards of all kinds. Shepherds do not belong to themselves and have no respite. It is easy to understand why householders of means hire salaried personnel. Now God decides to take charge of his innumerable flock in person. With him, his sheep will be assured of enjoying rest. Without having to keep wandering in order to find food, safe from all the dangers of vast deserted places, they will graze in "rich pastures'' ''and on the mountain heights of Israel shall be their grazing ground.''[9]

> Tell me where you go to graze your flock, so that I may find the pasture of salvation, feed on the heavenly food that everyone must eat in order to enter into life. May I run to you who are the source, in order to drink the divine beverage that you cause to well up as from a spring for all the thirsty ones.[10]

For shepherds, every sheep is valuable, whatever the size of the flock. Should only one be missing because it has wandered off, they immediately set out to look for it and do not come back until they find it.[11] God acts in this way because he is the shepherd of his people. His solicitude also appears in the manner in which he cares for the wounded or weak sheep. He attentively nurses the former and strengthens the latter so that all may rejoin the flock in the meadow. However, these special attentions that he lavishes on the weak and sick do not prevent the shepherds from tending the other sheep: ''I shall watch over the fat and healthy. I shall be a true shepherd to them.''[12] God accords to each one in all equity what he or she needs. In the community, we must behave in the same way toward each other; we should not use either our strength or our weakness in order to secure any privilege whatever. Each one must trust, with complete confidence, in the unfailing care of the Lord, who leads his people as the best of shepherds.

> *The Lord is my shepherd;*
> *there is nothing I shall want.*
>
> The LORD is my shepherd; I shall not want.
>   In verdant pastures he gives me repose;
> Beside restful waters he leads me;
>   he refreshes my soul.
> He guides me in right paths
>   for his name's sake.
> Even though I walk in the dark valley
>   I fear no evil; for you are at my side
> With your rod and your staff
>   that give me courage.
> You spread the table before me
>   in the sight of my foes;
> You anoint my head with oil;
>   my cup overflows.
> Only goodness and kindness follow me
>   all the days of my life;

and I shall dwell in the house of the LORD
   for years to come.
(Ps 23)

Christ Died for Us, Proof of God's Love

As a consequence of sin, the condition of humankind was tragic and hopeless. Nothing, not even the observance of the Law, could enable humankind to recapture, together with justice, the friendship of God lost
through sin. However, God did not abandon humans to their distress
and to the power of death, to which their sinful state submitted them.
In his mercy, God "helped all men [and women] to seek and find [him].
Again and again [he] offered a covenant to [humans], and through the
prophets taught [them] to hope for salvation."[13] When Christ came, "in
the fullness of time," the journey of humankind took another direction.
The future was no longer death but life. This radical change was due to
God's grace that alone justifies and to his limitless love (Rom 5:5b-11).[14]

"Indeed, only with difficulty does one die for a just person, though
perhaps for a good person one might even find courage to die." Such
heroic acts do happen sometimes. We hear of cases in which men and
women consciously risk their lives in order to save those of innocent
persons—of sick ones, for instance—or even to die in the place of others
unjustly condemned.[15] But Christ died "while we were still sinners,"
"enemies." Some were in sin for having turned away from God, had
despised his friendship, and broken his covenant. Some others, those
who did not know him—the pagans—were in a dead-end situation, "were
still helpless." God handed over his own Son for all. No one could ever
have imagined that God would go that far, that he loves us to such an
extent. Even after having received this proof, if we want to understand
something of the immensity of this love, we must be in harmony with
it: for only those who share in this boundless love—and its madness—
can understand it. Now this has been granted to us because "the love
of God has been poured out into our hearts through the Holy Spirit that
has been given to us."

We are no longer speaking of "proof," inasmuch as this word suggests
an intellectual, abstract knowledge, but of personal and intimate experience of God's love made possible by the movement of the Spirit.
When we want to speak of it and give an account of it, we are led to use
a language whose boldness and familiarity cannot surprise those carried
away by love.

> O love, you are attacking the very Heart of my Jesus, and with so rough a hand that you nail him to the cross, where he dies of love. O love, what are you doing? Where are the blows aimed at? You spare nothing, you do not stop before having helped the unfortunate. You do not know how to set limits to your tenderness. . . .
>
> This is enough, stop, O my love, do you not see that my Jesus, nailed on the cross, is lifeless? He is dead, really dead, so that life may overflow in me; dead so that the Father may adopt me with more tenderness as his child; dead so that my life may be happier. O death of Jesus, cherished death, you are my blessed heritage. O death, may my soul find in you the sweetest of refuges; you have produced fruits of eternal life; surround me entirely with such waters whence life wells up.[16]

Apparently, nothing is changed in the condition of believers who know what God's love has done for humankind. Their lives remain exposed to the same difficulties as the lives of everyone else. Like them, they are subjected to the implacable law of death. However, their condition has been radically transformed. "We are now justified by his blood," whereas before, "we were still sinners." "While we were enemies, we were reconciled to God through the death of his Son." This is what fundamentally changes everything. For it is a certainty, "we will be saved through him from the wrath. . . . [We will] be saved by his life." The horizon, yesterday completely blocked, now opens onto the infinity of eternal life; life, yesterday doomed to an irremediable failure, is now promised resurrection with Christ. "Already"—"not yet": what we are guarantees what we shall become; Christian hope bears upon the full unfolding of our present condition. Our assurance and our pride can be without limits, for they do not rest on ourselves, on our own merits, on any right conferred by a generous observance of the Law. "We boast of God through our Lord Jesus Christ, through whom we have now received reconciliation." "The breadth and length and height and depth" (Eph 3:18) of the love, of which God has given us the proof, are infinite. The open side of Christ on the cross reveals it. It is in it, and in it alone, that our faith and hope reside. The more we become aware of the meaning of this testimony of infinite love, the more we want it to be recognized by all.

> The wound in your side is large, Lord,
> and if you lend me a hand
> I shall make it larger still.[17]

God's Heart Full of Rejoicing in Forgiveness

The parable of the lost sheep, which the shepherd looks for through hill and dale, is one of the best known. It is an illustration of the immense mercy and tenderness of God, revealed through the way Jesus acted; it takes on its full meaning in the context of today's feast (Luke 15:3-7).[18]

"What man among you having a hundred sheep and losing one of them would not leave the ninety-nine in the desert and go after the lost one until he finds it?" As is usual in the parables, Jesus drew on his hearers' experience in order to elicit from them a judgment on the situation evoked or the attitude of the persons playing a part in it. Then his teaching built on this reaction. It had bearing on the types of behavior to imitate or to avoid.[19] All hearers of the parable Jesus narrated would have approved of the conduct of this man who set out to seek his lost sheep, even if they had no personal experience of such a situation.[20] Now, God acts like this shepherd: he goes searching for the smallest of his own and does not rest until he finds him or her.[21]

"And when he does find it, he sets it on his shoulders with great joy and, upon his arrival home, he calls together his friends and neighbors and says to them, 'Rejoice with me because I have found my lost sheep.'" If we had here only an ordinary story, we could admire the precision and exactitude of the description. The shepherd is overjoyed—his joy being the greater as his search has been the longer and the more anxious—when, at the end of his wandering, he at last finds the sheep he was looking for far and wide. He places it on his shoulders because he is in a hurry to bring it back home—he would tire the sheep if he pushed it ahead of him, obliging it to walk at his pace without tarrying along the way to nibble at some grass. Besides, everybody knows that it is a spontaneous reflex to clutch to oneself whatever was lost and is found. Lastly, it is equally normal to invite friends and neighbors to share in one's joy in such circumstances.[22] However, this accumulation of traits, observed and depicted with such accuracy, aims at making us understand the conduct of God toward those who stray.

"I tell you, in just the same way there will be more joy in heaven over one sinner who repents than over ninety-nine righteous people who have no need of repentance." Having known this parable for a long time and by heart, we do not find its conclusion surprising. However, if we take the trouble to think a little, we see here an absolutely astonishing teaching. With the whole force of his authority—"I tell you"—Jesus teaches that the solicitude of God toward his creatures goes far beyond what we could expect even after taking, on faith, the prophetic predictions. He is not content with affectionately watching over his own, gathering them, and leading them to rich pastures.[23] He takes pains to find any lost sheep.

To find it and bring it back home gives him so much joy that he shares it with the angels in heaven. "Here is the mystery of mysteries: God does not have our disgusts; God does not have any disgusts."[24] Jesus did not limit himself to teaching this in words that can always be explained away; he taught it in the most concrete manner by his way of behaving with sinners, with those whom the self-righteous of his time and all times abandon to their fate, whom they studiously avoid rather than seek. The import that this kind of teaching by actions is such that we can only accept it or reject it, thereby rejecting the teacher.

But what about the ninety-nine righteous who do not need repentance? Does God feel only coldness and indifference toward them? Does their perseverance in doing good cause him no joy? The parable speaks as one always does in similar cases. We rejoice over the recovery of a sick person, the return home of a lost child; but those in good health, those always around, are our everyday joy.[25] Not to have to worry about them is a blessing that allows us to devote time and energy to others who otherwise would be lost beyond help. The just ones must rejoice over God's solicitude toward sinners and participate in his joy when they are converted. Also, knowing that God acts in this manner toward sinners confirms the just ones in the certitude of being deeply loved too. Parents' love cannot be divided. They do not take from the one what they give to the other. This is even truer when we speak of God, whose love is infinite.

> The Good Shepherd, that is, the good shepherd.
> Through the lost sheep he has known anxiety.
> Through this one that did not stay with the ninety-nine others.
> The deadly anxiety.
> (The devouring anxiety in the heart of Jesus).
> The anxiety of not finding it. Of not knowing.
> Of never being able to find it. The human anxiety.
> The deadly anxiety of having to condemn it.
> But finally it is saved.
> He is saved from having to condemn it.
> How he breathes more freely.
> At least this one is saved.
> He will not have to condemn this soul.[26]

"This parable of the lost sheep suggests to us two traits of the merciful love of God: it is a love that worries and it is a love that acts. God knows the blessed fear of love, the fear well known to those who have truly loved in their lives: the fear of losing what one loves."[27] But if Jesus was able to speak in these terms, with equal simplicity and fervor, it was because he totally shared the intimacy of God's heart, because he loved with the same love as God all of humankind to which he was sent.[28] He went so far as to die in order "to gather into one the dispersed children of God" (John 11:52).

Already in the Old Testament, God revealed himself as the Good Shepherd who foresees the needs of his own and lavishes his care on them. Jesus used this traditional image to speak of the love of his Father, who unceasingly pursues the lost sheep and, full of joy, brings them back so that they may enjoy, in peace again, the goods he supplies in abundance to his flock. Being the perfect image of his Father, whose feelings and concern for all humans, especially those who are lost or at risk, he shares, Jesus realized God's plan by delivering himself to death in order to save us. He is the proof that God loves us, for in him, the Son, the heart of his Father and our Father is beating.

> We do not know your mystery,
> Infinite Love;
> But you have a heart,
> You who seek the lost child,
> And hold in a tight embrace
> This difficult child
> That is the world of humankind.
>
> We do not see your face,
> Infinite Love;
> But you have eyes,
> For you weep in the oppressed,
> And you rest upon us
> This look of light
> That reveals your pardon.
>
> We do not see your work,
> Infinite Love;
> But you have hands
> That lighten our labor,
> And you toil with us
> To make on the earth
> A way leading to your rest.
>
> We do not know your language,
> Infinite Love;
> But you are a cry
> That our brothers and sisters hurl at us.
> And the sinner's call

      Coming up from the abyss
      Toward the God of freedom.[29]

The three solemnities of the Holy Trinity, the Body and Blood of Christ, and the Sacred Heart were, in the beginning, devotional feasts. Their celebrations progressively spread, not without occasional reservations, and it was only after a long period that they were finally written into the universal calendar of the Latin Church. Besides, they were successively given several liturgical formularies. These facts teach us a few things worth remembering. First of all, we see that the Christian people play an active part, even take the initiative, in the development of the liturgy of the Church.[30] But we also see that the pope and the bishops, guardians of the faith that the liturgy expresses and promotes, exercise their responsibility of discernment.[31] They must be attentive to possible errors and deviations, encourage what is sound, see to it that the greatest number benefit by what is best.[32]

The fact that celebrations have been successively given different formularies shows that the understanding of a mystery can and must become more refined, that it is sometimes necessary to revise a liturgical expression excessively marked by the mentality or the sensibility of a given period or by the context of its origins. The feast of the Sacred Heart is a particularly eloquent example, but it is not isolated.[33] In any case, even if a few formularies have remained unchanged for a long time, all are inserted into history, into a living tradition.

The liturgy of the solemnities of the Holy Trinity, the Body and Blood of Christ, and the Sacred Heart of Jesus have received additional readings, since now there are three different sets of readings for Years A, B, and C. As a consequence, the perspectives of their celebrations are considerably enlarged. The mysteries are thus more clearly inserted into the dynamics of the history of salvation, and these feasts can no longer be regarded as mere devotions. The celebration of Trinity Sunday dwells on the fact that the unfolding of salvation in time is the work of the Father, the Son, and the Holy Spirit, one God in three Persons who act always and everywhere in perfect communion. The solemnity of the Body and Blood of Christ makes explicit the Eucharistic dimension of the Church and all believers; it makes them conscious of the presence of him who wanted to sacramentally remain among his own, Bread of eternal life, Wine of the new kingdom. Lastly, the solemnity of the Sacred Heart of Jesus celebrates the love of God revealed by Christ, who died so that we may have the life that for all humans flows from his pierced side.

Together, these three liturgies project a light that prevents us from yielding to the temptation of judging as monotonous and bland the long period of Ordinary Time, which is now beginning.

> God is the Ungraspable; left to ourselves, we would expect him to evade us, to be aloof from us, finite creatures, until he asks an account from us at his tribunal. But in Jesus Christ—in Jesus Christ alone, when everything is said and done—we experience a God who shares himself with us, with the reality of his Being; a God who forgives; the absolute proximity of the infinite Mystery. We discover by experience that the most intimate center of reality, the heart of all reality, is love, and not distance or judgment; it is gratuitous and merciful love.[34]

The Sanctoral Cycle

Solemnities and Feasts, Celebrated Even if Occurring on a Sunday

The celebrations of the Sanctoral Cycle[1] assigned to fixed days in the present[2] Roman Calendar are classified in four groups according to their importance: solemnities,[3] feasts,[4] obligatory memorials, and optional memorials.[5] Six of these solemnities,[6] the feasts of the Presentation of the Lord, the Transfiguration, the Assumption, the Dedication of St. John Lateran, All Saints, and All Souls are always celebrated on the day assigned in the calendar, even if it is a Sunday.

The special treatment accorded these solemnities does not deviate from the principle which states that "the Lord's Day is the original feast day . . . [and] is the foundation and nucleus of the whole liturgical year."[7] The Presentation of the Lord and the Assumption of the Virgin Mary, the Transfiguration and the Triumph of the Cross are all celebrations that refer to and illuminate the paschal mystery. The offering of the child Jesus in the Temple in conformity with the Law foreshadowed the offering on the cross, supreme expression of the total obedience that Christ gave his Father throughout his life. The transfiguration of the Lord, witnessed by Peter, James, and John, offers us—in a paschal icon—the celebration of Christ who, through his passion and resurrection, entered the radiant light of the Father, who glorified his Son's humanity. The feast of September 14 is in continuity with the adoration of the glorious cross on Good Friday, which cannot on that day be expressed with fitting splendor. The Assumption of the Virgin Mary celebrates her passage from death to life, she who believed in the fulfillment of God's promises: as she shared in the sufferings of him crucified, so is she associated with the glory of her risen Son. When celebrating All Saints, the Church proclaims their holiness and renders thanks to Christ our Lord "handed over for our transgressions and . . . raised for our justification" (Rom 4:24). On November 2 the Church prays for "our brothers and sisters / who have gone to their rest / in the hope of rising again,"[8] for all the dead "who have left this world in [God's] friendship,"[9] and for "all the dead whose faith is known to [God] alone."[10] God raised Jesus from the dead and "will give life to [the] mortal bodies also" of all the deceased.

On the birthday of John the Baptist, the liturgy, like the Gospels, turns our eyes toward him who came to save his people and whose forerunner John was. The Christian assembly sings its thanksgiving to the faithfulness, "the tender mercy of our God." He "has visited and brought redemption to his people." "He has raised up a horn of salvation / within the house of David his servant." He gave "his people knowledge of salvation . . . / to shine on those who sit in darkness and death's shadow, / to guide our feet into the way of peace" (Luke 1:68-79).

The feast of Sts. Peter and Paul, apostles, celebrates the mystery of the Church, whose cornerstone is Christ. Similarly, we remember the dedication of the basilica of St. John Lateran, built shortly after the end of the persecutions (ca. 320), because it is the cathedral of the bishop of Rome who "watches over charity,"[11] over the communion, in the same faith and hope, of all the churches scattered throughout the whole world.[12]

These nine feasts are really Days of the Lord: this is why Christians are invited to gather into festive assemblies to celebrate them. On the other days of the week, we limit ourselves to the Office and Eucharist of the current liturgical time: feasts have their own formularies.[13] However, the veneration of saints has not been minimized;[14] it is traditional in the Church.[15] Besides, a believer's piety may be very legitimately attached to this devotion that, well understood, remains a source of great spiritual profit.[16]

> Father, all-powerful and ever-living God, . . .
> You are glorified in your saints,
> for their glory is the crowning of your gifts.
> In their lives on earth
> you give us an example.
> In our communion with them,
> you give us their friendship.
> In their prayer for the Church
> you give us strength and protection.[17]

> We do well always and everywhere to give you thanks.
> [Your saints] inspire us by their heroic lives,
> and help us by their constant prayers
> to be the living sign of your saving power.
> We praise you, Lord with all the angels and saints in their songs of joy.[18]

The Presentation of the Lord

The fortieth day after the Epiphany is undoubtedly celebrated here with the very highest honour, for on that day there is a procession, in which all take part, in the Anastasis, and all things are done in their order with the greatest joy, just as at Easter. All the priests, and after them the bishop, preach, always taking for their subject that part of the Gospel where Joseph and Mary brought the Lord into the Temple on the fortieth day, and Symeon and Anna the prophetess, the daughter of Phanuel, saw Him—treating of the words which they spake when they saw the Lord, and of that offering which His parents made. And when everything that is customary has been done in order, the sacrament is celebrated, and the dismissal takes place.[1]

This testimony is that of a Christian woman of the fourth century who wrote down in her travel diary what she saw during her pilgrimage to the Holy Land.[2] Like many other feasts connected with specific places in Jesus' life,[3] that of the Presentation of the Lord in the Temple originated there; it was celebrated as a continuation of the birth of the Lord.[4] We read in Luke's Gospel (2:22), "When the days were completed for their purification according to the law of Moses, they took him up to Jerusalem to present him to the Lord."[5] After the birth of a boy, the purification of the mother took place after forty days (Lev 12:1-2, 6-8). This event was celebrated "on the fortieth day" after Epiphany.[6] When this feast spread to the West, in the second half of the seventh century, it was placed forty days after Christmas, that is to say, on February 2.

In Jerusalem, as attested by Egeria, the object of the feast was rigorously determined by the Gospel narrative. When it was adopted in Syria, in the sixth century, it received in Constantinople the name of "Encounter" (*Ypapante* in Greek). Later on, in the middle of the eighth century in Gaul, it received the title "Purification of the Blessed Virgin Mary," which it kept until 1969. But the procession instituted in Rome by Pope Sergius I (687-701)—it took place at dawn, before Mass, and people carried lighted candles—popularized the name *Chandeleur* in Gaul (Candlemas in English-speaking lands).[7] Now called "Presentation of the Lord,"[8] it has clearly returned to its original orientation: it is a celebration of the

Lord that concludes the solemnities of the Nativity, although Ordinary Time has already begun on the day after Epiphany.

The procession has lost much of its importance and may be replaced by a solemn entrance of the priest. After the singing of the antiphon "The Lord will come with mighty power, and give light to the eyes of all who serve him, alleluia,"[9] he blesses the candles.

> God our Father, source of all light,
> today you revealed to Simeon
> your Light of revelation to the nations.
> Bless these candles and make them holy.
> May we who carry them to praise your glory
> walk in the path of goodness
> and come to the light that shines for ever.

In order to ask God for his light, symbolized by the candles, he may use the following prayer.

> God our Father, source of eternal light,
> fill the hearts of all believers
> with the light of faith.
> May we who carry these candles in your church
> come with joy to the light of glory.

The singing of the canticle of Simeon—"Now Master, you may let your servant go / in peace according to your word" (*Nunc dimittis*)—rightly places the liturgical approach within the perspective of the gospel narrative and within the perspective of an encounter with Christ, "light of the nations." The same is true of the entrance antiphon in the missal:

> Within your temple we ponder your loving kindness, O God. As your praise reaches to the ends of the earth, your right hand is filled with justice.

The Preface states, "Our hearts are joyful / for we have seen your salvation / and now with the angels and saints / we praise you for ever." Finally, after Communion, we ask God "to prepare us to meet Christ / when he comes to bring us into everlasting life."

Despite the various names it has received in the course of ages, the feast of February 2 has remained rooted in the Eastern tradition of its origins: the first reading (Mal 3:1-40) and the Gospel (Luke 2:22-40) come from the original formulary. This is due to the fact that Pope Sergius I, who introduced the feast into the West along with other feasts of Mary—Birth of Mary (September 8), Annunciation (March 25), Assumption (August 15)—was himself an Easterner, a Syrian born in Sicily.

The feast of the Presentation of the Lord is a prolongation of the feast of the Nativity. But it has a definite paschal coloration: the acclamation of Christ as Light is a prelude to that which will flow unrestrained in the liturgy of the Easter Vigil: the Encounter with God coming among us, in his Son made human, has its prolongation and fulfillment in the encounter that the Risen Christ is preparing for us at the end of our earthly pilgrimage, in a pasch like his.

Light up your house, Jerusalem.
Welcome Jesus, your Lord
with Mary, his Mother, the Virgin of the new day:
she carries in her arms
the Son born of the Father before the light.

Sing and rejoice,
Daughter of Zion;
Here is your King and Savior.

Blessed are you, you who believed,
blessed the fruit of your womb.

Blessed are you, holy Virgin,
who bore the Creator of the world.

Blessed are you, you who welcome the Word,
Light for the world.

Sing and rejoice,
Daughter of Zion;
Here is your King and Savior.[10]

Going to Meet the Awaited One, the Light of the Nations

The Messenger of the Covenant Is Coming

The last of the prophetic writings, the Book of Malachi has captured the attention of its readers chiefly because of its insistence on the imminent coming of "the Day of the Lord," who will accomplish the purification of his people. We must prepare for it by living according to the law of the Lord in such a way that we may render him a pleasing worship. Then we shall be in a position to welcome the messenger whom God will surely send to open the way to himself (Mal 3:1-4).[1]

This prophetic oracle takes place in the climate of gloom and disappointment often besetting peoples and religious communities. It usually creeps in after a first period of euphoria following the dawning of long-expected days that have nourished one's dreams during years of trial, decadence, and oppression. Would it not be marvelous if, in a renewed world, liberation and peace, the restoration of past splendor and prosperity were to come about? One has courageously undertaken the work of rebuilding the ruins and making a new start. But soon one has to sing a different tune. The old difficulties and problems reappear, to which new ones are added, the more bitterly felt because one had been imagining a totally different scenario. It seems that no lesson has been learned from the harsh experience, that the generous projects worked up together are forgotten as soon as the time for implementing them comes.[2] The Book of Malachi attests to the situation that followed the resettlement of the exiles returning from the Babylonian captivity to their own land. The Temple had been rebuilt, but with less enthusiasm than expected (Hag 2:2-4); the priesthood and the worship had been restored, but the general mentality was again weighed down by religious formalism and soulless ritualism (Mal 2:1-9); families had been reunited, but social and familial relations were lamentable (2:10-17). It was high time, the prophet said, to awaken from one's slumber, to shake off one's apathy, to react against the prevalent easygoing ways, instead of timorously withdrawing into oneself, saying despondently, "Every evildoer / is good in the sight of the LORD, / And he is pleased with him" or "where is the just God?" (2:17).

The prosperity of the wicked has always been a subject of scandal.[3] The condoning silence of the very people who should have reestablished justice and their infidelity to the Covenant intensified the confusion in people's minds (Mal 2:1-8). To those who were forgetting the Law, the prophetic oracle directed a stern warning that was, for the others, an encouragement to persevere in doing good without losing patience:

> Lo, I am sending my messenger
> to prepare the way before me;
> And suddenly there will come to the temple
> the LORD whom you seek.[4]

To those who said "There is no God; he stands aloof; he hides; he will not avenge it" (Ps 10:4, 1); to those who every day heard it said "Where is your God?" (Ps 42:11); to the just threatened with discouragement, not knowing where to turn, the Lord revealed himself and answered "Here I am, I am coming."

This coming would happen in two phases: first the arrival of a messenger commissioned to prepare the way, then that of "the Lord" in person.[5] Of course, people have wondered about the identity of the messenger-forerunner announced by the prophet.[6] Today, rather than the answer to this query, it is the insistence on the coming of the Lord "to the temple" that rivets our attention.[7] The liturgy places side by side this prophetic oracle and the object of the feast celebrated, thereby suggesting that we see in the presentation of Jesus in the Temple the fulfillment of Malachi's prophecy. But we must go farther than the material facts if we want to perceive the whole meaning of this parallelism. The return of the glory of the Lord into the Temple is one of the characteristic themes of the prophets' preaching. God himself must come to purify the sanctuary, the place of his presence and, starting from there, the whole people (Ezek 43:1-9). He will act like the metalworker who subjects ore to the fire to rid it of its impurities, like the fuller who attacks stains on cloth with a potent agent. The prospect of this purifying intervention of the Lord must give us pause because it will reveal the deep worth of each person: "Who will endure the day of his coming?"

Since he comes "to the temple," the Lord will take his time purifying, in the first place, the priests and other ministers of the sanctuary: "the sons of Levi." The matter at hand is not only the correction of abuses that tarnish the worship but also the reform of the personal conduct of its ministers.[8] Indeed, God is offended when the offering is presented by priests who do not live a righteous life. At the same time, the reprehensible behavior of the priests and other ministers turns the people away from the Lord who, for his part, also withdraws from the Temple. On the contrary, the encounter with God takes place when praise comes from pure lips together with the offering of a life led in justice.

> One night, a man was crying, "Allah," until his lips became sweet with His praise. The Devil said to him, "O man of many words, where is the answer 'Here I am' to all these 'Allahs'?
>
> "No answer comes from the divine Throne. How long are you going to repeat 'Allah' with a somber face?"
>
> These words broke the man's heart. He lay down to sleep and saw in a dream Khadir surrounded by foliage who told him, "Listen, you stopped praising God. Why do you repent of calling him?" He answered, "No 'Here I am' reaches me in response. I fear being repelled far from the door."
>
> Khadir answered, "No. God says: ' "Allah" is my "Here I am"; and this sweetness, this fervor from you is my Messenger to you. Your fear and your love are the lasso to capture my grace:
>
> 'Under each "O Lord" from you is many a "Here I am" from me.' "[9]

Following numerous messengers, John the Baptist was sent by God to prepare the way of the Lord.[10] Jesus came. Still an infant, he was carried by his parents into the Temple of Jerusalem, in which he later frequently announced the good news, and out of which he one day expelled the merchants[11] before making of his body the temple of the new worship (John 2:22) "in Spirit and truth" (John 4:24).

> *Who is this king of glory?*
> *It is the Lord!*
>
> Lift up, O gates, your lintels;
>   reach up, you ancient portals,
>   that the king of glory may come in!
> Who is this king of glory?
>   The LORD, strong and mighty,
>   the LORD, mighty in battle.
> Lift up, O gates, your lintels;
>   reach up, you ancient portals,
>   that the king of glory may come in!
> Who is this king of glory?
>   The LORD of hosts; he is the king of glory.
> (Ps 24:7-10)

Jesus, Human Among Humans, Merciful High Priest

Jesus realized beyond all expectation the promises of a messenger of the Covenant sent to "purify the sons of Levi" so that they may be able to present a pure offering to God.[12] Jesus came to be the high priest of a new and eternal covenant. Son of God, he offered once for all the perfect sacrifice and reconciled humankind to their Lord by taking on the human condition (Heb 2:14-18).[13]

Jesus' solidarity with humankind was a total one. He took on a nature of "blood and flesh" like our own and submitted to the common law of death that entered the world as a consequence of sin into which the devil caused humankind to fall. But for him, the Just One, death was not a consequence of sin. On the contrary, he freely surrendered to it. He accepted it because of his flawless fidelity to God and his total obedience to the Father: thus, "made perfect, he became the source of eternal salvation for all who obey him" (Heb 5:7-9). His flesh, which was not for him a source of sin,[14] was glorified; the blood he poured out did not signify life lost forever: it became "a spring of water welling up to eternal life" (John 4:14).[15]

> [Jesus], though he was in the form of God,
> did not regard equality with God
>   something to be grasped.
>   Rather, he emptied himself,
> taking the form of a slave,
> coming in human likeness;
> and found human in appearance,
>   he humbled himself,
> becoming obedient to death,
>   even death on a cross.
> Because of this, God greatly exalted him
> and bestowed on him the name
> that is above every name.
> (Phil 2:6-9)

Jesus made of death a passage, a pasch that opens onto life and glory, and no longer onto darkness. Of course, this death was painful for him as it is for everyone; it remains a distressing trial that no one escapes. But, assured from now on that we are freed from the power of death, "that is, the devil,"[16] we are not "subject to slavery all [our] life" and are not leading an existence without any other perspective than that of the darkness toward which we are advancing.

I was not rejected although I was considered to be so,
And I did not perish although they thought it of me.

Sheol saw me and was shattered,
And Death ejected me and many with me.

I have been vinegar and bitterness to it,
And I went down with it as far as its depth.

Then the feet and the head it released,
Because it was not able to endure my face.

And I made a congregation of living among his dead;
And I spoke with them by living lips;
In order that my words might not be unprofitable.

And those who had died ran towards me;
And they cried out and said, Son of God, have pity on us.

And deal with us according to Thy kindness,
And bring us out from the bonds of darkness.

And open for us the door
By which we may come out to Thee;
For we perceive that our death does not touch Thee.

May we also be saved with Thee,
Because Thou art our Savior.

Then I heard their voice,
And placed their faith in my heart.

And I placed my name upon their head,
Because they are free and they are mine.
Hallelujah.[17]

"Surely he did not help angels but rather the descendants of Abraham."
This way of speaking does not imply any limit to the redeeming value
of Christ's death. He wanted "to reconcile all things for him, / making
peace by the blood of his cross, / whether those on earth or those in
heaven" (Col 1:20). But the author of Hebrews insisted on the reality of
the human condition of Christ and of his death that was like ours. He
was not an angel with a human appearance; he did not feign death like
an angel that death cannot reach. Similarly, he did not die just for those
who are among "the descendants of Abraham" by birth, but for all those
who belong to Abraham by faith.[18]

> O goodness, charity, admirable generosity! Where the Lord will be there
> the servant will be; could any greater glory be given to us? The servant will
> reign with the Lord. What can we render to you, Lord God, for so many
> benefits of your mercy? . . . For your Son, our King, has not taken charge

of angels but of the descendants of Abraham, having become like us except for sin (Heb 2:16-17). It is indeed human nature, not angelic nature, that he has assumed and, glorifying it by the gift of the holy resurrection and immortality, he has lifted it above all the heavens, above all the angels, above the cherubim and seraphim, and placed it in him, at your right.

It is human nature which the angels praise, the blessed spirits adore; it is human nature before which the powers on high bow and the innumerable heavenly creatures throb with delight. Here is my whole hope: in this human being who is Christ, there is a part of each of us, there is blood, there is flesh. And where a part of my being reigns, I believe that I also reign.[19]

By reason of his twofold nature, human and divine, Christ is the perfect high priest who, after having offered to the Father the sacrifice able "to expiate the sins of the people," efficaciously intercedes for us with God.[20] But he continues to exercise his mercy toward his brothers and sisters on earth, still in the throes of the hardships inherent to the human condition and of the daily difficulties confronting those who want to live according to God's law. "'Son though he was, he learned obedience through what he suffered" (Heb 5:8); he has "been tested in every way, yet without sin" (Heb 4:15). It is therefore knowingly that "he is able to help those who are being tested."

It is he who, still now, bears our weakness and our diseases, for he is himself human, exposed to all misfortunes and capable of taking upon himself the weakness which we would be unable to assume without him. It is he, yes, it is he who carries in us and for us the weight of the world in order to deliver us from it. Here is how strength gives its full measure in weakness (2 Cor 12:9). It is he who in you endures contempt, and it is he whom the world hates in you. Let us give thanks to the Lord, for he is brought to trial and he wins the victory (Rom 3:4). According to this word of Scripture, it is he who triumphs in us when, by taking on the condition of servant, he wins for his servants the grace of freedom.[21]

The Messiah of the Lord, Light of the Nations

What is called "Luke's Infancy Narrative," made up of seven tableaux,[22] is a sort of prologue to the whole book.[23] An attentive reading of these carefully crafted passages reveals their great doctrinal and spiritual riches. The story of the presentation in the Temple holds a special importance. It sketches some major traits of the Lord's mission and destiny; it underlines the importance of the Old Testament and the role of the Law (Luke 2:22-40).[24]

"When the days were completed for their purification according to the law of Moses, they took him up to Jerusalem to present him to the Lord."[25]

His way of introducing the story contains, in its very simplicity, several important teachings. First of all, we notice that attention is centered right away on Jesus: Mary's purification is simply mentioned, whereas the evangelist dwells on what concerns the infant.[26] The infancy narratives are really gospel, that is to say, announcement of the mystery of Christ that they unveil, if only a little. What is said here already sheds light on what the book will develop. The evangelist emphasized that Jesus, by submitting to the prescriptions of the Law imposed on first-born sons, manifested as soon as he entered this world his obedience to God, his Father (Luke 2:49).[27]

Second, we are struck by the place Mary occupies. Mother of the Savior, she is naturally prominent in the stories of the birth and the infancy of Jesus, but with a remarkable discretion and self-effacement. Luke recorded few of the Virgin's words: at the Annunciation (1:34, 38) and at the time when, with Joseph, she found Jesus in the Temple among the doctors (2:48). Luke also attributed to her the song of the Magnificat in response to Elizabeth's salutation (1:46-55), but this is all for the some three months she spent with her cousin (1:56). There was no word of hers at the birth or the presentation of Jesus. She was there, intensely involved in the mystery with which she is associated, but silently: "Mary kept all these things, reflecting on them in her heart" (2:19). Such would be her attitude during the whole ministry of Jesus. Luke did not even explicitly mention her among the faithful women who followed Jesus to Calvary (23:49). On the other hand, he noted her presence with the apostles, some women, and close relatives of Jesus in "the upper room" in Jerusalem where the little group dwelt after the resurrection and ascension of the Lord (Acts 1:14). She was there, always silent, when the Spirit, who came down upon her so that she might become the mother of Jesus (Luke 1:35), came down again so that the Church might be born.

Such is Mary in the unfolding of the plan of salvation, today as yesterday. Associated in a unique manner with her Son's work, she is self-effacing so that Jesus may be seen in the place of honor for which no creature can contend. Through her attitude of humble servant of the Lord, Mary shows the rightful place she is to occupy in Christians' piety, and how the Church, whose perfect image she is, must understand its own vocation and assume its God-given mission. "The Church does not hesitate to profess this subordinate role of Mary. She experiences it continually and commends it to the heart of the faithful so that encouraged by this maternal help they may more closely adhere to the Mediator and

Redeemer."[28] "The offices and privileges of the Blessed Virgin . . . are always related to Christ, the Source of all truth, sanctity and piety."[29]

"Now there was a man in Jerusalem whose name was Simeon. This man was righteous and devout, awaiting the consolation of Israel, and the holy Spirit was upon him. It had been revealed to him by the holy Spirit that he should not see death before he had seen the Messiah of God." This last notation and the advanced age of the prophetess Anna, who came upon the scene after him, have led interpreters to see Simeon as an old man. Be this as it may, Simeon was the representative of all the just of Israel full of the hope of seeing the One sent by God, announced by the prophetic oracles collected under the title of "Book of Consolation of Israel" (Isa 40–55). In order to express the object and spirit of Simeon's expectation, Luke used the same device he used in the narratives of the visit of Mary to her cousin Elizabeth (1:46-55) and the birth of John (1:68-79): he had Simeon sing a canticle of praise.

> Now, Master, you may let your servant go
>   in peace, according to your word,
> for my eyes have seen your salvation,
>   which you prepared in sight of all the peoples,
> a light for revelation to the Gentiles,
> and glory for your people Israel.

In the same line of inspiration as Isaiah,[30] Simeon saw salvation as the dawning of light on the nations. Luke could not but clearly affirm early in his narrative this universalism, foretold by the prophet (Isa 52:7-10), a theme to which he often returned in his Gospel and Acts. Together with Paul, the apostle of the nations, he observed how eagerly the pagans welcomed the good news and, in his Gospel, he willingly recorded that this universal mission was based on the will and command of the Lord himself.[31]

But this eager welcome on the part of many could not hide the fact that Jesus and his messengers would also be rejected. "Simeon blessed them," then he said to Mary, probably when he gave back the infant whom he had held for a while in his arms, "Behold, this child is destined for the fall and rise of many in Israel, and to be a sign that will be contradicted (and you yourself a sword will pierce) so that the thoughts of many hearts may be revealed." The reading of the Gospels and the Acts, as well as that of Church history from its beginning, plus numerous personal experiences, confirm that the necessity of opting for or against Christ brings division, even within one and the same family; that it initiates a judgment between those who welcome him and those who reject him.[32] For every person, Jesus can become the solid rock on which one builds a future that nothing can shake or the stumbling block against which one trips, the stone established in Zion for the believers or the stone of scandal that causes one to fall. Falling and rising: these two aspects that are already found in the certain prophecies[33] have been taken up in the New Testament.[34] Luke underscored them early on in his story of Jesus' presentation in the Temple.

What Simeon said to Mary, the mother of the Lord, has a general scope. Mary here represents all believers "who hear the word of God and observe it" (Luke 11:28). She is their model because she "believed that what was spoken to [her] by the Lord would be fulfilled" (Luke 1:45). All generations proclaim her blessed (Luke 1:48) because the living word of God, "effective, sharper than any two-edged sword," by penetrating to the deepest part of her soul, "even between soul and spirit, joints and marrow," manifested the thoughts of the heart (Heb 4:12)[35] of the Lord's perfect servant.[36] "No creature is concealed from him, but everything is naked and exposed to the eyes of him to whom we must render an account" (Heb 4:13). The word of God unveils the "thoughts of many hearts." For "not everyone who says to me, 'Lord, Lord,' will enter the kingdom of heaven" (Matt 7:21). Like Mary, we must open our hearts to the Word and put it into practice. We shall then be like the person who builds a house on rock: nothing, no storm, no trial, can shake it (Luke 6:47-48). It is not enough to speak to Christ: we must seize him, allow ourselves to be seized by him (Phil 3:12), receive him as word and bread of life.

> As long as I did not hold Christ, as long as I did not embrace him in my arms, I was imprisoned and unable to break free from my bonds. These words are not to be understood as those of Simeon only but as those of all humankind. If any leave the world, if any are freed from prison and the dwelling of captives in order to gain kingship, let them take Jesus into their hands and embrace him, let them hold him entirely in their hearts, and then leaping for joy, they will be able to go where they desire. . . .
>
> Those who dare to say, "I live, no longer I, but Christ lives in me" (Gal 2:20), possess Jesus. In order to be worthy of being delivered and going toward better realities, let us—we who stand in the Temple, holding the Son of God and pressing him in our arms—pray to the all-powerful God, let us also pray to the child Jesus himself with whom we desire to converse while holding him in our arms.[37]

After Simeon had finished speaking, a woman approached, "Anna, the daughter of Phanuel, of the tribe of Asher. She was advanced in years, having lived seven years with her husband after her marriage, and then a widow until she was eighty-four. She never left the temple, but worshiped night and day with fasting and prayer." Her heart leapt for joy at the sight of this child. She proclaimed the praises of God and hurried to share her exultation with "all those who were awaiting the redemption of Jerusalem." What did she say to them? Luke did not think it useful to tell us. She was a woman: the first of those who would recognize Jesus as the Savior; a woman like those who "on the first day of the week" would go to the tomb, would receive the angels' message, and would announce to the apostles that Jesus was risen (Luke 24:1-12). She was there as the second witness required by the Law. She corroborated what Simeon has explicitly declared. This was enough.[38]

"When they had fulfilled all the prescriptions of the law of the Lord, they returned to Galilee, to their town of Nazareth. The child grew and became strong, filled with wisdom; and the favor of the Lord was upon him." The presentation of Jesus in the Temple lasted only for the time of the fulfillment of the prescribed rites. But the light of this brief liturgical encounter had already revealed in the child Jesus the Lord who came to save the nations. Twelve years later, again in the Temple, he declared for the first time that he had come to do the work of his Father. At the time, his parents did not understand what he meant (Luke 2:49-50). For them to progressively accede to the understanding of his mystery, there would be need of more encounters, as there is always for all of us: in the silence of Nazareth, the assiduous reading of the Scriptures, the reception of the Eucharist in which we participate in the sacrament of his presence placed in our hand.

> God our Father,
> Joseph and Mary came to offer you
> their first-born,
> in whom we recognize the Savior of the world.
> May his presence in our lives
> be the sacrifice that we offer you in our turn,
> God blessed forever and ever.[39]

The feast of the Encounter—the name the Eastern Churches give to the Presentation of the Lord—unveils all its riches to anyone who attentively reads and ponders the scriptural texts offered by the liturgy.

God had promised to send a messenger to purify the Temple, the priesthood, and the people. He sent his own Son. A "merciful and faithful" high priest, this Son delivered humankind from the weight of sin and from the anguish of death at the end of a life of slavery. Light that il-luminates all nations, he enables all who welcome him to become chil-dren of light, children of God. His risen body is the new Temple into which everyone may enter to at last render to God a "worship in Spirit and truth."[40]

When Simeon held the child Jesus in his arms as Anna, a prophetess, watched filled with wonder, the Old and the New Testaments embraced each other. "The old man was carrying the child, but the child was lead-ing the old man," the liturgy of the feast sings.[41] It is by allowing itself to be led by the newness of Christ that the old world—that of today like that of yesterday—and the Church find their full completion. But, con-versely and simultaneously, there is no newness except after a slow matu-ration. The Church and Christians must never forget that their faith is rooted in the fertile soil of the Jewish tradition.

The feast of the Encounter has, moreover, another meaning shown by the joy of Simeon and Anna, whose eyes were enlightened when they caught sight of the child presented in the Temple.

> The feast of the Encounter is also that of age, decline, death. I rightly say "the feast" for decline can become metamorphosis and death in Christ is only the final rending of the veil of love. Simeon the New Theologian wrote, "I know that I shall not die since I am inside life and since I feel it entirely inside me."[42]

Old age can indeed appear as a shipwreck, especially when the diminu-tion of physical strength is accompanied by that of intellectual and men-tal faculties. Then people seek to counteract the ravages of age by illusory artifices, to hide and isolate the old because seeing them and realizing that all will be like them one day are frightening things to face. The feast of the encounter of Simeon and Anna, who was "eighty-four," with the child, who was the youth of the world, can teach us to transform the way we look at old age and the isolation to which we so often condemn it and which is one of the greatest and most unjust hardships of old per-sons. Then we shall see old age as the expectation of the great Encounter for which life prepares us, and we shall renounce the futile and sad game of a prolonged youth. Instead of pushing them far away from us, we shall help those who, in increasing numbers, know the long years of late life to serenely let go of all the secondary things that too often serve to de-fine us. By doing this, we shall learn from their example and help them to focus on that which is essential, revealed by the light of faith: "Now, Master, you may let your servant go / in peace, according to your word."

Those who want to be freed must come to the Temple, to Jerusalem, reach for the One anointed by the Lord, receive in their hands the Word of God and, as it were, hold it tight in the arms of faith. Then, having seen life, they will be liberated and will not see death.[43]

The liturgy of the feast also reminds us that the Son of God fully assumed human nature in order to become the high priest of the new covenant. "Because he himself was tested through what he suffered, he is able to help those who are being tested" (Heb 2:18). Presented in the Temple by his parents, Jesus would be back in Jerusalem to spend there the last days of his ministry (Luke 21:37-38) before fulfilling his pasch of death and resurrection. The light of Candlemas announces that of the paschal candle. Its brilliance that shines for all nations helps us to discover the true face of every human being, so often ignominiously disfigured, in which we must recognize the face of Christ, in whose image all have been created.[44]

This respectful recognition of the identity of everyone and of the differences between persons is the foundation of cultural and religious ecumenism, of peace in mutual understanding, and of the contribution of all to the building of a world into which the Savior can be welcomed with joy.

Finally, this feast presents a particularly significant image of Mary. The one who was all pure, the immaculate mother of the Son of God, submitted to the rite of purification enjoined on every mother soon after childbirth. She humbly obeyed this general prescription without raising any question, without wondering whether her divine motherhood did not exempt her from it. She thus appears as the perfect image of all women called to give birth to children who, while made of their own flesh, nevertheless belong to God. Daughters of Eve, they are also sisters of Mary. Their grandeur, like hers, is to lead those entrusted to them to meet the Lord, to grow, to become strong, to acquire wisdom, to open themselves to God's grace in order to become light-bearers for others. For Mary did not jealously keep her child to herself. In the same way she let Simeon take Jesus into his arms, she offers him to each one of us. She leads us to our Encounter with the Lord carried to Jerusalem, in the Temple, in order to fulfill the Law and the prophets.[45]

Light entered the world.
Zion, prepare your dwelling
to welcome your King, Christ.
Light of Christ,
we bless you.

In Mary, all pure Virgin,
the Word of God
was made flesh for us.
  Light of Christ,
   pure light,
  we glorify you.

Today the Mother of God advances:
she carries the King of glory,
Son of God begotten before the dawn.
  Light of Christ,
  light born of light,
  eternal joy in our hearts,
  we acclaim you.[46]

Joseph, Husband of Mary

It is not until about 800 that a martyrology,[1] from northern France, mentions for the first time the name of St. Joseph in conjunction with March 19. From that time on, a similar notation appears with increasing frequency in liturgical calendars of the same kind.[2] The title given to Joseph—Husband of Mary[3]—shows that from the start, the veneration accorded him was dependent upon devotion to the Mother of God, a devotion that developed in a considerable way throughout the Middle Ages. However, it is in the fifteenth century that the devotion to Joseph began to spread rapidly. St. Bernardine of Siena (1380–1444), a popular preacher; Pierre d'Ailly (1350–1420), chancellor of the University of Paris before becoming bishop of Le Puy (1395), then of Cambrai (1411); Jean Gerson (1363–1429), a theologian who also was chancellor of the University of Paris, contributed to the growth of this devotion because of the authority they enjoyed. Around that time, the feast was celebrated in Milan and in various localities in Germany, in Chartres (France) under the name of "Betrothal—or Marriage—of Mary and Joseph." Finally, the feast was approved by Pope Sixtus IV (1471–1484) and made obligatory for the Roman Rite in 1621 by Pope Gregory XV (1621–1623).[4]

This slow and late introduction of the feast of St. Joseph into the series of Christian celebrations can be explained and must be remembered. The pasch of Christ is the primitive nucleus of the liturgical year. The cycle of Advent-Christmas-Epiphany was the last to appear.[5] Besides, it is always Christ himself who is at the center of the celebration of salvation unfolding throughout time.[6] The veneration of saints—their "memory"— was born from piety toward brothers and sisters in Christ whose lives, shining with the Lord's grace, remained models in the community to which they belonged and whose tombs were venerated. For different reasons—in particular their greater fame in the Church at large or in places of pilgrimage—the devotion to certain saints spread more extensively.[7] But the first ones were the martyrs, who had shed their blood for Christ and thus were more closely associated with his pasch of death and resurrection. Because of her title of Mother of God, Mary, the one "full of grace'' in whom the Word became flesh, was very early venerated by Christians.[8] The devotion to Joseph appeared in connection with that of Mary, which, in its turn, is entirely subordinated to the celebration of the salvation worked by God in his Son, Jesus Christ the Lord. Every devotion, every form of veneration, derives its worth from this orientation; on the other hand, there is a deviation when the celebration of a saint loses its connection with the one who alone is the source of holiness and to whom alone we must render adoration.

The scarcity of information on Joseph in the Gospels did not lend itself to the growth of a special devotion and did not supply any elements for iconographic representations.[9] He is in the center of three Gospel stories. Matthew relates that an angel appeared to him three times: to dissuade him from withdrawing, as he had intended, when he saw that his fiancée was pregnant ''before they lived together'' (1:18-24);[10] to order him to flee to Egypt with Mary and the child whom Herod wanted to kill (2:13-15); to tell him that it was safe to go back home (2:19-23).[11] Luke implicitly mentions Joseph when he says that, at the age of twelve, Jesus went to Jerusalem with his parents for Passover and remained in the Temple where Mary and Joseph found him after three days (2:41-50).[12] The Gospels also note that Joseph was a carpenter (Matt 13:55) and that Jesus plied the same trade (Mark 6:3).[13] But the most important is what Matthew says of him: ''he was a righteous man,'' that is, a man who strove to please God in everything by faithfulness to the Law.

The little the Gospels tell us shows that Joseph was a virtuous man, obedient to God's calling and ready to do what was asked of him with a docility both total and simple. He discreetly shared the expectancy of the birth of the Savior and then silently witnessed it. He accompanied the mother carrying the infant to the Temple to present him to the Lord ''according to the law of Moses''; he heard Simeon's words and Anna's praises (Luke 2:22). He organized the departure for Egypt and the return home, then decided to go back to Nazareth, though perhaps he had intended to settle in Bethlehem, his ancestral city to which the census had recently brought him (Matt 2:13-23). If we except the brief mention of his plan of self-effacement on discovering that Mary was pregnant (Matt 1:19), nothing is said about Joseph's feelings and conduct; not a single word of his has been preserved. After having lived, humble and hidden—how long no one knows—in the shadow of Jesus and Mary, he left the world with the same discretion he entered it.[14] And this is what renders the character of Joseph so attractive. There is no need to invent legends or to rely on those that exist in order to find in this righteous man the particularly energizing model of humble and generous fidelity to the daily and unexpected calls of God. The little ones, the simple ones make no mistake about it.

> Joseph, son of David, rise!
> God's thoughts
> are not human thoughts.
> The Lord looks at the heart.
> The Lord chose you.
> He will make you great.
> It is he who builds your house.
> The lamp of David will shine before God;
> its light will expel the darkness.
>
> *The lamp of David will shine before God;*
> *its light will expel the darkness.*
>
> Lord, you are God!
> Your words are truth.
> You are making this beautiful promise to your servant.
> There is no one like you!
> Bless your servant's house
> that it may remain always in your presence.
>
> It is you who spoke to me!
> Through your blessing, Lord,
> your servant's house is blessed forever![15]

But the feast of St. Joseph does not present us only with the admirable example of a just man to whom God entrusted great things (Matt 25:21). It celebrates the mystery of salvation which, in every age, comes and humbly progresses with the cooperation of men and women who, without any self-seeking, silently accomplish the often unexpected mission that the initiative of God requires them to assume.

Blessed Are the Faithful Servants: God Entrusts His House to Them

"I Will Be a Father to Him, and He Shall Be a Son to Me"
In the biblical tradition of the Old and New Testaments, the figure of David stands out.[1] It evokes the ideal king according to God's heart, the one chosen by God to receive the messianic promises in conformity with the oracles of the prophet Nathan, recorded in the Second Book of Samuel, oracles of which today's reading contains the essential part (2 Sam 7:4-5a, 12-14a, 16).[2]

Now installed in Jerusalem and having made it the capital of his finally pacified kingdom, David thought the time had come to build a Temple to shelter the ark of the covenant, which was still under a tent, as during the march through the desert. Such a project was a credit to the king's piety: he thought it unseemly that he should dwell in a palace while God still had only the shelter of a nomad. Nathan, to whom David had told his intention, hastened to encourage the king to act upon it. But God disagreed with this initiative; he deemed it premature and sent Nathan to warn David to renounce his plan—Nathan had spoken a little too quickly. God sees the secrets of the heart and detects possible unconscious motives. Is not the royal project, which Nathan himself approved, tainted by too human a view of the circumstances and situation? "King David was settled in his palace, and the Lord had given him rest from his enemies on every side" (2 Sam 7:1). He saw his projects realized at last and he was expecting to enjoy peaceful days. Perhaps he was unconsciously thinking that God, having also realized his projects, was now able, like himself, to serenely settle among his people in a temple worthy of his majesty. If such was his thought, he was mistaken. God saw further ahead and had other ambitions for his elect. He destined him to be not only the king of this country but also the father of a lineage promised to an unsuspected future. God's views infinitely surpass human views.[3]

Whatever may have been the king's unconscious calculations, God, far from withdrawing his favor from him, promised him a successor in the near future. It is he who would build a house for the Lord. In fact, Solomon did build the first Temple, which would become the glory of Jerusalem and proclaim by its splendor the majesty of Israel's God (1 Kgs 5:15–6:38). But the divine promises go far beyond the short term. The oracle emphasized that God would establish the kingship and throne of David "forever"; his house would endure "forever." God alone can see so far and insure such a duration in spite of all the vicissitudes of human history. The sages of Israel correctly understood this. At the worst moments of exile, they reread Nathan's oracles. The psalmists never ceased meditating, and whispered in their hearts.

> If his sons forsake my law
> and walk not according to my ordinances,
> If they violate my statutes
> and keep not my commands,
> I will punish their crime with a rod
> and their guilt with stripes.
> Yet my kindness I will not take from him,
> nor will I belie my faithfulness.
> I will not violate my covenant;
> the promise of my lips I will not alter.
> Once by my holiness, have I sworn;
> I will not be false to David.[4]
>
> Your own offspring
> I will set upon your throne.[5]

Paradoxically, the disappointments caused by the kings, far from weakening this hope, sent it soaring further at every step of history. There would come a day on which God would cause an Elect of the Lord to be born from the posterity—"the house"—of David, an Elect who would establish "forever" the kingdom of God and his presence that no temple built by human hands could contain.

> Solomon fell, and thus gave a reason to hope for Christ. Not because God, who can neither be deceived nor deceive us and who foresaw Solomon's fall, placed on him the accomplishment of his promises, but because Solomon's fall obliges you to lift your eyes toward God and to entreat him for the realization of his promise. . . .

God took everything away from the first David so that we might not expect anything from that David. "Wait for what I have promised," says the Lord. David was not mistaken, for see what he says, "Yet you have rejected and spurned" (Ps 89:39a). Where is what he had promised? "[You have] been enraged at your anointed" (Ps 89:39b). Although he makes here a sad enumeration, nevertheless by this single word, he comforts us: what you have promised, O God, remains completely valid; for you have not taken away your Christ, but only postponed him.[6]

Nathan's oracle marks an important step in the messianic hope by specifying—something which was never forgotten—that the Messiah would be a descendant of David. The chief priests and the scribes answered Herod without any hesitation when he asked them where the Messiah was to be born, "In Bethlehem of Judea, for thus it has been written through the prophet: 'and you, Bethlehem, land of Judah' " (Matt 2:4-6). Similarly, when the crowds wondered about Jesus, some did not fail to refresh their memory, "Does not scripture say that the Messiah will be of David's family and come from Bethlehem, the village where David lived?" (John 7:42). Nathan's prophecy has lost none of its relevance. The Church reminds us of it by giving thanks for the coming of the Lord and by living in the hope of his return.

The son of David will live forever.

The favors of the LORD I will sing forever;
   through all generations my mouth shall proclaim your faithfulness.
For you have said, "My kindness is established forever";
   in heaven you have confirmed your faithfulness:
"I have made a covenant with my chosen one,
   I have sworn to David my servant:
Forever will I confirm your posterity
   and establish your throne for all generations."

"He shall say of me, 'You are my father, my God, the Rock, my savior.' "

"Forever I will maintain my kindness toward him,
   and my covenant with him stands firm."
(Ps 89:2-5, 27, 29)

Heirs of the Promises by Faith That Justifies

"Just in the eyes of God" is, in Scripture, the highest praise that can be attributed to anyone.[7] Those who played an especially important role in the history of salvation particularly deserved to be thus qualified and, as such, were proposed as references and models for all. It is therefore of the greatest importance to know how one becomes just in God's eyes. This is the grave problem that Paul treated in the beginning of the Letter to the Romans.[8] In order to elucidate it, he took the example of Abraham, the "father of us all" (Rom 4:13, 16-18, 22).

"It was not through the law that the promise was made to Abraham and his descendants that he would inherit the world, but through the righteousness that comes from faith." Indeed, some six centuries separate this promise (Gen 15:5) from the revelation to Moses on Sinai. Therefore, it is impossible to say that God chose Abraham because of his observance of the Law.[9] He owed his election to the sole grace of God. But he believed in the word of the Lord promising him a posterity as innumerable as the stars of heaven. He totally trusted that God would fulfill his promise, insane though it might have appeared. In fact, Abraham was childless and, owing to his age and that of his wife Sarah, could no longer have any hope of an heir. It is because of his trust that God deemed him just (Gen 15:1-6). What happened after shows the depth of Abraham's faith. God asked him to offer Isaac, the blessed son of the promise, as a sacrifice.[10] How was he not to conclude that God was going back on his solemn promise and therefore was untrustworthy? The nature of the demand increased the scandal: How was God able to exact a human sacrifice, this "abomination" that certain nations committed? In this tragic circumstance, Abraham again completely relied on God who, seeing this faith, solemnly renewed his former promise (Gen 22:1-18). "He believed, hoping against hope, that he would become 'the father of many nations.'"

We must share Abraham's faith—a gratuitous gift—in order to belong to his posterity and become heirs of the promise concerning "many nations." God expects from each of us, as he did of the father of believers, an absolute trust, whatever happens and whatever he asks, even if it should be what we hold dearest. In the last analysis, what is required of us is to trust, in all circumstances, the love of God, "who gives life to the dead and calls into being what does not exist," who leads us to a greater fullness of life, not despite the trial but through it; for faith is doubt overcome, hope is despair overcome. Abraham is the father of believers whom nothing leads astray from trust in God, who is the master of the impossible. Abraham's example comes back to mind every time one of these believers is mentioned.

The liturgy has a choice of two Gospel readings for the feast of St. Joseph. Both lift a corner of the veil covering the personality of the husband of Mary and at the same time shed light on the mystery of Jesus, the Child who, conceived "through the holy Spirit," showed at the age of twelve such an understanding of the things of God that even the doctors of the Law were astonished.

Mission of Joseph, the Just Man, Near Jesus and Mary

As presented by Matthew, the "book of the genealogy of Jesus Christ, the son of David, the son of Abraham" ends with Joseph,[11] to whom God revealed through an angel the role he had to play near Jesus and his mother.[12] It is the second part of this book—the announcement to Joseph—which was first selected for the celebration of March 19 (Matt 1:16, 18-21, 24).[13]

In the genealogy of Jesus Christ, Joseph played what could be called a second role, indispensable for the manifestation of the Lord as it had been announced in the Scriptures. Indeed, it was he who introduced the Savior, son of Mary, into the legitimacy of David's lineage. By giving him his name—Jesus—he welcomed him as his own son and, by recognizing him, he designated him from birth as the expected Messiah through whom "the Lord saves." Such was the place occupied in the plan of salvation by the husband of Mary, a place revealed by "the announcement to Joseph."[14] On the day of his feast, it is good to reread this Gospel and ponder the features of the human and spiritual personality of the one chosen to fulfill this mission. To do this does not mean in any way that we avert our attention from the mystery, or our eyes from the most holy Father to whom we give "thanks as we honor St. Joseph."[15] To do this is indeed to meditate on God, who sets in action his plan of salvation and requires the cooperation of those he has chosen.

Joseph is "a righteous man."[16] This adjective applies to all those who, today as yesterday, conduct themselves in conformity with the Law and God's will, who walk in his ways and reflect divine holiness in their lives and "give us an example."[17] Every righteous person witnesses to God and contributes to his reign in an original manner: the vocations and missions in the community of the world and the community of believers are diverse; we are all marked by our personal history, our age, everything that makes us unique persons in whom grace operates in all its diversity. The Gospel says that Joseph was "a righteous man" in order to explain his reaction when "Mary [who] was betrothed to Joseph, but before they lived together, . . . was found with child. . . . [U]nwilling to expose her to shame, [he] decided to divorce her quietly." This decision implies that he did not doubt Mary's virtue. Matthew is content to suggest this without giving any information on the feelings and eventual inner struggles of Joseph or on the moment he learned of Mary's pregnancy or on their conversation concerning these happenings. It is proper for us to respect Matthew's discretion; it is enough to know that God himself intervened to reveal to Joseph the mystery of the pregnancy of Mary who "was found with child through the holy Spirit" and that Joseph did not shirk his mission. The fact that Mary did not take the initiative of speaking first may be explained in several ways; "either because a woman is a poor witness in her own case, or through modesty, or because she understands that, in a divine work, one must leave the initiative to divine motion."[18] But what is the use of asking questions about a narrative whose sole aim is to record "the birth of Jesus Christ?"[19]

Everything is steeped in deep silence, a silence that is one of the most salient traits of Joseph's personality. Not a single word of his has been recorded, not even a "fiat" of assent to the angel's message. His silence is not that of a taciturn man, of a withdrawn man, but that of a man who lets God speak and answers by obeying eagerly without discussion, without asking the least question (even an explanation), without expressing the slightest objection: "He did as the angel of the Lord had commanded him."

> No longer doubt this mystery,
> Joseph, son of David;
> Receive the announcement after Mary:
> God is coming on earth,
> Your house will be his.
>
> You will tend the fire that is starting.
> It must set everything ablaze;
> Watch in the shadows,
> This flame still hidden,
> Its light will be yours.
>
> You will give to the Son of Man
> The name of God the Savior;
> He, who will be the Servant,
> Comes as a poor person,
> But he is our wealth.[20]

This silence, which we must not confuse with taciturnity, evokes that of the mystics, so attuned to God's word that the mere listening to it arouses many echoes in their hearts and fills them entirely. In a world overwhelmed by a tumultuous flood of words and noises, we risk losing the taste for silence, denying God the possibility of getting a word in edge-ways, denying the Word the chance to be heard. Prayer and liturgy them-selves often become babble. The least moment of silence seems an insufferable dead time, a frightening void.

> Man of silence,
> the Word comes to you,
> the unheard voice
> of the haltingly speaking Word![21]

Joseph, Mary's husband, appears three times in the first two chapters of Matthew's Gospel. Afterwards, his existence is never mentioned again.[22] The conclusion is that, for Matthew, Joseph's mission rigorously concerned Jesus' infancy from which Mary is inseparable: by taking into his home his wife "found with child through the holy Spirit," he gave to the Savior his legitimacy in David's lineage (1:16-21), he saved the child from Herod who wanted to kill him, and lastly he brought him back from Egypt and settled in Galilee with the child and his mother (2:19-23). Two things are striking in these three narratives. First of all, Joseph took no initiative in any of these circumstances; he strictly did what God asked of him at the proper time. This in no way lessens Joseph, much the con-trary. He appears thus as the direct and personal representative of the Father at the side of his Son come to earth, the guardian whom the Fa-ther chose because he could totally trust him and with whom he remains in close touch to show him what he must do.

The second thing that strikes us is that God wanted to communicate with Joseph through an angel who appeared "in a dream."[23] We are tempted to pay little attention to this fact, whether because we accord scant importance to it or because such insistence on dreams makes us uncomfortable. First of all, we must note that as depicted in the Gospel, Joseph was anything but a dreamer, a visionary. On the contrary, he was a man of decision, a realist who confronted situations and coped with them with determination and efficiency: the successful flight to Egypt, the return to the homeland, and the settlement in Nazareth are proofs of this. In any case, it is not surprising that he should have been such a capable man, since he was a carpenter and cabinetmaker and had to use his know-how in the service of a variety of needs in his village. When one needs a tool, a house, or a cradle made or repaired, one does not call on a dreamer. On the other hand, dreams have always been taken seriously. Today, they play an important role as a means of uncovering impulses and feelings repressed in the waking state, but able to reveal the inner recesses—the unconscious—of the personality. In antiquity, and particularly in the Bible, they were seen as a way for God to communicate his will, to make a revelation.[24] The revelations received in dreams usually concerned the unfolding of God's plan—the patriarchs were especially favored in this regard.[25] Joseph belongs in their ranks: "He is the conclusion of the Old Testament; the dignity of patriarchs and prophets receives the promised fruit in him. He alone possessed in reality what divine goodness had promised them."[26]

Dreams are not daydreams indulged in by voluntarily letting the imagination or emotions have the upper hand. Under the movement of the Spirit, they can become a road to the knowledge of God and the understanding of his words, as the prophet Joel foretold (3:1):

> Then afterward I will pour out
>   my spirit upon all mankind.
> Your sons and daughters shall prophecy,
>   your old men shall dream dreams,
>   your young men shall see visions.[27]

On Pentecost, Peter quoted this oracle in his discourse, "This is what was spoken through the prophet Joel" (Acts 2:16-17). Because of his mission concerning the Son of God, who came to inaugurate the end times announced by the prophets, and his perfect readiness to discharge it as a good and faithful servant, Joseph was, more than any other person, instructed in dreams. As a consequence, he is the model of all believers. Each one can be assured of receiving instructions at the proper time, in one way or another, concerning what must be done in order to respond to his or her personal vocation in the world and the Church. Joseph's example shows us that the most humble persons, when they are open to the unexpected coming from God and obedient to his calls, become capable of doing the greatest things for the advent of God's kingdom.

Jesus, His Father, and Mary and Joseph

Luke's Gospel stresses that the child Jesus "grew and became strong" and "advanced [in] wisdom and age," that "the favor of God was upon him," that he "was obedient" to Mary and Joseph.[28] Now we see the narrative of the years of childhood, which is very reserved, end with an episode that acts as a transition between "The Infancy Narrative" and the public manifestation of the Lord.[29] Afterwards, indeed, Luke treats of the ministry of Jesus: after his baptism by John and his forty-day retreat in the desert, he came back to Nazareth, "where he had grown up," in order to announce the good news of an era of grace.[30] This Gospel passage also reveals an unexpected aspect of Jesus' relations with his parents that the context of today's feast sets off. But Luke probably did not relate this story only to show this aspect. The Lord is in the foreground. His initiative, which disconcerted Mary and Joseph, their reaction, and the answer they receive—the first words of Jesus recorded in a gospel—illuminate the mystery of the Son of God incarnated, and teach us how each believer must seek to understand it (Luke 2:41-51a).

Having reported that, after his birth, Jesus was presented in the Temple "according to the law of Moses" (2:22-23), Luke thought it important to mention that Jesus went to Jerusalem in pilgrimage "for the feast of Passover . . . when he was twelve years old." Since his parents were going to Jerusalem "each year," they must have taken the child along all those years. But at twelve, Jesus passed from the category of children to that of "the sons of duty or enjoinder."[31] The pilgrimage of that year was therefore particularly important: it marked the fact that the Lord was from then on subject to God's Law. Besides, by tarrying in the Temple after the departure of his parents and their party, Jesus manifested his strong attraction to the holy place. During the last days of his life, it was in the Temple that Jesus, having purified it (Luke 19:46), would continually remain to teach.[32] He would then meet again with the teachers of the Law, among whom he had sat at the time of this memorable pilgrimage. The exchange of questions and answers would continue, but in an altogether different atmosphere. All those who heard him at twelve "were astounded at his understanding and his answers." At the end, no one would be able to find fault with his words and the whole people would hang on his teaching and throng to listen to him with wonder (Luke 19:47-48). The picture Luke painted has nothing of the moving and maudlin scene of a "little Jesus" as a child prodigy around whom a gathering of old scholars sits transfixed with admiration.[33]

Jesus remained in Jerusalem unbeknown to his parents, who discovered his absence only at the evening regrouping of families. Worried, they returned to Jerusalem "to look for him" and finally found him again in the Temple "after three days." This breathless search on the part of Mary and Joseph is touching. We immediately think of parents alarmed at discovering the disappearance of their child, the more so because that child was unfailingly docile and thoughtful toward them. They fear the worst, since an escapade seems so improbable.[34] Finding Jesus in the Temple, Mary and Joseph were relieved; but his mother could not help saying:

"Son, why have you done this to us?[35] Your father and I have been look-ing for you with great anxiety." Expressed with tenderness and delicacy, this reproach showed the painful surprise of parents who never dreamt such unusual behavior possible. If it were a mere anecdote, the narrative might have stopped here with the return of Mary and Joseph, accompa-nied by Jesus become again his customarily obedient self. But he said to them: "Why were you looking for me? Did you not know that I must be in my Father's house?"[36]

Mary and Joseph "did not understand what he said to them." Luke's remark here suggests that Jesus' words were not really his response to the reproach addressed by his parents. Otherwise, we would have to see in them a rather harsh rebuke that would have hurt them and, besides, would not have contributed to any increased esteem for them on the part of Luke's readers. Luke adds that "his mother kept all these things in her heart" (2:51),[37] as he had said in almost the same terms at the end of the account of the birth of the Lord (2:19). It is only progressively that we advance in the understanding of the events of salvation and of the person of the Lord. Mary and Joseph did not escape this law. The mean-ing of a word at first sight enigmatic, of an event at first sight disconcert-ing, even disturbing, is attained only by the light of other words, other events. It is the way faith grows and deepens, the way the mystery is revealed.

Mary and Joseph experienced this very early, starting with Jesus' in-fancy, thanks to the assiduous and intimate relationship with the Lord they had the privilege to enjoy. For others, beginning with the apostles, the road would be longer. Several times, Jesus announced to the apos-tles his passion and resurrection, "The Son of Man must suffer greatly and be rejected by the elders, the chief priests, and the scribes, and be killed and on the third day be raised" (Luke 9:22).[38] But they did not un-derstand the meaning of these words and did not dare to ask him.[39] In the admirable story of the disciples at Emmaus (24:13-35), Luke reminds us that the paschal faith itself was long in maturing in the disciples' hearts. We must therefore not be too surprised if we do not immediately under-stand all of the Lord's words. The example of Mary and Joseph is a con-stant encouragement for us and helps us not to be put off by an initial lack of understanding. We must look for the Lord in his Father's house, to which, faith assures us, he has ascended in order to become and re-main closer to us on our lives' roads. Nothing, even the most legitimate bonds, must keep us from pursuing this quest. "If anyone comes to me without hating his father and mother, wife and children, brothers and sisters, and even his own life, he cannot be my disciple" (Luke 14:26).[40]

The Gospels say very little about "Joseph, the husband of Mary." When they do speak of him, they say that he was "righteous." This is a prestigious adjective; it includes all the qualities that make a human being precious in the eyes of God. But many people can be recognized as "righteous." Joseph, however, occupies a place apart. God chose this humble village craftsman to be the guardian of his Son made human and of Mary, his mother full of grace. Through him, the eternal Father accomplished the prophecies announcing that the Messiah would belong to David's lineage. From the day on which God told him to take into his home Mary, his wife "with child through the holy Spirit" "before they lived together," Joseph, like a good and faithful servant, did everything God asked, in complete trust in the Lord's word. In the Church, he is the model of faith and hope on which God can build his house.

Joseph, like a good servant, fulfilled his mission in silence without ever attracting attention to himself, looking for no other reward than that of work well done. As a consequence, the Church renders thanks to God for the carpenter of Nazareth who "with fatherly care watched over Jesus Christ [his] Son."[41]

> Blessed the man with a pure heart,
> To whom God entrusts the new Eve.
> Blessed the obscure servant,
> For whom the day dawns.
>
> At night, the angel comes,
> Pushing away the shadows of silence.
> Joseph glimpses from afar
> His role in the covenant work.
>
> Jesus is entrusted to him,
> This child asleep in Mary's arms.
> Mary is the enclosed garden,
> Where God calls forth a spring.
>
> Blessed the man who knows how
> To welcome the Word of light.
> When looking at Joseph, Jesus
> Will see the image of the Father.[42]

Annunciation of the Lord

The incarnation of the Son of God is the fundamental mystery of the Christian faith (John 1:14) that the Church has proclaimed since the second century, and even since apostolic times, by saying, "Jesus Christ . . . conceived by the power of the Holy Spirit, was born of the Virgin Mary."[1] This article of the Creed simply expresses, without any addition, what we read in the Gospels, how the good news was announced to Mary (Luke 1:35) and Joseph (Matt 1:21). The Church Fathers reminded their hearers of this when they preached on the nativity of the Lord.[2] But this does not mean that a feast of the annunciation was already celebrated in patristic times. The first mention of such a celebration appears in a text from the Council of Toledo in 656. Some thirty years later, the feast came to Rome. All this means that the feast had a more ancient origin; but we are unable to be more specific.[3] Besides, the date of March 25 did not immediately gain general acceptance. In Spain, as late as 1000, and in other rites as well, they celebrated a feast on December 18, that is, one week before Christmas.[4] From these beginnings,[5] we learn that the feast of the Annunciation was instituted in direct and close relation to the celebration of the Nativity of Christ.[6] It is therefore right that since the liturgical reform of Vatican II, the feast is again called the Annunciation of the Lord, which explicitly qualifies it as a feast of the Lord.

This shift of emphasis in the celebration of the Annunciation—now a feast of the Lord—corresponds very closely to the spirit of a sound Mariology and to the spirit of the liturgy. Mary is the mother of the Son of God who came into this world to announce the good news of salvation for all human beings and accomplish it by his pasch of death and resurrection. Her unique place in sacred history and the Church is due to this divine motherhood for which God chose her and lavished grace on her. The story of the annunciation as Luke reports it (1:26-38), the prophetic oracle of Isaiah (7:10-14) on the birth of the son called Emmanuel, and the remarks of the Letter to the Hebrews (10:4-10) on the self-offering of Christ upon coming into the world, turn the eyes of the Christian assembly toward the Son of God who was born of the Virgin Mary: "The

Word became flesh / and made his dwelling among us, / and we saw his glory'' (John 1:14).

At the beginning of the celebration, as after the first reading, we sing the psalm verse that the Letter to the Hebrews places in Jesus' mouth when he came into this world: ''Behold, I come to do your will.''[7] The Church does not forget that it began when ''[God's] Son became man.''[8] By recognizing in him ''our redeemer, God and man,'' Christians ask to ''become more like Jesus Christ.''[9] Really, the feast of the Annunciation celebrates the mystery of the Son of God, whom the Virgin conceived in her womb in order to give him a body; this body enabled him to bring us to salvation by dying and rising for us.[10]

> He came to save [humankind] by becoming a human himself.
> The Virgin Mary, receiving the angel's message in faith,
> conceived by the power of the Spirit
> and bore your Son in purest love.[11]

The Good News
of the Incarnation
Announced to Mary

The Pregnant Young Woman: God-with-Us

Every prophetic oracle had a twofold aim. On the one hand, it was directed to a state of affairs, to types of behavior of which the prophet was an eyewitness and which the prophet denounced as evil, as not being in conformity with the will, the expectations of God. On the other hand, the prophet announced what God was about to do, an initiative he held in reserve, an event that not only was to rectify the present deviations, but was also to advance his reign in an unexpected and marvelous manner, in a new and often unheard of situation. The circumstances, the facts that brought about the prophet's intervention, show the object and the reasons for the denunciation, which regains its full pertinence whenever similar events occur. However, it remains always risky to pretend to pinpoint the particulars of the foretold future and the time of its manifestation. The prophecy is a key to the interpretation of the events as they happen and allows the participants to cope with them with discernment. It prevents them from believing already here what is still to be awaited and from losing patience. Prophets are persons of hope, hope that the constant reading of their oracles extends farther and farther. Finally, when the announced events do come, prophecies help people to recognize these events in faith and to assume their part of responsibility for them, their eyes lifted to what is still to happen. Understood in this way, the prophecy from the Book of Isaiah we read today proves its absolute relevance (Isa 7:10-14).[1]

Like many people before and after him—among whom we are—King Ahaz esteemed himself able to do without God in the conduct of his affairs and those of his people. He was counting on his own judgment, on values and alliances human wisdom deemed reliable. Clever human calculations were safer, he thought, than betting on a hypothetical divine intervention: "I will not ask! I will not tempt the LORD!" Ahaz had little use for signs from the Lord "deep as the nether world, or high as the sky." No need to trouble God, he said. To negotiate with a powerful leader of this world, to conclude an alliance with him against weaker adversaries would be a surer way to gain the upper hand.[2] He did not take into any account the Lord's warning: "Unless your faith is firm / you shall not be firm" (Isa 7:9). Nevertheless, God did not renege on his promises to the "house of David" that constantly disappointed him; he was about to take another initiative.

"The LORD himself will give you a sign: the virgin shall be with child, and bear a son, and shall name him Emmanuel," that is to say, God with us.[3] This announcement strikes us with its unusual, enigmatic, and solemn expression. We find in the Bible similar promises, but couched in simpler terms, more normal terms: "A child will be born to you (or to your descendants)." As a rule, the mission of the child is described: for example, this child will restore the compromised state of affairs now prevailing through the father's fault, will reestablish the authority of the kingship or the observance of the Law. Here, we have nothing of the sort: the child announced will himself be a sign, which suggests the extraordinary character of his birth. Moreover the present and an imprecise future seem to meld, and the identity of the pregnant young woman seems to remain hazy. We have here a typical case of an oracle whose outline and meaning remain blurred even to the prophet himself. He glimpsed a "sign" arising on the horizon, where the full sunlight had not yet dissipated the morning haze. It is a "virgin" who would give birth to a child with an exceptional destiny. His birth, worked out by God, would be a decisive event for salvation. He could not say more, but he was sure that the event would take place and that he had been chosen to announce it (Isa 6:1-13). This initial prophecy remained deeply imprinted on Isaiah's mind, as is shown by the series of oracles rightly called "Immanuel Prophecies" (Isa 6:1–12:6). Other prophets would return to this promise, Micah in particular:

> But you, Bethlehem-Ephrathah,
>   too small to be among the clans of Judah,
> From you shall come forth for me
>   one who is to be ruler of Israel;
> Whose origin is from of old,
>   from ancient times.
> Therefore the Lord will give them up, until the time
>   when she who is to give birth has borne. . . .
> (Mic 5:1-2)[4]

Read over and over again, Isaiah's oracle kept alive the Messianic hope and rekindled it in times of crisis. The meaning of the oracle gradually became more and more explicit until, finally, Matthew's Gospel recorded its fulfillment in the virginal conception of Jesus (1:23).[5]

Authentic prophecies are neither precise descriptions made by a so-called extra-lucid visionary, nor announcements so confused and general that they can apply to anything; they uncover the "not yet" of which the "already" is the bearer. Seized by the Spirit, prophets utter oracles whose meaning and scope they themselves do not grasp, oracles that do not allow them to imagine today what tomorrow will be, as though they were projected into the future. The full significance of prophecies is revealed by degrees to the eyes of those who, following the prophets and like them under the movement of the Spirit, decode the "signs of the times" by the light of the Scriptures and scrutinize the Scriptures by the light of the successive events of salvation history.[6] Now, the major event is Christ, who gives Scripture its ultimate meaning. The liturgy is based on this reading of Scripture. The texts of the Old and New Testaments that are proclaimed during the liturgy project their converging and complementary lights on the mystery being celebrated that, in turn, concretely reveals the depth of their meaning. "God with us" himself is present with his whole power of salvation.

> *Here am I, Lord; I come to do your will.*
>
> Sacrifice or oblation you wished not,
>   but ears open to obedience you gave me.
> Holocausts or sin-offerings you sought not;
> then said I, "Behold I come;
>   in the written scroll it is prescribed for me.
> To do your will, O my God, is my delight,
>   and your laws are within my heart!"
> I announced your justice in the vast assembly;
>   I did not restrain my lips, as you, O LORD, know.
> Your justice I kept not hid within my heart;
>   your faithfulness and your salvation I have spoken of;
> I have made no secret of your kindness and your truth
>   in the vast assembly.
> (Ps 40:7-11)

The Body of Christ for Our Salvation

Many elements of the Letter to the Hebrews disconcert modern readers: evocation of sacrificial rites of which we no longer have any experience, modes of reasoning, discussions of points that today have no interest, although they are important in the author's eyes. Nevertheless, we are struck by the riches and depth of the author's thought; suddenly, it appears surprisingly timely and sheds a bright light on the mystery of salvation accomplished by Christ, and, as a consequence, on the Christian condition at all times.[7] Thus the passage chosen for the feast of the Annunciation shows with remarkable vigor the central place of the incarnation of the Son of God in the realization and unfolding of the plan the Father pursues in order to make all humankind into a holy people (Heb 10:4-10).[8]

Beyond the changes of culture and religious sensibility, we can understand, through the reading of the Bible and especially the psalms, the sincere and deep feelings that found their expression in offerings and sacrifices. The minutiae of the ritual prescriptions of this worship must not fool us. Those who observed these regulations in the spirit of the Law knew it well: the sacrifice pleasing to God is a contrite heart (Ps 51:19), a life led with generosity and sincerity according to the precepts of the Lord.[9] But the worth of the sacrifices instituted by God himself proved to be too dependent on the changing dispositions of the human heart. Their multiplication caused their limitations to become clear, "for it is impossible that the blood of bulls and goats take away sins." This is why God sent Christ.

> For this reason, when he came into the world,
> he said:
> "Sacrifice and offering you did not desire,
>   but a body you prepared for me;[10]
> holocausts and sin offerings you took no delight in.
> Then I said, 'As is written of me in the scroll,
>   Behold, I come to do your will, O God.' "

The Son of God took a body in order to obey his Father and thus be able to offer himself as a holocaust. In other words, the incarnation was directed toward the paschal sacrifice of Christ. Thanks to the offering of his body, done once for all on the altar of the cross, we are sanctified. There is no point now in repeating sacrifices. Our Eucharists indefinitely offer, without adding anything, the sacrifice of Christ, which redeemed the whole world and in which each one of us takes part.

> We recall Christ's death, his descent among the dead,
> his resurrection, and his ascension to your right hand;
> and, looking forward to his coming in glory,
>   we offer you his body and blood,
> the acceptable sacrifice
>   which brings salvation to the whole world.[11]

"Conventional gestures, the old sacrifices were not able to deeply purify human conscience or lift humans to God. On the contrary, the death of Christ is a perfect personal offering; it takes the whole person and submits it entirely to God's will. At the same time, it completely renews humans and establishes them in God's intimacy."[12] The inauguration of a new economy, replacing the preceding sacrificial economy, which proved ineffectual, was accomplished by the Father and the Son in perfect accord. The author of the Letter to the Hebrews speaks of a sort of dialogue, at the end of which the Son, who received the body given by his Father, declares, "Behold, I come to do your will, O God." The whole life of Christ was, from this moment and until his death, a constantly renewed consent to the Father's will. Similarly, at the time of the announcement of the angel, Mary said: "Behold, I am the handmaid of the Lord. May it be done to me according to your word" (Luke 1:38). From its beginning in heaven to its advent on earth at the virginal conception of Mary to the redeeming death of Christ, the mystery of the incarnation is characterized by obedience. All believers must act in the same way. From the initial "Yes" when receiving baptism to the last "Yes" when committing their souls into God's hands, their lives are punctuated by the Amen of prayer and sacraments that recapitulates, activates, renews and, when necessary, redirects the Amen of their daily faithfulness to the will and calls of the Lord. "Blessed are those who hear the word of God and observe it" (Luke 11:28).

The Son of God knows his Father's will from all eternity and is unalterably attached to him: "I do know him and I keep his word" (John 8:55).[13] But having become a human being, he also learned from Scripture, which speaks of him, what the Father expected him to do.[14] It was in prayer that, like other human beings, he listened to the word of God, adjusted his own will to God's, expressed his absolute obedience, whatever the cost. "In the days when he was in the flesh, he offered prayers and supplications with loud cries and tears to the one who was able to save him from death, and he was heard because of his reverence. Son though he was, he learned obedience from what he suffered; and when he was made perfect, he became the source of eternal salvation for all who obey him" (Heb 5:7-9).[15] The Book of Psalms, the prayer of Israel, was the privileged place and the principal mode of expression of this dialogue between the Son of God made human and his Father. Augustine said that Jesus had been and remained the cantor par excellence of the Psalter. This is why, in the Church, we still can pray the psalms today with Christ by making them our own as he did.

> May Christ, our cantor, sing in everyone of you and may everyone be this cantor. For when everyone sings this song, it is one single person who sings, since we are one in Christ.[16]

Like Christ, the Church, which is his body, continues to sing psalms—and more generally to read the whole of Scripture—by interpreting them in relation to the unfolding of salvation history and the "signs of the times." We have here one of the dimensions of the incarnation, and not the least important: the word of God that the Church scrutinizes and proclaims is also, in some way, the dwelling of the Son of God become human.

The "Yes" That Made Mary the Mother of the Son of God

The Gospel narrative of the annunciation manifests an already sophisticated reflection on the mystery of the incarnation of the Son of God. We must read it with this in mind and not only as the marvelous story of what happened to this young woman, a "virgin" called Mary, whose destiny was most extraordinary (Luke 1:26-38).[17]

In the scene occurring in "a town of Galilee called Nazareth," in the house of Mary "betrothed to a man named Joseph,"[18] it is God's initiative, announced by the angel, that occupies the first part of the story.[19] The angel's message is addressed to Mary. But the angel's words are words of revelation concerning the mystery of the incarnation of the Son of God, transmitted by Luke to all believers. They must know before all that everything comes from the divine initiative: the choice of Mary, the "favored one," that she might be prepared for the mission God had in view; the announcement of the birth of the Messiah to this young woman who is asked to become his mother.[20] At the same time, Luke reminds us of what faith proclaims: the child conceived by and born of Mary is the "Son of the Most High," "God saves" according to the meaning of his name, the descendant of David promised by the prophets,[21] the Lord whose reign will have no end; he was conceived by the power of the Holy Spirit acting in a young woman, a "virgin."[22] This is what our creed says. The virginal conception of the child is the sign given by the angel and confirmed by the approaching delivery of Elizabeth. She was called "barren." And now, she "has also conceived a son in her old age . . . for nothing is impossible for God."[23]

Luke's Gospel does not say that Mary had intended to keep her virginity: besides the fact that such a vow was unknown in ancient Israel, it was most unlikely since she was "betrothed to . . . Joseph."[24] On the other hand, the Gospel insists on the fact that, being a virgin at the moment the angel Gabriel was sent to her, she conceived Jesus because "the holy Spirit [came] upon [her], and the power of the Most high" overshadowed her. She is the virgin mother of the Son of God. This virginity expresses the total and unparalleled purity fitting for the woman who was to conceive and bear him who is "holy, the Son of God." This is what will find expression later in the proclamation that the Virgin Mary was "immaculate from the first instant of her conception."[25]

To this announcement of the birth of the Lord whose mother she is becoming, Mary gives her unconditional consent in full and informed freedom: "Behold, I am the handmaid of the Lord. May it be done to me according to your word." The Virgin of Nazareth relies entirely on God, without a thought about what will happen to her. God has spoken through his angel; it is enough. The "Yes" of Joseph will echo hers (Matt 1:18-25). The mystery of the incarnation is entirely characterized by obedience: that of the Son of God who took a body to answer the Father's will, that of Mary and then that of Joseph, two righteous persons who welcomed the word of the Lord transmitted by the ministry of an angel.[26]

> Everything is contained in a single word: obedience
> Not that of the enslaved and heavy soul
> The bovine effort, dead set, the eye swarming with flies
> The yoke,
> But the dazzling face-to-face
> Of one and the same Yes.
> Everything is contained in this woman's look upon Him
> Who knows her.
> Face open to ages upon ages
> Magnificat for ages upon ages
> Yes to everything. The young woman
> Dared to do this.
> To be the mold, the crucible
> In which the eternal misery of humans
> In which the eternal misery that humans are
> Becomes God.[27]

"The announcement of the divine incarnation to the blessed Virgin Mary": this was the formula used in some ancient martyrologies to designate today's feast.[28] This title has been resumed today, although in a less explicit form: Annunciation of the Lord. But the readings that have been chosen for the celebration leave no doubt whatsoever on the object of this feast. Incessantly reread, Isaiah's prophecy kept alive for centuries the ardent hope for the birth of a son of David, through whom the

Lord would at last be in the midst of his people: "God with us." In to-day's liturgy, this prophecy functions like those beams that converge to reveal onstage the announced presence of the main character who suddenly appears in full light (First Reading).

It is Christ, who immediately proclaims:

> Sacrifice and offering you did not desire,
>   but a body you prepared for me;
> holocausts and sin offerings you took no delight in.
> Then I said, "As it is written of me in the scroll,
>   Behold, I come to do your will, O God."
> (Second Reading)

As the assembly sings the psalm from which Christ quoted, the light softens, creating an atmosphere of meditation and contemplation. An angel appears who delivers to the young woman a surprising message. A virgin, she will conceive and bear a child, the Son of the Most High, the Son of God, Jesus. Although we do not lose sight of Mary, the "favored" one, who declares herself the "handmaid of the Lord"—"May it be done to me according to your word"—our attention is directed to the contents of this good news and all its connotations in the memories of believers: the manifestation of the Holy Spirit and the word of the Father at Jesus' baptism on the banks of the Jordan, his transfiguration on the mountain, his pasch and ascension, but also the multiple signs worked during his ministry, signs that progressively revealed this man, born of a woman, who called God his Father (Gospel).[29]

The Annunciation is truly the celebration of the mystery of salvation in its decisive moment,[30] the incarnation of the Son of God who, in Nazareth, took flesh from a "daughter of Israel," the Virgin Mary "betrothed to a man named Joseph, of the house of David." This is the celebration of God's faithfulness: Christ accomplishes his Father's will, with which he has been in accord from all eternity and which he concretizes for us by becoming human through the Holy Spirit that made Mary, "the handmaid of the Lord," the mother of the Savior. It is the celebration of the first day of the new era of creation.

> O Father of the ages of the world
> Now the last-born of days is coming
> To encounter through us
> The First-born of your Love.
>
> It is he who made dawn blossom
> It is he who before you was singing dawn

When there were not yet any humans
To share in its beauty.

Through him everything remains nascent,
Our days in their senescence arise
Toward his youth
For his light breaks in the East.

It is he who unceasingly revives,
It is he who over the ages maintains this hymn
Marveling from the beginning
At the work of your hands.

Here comes the new light
Ascending in the most secret recesses of our bodies,
O Father,
Send on the earth the breath
Of the First-born among the dead.[31]

Birth of John the Baptist

The four Gospels speak of John the Baptist several times: John announced and baptized Jesus; he pointed him out to his own disciples from among whom the Lord chose his first followers. They give an account of the testimony John rendered to the one whose way he was preparing. They record his imprisonment by Herod and his execution. They also underline the esteem in which Jesus held him. Lastly, Luke's Gospel draws a parallel between the announcement to Mary and the birth of Jesus and the annunciation and birth of John, whose mother, the Gospel points out, was Mary's relative.[1] Therefore, the Gospel begins with the coming of John and the beginning of his ministry, as Mark explicitly says (1:1-2). Besides, Jesus began to preach when John, in prison, was prevented from doing so (Matt 4:12; Mark 1:14), taking up John's message, "Repent, for the kingdom of heaven is at hand" (Matt 4:17; Mark 1:15). After the ascension, Peter stated the necessity of choosing a successor for Judas, someone who had accompanied the Twelve "the whole time the Lord Jesus came and went among [them], beginning with the baptism of John until the day on which he was taken up" (Acts 1:21-22). Finally, the Acts often report how, in different circumstances, the apostles in their preaching cited John's testimony and reminded their hearers of the meaning of his baptism which announced the one Jesus instituted.[2] It is therefore entirely normal that, in Christian memory and piety, John the Baptist has always held an important place, and that the celebration of his birth has been linked with that of the Lord.

In the fourth century, we find the first mention of a liturgical celebration of the Nativity of the Lord, first with a Mass at the grotto presumed to be the place of his birth.[3] Quite naturally, at about the same time, Christians began to remember John's birth six months before and to localize this memory. Several locations were competing for the honor, in particular Ain Karim, some seven kilometers north of Jerusalem, where a Byzantine church was built in the fifth or sixth century.[4] The date on which it was fitting to commemorate the birth of John the Baptist was debated for a long time in the East. In the West, on the contrary, June 24 was readily adopted without problem.⁵ Besides, the dates of the two births had symbolic values: the winter solstice was perfectly appropriate to the birth of Christ, the rising sun that illuminates the world; the summer solstice reminded Christians that John's vocation, "a burning and shining lamp" (John 5:35), was to "decrease" when the Light would appear (John 3:30).⁶ This subordinate role makes John "more than a prophet" (Matt 11:9). Not only did he announce the Savior, but he baptized him; he pointed him out coming and going on the banks of the Jordan; he directed to him those who became his first disciples (John 1:35-42). Along with Jesus and Mary, he is the only one whose birth the liturgy celebrates. In Eastern churches, above the royal door of the iconostasis, the door reserved for the bishop or the priest, we can see Christ in glory with Mary at his right and John at his left: the woman who gave the Lord to the world, the man who designated Jesus as "the Lamb of God, who takes away the sin of the world" (John 1:29).

The Roman Missal restored by decree of the second ecumenical council of the Vatican, promulgated by Pope Paul VI on April 3, 1969, has two Masses for the Birth of John the Baptist: that of the eve and that of the day. In his mercy, God "helped all [human beings] to seek and find" him. "Again and again [he] offered a covenant to [humankind], / and through the prophets taught [it] to hope for salvation.'"⁷ The solemnity of June 24 celebrates the faithfulness of God, who pursues the development of the work of salvation by sending prophets into the world. John the Baptist takes his place among these innumerable emissaries, but he also remains the model of the forerunner-prophets sent at all times to humans who do not yet know the Lord. They show Jesus present in their midst, coming and going on the bank (John 1:36). But no one arrogates to himself or herself the prophetic mission; it is received through a call from God, like that of the priesthood (Heb 5:4). This is most clearly shown by the example of John the Baptist being chosen by the Lord from his mother's womb.

Forerunner of the Lord, Messenger of Joy

My Words in Your Mouth

Every prophetic vocation is due to the absolute initiative of God that manifests itself equally in the choice of those he decides to send and in the specification of the missions he entrusts to them. Jeremiah's case is especially exemplary. On the one hand, nothing is said about the concrete circumstances of his calling: we know neither where nor at what moment of his life God's word was addressed to him for the first time.[1] On the other hand, the narrative shows the hesitations of Jeremiah, who seeks to escape by using the excuse of his youth and his lack of aptitude for fulfilling the task God wants him to undertake: willy-nilly he becomes a prophet (Jer 1:4-10).

It is common enough to connect God's call with a particular place or event. For instance, Isaiah remembers that for him all began with a vision in the Temple of Jerusalem (6:1-13).[2] Amos remembers that he "was a shepherd and a dresser of sycamores" when God ordered him to go and prophesy to Israel (7:14-15).[3] The same is true for all who remember the origins of their vocations, whatever they are: it was such and such a day, in such and such a place, in such and such circumstances.[4] The evocation of these landmarks whose memory is ineradicable does not obscure the fact of which one remains perfectly conscious: God's initiative is at the origin of the call. But in Jeremiah's case, this is all we hear about: "Before I formed you in the womb I knew you, / before you were born I dedicated you." Whatever other factors entered the equation, nothing besides this mysterious predestination remained in Jeremiah's memory. The psalmist, who also goes to the heart of the matter, speaks in similar terms.

> You have been my guide since I was first formed,
>   my security at my mother's breast.
> To you I was committed at birth,
>   from my mother's womb you are my God.
> (Ps 22:10-11)

When announcing to him his election, God unveiled for Jeremiah what he had in mind for him: "a prophet to the nations." We know what the prophetic mission consists in: to speak in God's name, to proclaim his oracles. But what does "to the nations" mean? God did not add any specification, but stated that he was entrusting his spokesperson with an extensive ministry. "To whomever I send you, you shall go; / whatever I command you, you shall speak."[5] Therefore, God required of Jeremiah an unconditional availability for missions to be specified one after the other at the proper time. Who would not be frightened to have to make such a commitment? " 'Ah, Lord God!' I said, / 'I know not how to speak; I am too young.' " Aware of his weakness, confronted all his life with more and more difficult missions, bearer of threatening messages against his own people that would come to consider him a traitor, misunderstood and persecuted, Jeremiah would, throughout his life, beg God to be relieved of his duty. However, he would discharge it to the end.[6] For, while confirming him in his mission every time, the Lord would repeat to him with the same accents of tenderness and the same reassurance that consoled him, "Have no fear before them, / because I am with you to deliver you."[7]

This assurance given to Jeremiah is confirmed by an investiture that is sacramental in character.

> Then the LORD extended his hand and
> touched my mouth, saying,
>
>> See, I place my words in your mouth!
>>   This day I set you
>>   over nations and over kingdoms,
>> To root up and to tear down,
>>   to destroy and to demolish,
>>   to build and to plant.
> (Jer 1:9-10)

The laying on of hands is a gesture commonly used to bless, to express a taking of possession, to transmit a power, to confer an investiture.[8] God established Jeremiah in his function of prophet through this very expressive gesture of ordination. By touching the mouth of this man who did not "know how to speak," he made Jeremiah the speaker of his own word. Jeremiah was acutely conscious of this.[9] Every one of his messages was punctuated by the same powerful formula: "says the LORD."[10] Thus, the spokesperson's weakness emphasized the fact that he did not speak on his own. In any case, this is a constant of God's conduct: he manifests his power by relying on weak individuals to whom he entrusts missions that are totally out of proportion with their personal resources.[11] This is evident here. God gave to Jeremiah his own authority "over nations and over kingdoms," and also his power to "root up and to tear down, / to destroy and to demolish, / to build and to plant"; whereas he, and he alone, is the master of life and death, the creator and the redeemer.[12] Because of this mission, Jeremiah has been called "a prophet of doom." In fact, he announced the ruin of Jerusalem, the destruction of the Temple, the end of a corrupt worship. Powerless witness and victim, he saw the collapse of the Kingdom of Judah and its dynasty. He did all this, just like all the prophets who vehemently denounced sin and, with a heavy heart, announced the calamities that impiety brought on the world and humankind. But it was in view of their conversion and with the hope of a new covenant and creation. The same thing would happen with the preaching of John the Baptist and that of Jesus on the judgment to come. Today, these prophetic messages still resound like calls to hope and repentance, from which the expected salvation will come.

> *Since my mother's womb, you have been my strength.*
>
> In you, O LORD, I take refuge;
>   let me never be put to shame.
> In your justice rescue me, and deliver me,
>   incline your ear to me, and save me.
> Be my rock of refuge,
>   a stronghold to give me safety,
>   for you are my rock and my fortress.
> O my God, rescue me from the hand of the wicked. . . .
> For you are my hope, O Lord;
>   my trust, O God, from my youth.
> On you I depend from birth;
>   from my mother's womb you are my strength.
>
> ────────────
>
> My mouth shall declare your justice,
>   day by day your salvation.
>
> ────────────
>
> O God, you have taught me from my youth,
>   and till the present I proclaim your wondrous deeds.
> (Ps 71:1-4a, 5-6a, 15a-b, 17)

Salvation, Glimpsed Yesterday, Now Accomplished

Christians live in a situation that is paradoxical from all points of view. They do not yet possess what is theirs in faith; they are acquainted with trials, although they have all the possible reasons to be joyous at the thought of the salvation acquired by Christ and in which they have the assurance of fully participating (1 Pet 1:8-12).[13]

"Although you have not seen him you love him; even though you do not see him now yet believe in him, you rejoice with an indescribable and glorious joy, as you attain the goal of [your] faith, the salvation of your souls." This way of speaking is in accord with that of the Letter to the Hebrews, which says, "Faith is the realization of what is hoped for and evidence of things not seen" (Heb 11:1).[14] The difference is that Peter speaks of the love relation that already now unites believers to Christ known in faith. But both texts show that faith is not simply an inner, subjective conviction, well-established as it might be; it enables us to possess already "things not seen"; it places us in an objective relation with the Lord "though [we] do not see him now." In the same way, hope is something other than a passive waiting for what is to happen. The way the letter of Peter expresses itself is difficult to translate. He said in fact, "You are going to gain the prize toward which your faith is straining." The words he used belong to the vocabulary of sports. "To gain the prize" evokes what the runners in the stadium are after. The aim is the objective to reach, the finish line. Believers are comparable to marathon runners who catch sight of the finish line; victory and "the prize" cannot now elude them. They are still exerting themselves to the utmost, but "an indescribable joy" already suffuses their faces, still taut from the effort, and transfigures them. It is impossible to evoke the impetus of faith in a more dynamic manner. Paul made use of the same image when he wrote, "Forgetting what lies behind but straining forward to what lies ahead, I continue my pursuit toward the goal, the prize of God's upward calling, in Christ Jesus" (Phil 3:13-14).

All of Scripture speaks of this salvation accomplished by Christ. Jesus reminded the two disciples going to Emmaus, on the evening of his resurrection, that the prophets announced "that the Messiah should suffer these things and enter into his glory" (Luke 24:13-35).[15] God had also revealed "that they [the prophets] were serving not themselves but you with regard to the things that have now been announced to you by those who preached the good news to you [through] the holy Spirit sent from heaven." In fact, the apostolic preaching often appeals to the prophetic testimony[16] that the Church cannot do without; for as Christ is the key of the interpretation of Scripture, so are the prophetic oracles a help in the understanding of the mystery of Christ. The same is true of the psalms: they speak of him and prove to be irreplaceable guides for Christian meditation and contemplation. By reintroducing large excerpts from prophetic texts and psalms in the Sunday liturgy, the Lectionary of Vatican II has come back to the tradition of the Synoptic reading of the Old and New Testaments.[17] This reading allows Christians to perceive the permanent relevance of prophetic oracles: their light is indispensable to the understanding of the fulfillment now proclaimed. But the passage of the First Letter of Peter read today contains still another teaching. In the same way "the Spirit of Christ within [the prophets] indicated . . . the sufferings destined for Christ," the accomplishment of the prophecies "now" is proclaimed by the preachers of the gospel through "the holy Spirit sent from heaven."

> Jesus perfected revelation by fulfilling it through His whole work of making Himself present and manifesting Himself . . . especially through His death and glorious resurrection from the dead and final sending of the Spirit of truth. Moreover, He confirmed with divine testimony what revelation proclaimed: that God is with us to free us from the darkness of sin and death, and to raise us up to life eternal.[18]

You Shall Name Him John: "God Has Shown Favor"

"In the days of Herod, King of Judea, there was a priest named Zechariah of the priestly division of Abijah; his wife was from the daughters of Aaron, and her name was Elizabeth." What starts like a beautiful story is the beginning of the good news—the gospel—of which Luke intends to be the witness (1:5-10).[19]

This opening sentence shows the evangelist's purpose. He undertook to write "after investigating everything accurately anew" so that his readers "may realize the certainty of the teachings [they] have received" (Luke 1:5-10).[20] He began by giving the names of the two characters he was placing on stage, indicating with precision their lineage and the period in which they lived: "in the days of Herod, King of Judea."[21] But Luke was writing a Gospel. His insistence on the fact that Elizabeth and Zechariah both belonged to priestly families already suggests that he placed himself in the perspective of salvation history. This is confirmed by what follows: "Both were righteous in the eyes of God, observing all the commandments and ordinances of the Lord blamelessly." "But they had no child"; whereas, fecundity was regarded as a sign of divine blessing.[22] What is worse, they could not look forward to having this consolation "because Elizabeth was barren and both were advanced in years." We immediately think of the similar circumstances of other just persons who played important roles, Abraham and his wife Sarah to begin with.[23]

The event, of which this introduction gives us intimations, took place in Jerusalem, in the Temple, in which Zechariah "was serving as priest in his division's turn before God."[24] According to the practice of the priestly service, he was chosen by lot to enter the sanctuary of the Lord to burn incense."[25] This daily offering was an important time of prayer that gathered all the people, who stood outside while the priest accomplished the prescribed rites. Those who were unable to take part in this liturgy joined in it through prayer: "Let my prayer come like incense before you; / the lifting of my hands, like the evening sacrifice" (Ps 141:2). Then "the angel of the Lord appeared to him, standing at the right of the altar of incense. Zechariah was troubled by what he saw, and fear came upon him."[26] As always, the divine messenger began by reassuring him. "Do not be afraid" is equivalent to "You are not the victim of an illusion; I am the bearer of good news."[27] And he added, "Your prayer has been heard. Your wife Elizabeth will bear you a son." Zechariah's reaction upon hearing of this birth that seemed impossible to him (1:18-20) suggests that he had ceased to pray for this intention. But he was a priest; he was offering the evening sacrifice directed toward the expectation of the Messiah: the good news was God's answer to the prayer of "the whole assembly of the people" that Zechariah was lifting toward heaven like the smoke of the incense he was burning on the altar of the sanctuary. The angel who spoke to him was Gabriel (1:19), who explained to Daniel the events of the end of time and the vision of the seventy weeks at the end of which the Messiah was to come.[28] As a consequence, although Zechariah was directly concerned with the angel's message, the good news of this birth was for the whole people to which it would bring joy and gladness. The child to be born would not belong to his parents. His father would not choose a name for him; the child would bear the name God imposed on him: "You shall name him John," which means "God has shown favor."[29] "Great in the sight of [the] Lord . . . filled with the holy Spirit even from his mother's womb," he would be a "Nazirite"[30] all the days of his life: "He will drink neither wine nor strong drink."[31]

At the end of his message, the angel specified the mission for which the child was "filled with the holy Spirit even from his mother's womb," the mission that justified the name of "God has shown favor," and made him "great in the sight of the Lord." "He will turn many of the children of Israel to the Lord their God," thus realizing the ideal of the perfect priest (Mal 2:6). "He will go before [the Lord] in the spirit and power of Elijah.'' He would not be Elijah himself, but his mission was akin to that of the great prophet and defined in the same terms.[32] He would preach conversion ''to prepare a people fit for the Lord.'' John's mission announced that of Jesus and the Church whose call never ceases to resound: ''Repent!''[33]

> *Since the days of John,*
> *Penance prepares us!*
> *The kingdom of heaven belongs to the violent who seize it!*
>
> He teaches us the desert,
> he teaches us that the fruits of abstinence revive us.
> He goes ahead, in open view.
> To follow him is to advance toward the Presence!
>
> With a great sign, he shows the One who is coming
> to satisfy all justice: ''He stands among all of you!''
> And it is the Lamb of the sacrifice that he is pointing out!
>
> Let the old self diminish!
> In us, Christ must increase without measure!
> At each moment of his coming,
> it is our toil that his grace transfigures![34]

As John, the son of the priest Zechariah, ''of the division of Abijah,'' and his wife Elizabeth, ''from the daughters of Aaron,'' comes upon the scene ''[in] the days of Herod,'' a threshold in salvation history is passed. ''Filled with the holy Spirit even from his mother's womb,'' vowed to the Lord throughout his whole life, John is at the juncture of the Old Testament and the New.

> He appears as a boundary between the two Testaments, the Old and the New. The Lord himself attests that he is a sort of frontier when he says, ''The law and the prophets lasted until John'' (Luke 16:16). Therefore, he is a personage of the old order and the herald of the new. Because he represents the old order, he was born of aged parents; because he represents the new order, he shows himself a prophet in his mother's womb. . . . Even there, he was designated for his mission, designated before his birth. He already appears as the forerunner of Christ before the latter can see him. These things are divine and surpass the capacity of human weakness.[35]

John's election resembles Jeremiah's (First Reading); his life of ''Nazirite,'' Samuel's; his martyrdom, a great number of persecuted prophets'.

> The last of the prophets, the greatest, according to Jesus, was the prophet of Israel in so exemplary, excessive, expressive a manner that he seems to be stuck there at the threshold of the gospel, as the very prototype of the function of prophecy.[36]

The one who was designated the Lamb of God, Jesus Christ, fulfillment of the promises proclaimed "now"—we love him "although [we] have not seen him," believe in him whom we "do not see . . . yet," and through him are assured of obtaining salvation, "the goal of [our] faith" (Second Reading).

John the Baptist came "to prepare a people fit for the Lord" (Gospel). From that time, this has been the mission of the Church commanded to announce the good news to all nations. All Christians, weak and lacking in eloquence though they may be, have the duty to assume the task of forerunners of the Lord toward their brothers and sisters and of messengers of joy.[37] "Amen, I say to you, among those born of women there has been none greater than John the Baptist; yet the least in the kingdom of heaven is greater than he."[38]

A Man Sent from God: His Name Was John

Listen, O Distant Peoples

In the poem-oracles called "Songs of the Suffering Servant," Isaiah introduced a mysterious Servant of God.[1] He is the object of a special election on the Lord's part; he exhibits a flawless obedience; nothing can lead him astray. Doomed to a tragic destiny, he will know a spectacular reversal of his situation and will become a cause of salvation for the multitude.

Taken together, these features that characterize this extraordinary "Servant" gave rise to the biblical interpretation that saw in him the figure of the Messiah to come and to the Christian tradition that recognizes in him a striking prefiguration of Christ dead and risen for the salvation of humankind. But some of these traits also evoked the figure of such and such a prophet who by his or her life and teaching prepared people in a particular manner to recognize the one who was to come. This is true of John the Baptist to whom the liturgy applies the "Second Song of the Servant" (Isa 49:1-6).

"The LORD called me from birth, / from my mother's womb he gave me my name." Certain persons have been much more aware than others, and very early, that God was thinking of them, long before communicating to them the explicit call that determined their vocation.[2] But all believers, at one time or another, acquire through faith a similar conviction and hope that one day God will give them "a white amulet upon which is inscribed a new name, which no one knows except the one who receives it" (Rev 2:17).[3] In this sense, all are called to foreshadow, through certain traits of their persons or lives, the face of him through whom they have been predestined. No one however, even if established as a prophet before birth, can alone give a perfect image of the one he or she prefigures: "I am not the Messiah" (John 3:28). The Servant was an instrument in the Lord's hand, "a polished arrow," hidden "in his quiver," a weapon kept in store to be used at the proper time. The Servant's vigor and efficacy were solely due to "the word of God . . . living and effective, sharper than any two-edged sword'' (Heb 4:12) given by the Lord and making the Servant's word also a "two-edged sword."

The task entrusted to the Servant remained nonetheless strenuous, exhausting, even discouraging: "I thought I had toiled in vain, / and for nothing, uselessly, spent my strength." However, deep down, the Servant kept the certitude that "my reward is with the LORD, / my recompense is with God," that the Lord "formed me as his servant from the womb" so that God might be glorified. This assurance kept the Servant's discouragement from turning into despair: he could rely on one stronger than himself. Those sent by God often experience this: "I know in whom I have believed" (2 Tim 1:12). "When I am weak, then I am strong" (2 Cor 12:10). In the most painful moment of his trial, the Servant of whom the Book of Isaiah speaks heard God renew his confidence in him and even extend unexpectedly the field of his mission.

> It is too little, he says, for you to be my servant,
>   to raise up the tribes of Jacob,
>   and restore the survivors of Israel;
> I will make you a light to the nations,
>   that my salvation may reach to the ends of the earth.
> (Isa 49:6)

This is why his message was addressed to the whole earth, "Hear me, O coastlands, / listen, O distant peoples."

All prophets, all spokespersons of God, all missionaries of the good news exercise their ministry for a relatively short time; in the immediate future, their voices do not carry very far; their testimonies during their lifetimes reach only a limited number of persons. But because they are instruments in the hands of the Lord who chose them, their interventions, though humble and apparently ineffective, contribute, beyond human imagining, to the extension of the kingdom of God "to the ends of the earth."

> *I praise you for I am wonderfully made.*
>
> O LORD, you have probed me and you know me;
>   you know when I sit and when I stand;
> you understand my thoughts from afar.
> My journeys and my rest you scrutinize,
>   with all my ways you are familiar.
>
> ---
>
> Truly you have formed my inmost being;
>   you knit me in my mother's womb.

I give you thanks that I am fearfully, wonderfully made;
   wonderful are your works.
My soul also you knew full well;
   nor was my frame unknown to you
When I was made in secret,
   when I was fashioned in the depths of the earth.
(Ps 139:1-3, 13-15)

The Promise Made to David and the Testimony of John

The apostles' discourses, echoes of which the Book of Acts have transmitted to us, rightly recall the homogeneous development of salvation history that culminated in the sending of a savior, Jesus Christ.[4] Paul did just this when, in the course of his first missionary journey, he addressed the Jews in the synagogue of Antioch in Pisidia.[5] Having recapitulated the stages that led to David' election, he announced that Jesus was the expected Savior (Acts 13:22-26).

''God raised up David as their king; of him he testified, 'I have found David, son of Jesse, a man after my own heart; he will carry out my every wish.' ''[6] The Bible has not concealed the faults and sins of David, nor have these shadows marred his image. We forgive his weaknesses on account of his repentance, magnanimity, and loyalty; of his piety shown in those psalms attributed to him; of a multitude of actions that cannot but be admired. Chosen by the Lord to unify his people, he received the promise of an endless dynasty (2 Sam 7:16). Idealized by the biblical tradition in chronicles that are apologies, David became the figure of the Messiah himself.[7] Now, Paul proclaimed, Jesus is the savior whom God ''has brought to Israel'' from David's posterity.[8] ''John heralded his coming by proclaiming a baptism of repentance,'' the ultimate call of God before the manifestation of the promised Messiah.

But we must remember that John rendered an explicit testimony to Jesus. At the end of his career, he said: ''One mightier than I is coming after me. I am not worthy to stoop and loosen the thongs of his sandals.'' (Mark 1:7). What John was saying about himself, his care to nip in the bud any mistaken idea about himself—things that the New Testament[9] writings note several times—give to John an unequaled stature.

> This mission of John, this role of witness, are of an incomparable grandeur, for we can give testimony to a reality only in the measure in which we participate in it. Jesus said, ''We speak of what we know and we testify to what we have seen'' (John 3:11). To render testimony to the truth supposes that we know this truth. It is why Christ also had this function of witness: ''For this I was born and for this I came into the world, to testify to the

truth'' (John 18:37). But Christ and John had this role in different ways. Christ possessed this light in himself; what is more, he was this light, whereas John only participated in this light. Therefore, only Christ gives a complete testimony and perfectly manifests truth. John and other saints do this only inasmuch as they receive this truth.

Sublime mission of John: it implies his participation in God's light and his resemblance to Christ who also fulfilled this mission.[10]

John's testimony still resounds today: he urges us to turn toward the one he announced, Jesus Christ, the good news of salvation.

"John Is His Name"

Luke established a relation between the events of John's birth and infancy and Jesus'.[11] This relation does not mean that there is a real parallelism between the vocation and destiny of the two children. On the contrary, by presenting these stories in a synoptic manner, Luke wanted to show the bond of dependence established, from the announcements of their births, between the forerunner and the one he preceded to prepare the way. The narrative of John's birth and circumcision that concludes the cycle of his infancy, proceeds from the same intention on Luke's part (Luke 1:57-66, 80).

"When the time arrived for Elizabeth to have her child she gave birth to a son. Her neighbors and relatives heard that the Lord had shown his great mercy toward her, and they rejoiced with her." This birth is evoked in classical biblical terms, according to a stereotyped formula.[12] The joy could have been simply that which all families feel at the birth of a child, a joy that the relatives and neighbors share when they come to congratulate the happy parents. The joy in this instance was even greater because of Elizabeth's lifelong barrenness and the advanced age of the couple. This birth was miraculous. Besides, in the biblical mentality, fecundity was a sign of divine blessing, and childlessness was painfully felt to be, if not a true curse, at least a sort of disgrace imposed by God. Consequently, the late maternity of Elizabeth, the barren woman, meant that God "had shown his great mercy toward her." However, we can also see in this an allusion to the Messianic joy announced by the prophets[13] and mentioned in several passages of Luke's infancy narrative.[14]

"They came on the eighth day to circumcise the child."[15] This was the occasion when the newborn boy received his name. People thought that the infant would be named Zechariah after his father; Zechariah, meaning "God has remembered," would have been the perfect name for a child granted through divine mercy. But the mother replied, "No. He will be called John." General surprise: "There is no one among your relatives who has this name." The father was consulted. "He asked for a tablet and wrote, 'John is his name.' " This categorical decision aroused even more astonishment[16] among the relatives and friends gathered for the newborn's circumcision, but it does not surprise the readers of the Gospel. They know that God himself had decided on the child's name (Luke 1:13): Zechariah and Elizabeth could not have chosen another name for the son God was giving them and who was destined for a great mission (Luke 1:17). The fact that Zechariah recovered the use of his tongue is significant. Elizabeth's pregnancy proved to him that the divine messenger had told the truth. He therefore had no merit in relinquishing his first incredulity (Luke 1:21). But he had had ample time to repent: his cure was an absolution. But there is more.

As soon as he was capable of speaking again, Zechariah blessed God, gave thanks to him, sang his praise in the "joy and gladness" the angel had promised (Luke 1:14). He thus was the first of all those whom the announcement of the good news would delight, as Luke loved to emphasize.[17] At this time too, "fear"—an attitude made of respect and religious astonishment before the divine—manifests itself, that fear which falls upon the witnesses of Jesus' miracles and the apostles at the appearances of the risen Christ.[18] This fear led people to ask themselves when they saw God's action: " 'What then will this child be?' For surely the hand of the Lord was with him."[19] This will happen again with Jesus.[20]

Questions caused by what one sees continue to be a first step on the road to faith even today, inasmuch as one pursues relentlessly and sincerely the answers to the questions the signs have provoked. As for those who have recognized God's presence, who have met him, they cannot keep the good news to themselves; they hasten to share it with others. The witnesses of what happened at John's circumcision immediately spread the story. The whole "hill country of Judea" was informed, according to Luke. In the same way, Jesus' renown spread not only in "the hill country of Judea" but elsewhere: in Galilee, the Decapolis, Jerusalem and beyond the Jordan, even to "all of Syria" (Matt 4:24-25).[21] And Luke devoted the second part of his work—the Book of Acts—to showing how, from the testimony and preaching of the first disciples, the good news of salvation reached the ends of the earth.

"The child grew and became strong in spirit." This stereotyped biblical formula evokes the harmonious development of a child marked before birth by divine grace and on whom "the hand of the Lord" reposed.[22] But Luke added, "He was in the desert until the day of his manifestation to Israel." We have here a discreet allusion—but one understood by the readers of the Gospel—to what would become of this child about whom all wondered. Indeed, the desert is more than a geographical location. It is the place where God tests, forms, and prepares for their mission those he has chosen. Moses sojourned in the desert (Exod 2:15-22), and it was in this wilderness that he received the vision of the bush that burned without being consumed (Exod 3:1-2). Jesus was in the desert for forty days before undertaking his mission (Luke 4:1-2). After his conversion, Paul spent three years in the desert of Arabia (Gal 1:17). From the time of his youth spent in the desert, John would always keep the habits of ascetical life and the appearance of an austere prophet; he would appear in this manner on the banks of the Jordan in order to give a baptism of conversion and announce the imminent coming of the judgment (Matt 3:1-10).[23]

When they saw that the mute who had been brought to Jesus was able to speak, the crowds were astonished.[24] On the day of the circumcision of John, who defined himself as "the voice of one crying out in the desert,"[25] this Messianic sign gave a hint of what this child would be.

> At the very moment when, out of her womb,
> Elizabeth was releasing John,
> He, walking before his God like Elijah,
> Was opening a living path for him.
> It was John who cut the tie
> Holding Zechariah's tongue
> To announce him who was coming.[26]

After the announcement of his birth, the circumcision of John the Baptist reveals the mission for which God chose him from his mother's womb. On that day, his father renounced his right to name him and gave him the name God himself had chosen. By this act, Zechariah acknowledged, and indicated to all, that this child belonged to the Lord for the mission, still unknown at the time, that he had in store for him. The birth of this son granted through divine mercy to Zechariah and Elizabeth filled with a great joy not only his parents but also their neighbors who announced the good news throughout the whole region: a child had just been born on whom the Lord's hand rested (Gospel).

This particular divine protection was to make of him a faithful prophet and a fearless preacher of the salvation that God wanted to see extending "to the ends of the earth" (First Reading).

After years spent in the desert, John manifested himself on the banks of the Jordan to proclaim a baptism of conversion and prepare the way of the Savior, Jesus, son of David (Second Reading).

The Christian assembly celebrating John's birth sings its thanksgiving to God who, in his tenderness and love, "has visited and brought redemption to his people" (Luke 1:68-79).[27] By his person and message, John the Precursor remains inseparable from Jesus and from the announcement of the good news addressed to all humans whom God loves.[28]

Like Jesus, and according to his commandment, the Church incessantly preaches conversion and the forgiveness of sins "to all the nations" (Luke 24:47). The Church remembers John the Baptist, the model of true dissenters "who, eyes fixed on the truth of which they hear the murmur, do not seek to please,"[29] even though they should have to seal with their blood the testimony they give to the Light.

John is there also to remind the Church, the preachers of the gospel, and all believers, that they must make way for the one they announce and whose path they prepare; they must keep pointing out Someone greater in order to show him to those who seek him. Their joy is that the seekers should find him. And when the encounter takes place, they disappear.

> You who watch in the night,
> Joyous is your light!
> You are the lamp that burns and shines
> Until the coming of the dawn
>   Expected for centuries.
>
> You precede daylight,
> You bear hope;
> Do enlighten humankind seeking love
> And lead its heart
>   Back to innocence.
>
> For the Pasch of God
> Do prepare our earth!
> You announce to us a baptism of Fire:
> May it set aflame the life
>   Of all beings!
>
> Your light is waning,
> Another is revealed;
> It is God who rises and overtakes you:
> In the dawn of Christ,
>   Perfect joy.[30]

Peter and Paul, Apostles

The oldest "Roman Calendar" that has come down to us goes back to the year 354.[1] It mentions, on February 22, a feast of the "Chair of St.Peter" and, on June 29, "Sts. Peter and Paul." On February 22, what was commemorated was the day Peter assumed the charge of the Church of Rome. But it seems that the origin of this memorial[2] is to be sought in a funerary custom of old Rome. On February 22—the eighth day before the "kalends" of March[3]—each family commemorated its dead relatives.[4] All family members gathered in the house for a banquet and, near the family grave site, for a funerary meal called *refrigerium*. In these cemeteries, a seat (*cathedra*) was often hollowed out of the rock where the dead person being venerated was supposed to sit.[5] Roman Christians became accustomed to celebrate on this day the memorial of the apostles Peter and Paul, the "founding fathers" of the community.[6] But in the beginning of the fourth century, Christians were forbidden to celebrate funerary meals, deemed too close to the pagan worship of ancestors; and besides, the banquets organized for those occasions risked giving rise to excesses. However, as is often the case, authorities were not content with a pure and simple prohibition. Instead of imposing the suppression— always uncertain—of this deeply ingrained custom, they gave it another object. Thus, February 22 was assigned to memorialize the day on which Peter took possession of his "chair" (*cathedra*) in Rome. Nevertheless, the origins of this feast prove that, very early on, Peter and Paul were associated in the memory and liturgy of the Church.

The *Chronographer of A.D. 354* also mentions on June 29—the third day before the kalends of July—the celebration of Peter "in the catacombs"[7] and Paul "on the Ostian Way."[8] It links the celebration of this feast to the consulate of Tuscus and Sassus, in 258. We still do not know what event happening in that year could have contributed to the institution of the celebration of the feast of Peter and Paul on June 29. Whatever the case, this feast rapidly spread throughout the West, beginning with Africa: several sermons of Augustine (354–430) attest it. Numerous churches were built in honor of Peter and Paul in Italy, Spain, Gaul, and later on in England (Canterbury). "Monks were influential in spreading the devotion to the Prince of the Apostles: Most place-names mentioning St. Peter signal the existence of a Benedictine monastery"[9] that gave its name to the village or the nearby town.

Everywhere, the feast of June 29 associated the memory of the two apostles; it took on a particular solemnity in Rome. The *Leonine Sacramentary*, a compilation of liturgical texts from the fifth and sixth centuries, contains twenty-eight formularies for the Mass of this celebration that also had an octave.[10] At that time, the Pope celebrated twice: in the Vatican Basilica, then at St. Paul Outside the Walls, but in each basilica in honor of both apostles. In the course of the seventh century, two festive days replaced the one to avoid the necessity of going on the same day to two opposite extremities of the city. June 29 was reserved for Peter and June 30 for Paul.[11] The *Missal of Paul VI* (April 3, 1969) returned to the ancient tradition of one single feast on June 29. Besides, it contains an evening Mass for June 28, corresponding to the Mass the Pope used to celebrate at dawn on June 29 near the tomb of Peter. For lack of space, few persons were able to participate. The great gathering of the Christian community of Rome took place later in the day, in the basilica.

Peter and Paul are the two pillars of the Church, the one the shepherd of Christ's flock who governs from his "chair" at Rome, the other the missionary, the "Apostle of the Nations" who went all over the world to found ecclesial communities everywhere and strengthen, in the course of his apostolic journeys, those he had already established. The common celebration of their memorials helps us to become more aware of the twofold dimension of the Church of Christ, one and universal—catholic— thanks to the diversity of complementary vocations and ministries represented by Peter and Paul: the concern for cohesion does not have to restrain apostolic audacity and does not impede the communion of the Churches scattered throughout the whole world.

> Father, all-powerful and ever-living God,
> we do well always and everywhere to give you thanks.
> You fill our hearts with joy
> as we honor your great apostles:
> Peter, our leader in the faith,
> and Paul, its fearless preacher.
> Peter raised up the Church
> from the faithful flock of Israel.
> Paul brought your call to the nations,
> and became the teacher of the world.

Each in his chosen way gathered into unity
the one family of Christ.
Both shared a martyr's death
and are praised throughout the world.[12]

Peter and Paul, Pillars of the Church

Peter in the Temple: First Miracle

As its name indicates, the Book of Acts reports the activity of those whom the Lord chose and sent on a mission into the whole world. On the very day on which the Spirit came down on them, they addressed the crowd in order to proclaim the Lord's resurrection, preach conversion and baptism for the pardon of sins. A small community formed and increased day by day. "They devoted themselves to the teaching of the apostles and to the communal life, to the breaking of the bread and to the prayers" (Acts 2:42).[1] After this presentation of the original nucleus of what will be called the Church, the narrative of the Acts of the Apostles begins; it is inaugurated by a cure worked by Peter (Acts 3:1-10).

"Now Peter and John were going up to the temple area for the three o'clock hour of prayer." In the beginning, Christians continued to frequent the Temple, although they had their own meetings in their homes (Acts 2:46). They did as Jesus did during his ministry: when he was in Jerusalem, he went to the Temple with his disciples to pray and teach the crowds, and to the synagogue in the towns and villages where he happened to be; but he also gathered his own in the intimacy of the house where, on occasion, other people joined them in great numbers.[2] This first going out, official as it were, manifested the continuity between their behavior and that of the Master, between the life of the paschal community and that of the original group of the disciples around the Lord. As is often the case, John was accompanying Peter,[3] but the latter played the leading role. Always named in the first place in the lists of the Twelve,[4] it was Peter who, here as on other particularly important occasions, took the initiative and spoke.[5]

At the moment of their arrival, "a man crippled from birth was carried and placed at the gate of the temple called 'the Beautiful Gate.'" He was put there every day at the gate opening onto the first inner court in the sacred precincts where only Jews could enter.[6] He thus remained outside this inner court because of his infirmity, which constituted a "legal impurity" forbidding him to go any farther.[7] But the place was a good one: the Gentiles in their court and the people coming and going through this gate added up to a fair number of persons from whom he could ask alms. His presence at this spot for long years probably had earned him a certain popularity, and no doubt some people were in the habit of regularly giving him a mite. He begged from the two men who just entered. Now they stopped and the older of the two said, "Look at us." Alerted by this, he was expecting to receive something, and maybe a little more than the usual small coins. What Peter first told him was not very encouraging, "I have neither silver nor gold." But what followed left him speechless, "What I do have I give you: in the name of Jesus Christ the Nazorean, [rise and] walk." Before he had time to react, "Peter took him by the right hand and raised him up, and immediately his feet and ankles grew strong. He leaped up, stood, and walked around." Freed from his legal impurity, he went with them into the Temple "walking and jumping and praising God." This unusual behavior attracted notice. Besides, many people "recognized him as the one who used to sit begging at the Beautiful Gate of the temple, and they were filled with amazement and astonishment at what had happened to him."

Whoever is familiar with the Gospels notes that this cure worked by Peter strangely resembles that of the paralytic to whom the Lord also said, "Rise and walk." The immediate reactions were identical: the cured man glorified God and so did the crowds struck with awe.[8] But there is a considerable difference. Jesus' miracles reveal his personal authority: "But that you may know that the Son of Man has authority on earth to forgive sins—he then said to the paralytic, 'Rise, pick up your stretcher and go home.' "[9] On the contrary, if Peter gave the same command to the crippled man, it was "in the name of Jesus Christ the Nazorean." He had no more personal power than silver or gold. But he had the Lord's power at his disposal.

> What is more sublime than this humility? What richer than this poverty? They do not have the use of money, but have the gifts of nature. With one word Peter made whole a man who was crippled from birth; and he who did not give any coin in the image of Caesar restored to this man the image of Christ.

> Now this man to whom the ability of walking was given back was not the only one to benefit by the riches of such a treasury: five thousand persons believed in Peter's words because of this miraculous healing (Acts 4:4). And

this poor man who did not have anything to give the beggar conferred divine grace in such profusion that, after having given back to one man the use of his legs, gave back to thousands of believers health of heart and transformed [them] into light-footed persons in Christ. . . .[10]

Peter, who from the beginning assumed the roles of spokesperson for the apostolic college and of recognized leader of the Christian community, is also, according to the testimony of the author of Acts, the first one to free "in the name of Jesus Christ" a man prevented by his innate infirmity from taking part in the Temple worship. Soon afterwards, thanks to a vigorous nudge from the Holy Spirit, he was the first to confer baptism "in the name of Jesus" to pagans and allow them to enter the Church and receive their full share of the grace of salvation. It was not easy for him to let go of his prejudices and hesitations (Gal 2:11-14). Finally, he came to understand: "In truth, I see that God shows no partiality. Rather, in every nation whoever fears him and acts uprightly is acceptable to him" (Acts 10:34-35).[11] At that time, Peter vindicated Paul's ministry with the Gentiles and defended him against his detractors and those who "distort[ed]" the meaning of his teaching.[12] This progressive opening of Peter and, through him, of the whole Church, to the universality of salvation is a manifestation of God's power. It never stops giving joy to the community of believers scattered throughout the whole world.[13]

> *Their message goes out through all the earth.*
>
> The heavens declare the glory of God,
>   and the firmament proclaims his handiwork.
> Day pours out the word to day,
>   and night to night imparts knowledge;
> Not a word nor a discourse
>   whose voice is not heard;
> Through all the earth their voice resounds,
>   and to the ends of the world, their message.
> (Ps 19:2-5ab)

Paul: the Zealous Persecutor Becomes Apostle of the Pagans

It is not rare for us to evoke the past, either because it is useful as a point of reference to justify, by fortunate or unfortunate experiences, our present analyses and positions, or because, being the story of our conversion, it is likely to edify the hearers. Similarly, Paul spoke of his former religious activity to show how he was chosen and called by God for the apostolate that he was now exercising (Gal 1:11-20).[14]

The gospel message is so extraordinary, it questions so many things and so profoundly disturbs life that we must be assured of its authenticity. This demand of guarantee does not concern only the initial announcement. For it can happen that self-appointed preachers sow confusion in the hearers' minds by spreading ideas contradicting what has been learned. Those responsible for creating such a situation are not always innovators, "liberals" as we would say, but sometimes persons who, on the contrary, advocate a return to the past, an equally harmful idea. This was already the case with the Galatian communities to which Paul wrote. Christians who did not know or did not accept the decisions of the "council" of Jerusalem (Acts 15:28-29) were preaching the necessity of observing prescriptions and customs that the Church had clearly and solemnly declared no longer applicable. "It is the decision of the holy Spirit and of us not to place on you any burden beyond" what is necessary (Acts 15:28).[15] Paul reacted with vehemence because the stakes were high: what was in question was the purity of the gospel and, as a consequence, the object of Christian faith.

"Now I want you to know, brothers, that the gospel preached by me is not of human origin. For I did not receive it from a human being, nor was I taught it, but it came through a revelation of Jesus Christ." We could not imagine a better guarantee of authenticity for the teaching of any preacher. But how could Paul speak about himself in these terms that set him apart from all others? For those whose authority he was contesting would not have had any influence had they not claimed to be the defenders of the true tradition and the champions of the strictest orthodoxy.[16] If they intervened, they said—and still say—it was to rectify deplorable deviations. In comparison with them, Paul could boast a singular destiny, and he was not slow in doing so. More than most persons of his people and generation, Paul had been "a zealot for [his] ancestral traditions," going so far as to have persecuted "the church of God beyond measure" in order to destroy it. He could not be accused of having abandoned the ancient customs through lukewarmness or desire to escape their burden. Humanly speaking, nothing could have given anyone any hint that he would become a believer in Christ. Christians themselves could not believe that the fierce persecutor had been converted, and it took quite a long time for them to accept him with confidence into their community (Gal 1:22-23). But God "from [his] mother's womb had set [him] apart and called [him] through his grace."[17] He seized him at the most unexpected moment: while on the way to Damascus, where he was going with authority to arrest and imprison the Christians of that city. All this manifested most clearly the divine initiative. But when and how did God manage "to reveal his Son" to this convert? Paul's letters attest to his zeal to instruct those who were coming to the faith; he was conscious that the new believers needed an on-going catechesis. But for his part, he "did not immediately consult flesh and blood, nor did [he] go up to Jerusalem to those who were apostles before [him]; rather [he] went into Arabia" before returning to Damascus.[18] Only after three years did he go "up to Jerusalem to confer with Kephas." He "remained with him for fifteen days" only. And he "did not see any other of the apostles, only James the brother of the Lord."[19]

The case of Paul, like those of the other apostles, is quite exceptional. There was a radical change between what they were as the Gospels depict them and what they became overnight after Pentecost. They understood immediately what they had never succeeded in comprehending in spite of the care Jesus took to teach them. Such a transformation had only one explanation: the decisive and efficacious action of the Spirit that was abundantly communicated to them in order to enable them to exercise their ministry. The same thing happened to Paul. However, in his case, we must take into account elements of his preparation in his thorough formation "at the feet of Gamaliel" (Acts 22:3). In his contact with this renowned and highly spiritual master (Acts 5:34), he had acquired an uncommonly advanced knowledge of Scripture. The flash of light that threw him to the ground on the way to Damascus revealed the meaning of Scripture. This event must have caused a kind of chain reaction, a powerful dynamic inspired by the Spirit. Is not this explanation sufficient?

> Why are you going to waste your time asking useless questions? . . . Let us learn from this example that nobody, including Paul himself and those who preceded him, has ever found Christ by his or her own strength: Christ always manifested himself first. Hence this word: "It was not you who chose me, but I who chose you" (John 15:16). Why did he not believe when he saw the dead rise in the name of Jesus Christ? He saw the lame walk, the demons take flight, the paralytics recover the use of their limbs, but that did not do him any good. He was not unaware of these miracles, he so curious about everything that had to do with the apostles. Stephen was stoned to death in his presence; he saw his face like the face of an angel, but it served no purpose at all. How is it that it served no purpose at all? Because he had not yet been called![20]

Many are those who have had an experience similar to Paul's. For years, we live in a distracted manner through circumstances apparently devoid of meaning; we witness objectively extraordinary facts, but we do not pay them any attention. And then, one fine day, something suddenly strikes us: an encounter apparently like many others, a word, a look, even a silence. All of a sudden, everything changes, everything takes on a new meaning that we wonder at not having seen earlier. What happens thus on the human level is verified in a more marvelous way in the religious domain. We see people go overnight from indifference or unbelief to faith, from an allergy to spiritual realities to the most sincere zeal for God and the things of God. Witnesses of these radical conversions do not believe their eyes; those thus seized by grace are also mightily amazed at what is befalling them. One day, Christ came to meet them and showed himself on the road: this is all they can say. Paul, the Apostle of the Nations, is the first of those great converts. The Lord transformed a persecutor into a pillar of his Church.

> Who is this traveler
> whom the Lord awaits on the road
> and throws down with his light?
> Who is this violent one
> whom the Lord chose among all
> in order to make known forever
> the force of his Word?
>
> *Victory of Christ in his Apostle!*
>
> Against Jesus, he was going to Damascus
> for Jesus he will crisscross the world.
>
> In the justice of the Law he put his trust,
> the grace of the Spirit will be his sole pride.
>
> To know Jesus and him crucified:
> from now on nothing else will count for him.
>
> He will share the hardships of his Lord
> to partake also of the glory of his resurrection.[21]

Shepherd of the Lambs and the Sheep

Peter occupies an important place in the writings of the New Testament. His role is particularly emphasized in the two books written by Luke, his Gospel and the Acts of the Apostles.[22] However, it is at the end of John's Gospel that we find the narrative of the explicit investiture of Peter to whom the risen Christ entrusted the whole of his flock (John 21:15-19).[23]

The scene is at the Sea of Tiberias. Simon Peter, Thomas, Nathanael, "Zebedee's sons, and two others of his disciples" had spent the night fishing without catching anything. In the early morning, a man standing on the shore asked them whether they had any fish. "No," they answered. Then the man told them to throw the net over to the right side of the boat, which they did. Then they caught so many fish that they were unable to pull in. When they were "only about a hundred yards"—a little less than one hundred meters—"the disciple whom Jesus loved" was the first to recognize the Lord and told Peter. Without any ado, Peter "tucked in his garment, for he was lightly clad, and jumped into the sea" to rejoin the Lord.[24] A "charcoal fire was already lit with fish on it and bread." Jesus asked them to bring some of the fish just caught. Then Peter went over to the net left in the water and succeeded to drag all alone onto the bank what his companions had had trouble pulling in the lake. The Lord took what Peter brought and invited the seven disciples to eat with him.

After breakfast, Jesus turned to Peter and abruptly asked, "Simon, son of John, do you love me more than these?" Peter's answer to this direct question was full of humility. "More than these?"—he avoided affirming it.[25] He simply said, "Yes, Lord, you know that I love you." Then Jesus declared, "Feed my lambs." A second time, Jesus addressed Peter, "Simon, son of John, do you love me?" Peter's response was identical to the first, "Yes, Lord, you know that I love you." Jesus said, "Tend my sheep." Jesus repeated the same question a third time, to Peter's distress. He repeated his preceding statement, appealing to the wisdom of Jesus who knew the feelings of his disciple better than he himself, without needing to hear them expressed in words, "Lord, you know everything; you know that I love you." Peter must have read on the face and in the eyes of Jesus that indeed he knew his disciple's sincerity. The tone of voice also probably confirmed this certitude: "Feed my sheep."

Spontaneously, we link Peter's three declarations with his threefold denial. Indeed, it is possible that Jesus wanted to give Peter an opportunity to publicly proclaim that his failing of one day had not affected his deep attachment to the Lord. But Jesus knew full well that Peter had immediately repented. While crossing the courtyard of the high priest's house, he had turned and looked at Peter. Becoming aware of his cowardice—"I do not know this man. I am not a disciple of his. I do not know what you are talking about"—Peter "went out and began to weep bitterly" (Luke 22:54-62). Jesus had seen those tears and had forgiven his repentant disciple. If the triple question did revive in Peter's heart the memory of his fault, it is sure that Jesus was not seeking to publicly humiliate his disciple. The Lord does not behave like those persons who do forgive but do not forget, and show it. Whatever the other considerations this scene might suggest, what the author described here is a solemn investiture. Peter, conscious of his weakness but also of his profound attachment to the Lord, sees himself publicly, and we might say, officially, entrusted with the duty of shepherd of the whole flock, the Church of Jesus Christ.[26]

Peter did not merit to receive the pastoral charge of the whole flock because of his love—or his greater love[27]—for the Lord, as a reward so to speak. Nonetheless, the relation between attachment to Christ and the duty of leading the Church is strongly emphasized. Tradition well understood this and explicitly taught it. It is likely that Peter had been dead for a while by the time the conclusion of John's Gospel was set down in writing.[28] Now, very early, the bishop of Rome was seen as the one who "watches over charity,"[29] that is, the one who exercises his ministry for the benefit of the Church, the community founded on love for Christ. He watches "over the unity of the Church whose bond is charity."[30] Consequently, the pope must be an example for all of the love we have for Christ and a witness of the charity of Christ in the exercise of his primacy. Peter's ministry "is before all a matter of knowledge and love, faith and charity. Of these two virtues, the one comes first and the other is the most important of all."[31]

As a conclusion of this narrative of investiture, the author recorded two other words of Jesus concerning Peter. First, he said to him, "Amen, amen, I say to you, when you were younger, you used to dress yourself and go where you wanted; but when you grow old, you will stretch out your hands, and someone else will dress you and lead you where you do not want to go." These expressions could have been understood as applying to any constraint severely limiting the autonomy of movement. But the author added, "He said this signifying by what kind of death he would glorify God." This was a way of evoking Peter's martyrdom. After the incident in Antioch alluded to in Paul's Letter to the Galatians (2:11-14), and which can be placed in 48-49, we know nothing of Peter's travels. He must have arrived in Rome after the redaction of the Letter to the Romans, which can be dated from the winter of 57–58. According to the tradition confirmed by the excavations made under the basilica of the Vatican,[32] it is there that Peter underwent martyrdom at an uncertain date that could be either 64 or 67. Whatever "the kind of death" he knew, Peter walked in the footsteps of the Pastor of pastors, of the good and true Shepherd who laid down his life for his sheep.[33] He owed this faithfulness unto death to the Lord, who prayed for him that his faith might not fail despite the attacks of Satan and that he might, in conformity with the mission received, strengthen his brothers and sisters (Luke 22:31-33).

> So I exhort the presbyters among you, as a fellow presbyter and witness to the sufferings of Christ and one who has a share in the glory to be revealed. Tend the flock of God in your midst, [overseeing] not by constraint but willingly, as God would have it, not for shameful profit but eagerly. Do not lord it over those assigned to you, but be examples to the flock. And when the chief Shepherd is revealed, you will receive the unfading crown of glory (1 Pet 5:1-4).

The celebration of Sts. Peter and Paul turns the eyes of Christians toward the mystery of the Church of Christ that unites them. For his building, Jesus has chosen human beings who, in spite of their weakness, he has made the pillars of the structure. He has instituted as shepherd of the whole flock Peter, the fisherman of the sea of Tiberias, so that he might "watch over charity" and keep in unity the multitude of God's children. He has chosen Paul to announce Christ among pagan nations. The two inseparable apostles represent the twofold face of the Church, strongly anchored in ancestral tradition but resolutely and boldly open to the universal and the new under the guidance of the Spirit whose initiatives often upset the Church's prejudices and direct it into unexpected ways.

> Truly it is right and just to praise you in honor of your blessed apostles and martyrs, Peter and Paul, whom you deigned to choose and consecrate to yourself.
>
> You changed Peter's fishing skill into a divine science, since by the nets of your commandments, you free humankind from the depths of this world. You changed both the name and the spirit of his co-apostle Paul, since the Church rejoices to have now as a teacher of your heavenly commandments the very person it formerly feared as a persecutor.
>
> Paul was blinded, the better to see; Peter denied, the better to believe. To the one, you entrusted the keys of the kingdom of heaven; to the other you granted the knowledge of divine law so that he might call the nations. The one opens, the other ushers people in, and both receive the eternal reward. . . .
>
> The one broke the gates of hell; the other overcame the sting of death.
>
> Paul was beheaded because he had shown himself the head of the Gentiles turned believers.
>
> As for Peter, by undergoing in his turn the torment of the cross, he followed him who is our head, the head of all, Christ.[34]

Peter and Paul, Mirrors of the Church

The Pasch of Peter and the Church

Very soon after Pentecost, the Book of Acts tells us, the apostles got into difficulties with the religious authorities in Jerusalem. After the death of Jesus, they had believed that all would return to order despite the enigma of the tomb found empty on the third day. Even though nothing had been officially clarified, the disappearance of the body of the crucified Christ seems not to have caused any problem. People would surely soon forget the explanation of a handful of his disciples who were talking about a resurrection. When they began to foster this idea after the healing of a cripple, the authorities were sure that intimidation would be enough to silence them.[1] When this tactic failed and the apostles continued to rally people in great numbers, they were again arrested and thrown in prison to await their appearance in court the following day. But when the tribunal was ready to hear the case, it was discovered that the apostles had mysteriously disappeared from the dungeon. Again, they were found preaching at the Temple and brought back before the judges, but escaped being condemned to death through the intervention of Gamaliel. Instead, the authorities had to be content with having them beaten with rods and forbidding them henceforth to pronounce the name of Jesus.[2] But the actions of a preacher of the new doctrine, the deacon Stephen, caused the authorities to proceed with greater vigor. In fact, the impact on the people of the "signs" and other wonders generated by this man with the Greek name aroused a violent reaction on the part of the members of a synagogue. Individuals were suborned to attest that he had spoken against Moses and against God: blasphemy, for which the punishment was death. Stephen was stoned without a trial, and became the first martyr of the nascent Church.[3] A violent persecution followed and led to the dispersal of the Jerusalem community, with the exception of the apostles. This exodus led to the gospel's being preached outside the city, in Caesarea, in Samaria, and even as far as Antioch, where a Christian community was formed.[4] Those who stayed behind had only a brief respite,[5] for their persecutors lost no time in pursuing the leaders of the community of Jerusalem (Acts 12:1-11).[6]

"About that time King Herod laid hands upon some members of the church to harm them.[7] He had James, the brother of John, killed by the sword,[8] and when he saw that this was pleasing to the Jews he proceeded to arrest Peter also." There is a striking symmetry between the way in which our text refers to the execution of the first of the martyred apostles and the imprisonment of their leader, both at the initiative of Herod. But while James is only mentioned briefly in passing, the reader senses that the incarceration of Peter is going to be the subject of a whole story. The text says "about that time"—in other words, this episode takes place within the framework of the persecution that once again broke out against the apostles who remained in Jerusalem (Acts 8:1-2). The author does not specify the year in which these things took place.[9] On the other hand, he notes carefully that it was during the week of Passover. The cruel treatment that Herod inflicted on the Church recalls the persecutions of the people of God at the hands of Pharaoh.[10] But we should note that Peter was arrested at about the same time of the year as Jesus (Luke 22:41).[11] Herod "intended to bring him before the people after Passover." This public appearance presented a double advantage. It provided the king with an opportunity to prove his good will toward those whom he wished to win over; and at the same time the public nature of the trial and condemnation would intimidate the people. So Herod had Peter locked up under heavy guard: "four squads of four soldiers."

"Peter thus was being kept in prison, but prayer by the church was fervently being made to God on his behalf." When "the kings of the earth rise up, and the princes conspire together against the LORD" (Ps 2:2),[12] the Christians, like the ancient Hebrews in Egypt, turn toward God (Exod 2:23).[13] The Church appeals urgently to the Lord because it realizes that without him it has no way out of its tragic situation. But the Church is also the expression of deep and total trust: God never abandons his own, who can—and must—trust in him to intervene; when and how, only he can decide in his own wisdom. In these cases we do not tell him what he should do, what we think is the most important and the most urgent. We cry out to him, saying "Deign, O God, to rescue me; O LORD, make haste to help me" (Ps 70:2).[14]

While the community kept a vigil of prayer, Peter, in prison, "was sleeping between two soldiers" to whom he was "secured by double chains."

How can we explain this deep and peaceful sleep of a prisoner the night before he is to appear publicly for a judgment that he can only expect to be against him? Depending on our own particular temperament, we might be inclined to ascribe to Peter a remarkable psychological equilibrium, given his total lack of understandable anguish; or we might speak of his astonishing heedlessness or even of his being unaware of his own danger. The author of the passage certainly does not seek to describe Peter's various inner states. His sound sleep corresponds to the attitude and conviction of the praying community: no matter how bad things look, we are in the hands of God and his providence; whatever happens, "We know that all things work for good for those who love God, who are called according to his purpose" (Rom 8:28). In fact, his supreme intervention takes place without the slightest effort on Peter's part: he is asleep. This is undoubtedly what the author intends to bring out.

"Suddenly the angel of the Lord stood by him."[15] A bright light illumined the cell. The angel awakened Peter and told him to get up "quickly." Peter's chains fell from his wrists. At the angel's behest he put on his belt, his sandals, and his cloak, and followed the messenger. With him he passed through a first and then a second guard post. The iron gate opening on the city opened all by itself and, still accompanied by the angel, he walked for a minute down a street. All this took place as if in a waking dream or a vision; Peter acted like a sleepwalker, capable of precise behavior but somehow standing outside of himself. Suddenly outside, he regained his senses only for the angel to leave him. At that particular moment he finally realized what had happened: "Now I know for certain that [the] Lord has sent his angel and rescued me from the hand of Herod and from all that the Jewish people had been expecting." This last reflection put into Peter's mouth is less banal than it might appear: "from the hand of Herod" is an expression that recurs several times in the Greek translation of the Bible.[16] When Moses tells Jethro of the Exodus, Jethro exclaims "Blessed be the LORD . . . who has rescued his people from the hands of Pharaoh and the Egyptians" (Exod 18:10).[17] When Nebuchadnezzar realizes that the three young men whom he had thrown into the blazing furnace came out unharmed, he cries out "Blessed be the God of Shadrach, Meshach, and Abednego, who sent his angel to deliver the servants that trusted in him" (Dan 3:95). Lastly, the same expression is found in the canticle of Zechariah: "Blessed be the Lord, the God of Israel . . . He has raised up a horn for our salvation . . . salvation from our enemies and from the hand of all who hate us" (Luke

1:68-71).[18] Whether Luke uses the expression in his account of Peter's deliverance intentionally or not, this phrase "from the hand of" is typical of the vocabulary of divine intervention at the time of the Exodus, which is commemorated during the paschal vigil. But in Jewish tradition this Passover night had for a long time evoked all those other nights when the Lord intervened on behalf of the just, as well as the night when the Messiah will appear in the company of Moses and Elijah.

> What is the meaning of "a night of vigil"? A night during which God has done great things for the just, as he had done for the Israelites in Egypt. It is during this night that he saved Hezekiah, Hananiah, and Daniel in the lions' den, and it is during this night that the Messiah and Elijah will manifest their power.[19]

"It was [the] feast of Unleavened Bread." This was during the week of the Passover. This comment at the beginning of the account seems at first of little importance, but it is actually very significant. The deliverance of Peter, whom God frees from prison at night, and precisely at this period of the year, assumes the value of a parable. For the Church, it is still the time of the Exodus. During the night of this world, it prays with confidence, remembering the pasch of Christ and giving thanks for the marvels God has accomplished, including thanksgiving ahead of time for the crowning marvel: when Christ himself, and no longer an angel, will come back "to snatch her finally and forever from the hands of all her enemies."

> *Their message goes out through all the earth.*
>
> The heavens declare the glory of God,
>   and the firmament proclaims his handiwork.
> Day pours out the word to day,
>   and night to night departs knowledge;
> Not a word nor a discourse
>   whose voice is not heard;
> Through all the earth their voice resounds,
>   and to the ends of the world their message.
> (Ps 19:2-5)

In Life as in Death, God Never Abandons Us

The Second Letter to Timothy is the last that St. Paul wrote.[20] He is in Rome, a prisoner under humiliating conditions.[21] He entertains no illusions as to the outcome of his trial: he will be condemned to death. We can still read today the last paragraphs of this moving letter addressed to his most faithful co-worker, in which the apostle looks rapidly over his life and speaks of his upcoming martyrdom (2 Tim 4:6-8, 17-18).[22]

"As for me, my life is already being poured away as a libation, and the time has come for me to be gone" [JB]. The two images that St. Paul uses to evoke his death should hold our attention. The first has to do with the cult, and must be seen in the light of what the apostle writes elsewhere, also in the same perspective of the cult. For him, a Christian life lived according to the gospel has the value of worship: "I urge you therefore, brothers, by the mercies of God, to offer your bodies as a living sacrifice, holy and pleasing to God, your spiritual worship" (Rom 12:1).[23] This is why the exercise of the apostolate is, in itself and its objectives, a function of worship—we might even call it priestly. All the baptized are called to exercise it, as the apostles do in their special mission in the Church.[24] St. Paul writes: " . . . I serve with my spirit in proclaiming the gospel . . . " (Rom 1:9). And again, " . . . to be a minister of Christ Jesus to the Gentiles in performing the priestly service of the gospel of God, so that the offering up of the Gentiles may be acceptable, sanctified by the holy Spirit" (Rom 15:16). And he also says, "But, even if I am poured out as a libation upon the sacrificial service of your faith, I rejoice and share my joy with all of you. In the same way you also should rejoice and share your joy with me (Phil 2:17-18). This offering to which he had long ago given his full consent is going to be expressed now in the libation of his blood, in the sacrifice of martyrdom.[25]

Paul then goes on to describe his upcoming death as his "departure." This second image must also have been familiar to him. He considers the death of every Christian as a passage, a Pasch, toward the homeland: "Then we who are alive, who are left, will be caught up together with them in the clouds to meet the Lord in the air" (1 Thess 4:17), for Christ "died for us, so that whether we are awake or asleep we may live together with him" (1 Thess 5:10). From this point on "we would rather leave the body and go home to the Lord" (2 Cor 5:8). For this reason St. Paul was torn between wanting to join Christ as soon as possible and the duty of remaining to carry out the mission entrusted to him:

> For to me life is Christ, and death is gain. If I go on living in the flesh, that means fruitful labor for me. And I do not know which I shall choose. I am caught between the two. I long to depart this life and be with Christ, [for] that is far better. Yet that I remain [in] the flesh is more necessary for your benefit (Phil 1:21-24).

When he wrote these words, St. Paul was a captive, unsure of his fate.[26] The Second Letter to Timothy is five or six years later than this.[27] He is no longer wavering between what seems "preferable" or less preferable to him, for the time of departure has come. But the prisoner about to be martyred can, however, reflect briefly on his life's work: "I have competed well; I have finished the race; I have kept the faith." He often described life in Christ as a combat,[28] a race.[29] But this last look that he takes at his life bears no resemblance to that of a former athlete who thinks with nostalgia of his past prowess.[30] Victory in the last fight and at the end of the race is now assured: "From now on the crown of righteousness awaits me, which the Lord, the just judge, will award to me on that day, and not only to me, but to all who have longed for his appearance." No nostalgic reliving here, no self-satisfaction over past success. To the very end the apostle is "straining forward to what lies ahead" (Phil 3:13) and takes into consideration, as no one else, Christ and the glory of God. There is nothing here, either, of the resignation of a man who has lost all his illusions and awaits, intrepid and stony-faced, an end that he is helpless to avoid.

Paul does not know when the time to take his departure will arrive, but he intends to spend the time that is left to him as profitably as possible. When Mark and Timothy join him, they will be, along with Luke who is already there, a precious source of comfort. Thanks to them, he will still be able to exercise some sort of ministry. Books and parchments left at Troas will allow him to keep on working (2 Tim 4:9-13).[31] Even though he has forgiven those who have hurt him— "May it not be held against them!" (2 Tim 4:16)—some wounds still hurt him: "Everyone deserted me." But he refers to this ordeal above all to encourage his disciple, who is bound to face similar trials, because he finds in it a new occasion to give thanks and to hope: "But the Lord stood by me and gave me strength, so that through me the proclamation might be completed and all the Gentiles might hear it. And I was rescued from the lion's mouth. The Lord will rescue me from every evil threat and will bring me safe to his heavenly kingdom. To him be glory forever and ever. Amen."[32] God himself had told his apostle that he would have to suffer much for the sake of his name (Acts 9:16). It is certain that from his first trial Paul's defense took the shape of a proclamation of the gospel, as it had at other courts, as at Jerusalem before the magistrates (Acts 22:1-29), at Caesarea before the governor Felix (Acts 24:10-21), and before Agrippa and Bernice (Acts 26:1-32). He also took advantage of the respite granted him to con-

tinue to make his message heard, a message to which his very imprisonment gave witness. Through his epistles that have been read, re-read,
and meditated upon, as through his example as the tireless apostle, prisoner, and martyr, St. Paul remains, in the Church, the greatest preacher
of the gospel.

> Let us not look only at the greatness and the weight of his merits, but let
> us also look at the vigor, the energy that has brought him such grace, and
> let us not forget our common nature with him, for he shared everything
> with us, without exception. And then, acquiring his merits, which is very
> difficult, will seem an easy thing to us, and after having striven for such
> a short time in this world, we will live with this incorruptible and immortal
> crown there above, forever, through the grace and mercy of our Lord Jesus
> Christ, to whom belong glory and power now and forever.[33]

The Investiture of Peter at Caesarea Philippi

In the three Synoptic Gospels, Peter's confession of faith at Caesarea
Philippi, followed by the pronouncement of the conditions for following
Jesus and the foretelling of his transfiguration, marks a turning point in
the ministry of Jesus.[34] The Gospel According to Matthew adds that, after
having confessed the faith in the name of the disciples, Peter was invested
by Jesus with the charge that he would assume in the Church (Matt 16:13-
19).[35]

People had been wondering who Jesus was from the very beginning.
Even during his lifetime the most diverse opinions circulated. Some
thought he was John the Baptist risen from the dead, as did Herod, while
others thought he was Elijah who, it was said, had to come back to prepare the way for the appearance of the Messiah in the world;[36] still others
thought he was Jeremiah of immortal memory (2 Macc 2:1-8) or one of
the prophets, or perhaps the one Moses had promised would come,
someone like unto himself (Deut 18:18). "But who do you say that I am?"
Jesus asks his disciples this question, not to find out their position in all
this debate, nor to let them express their own opinion, but to have them
profess their faith.

> If I speak of faith, and not some simple adherence to a given belief, I must
> make the same interior journey as the disciples and the apostles; I must
> relive this same critical moment, this radical inner change of state. For if
> I do not, my faith remains a matter of language, of the letter—perhaps quite
> exact—but not necessarily true for me.
>
> What I am talking about is a certain passage, the passage from mere lan-
> guage to the word, to my word, the word with which I commit myself.

> This true commitment is not made through the means of a common lan-
> guage; usually it is quite the opposite: I join or quit in order not to be my-
> self.[37]

"You are the Messiah," Simon Peter answered, "the Son of the living God." Jesus seems in admiration, if not actual surprise, at this remarkable profession of faith. Thankfulness must have welled up in his heart as on the occasion when he said "I give praise to you, Father, Lord of heaven and earth, for although you have hidden these things from the wise and the learned you have revealed them to the childlike" (Matt 11:25). What he does say here is in fact full of the same sentiments: "Blessed are you, Simon son of Jonah. For flesh and blood has not revealed this to you, but my heavenly Father." Peter answered for all the disciples when Jesus asked them "But who do you say that I am?" It is for the benefit of the entire Church that the Father "revealed" this to Peter, and in him Jesus continues to proclaim "blessed" all the faithful who believe in him. In the light of the paschal mystery—Easter and Pentecost—all Christians make the same voyage as the apostles, and make their own Simon Peter's profession of faith; all Christians have realized that Jesus Christ, the "Son of Man," is truly and absolutely the "Son of the living God" in a way that applies to no one else.[38]

After having proclaimed that the heavenly Father is the one to thank for Peter's faith, Jesus adds: "And so I say to you, you are Peter, and upon this rock I will build my church, and the gates of the netherworld shall not prevail against it." The invisible foundation of the Church is the resurrected Lord. When Simon is given the surname of Rock, he is assigned the function of that bedrock upon which the edifice is constructed: the Church of Jesus Christ.[39] This particular expression evokes an oracle of the Book of Isaiah (28:16): "Therefore, thus says the Lord GOD: / See, I am laying a stone in Zion, / a stone that has been tested, / a precious cornerstone as a sure foundation; / he who puts his faith in it shall not be shaken." This oracle, which was understood as referring to the Messiah,[40] is now fulfilled. The Son of God, and he alone, is the cornerstone[41] upon which the Church rests, the Church that Jesus has himself built upon Peter. Whoever trusts in it will not be shaken.[42] It has, in fact, the assurance that the "powers of evil"—that is, Satan,—will never be able to tear it down.

Jesus continues speaking to the one who spoke in the name of all the disciples and professed the faith of the Church, and he says: "I will give you the keys to the kingdom of heaven." This image is connected to the preceding one. The Lord is going to depart. Until he returns, he entrusts to Peter the keys of the building that he has constructed and that remains his property.[43] This is, even today, a symbolic way of entrusting one's goods to another.[44] It is an act of confidence: Whoever receives the keys of the house conducts himself not as a master, but as a steward. So much is obvious. Behaving in any other way would be tantamount to betraying the trust of the owner and would induce him to take the keys back and never entrust them again. The apostles know full well that they must behave as faithful stewards: a strict accounting of their stewardship will be asked of them.[45] They were given their authority only for the service of their brethren (John 13:13-17).

The power to bind and to loosen is to be understood in the same light. Its object is the interpretation of the Law, consequently of the gospel, and more concretely, the forgiveness of sins that opens up, within the Church, the gates of the kingdom of God. And here this power is given to Peter, who represents the group of the apostles (Matt 18:18). For it is to the group of apostles gathered together on Easter Day that Jesus declared: "Receive the holy Spirit. Whose sins you forgive are forgiven them, and whose sins you retain are retained" (John 20:22-23).

> It is because he all alone personified the Church that Peter had the joy of hearing said to him: "I will give you the keys of the kingdom of heaven."
>
> But in fact it was not to him as one man alone that the keys were given, but to the united Church. This emphasizes the preeminence of Peter, for he represents the universality and unity of the Church when it was said to him, "I will give to you," when actually those words meant that the keys were given to all. In fact, in order for you to understand that it is the Church who has received the keys of the kingdom of heaven, hear what the Lord says to all the apostles in another passage: "Receive the holy Spirit." And he adds immediately: "Whose sins you forgive are forgiven them, whose sins you retain are retained" (John 20:22-23).[46]

This is truly a formidable responsibility entrusted to Peter and to the group of apostles in solidarity with him, in the Church![47] It requires unflagging discernment in order not to confuse human tradition with commandment of God (Mark 7:8). Having received "the care of sick souls, and not the power of a tyrant over healthy ones,"[48] it is their task "to serve, more than to rule,"[49] and they must "strive to be loved more than feared."[50] In their role as faithful "stewards of the mysteries of God" (1 Cor 4:1-2), those who hold the place of Christ in the community must so fulfill their role that they may say, when they open or they close, when they bind or they loosen, "It is the decision of the holy Spirit, and of us" (Acts 15:28).[51]

Peter and Paul, with their contrasting charisms put at the service of one and the same gospel, illustrate the nature of the Church of Christ and of the ministry entrusted to those whom the Lord choses. Through the faith of which the apostles are witnesses and guides, the community of believers is solidly founded on Christ, "the cornerstone" that nothing can dislodge. Whatever may happen, despite all the trials, God delivers his friends as he freed his Christ from "the power of death." Like their Master and Lord, those who exercise their responsibilities in the Christian community have only one ambition, to "stay the course," to remain faithful to their mission as stewards of the mysteries of salvation, and to make themselves, without counting the cost, the servants of the servants of God, the messengers of his love.

> Truly it is just and good to praise you, for in your providence and your goodness you have given us this feast day on which we celebrate each year the triumph of the blessed Peter and Paul.
>
> The whole world venerates them as well, for, while one was the first called to the apostolate and the other the last, both have shared in the same grace and the same passion.
>
> The one may have been the first to confess the faith, but the other shone in its defense and its clarification.
>
> Inspired from above, the one proclaimed Christ the Son of the living God, but the other was chosen to recognize in this same Word the wisdom and the power of God.
>
> The one recruited the first community among the Jews, while the other became the Apostle and the physician of the nations.
>
> And so, each in his own way, they brought together the unique family of Christ, and although they did not die at the same time, a same feast day and a same glory unites them forever.[52]

On the day of the Solemnity of Saints Peter and Paul, all the Christian communities of the East and the West join in the same prayer for the Church of Christ spread out in the universe, and for those whose task it is to be stewards of the kingdom of heaven among their brethren, with the power of binding and unbinding.

Different as they were in temperament, social, cultural, and religious origin, Peter and Paul nevertheless share a number of similar characteristics. One denied his Master during the passion, while the other persecuted Jesus in the persons of his disciples. Peter was a man of impetuous generosity, to the point of presumptuousness, sometimes hesitant, but of solid loyalty. Paul was proud of his Roman citizenship and did not hesitate to demand his title as Apostle, but was conscious of being as fragile as a "pot of clay." The former was attached to the old reassuring institutions but did not resist the Spirit who upset his convictions and led him where he did not want to go. The latter resolutely turned to the nations but was torn within by the resistance of his own people.

Won over by Christ, to whom they gave their faith and their love, both gave the supreme witness of martyrdom. In them the Church sees what it should and would be, by its faith and its love of Christ, and its mission.

> [Through the] power of your mercy,
> O Jesus, Son of God:
> To this disciple who had denied you,
> You entrust the gate of heaven,
> And the persecutor of your Church,
> Here he is spreading her far and wide!

> Victory which your grace has prepared
> And upon which your cross has set its seal:
> Out of Simon Peter, stumbling on the waters,
> You have made the rock of the faith,
> The leader and the shepherd of all his brothers,
> The watchman who keeps them in your ways.
> You alone could discern the apostle
> In the ardent Pharisee,
> And Paul longs to lose all for your sake,
> Because your breath fills him with ardor.
> He explores and reveals to all the peoples
> The infinity of the kingdom that is to come.
> Blessed is the day when both apostles
> Followed you unto death:
> You receive them in the paschal offering
> Of your Blood poured out for your Body.
> They share in your joy and your light,
> Their praise has found its wings.[53]

The Transfiguration of the Lord

Each year, the Sunday liturgy of Lent sets out from the desert where Jesus triumphed over the temptations of the devil[1] to the mountain where he was transfigured in the presence of the three apostles Peter, James, and John.[2] This stop at Mount Tabor, six weeks before Easter, prepares Christians to "raise their eyes" toward the Crucified of Calvary, acknowledging him, in faith, as the Lord of glory. And now forty days before the feast of the Triumph of the Cross,[3] the Church celebrates the transfiguration of the Lord.

This feast originated in the East in the fourth century, among the Christian monks who lived in the desert.[4] The mystery of the transfiguration held an important place in the spirituality and mysticism of these ancient monks.[5] They applied themselves to the contemplation of the glory of God appearing in the transfigured Lord, as in solitude they led a life unified in peace by prayer, and in particular by the constant repetition of the name of Jesus.[6] The feast of the Transfiguration was celebrated as early as the tenth century by a few churches in Spain, in particular those of Vich, in Catalonia, as well as a good number of dioceses in France and Italy. Peter the Venerable instituted it very early on at Cluny, where he was abbot 1122–1156. He even composed an entire office for this celebration, which may reflect memories of a trip to Spain. Callistus III, who had spent a long time in the diocese of Lerida, near Vich, introduced it in Rome before he became Pope (1455–1458)[7] and prescribed, in 1457, that it be thenceforth celebrated throughout the entire Latin Church.[8]

On the Second Sunday in Lent the Gospel of the transfiguration anticipates to some degree the celebration of Easter by reminding us that the humiliation and passion of Christ must never be considered or celebrated without recalling that, through his death, he entered into glory. For this reason the liturgy of Good Friday itself, at the moment when the cross is adored, has the faithful sing hymns that are preludes to the *alleluias* of Easter night.[9] The light of Easter completely fills the celebration of August 6: "In the shining cloud the Spirit is seen."[10] By celebrating this mystery, the Church gives thanks for her participation in the brilliant light that transfigured the face of Christ,[11] and prays that all who communicate in the body of the Resurrected One may one day be radiant with his glory.

> Lord,
> you revealed the true radiance of Christ
> in the glory of his transfiguration.
> May the food we receive from heaven
> change us into his image.[12]

Hoping for the Day When the Morning Star Will Rise

The Vision of the Son of Man in the Glory of God

The prophetic oracles can be read on at least two levels. First of all there is what the prophet himself has said and what he personally saw. Reading on this level attempts to grasp the meaning and significance of the oracle by referring to what is known, in particular, about the personal experience of the prophet and the actual circumstances under which he made his statements. In this way one can get a glimpse of the kind of future that he is announcing, but without being able to describe it precisely. The prophet is, in fact, an inspired person who tries to pass on what he has heard or seen. He does not behave like a diviner, who claims that he can foretell the future exactly. The words that the prophet has heard have a fullness of meaning that escapes him; his visions, for all their richness and allusive quality, possess a depth of symbolic meaning that goes far beyond what he can understand. He knows this and does not hide it. Bit by bit, events bring clarification of the hidden meaning, while the prophecy for its part helps the events to be understood.

This brings us to the second level of understanding prophetic oracles, which is linked to the first. The Bible itself is full of this sort. It has better perceived the significance of previous prophecy in the light of the present, and it has decodified the meaning of the present in the light of the prophecies. The New Testament continues in this tradition, but the event that is Jesus Christ—his person, his teaching, and his pasch—appears from that time on as the fulfillment and the key of all Scripture, while at the same time it throws decisive light on the future. And finally, the liturgy proclaims the biblical texts and inserts them into a new and original context—that of celebration. This does not represent a third level of meaning, properly speaking, because it is the integration of the previous two. The Church makes its own the texts that it chooses because they help to clarify the meaning and significance of the mystery being celebrated. This is the reason for the inclusion of the vision of the prophet Daniel on the feast of the Transfiguration of the Lord (Dan 7:9–10:13-14).[1]

Isaiah 6:1-13 and Ezekiel 1:4-28 also had visions. But the theophany that they speak of concerned their calling. Isaiah's vision that took place in the Temple was strongly imbued with the exalted ambiance of the sanctuary (Isa 6:1). The vision of Ezekiel in the land of exile (Ezek 1:3) had a wider perspective than just the confines of the Holy Land. The vision of Daniel does not concern his vocation. It is a revelation, and the scene has the heavens for its theater. In the eyes of the prophet, what happens up there reveals the hidden face of the events lived today by the people of God, who are dominated, oppressed, and persecuted by the powerful of this world. God seems absent or reduced to impotence. But it would be a grave error to believe this. What is more, although the images exhibit a sort of surrealism natural to scenes of this type, their description remains remarkably sober: one can visualize them, which is totally impossible in the case of the visions of Isaiah and Ezekiel.[2]

"In the vision I saw during the night," Daniel takes part in the setting up of a tribunal. "Thrones were set up and the Ancient One took his throne." The image calls to mind a personage of exceptional majesty, bearing no resemblance to an elderly person crushed under the weight of years. On the contrary, he is ageless. His hair, "as white as wool," and his garment "white as snow," make him seem to radiate a brilliant light. His throne "was flames of fire, with wheels of burning fire," and "a surging stream of fire flowed out from where he sat," giving the scene an indescribable splendor. In the background "thousands upon thousands were ministering to him," and "myriads upon myriads" were attentive to his pronouncements in judgment. All were concerned, even already judged, because in the books that were being opened at that moment all the good and all the evil actions of each one were being inscribed.[3] And now there came forward, "on the clouds of heaven," "one like a son of man," who "reached the ancient One and was presented before him."[4] To him was given "dominion, glory, and kingship" over all the peoples of the earth. This power that is solemnly invested in him by the Ancient One who is seated on the throne will be, unlike all other power, "everlasting."

In its primary meaning, and the one still in acceptance today, the expression "son of man"[5] applies to every member of the human race. But it has gradually come to mean the Man par excellence, "the primordial Man," both perfect image of God and, because he is that, the qualified representative of humanity in keeping with the thought of God:[6] " . . . One . . . coming on the clouds of heaven," the new Adam "is from heaven," whereas the first was "from the earth" (1 Cor 15:47-48). It is therefore not surprising that Jesus himself should be called the Son of Man.[7] As such, he is master of the sabbath[8] and pardons sins.[9] His death on the cross will, paradoxically, make manifest his glory[10] and his heavenly origins (John 3:13). He will go back where he came from (John 6:62), and he will come back on the clouds of heaven.[11] He will be seated on his throne of glory to judge the living and the dead.[12] But it is even now that the Lord exercises his powers to save his people (John 5:21-30), in particular, by giving them his flesh as food for eternal life (John 6:51).

> One day, the gospel tells us, the tension gradually accumulated between humanity and God will touch the limits prescribed by the possibilities of the world. And then will come the end. Then the presence of Christ, which has been silently accruing in things, will suddenly be revealed—like a flash of light from pole to pole. Breaking through all the barriers within which the veil of matter and the water-tightness of souls have seemingly kept it confined, it will invade the earth. And, under the finally liberated action of the true affinities of being, the spiritual atoms of the world will be borne along by a force generated by the powers of cohesion proper to the universe itself, and will occupy, whether within Christ or without Christ (but always under the influence of Christ), the place of happiness or pain designated for them by the living structure of the Pleroma. *Sicut fulgur exit ab Oriente et paret usque ad Occidentem . . . Sicut venit diluvium et tulit omnes . . . Ita erit adventus Filii hominis.* Like lightning, like a conflagration, like a flood, the attraction exerted by the Son of Man will lay hold of all the whirling elements in the universe so as to reunite them or subject them to his body.[13]

The liturgical context of this passage from Daniel gives it extraordinary fullness of meaning. But at the same time, this vision casts a brilliant light on the testimony of those who saw Christ transfigured. When she acclaims Christ the Lord, the Church acclaims its faith and its hope. The powers of evil in the world try in vain to bring their force to bear on the just, they do not succeed, and their days are numbered (Dan 5:26-27). It is the Son of Man who exercises the true power over "all the peoples, all the nations, and all the tongues," because God invests him with a kingship "which will not be destroyed."

> *The Lord is king, the most high over all the earth.*

> The LORD is king; let the earth rejoice;
>   let the many isles be glad.
> Clouds and darkness are round about him,
>   justice and judgment are the foundation of his throne.

The mountains melt like wax before the LORD,
 before the Lord of all the earth.
The heavens proclaim his justice,
 and all peoples see his glory.

Because you, O LORD, are the Most High over all the earth,
 exalted far above all gods.
(Ps 97:1-2, 4-6, 9)

The Prophets and the Transfiguration Bear Witness

Christian tradition accords particular importance to the transfiguration
of the Lord, witnessed one day by Peter, James, and John. This event
was, in fact, a revelation that followed in the tradition of the prophetic
oracles. It confirms their truth, and at the same time it calls for their testimony. The prophets and the transfiguration together support the veracity
of the apostles' message (2 Pet 1:16-19).[14]

From its beginnings, the Church has had to deal with gnostic tendencies. They took various forms depending on the era, but they were rarely
absent. This is true today. Gnosticism is not always, or even usually, a
structured doctrinal system. Many people would be astonished to be told
that their thinking or their way of talking is riddled with gnosticism. As
a matter of fact, few people are familiar with the term, or would at least
be at a total loss if they were asked to explain what it means. It is a fact,
however, that their religious ideation, and in particular their way of understanding and discussing the mystery of Christ is to varying degrees
far removed from the purity of Christian revelation as found in the
Gospels. This is mostly due to the power of concepts that come from alien
philosophical or religious worlds, that operate on a conscious or unconscious level and often poorly understood and assimilated. This amalgam,
which is often incoherent if not totally aberrant, constitutes a sort of
gnosis—that is to say, a body of knowledge that believes, and wants to
believe, that it is superior, because it has been acquired by its initiates
alone and because it pretends to transcend all religions, considered as
fragmentary and parochial.[15]

"We did not follow cleverly devised myths when we made known to
you the power and coming of our Lord Jesus Christ, but we had been
eyewitnesses of his majesty" (2 Pet 1:16). In these and similar terms the
apostles often proclaimed that what they taught, they had seen with their
own eyes, heard, even touched with their hands (1 John 1:1). They do
not even hesitate to acknowledge that the words of the Lord have even

sometimes shocked them, and that it took them some time, even a long time, to understand what they meant. Even their first reaction to the resurrection itself was one of incredulity. They finally were convinced by the evidence. And then and only then did they remember what had happened on the mountain of the transfiguration. One cannot separate this transfiguration of the Lord from the apparitions of the resurrected Christ: It was one and the same experience, witnessed in the first instance by Peter, James, and John, and in the second, the apostles all together. In both cases the words used are "we have seen." This double testimony has nothing in common with what the Second Letter of Peter calls "cleverly devised myths."[16] "The Lord has truly been raised and has appeared to Simon!" (Luke 24:34). "He received glory and praise from God the Father": Peter, James, and John have seen him in his majesty and heard at the same time, coming from the radiant glory of God, a voice that said, "This is my beloved Son, with whom I am well pleased; listen to him." This is what the apostles attest to.[17] The faith of the Church rests on their testimony:

> We believe in one God, the Father, the Almighty, . . . and in Jesus Christ his only Son . . . Crucified for us under Pontius Pilate, he suffered, died, and was buried. He rose again on the third day according to the Scriptures, and went up to heaven; he is seated at the right hand of the Father. He will come again in glory to judge the living and the dead.[18]

As apostolic tradition holds, and as the Christian profession of faith proclaims, the resurrection of the Lord and his entrance into the glory of the Father "confirms for us the words of the prophets." This affirmation is of capital importance and consequence. Through his life and his teaching, crowned by his pasch, the Lord carries out the words of Scripture and reveals their deepest meaning. Conversely, to understand the acts of the Lord during his life, and above all his pasch, we have to be attentive to the teachings of Scripture. From Pentecost on, and in the very earliest catechesis, as we see in Luke's Gospel, apostolic teaching has done just that (Acts 2:14-36).[19] In fact, in the story of the pilgrims of Emmaus we read: "Then beginning with Moses and all the prophets, he interpreted to them what referred to him in all the scriptures." The revelation of the gospel unveils the meaning of the prophecy and is rooted in it.[20] Both the Old and the New Testaments are indispensable for our faith, which needs their converging illuminations.

> This sacred tradition, therefore, and sacred Scripture of both the Old and the New Testament are like a mirror in which the pilgrim Church on earth

looks at God, from whom she has received everything, until she is brought finally to see Him as He is, face to face.[21]

Scripture, however, turns the eyes of believers not toward the past, but toward the future. It shows the royal way that the glory of God has traced through the world, in Jesus, whom the apostles saw on the mountain of the transfiguration. But, no matter how brilliant that light was, it remains a "lamp shining in dark place" of time, "until day dawns and the morning star," Christ glorified,[22] "rises in your hearts."

> The end and the fruit of Holy Scripture is not just any unspecific thing, it is plenitude and eternal felicity. For it is the Scriptures in which we find the words of eternal life; therefore it is written, not only so that we might believe, but also so that we might possess eternal life in which we shall see, we shall live, and in which our desires will all be fulfilled.[23]

And finally, through Scripture, "the dialogue between God and man" is established;[24] inseparable from the Eucharist, Scripture is a "sacrament" of the presence of God and of Christ for this intermediary time between the return of Christ to the Father and his glorious return among us.

> The Son of God, who took away from us that visible appearance yet desired to remain yet among his faithful, took a sort of second body, by which I mean the word of the gospel, which is in fact like a body clothing its truth. And in this new body he lives and converses with us, he acts and he works still for our salvation, he preaches and he gives us every single day teachings about eternal life, and he makes new to our eyes all his mysteries.[25]

Three Reports of the Same Event

The three Synoptic Gospels—Matthew, Mark, Luke—report the event of the transfiguration that was witnessed by Peter, James, and John. All three show much similarity. Nevertheless, it is not possible to perfectly superimpose them one on the other in order to obtain a single account, with the exception of only a few insignificant details. In fact each Gospel account presents its own peculiarities that tell us a great deal about its author's way of seeing the event.[26] For this reason it is good that the liturgy has seen fit to give us all three accounts successively.[27]

The three evangelists bear witness to a real event that happened in the course of Jesus' public life, more precisely, after his first mention of his passion and resurrection: "After six days," according to Matthew and Mark, "about eight days after," according to Luke.[28] This places the event of the transfiguration in direct relationship with Christ's pasch.[29]

To attempt to give an account of such an event, in itself ineffable, the evangelists had recourse to a double literary structure. On the one hand, they borrow the two great pilgrims of God, Moses and Elijah, who figured in some of the manifestations of God in the Old Testament—theophanies —on their journey toward "the mountain" where God reveals himself.[30] On the other hand, for their accounts of the transfiguration of the Lord, they take inspiration from the visions reported in the Book of Daniel[31] and the apocalypses.[32]

The basic elements that form the web of the story are found in all three Synoptics. Jesus takes with him, up the mountain, Peter, James, and John, who will be the witnesses of his prayer at Gethsemane on the Mount of Olives. Suddenly he appears transfigured by the brilliance of a bright light, while Moses and Elijah come beside him. Peter speaks up. He is clearly overwhelmed, and does not realize what is happening. And then, from within a cloud, comes a voice that repeats the same words it had proclaimed at Jesus' baptism. But this time the voice is addressed to the apostles. Then suddenly the vision disappears. Peter, James, and John find themselves alone again with Jesus. As if nothing had happened, they go back down the mountain with him. At that time, not understanding the meaning of the vision and the words that they had heard, they do not say anything about it to anyone. But they were too affected and stunned by what they had seen to forget it. They would speak about it after the resurrection of Jesus; the two events, juxtaposed, shed light on each other.

The account of the transfiguration of the Lord is full of biblical reminiscences and is presented as a sort of preview of the glory of the resurrected Christ. Peter, James, and John were chosen to be present, to the exclusion of all the others. After Easter, when they shared this experience with all the disciples, it became their common property. The words that came from heaven will from then on be "proclaimed on the rooftops,"[33] and will echo down the ages until the end of time: "This is my beloved son, listen to him." This is why all the disciples of Christ must keep the memory of the transfiguration of the Lord engraved on their hearts. While only three of them were actually witnesses that one day, they were given this experience for the sake of all. All Christians must summon up from their innermost depths the memory of this revelation whenever they see the Son of God dead on the cross, or the Church in agony, or when they are overwhelmed by personal tribulations, or on the edge of despair or of losing the faith. If they do, they will find the strength to pull themselves up from these depths and climb the heights of the mountain, no matter how difficult the way. Through mists and tears they too will be graced with a glimpse of the figure of the resurrected Christ surrounded by light.

> Let us go up to Tabor with Him; Jesus is ready,
> The host will be elevated for an instant; here
>   is the center of the Holy Mysteries.
> The perfect man in Christ attains his perfect form,
> And his feet, of themselves, leave the earth.
> The grain is hard, the grape has swollen, it is summer.
> Man is the perfect creature, Jesus is consummate man,
> Every living form in him attains its supreme example.
> What there is of clothing becomes white as snow, and
>   what there is of flesh shines like light.
> The Law and the Prophets disappear instantly in his presence,
> Like the iris where there is sun, and the Son when the Father is nigh:
> "You are my beloved Son in whom I am greatly pleased."
> Do we read that at this moment our brother has changed?
> His face, his eyes—his heart—his feet that we have touched?
> Nothing has changed in Christ, but all is transfigured,
> The face responds fully to the allegorical symbol.
> It is ourselves, forever! It is our body itself and it is our measure!
> It is the son of Mary and Joseph, and it is
> Where the heart beats in which a single Jesus is made of a double nature
> The second Person of the Trinity who says to the Father what He is.[34]

A Vision of the Christ of the Last Days

The Gospel According to Matthew presents the Christ of the transfiguration as the Lord who is going to manifest himself at the end of days (Matt 17:1-9—Year A).

The kingdom of God—prepared for, proclaimed, and established[35]—holds an important place in Matthew's thought. He had a solid foundation in the tradition of the Old Testament,[36] and he reports that Jesus solemnly declared to his disciples: "Amen, I say to you, there are some standing here who will not taste death until they see the Son of Man coming in his kingdom" (Matt 16:28). These words are in themselves rather enigmatic. In fact, they leave us in doubt as to just when this manifestation is to take place. But they follow the announcement of the passion and the resurrection of the Lord and his glorious appearance at the end of time. Several of the disciples to whom Jesus was speaking saw him resurrected, whereas not a single one of his contemporaries saw him return in glory—we are still waiting. But there was that one day when three of them saw the Lord radiating the glory of the Father. Moreover, from Matthew's perspective, the paschal mystery ushers in the kingdom.[37]

Through his resurrection Christ entered into the glory of God, from whence he will come to judge the living and the dead. Without seeing him, we confess that he is the beloved Son of the Father. Thus we prepare ourselves to recognize him when he returns in full splendor.

The temptation of Jesus (Matt 4:8), his great inaugural sermon (Matt 5:1), and the sending of the apostles on their mission throughout the whole world (Matt 28:16) all take place on a high mountain. Mount Tabor, where he appeared transfigured to the three apostles, evokes the "high mountain" where, on the last day, the innumerable nations will gather together on their march toward the light of the Lord that will shine forever.[38] We recall, in fact, Jesus' words at the end of the explanation of the parable of the weeds growing among the wheat, which recalls this assembly of the nations: "Then the righteous will shine like the sun in the kingdom of their Father" (Matt 13:43). This transfiguration of the elect is expressed in exactly the same terms as that of the face of Jesus, which had "shone like the sun." That is how he appeared on Mount Tabor, and that is how he will appear as Lord, on the mountain that the believers are climbing to participate in the ultimate manifestation of his return.

Moses and Elijah represent the Law and the Prophets—"the whole of Scripture"—who bear witness to Jesus and now see at last the full realization of what he had foretold, as the Lord himself had explained the evening of Easter to the two disciples of Emmaus (Luke 24:27).[39] The apostles will understand this in their turn, and will proclaim it in their preaching. For the vision and contemplation of the transfigured Christ only send us right back to earth and the time of the Church, in its naked faith. "This is my beloved Son." Without seeing him we believe him, because the voice from heaven proclaimed it to us. But it is not yet the time to set up our tents and sit down in the enjoyment of the vision and the endless celebration, with palm fronds in our hands, of "the salvation granted by our God, he who is seated on the throne, and by the Lamb." Then there will arise the eternal song of all those who will be gathered together in the heavenly Jerusalem:

> Amen! Blessing and glory, wisdom and thanksgiving,
> honor and power and might
> be to our God forever and ever. Amen.
> (Rev 7:12)[40]

Jesus himself intervenes to bring the apostles back to the reality of the present. He "came and touched them, saying, 'Rise, and do not be afraid.' " Each of the verbs quoted here has its own resonances and harmonics that are very rich in meaning. They recall the way Jesus acted with the sick whom he "touched" and told him to "rise"—to resurrect?—as well as the vocabulary of the Easter visions: "Do not be afraid!" But this vocabulary is also that of the days of the Church's march toward the return of the Lord who "is coming"; these are words that ask us believers, now that we have gotten up—"resurrected"—to forge ahead without fear, and to keep watch confidently, as we accomplish the task that is for now ours. This is how we can work for the coming of the kingdom, and prepare ourselves to enter in.

> Today, surrounded with light, Jesus,
> You reveal your glory to the witnesses
> Chosen by the Father.
> Tomorrow, stripped of everything
> Before your brothers,
> When upon the cross
> You will stretch out your arms,
> You will be humiliated.
>   Come the third day,
>   You will rise from the dead,
>   Clothed in light![41]

A Vision of the Risen Christ Shining with Glory

Mark's Gospel ends abruptly with the discovery of the empty tomb "on the first day of the week" by the women who had come to anoint the body. They were so frightened that Mary Magdalene, Mary the mother of James, and Salome said nothing to anyone, even when they saw "a young man . . . clothed in a white robe" who asked them to go and announce the resurrection of the Lord to "his disciples and Peter."[42] In Mark, the transfiguration is inserted exactly into the middle of the Gospel story, which unrolls like a drama, and the last scene is the discovery of the empty tomb by the frightened women and the invitation to go to Galilee to see the resurrected Christ.[43] From this perspective, the transfiguration of the Lord appears as the key to the understanding of the tragic destiny of Jesus and the enigma of the empty tomb (Mark 9:2-10—Year B).

Mark insists particularly upon the paradox between, on the one hand, the hostility provoked by the teaching and behavior of Jesus that culminates in his trial and death and, on the other hand, the enthusiasm of the crowds who sense an exceptional being in him, impressed by the authority of his words. In this regard the transfiguration represents a figurative point of equilibrium between these contrasts, or rather the solution of their apparent contradiction. What Jesus suffered does not constitute a true series of defeats that led up to his death. What they do represent is an itinerary toward glory. The transfiguration points toward the profession of faith of the centurion who, seeing "how [Jesus] [had] breathed his last" declared "Truly this man was the Son of God!" (Mark 15:39).

In Mark's account of the transfiguration, Elijah figures more prominently than Moses. This emphasis on the one who was to come before the Messiah could manifest himself is certainly intentional. In fact, immediately afterwards (Mark 9:11), Peter, James, and John ask Jesus questions about the teaching of the scribes on this point. "But I tell you that Elijah has come and they did to him whatever they pleased, as it is written of him" (Mark 9:13). To identify Elijah with John the Baptist by referring to the death of the precursor is another way of insisting on the necessity of the passion of the Lord, a life passage necessary to "restore all things" (Mark 9:12) at his resurrection.[44]

When he suggested setting up three booths, "Peter was being impetuous; he spoke without thinking because he wanted to take part in the kingdom before its time, before the passion of the Lord."[45] Mark speaks often of this sort of incomprehension on the part of the disciples that only faith in the resurrection can dispel. But this faith is achieved always at the end of a long journey strewn with moments of agony.

> Today, full of gladness,
> Jesus,
> You hear a voice confirming
> The promise in you.
> Tomorrow, silent,
> In deep distress,
> When pain
> Will drown your heart,
> You will be far from God.
>   But come the third day
>   You will rise from the dead
>   Full of gladness![46]

The Elect of God, Glorified While He Prayed

The account of the transfiguration of the Lord as we read it in Luke's Gospel differs very little from those of Matthew and Mark. It does, however, contain a few features peculiar to it alone (Luke 9:28b-38—Year C).

Luke places the event in a more exclusively paschal perspective than either Matthew or Mark. The transfiguration takes place after the promise of Jesus, who declares to those around him: "There are some standing here who will not taste death until they see the kingdom of God" (Luke 9:27).[47] Now for him, to "see the kingdom"—or rule—"of God" is to acknowledge the Lordship of the risen Christ.[48] Moreover, the evangelist specifies that this took place "about eight days after" he had said this (Luke 9:28).[49]

> What does he mean when he writes "eight days after" these words? Does he not mean that he who hears and believes the words of Christ will see the glory of Christ in his resurrection? For the resurrection took place on the eighth day. Or perhaps, having said that sacrificing one's life for the word of God is to save it, he means to show that he would fulfill his promises at the resurrection.[50]

"The mountain," without further identification, is the place where, according to Luke, Jesus liked to go apart to pray, sometimes accompanied by his disciples.[51] This time he went there with Peter, John, and James,[52] and while he prayed his face suddenly "shone like the sun" and his clothing became "white as light." Luke does not use the word "transfiguration," a term that could have evoked for the Greeks, for whom this Gospel was intended, the metamorphoses of the gods found in the mythology of Hellenistic religions. The change in Christ's appearance, his glorification, could on the other hand remind readers of Moses, whose face was shining when he came down from Mount Sinai (Exod 34:29-30); it could also evoke the glory of the resurrected Christ.[53] Moses and Elijah also appear "in glory," like heavenly beings. Luke is alone in specifying the subject of their speech with Jesus: " . . . they spoke of his exodus that he was going to accomplish in Jerusalem." And in fact, shortly after this passage, there begins a long section of Luke's Gospel that is called "the ascent to Jerusalem."[54] After traversing death, this exodus will bring Jesus to the glory of the resurrection and his ascension to the Father. The three apostles, on the mountain, contemplate this ending ahead of time.

This scene must have taken place at night, for Jesus habitually spent the night in prayer (Luke 6:12); moreover, the evangelist notes that "Peter and his companions had been overcome by sleep." When they awoke, Moses and Elijah were taking their leave. Peter wanted to keep them there and set up three booths: one for Jesus, one for Moses, and one for Elijah. But "he did not know what he was saying." He was still speaking when a cloud, such as those appearing in theophanies, came down and covered them with its shadow.[55] They "became frightened" when they found themselves in the dark. And from the cloud[56] a voice was heard, saying "This is my chosen Son; listen to him." At Calvary, those who mocked Jesus on the cross jeered and said: "He saved others, let him save himself if he is the chosen one, the Messiah of God" (Luke 23:35). "Yes," says the voice coming from the cloud. "Jesus is my Son, my Elect, the one I have chosen." Peter did not understand the meaning of this at the time. But on Pentecost, " . . . Peter stood up with the Eleven, raised his voice, and proclaimed to them, 'You who are Jews, indeed all of you staying in Jerusalem. Let this be known to you, and listen to my words. . . . God has made him both Lord and Messiah, this Jesus whom you crucified' " (Acts 2:14, 36).

> Today, shining with power, Jesus,
> You raise with joy your friends
> Whose expectations are fulfilled.
> Tomorrow, pierced
> By the lance,
> When the shadow of death
> Will cover your body,
> You will be abandoned.
>> But come the third day,
>> You will raise yourself from the dead,
>> Shining with power![57]

The feast of the Transfiguration celebrates the Lord come into his glory at the end of his paschal journey, when he invites his own to join him. The sufferings of the passion and the death on the cross are not forgotten; quite the contrary. Contemplation and the liturgy both consider the death and resurrection inseparably, as the two facets of the same mystery. Jesus is revealed as the beloved Son of the Father, his Elect, just as much on the cross as when he ascends to heaven. He will come back on the clouds, surrounded by a brilliant light, to judge the living and the dead, and to bring into glory those who have listened to him. The contemplation and the celebration of the transfiguration of the Lord give the Church fresh hope.

> All you who seek Christ,
> raise your eyes to the heights:
> there you shall be able to see
> the sign of eternal glory.[58]

The tradition of the Gospels reports two theophanies. The first takes place at the baptism of Jesus on the banks of the Jordan, and the second on the mountain of the transfiguration in the presence of Peter, James, and John.[59] They mark a progression in the revelation of the mystery of Christ.

> Both times Jesus was glorified; but the first time, it was in the desert; and the second time was on a mountain. The first time, it was like the entrance of the faith upon the stage; the second time it was its exit, so to speak, since his purpose had been made manifest. And so we could apply to the first those words of Paul: "At present we see indistinctly, as in a mirror" (1 Cor 13:12); and to the second, those of John: " . . . And we saw his glory, / the glory as of the Father's only son" (John 1:14).[60]

Similarly, the celebration of the feast of the Transfiguration offers Christians, gathered together year after year for the liturgy, a path of progress in the faith. All are invited to enter resolutely upon this way, even if they must recognize that they have made scant progress since the year before, or even slipped back. Every realization, in conscience, of one's failings or sins is, in fact, an agent of progress, so long as one turns back to God. Moreover, what Paul says of the apostles is true for all the faithful: "All of us, gazing with unveiled face on the glory of the Lord, are being transformed into the same image from glory to glory, as from the Lord who is the Spirit" (2 Cor 3:18). This transfiguration begins at baptism, which was called "illumination" in antiquity. "Although our outer self is wasting away, our inner self is being renewed day by day. For this momentary light affliction is producing for us an eternal weight of glory beyond all comparison" (2 Cor 4:16-17). And finally, we could never forget that participating in the liturgy, and especially in the Eucharist, gives us a share in the sufferings and the glory of the resurrected Christ, even now, and in a very real manner.

> Eat of the bread that makes your nature over anew,
> Drink the wine whose bouquet is immortality.
> Eat the bread that frees from the old bitterness,
> And drink the wine that dispels the pain of the body.
> This is the place where your nature is healed,
> Here is the pomp against all that wounds.
> For your sakes I became like unto you,
> And I have not changed my nature,
> So that, through me, you might share in my divinity.
> Be therefore transfigured by this beautiful change
> That converts you in a blessed manner from the earth to God
> And from the flesh to the Spirit.[61]

AUGUST 15

The Assumption of the Blessed Virgin Mary

Even after they were converted, early Christians continued to honor their dead and celebrate their memory and the anniversary of their death (or their birth depending on local custom), as they always had. By purging these customs of all taint of paganism, they made them into the expression of their faith in Christ and in his resurrection.[1]

The "feel" and the meaning of these commemorative celebrations were profoundly altered: hymns to Christ and songs of hope replaced the old libations to the gods and the ritual lamentations.[2] This cult of the dead led to family celebrations near the tomb of their ancestors. When Christians gave their life's blood for the faith, the commemoration of their admired martyrdom took the form of a cult centered on their burial site. As early as the second century their tombs were visited on the anniversary of their victorious combat, called their *dies natalis* ("birthday") in heaven. These commemorations then led to celebrations in the local Church. Gradually the cult of the most famous martyrs spread widely throughout the Church.

From the times of the persecutions on, the veneration shown the martyrs was spread to the "confessors of the faith" whose blood was not spilled in martyrdom but who had suffered in prison or in forced labor or had died in deportation or exile. After this period, virgins and ascetics who had consecrated themselves to the exclusive service of the Lord, in solitude and prayer, were venerated on the basis that this form of life was from now on a form of martyrdom—of bearing witness—even though it was not bloody. This was the origin of the cult of the saints.[3]

The cult of the Virgin Mary arose later. The reason for this lies in the fact that, aside from the "gospels of childhood,"[4] the Scriptures have little to say about the mother of the Savior, and nothing whatsoever after Pentecost. Once she had brought her son into the world and seen to his early upbringing, it seems that her role was ended.[5] It is not that she was totally absent from the piety of the Christians. The famous prayer *Sub tuum praesidium*—"Under your protection, Our Lady"[6]—is attested as early as the third century.[7] But it was the third ecumenical council at Ephesus in 431 that provided the impetus for the cult of the Virgin Mary. By condemning the doctrine of Nestorius, a priest of Antioch and then patriarch of Constantinople (428–440),[8] this council clearly defined that within the unity of a single person, Christ was both God and man. From this time on, the Virgin Mary is the "Mother of God," *Theotokos*.[9] Shortly afterward Pope Sixtus III (432–440) had built in Rome the first basilica in the West to be named for the Mother of God. It is still in existence, under the name of St. Mary Major. The first liturgical feasts celebrating Mary first appeared in both the East and the West in relationship to the celebration of the nativity of the Lord.[10] The origins of the feast of the Assumption are more obscure.

A fourth-century apocryphal writing, "The Assumption of Mary," tells that Jesus appeared to his mother two years after his ascension to tell her of her approaching assumption. Indeed, Mary dies and many miracles happen near her body. She is reanimated and carried up to paradise.[11] But other, older apocrypha also recount the death of Mary and her being carried up to heaven.[12] However, St. Epiphanos, bishop of Salamis in Cyprus (367–403), who was otherwise a well-informed person, seems not to have been familiar with these Palestinian traditions. In any case he refers to the event as if those accounts of it did not exist, or as if he did not want to acknowledge that he knew them.

> One does not find the death of Mary in the holy books, whether she was buried, etc. . . . Scripture has kept complete silence on this matter because of the greatness of the prodigy and in order not to overly astonish the minds of humans. As for me, I dare not speak of it. I keep my thoughts to myself, and I remain silent.[13]

In any case, the roots of the feast of August 15 are to be found in Jerusalem. It was first celebrated not far from the city at the place where legend has it that Mary rested before arriving in Bethlehem. The Greek word *koimēsis* was used, which could mean a going-to-sleep for the purpose of rest or the sleep of death. Toward the end of the fifth century, this feast was celebrated at Gethsemane in the basilica where Mary's tomb was venerated. Henceforth it was known as the Dormition, recalling her death and entrance into heavenly glory. At the end of the sixth century, the emperor Maurice (539–602) made the celebration of the Dormition of Mary an obligatory feast for the entire Eastern empire.

In the West the feast knew a similar evolution. By the sixth century in Rome, there was a quasi-feast dedicated to Mary that was observed on the first day of January: it honored her maternity. Around 650 the August 15 feast was adopted, celebrating the glorification of the Virgin. The term "dormition" was used under the pontificate of Pope Sergius (687–702), who was of Syrian origin. The term "assumption" appeared toward 770. But in the ninth century we see arise a certain reticence—the corporal glorification of the Mother of God was not denied, but in the absence of authentic witnesses, it was not insisted upon. And, in fact, the liturgical prayers do not go into much detail.

> For a long time the magisterium remains silent: It silently observes the dialogue between the intuitions of the "lovers" of Mary and the reticence of the theologians, who respect above all the witness of the word of God, including its silences.[14]

It is a fact that the Roman See, which held authority in the matter, was content with overseeing, quite liberally, the liturgical expression of piety toward the Virgin of this feast, as well as diverse Marian traditions originating in many different places and varying a good deal in authenticity—a number of these arose in connection with a particular sanctuary. It is for this reason that the universal Roman Calendar in force up to January 1, 1970, contained nearly twenty feasts of the Virgin Mary.[15] When Pius IX defined the Dogma of the Immaculate Conception on December 8, 1854,[16] and then Pius XII that of the Assumption on November 1, 1950,[17] the magisterium of the Church committed itself more decisively. These two definitions "represent an extreme point of dogmatization, like the foamy crest of a deep sea wave—the swell of Marian piety—reaching the Pope himself.[18]

The Roman Calendar promulgated by Pope Paul VI on February 14, 1969, was worked out from the same perspective.[19] The list was revised along with the relative degrees of importance of the various Marian celebrations.[20] What is more important, they were integrated in a clear way into the mystery of salvation through Christ, the true object of Christian faith and worship.

> She [Mary] stands out among the poor and humble of the Lord, who confidently await and receive salvation from Him. With her, the exalted Daughter of Sion, and after a long expectation of the promise, the times were at length fulfilled and the new dispensation established. All this occurred when the Son of God took a human nature from her, that He might in the mysteries of His flesh free [us] from sin.[21]

Predestined from all eternity to be the mother of the Son of God become man for our salvation,[22] she was totally dedicated to the person and the work of her Son,[23] and by doing so she prefigures the Church in its ultimate reality[24] and is the model of perfection for the faithful. This is why, in the Eucharistic Prayer, we ask God to make us, along with Mary, "worthy to share eternal life";[25] and we ask God, "from whom all good things come,"[26] to let us "enter into our heavenly inheritance."[27]

Our present-day Missal and Lectionary present us with a liturgy of the Assumption of Mary that was composed in accordance with the Marian doctrine of Vatican II. There are two Masses, as there were before. The first, for the evening before, replaces the Mass formerly celebrated on August 14 in the morning, on the vigil of the feast. The second is for the day of the feast itself.

In the Mass of the Vigil, one formerly read verses from Sirach (24:17-22)[28] from the passage where Wisdom sings her own praises: "I bud forth delights like the vine, my blossoms become fruit fair and rich. . . . He who obeys me will not be put to shame, he who serves me will never fail." In the place of this reading we read today two passages from Scripture. The first is taken from the Old Testament, the story of the carrying of the ark of the covenant up to Jerusalem and its installation in the tent set up by David (1 Chr 15:3-4, 15-16; 16:1-2). The second is a passage taken from the First Letter of Paul to the Corinthians (1 Cor 15:54-57): Death will be finally conquered for good on the day when " . . . this which is corruptible clothes itself with incorruptibility and this which is mortal clothes itself with immortality." The Gospel has remained the same (Luke 11:27-28): the day when a woman cried out, "Blessed is the womb that carried you," and Jesus replied: "Rather, blessed are those who hear the word of God and observe it." The Scriptural texts of the former Mass of the Vigil of the Assumption focused on the personal glory of Mary, who received the praises given to Wisdom. The readings we have today for the Vigil Mass reveal the fullness of Mary's glory and her significance in the history of salvation. The Mother of our Savior, the Son of God, is already elevated to the glory of the elect, where she bears witness to the victory over death that will shine for all those who follow Christ, who hear the word of God, and observe it.

Before Vatican II the readings for the Mass of the Day of the Assumption were the praise of Judith, to whom God had given victory over the enemy of her people (Jdt 13:22-25; 15:10). The Gospel is that of the visitation (Luke 1:41-50).[29] Since the Council, we read in Revelation the vision of the "sign" of the woman who appears in the sky (Rev:11:19a; 12:1-6a, 10ab) and then the passage from the Letter to the Corinthians where Paul reminds his readers that Christ is now "raised from the dead, the firstfruits of those who have fallen asleep" and is the promise of the resurrection of all (1 Cor 15:20-27a). The Gospel is the same as on the preceding evening, but it continues this time up to the end of the *Magnificat* (Luke 1:39-56). As on the evening before, the liturgy invites Christians to see in the Virgin raised to heaven the icon of the Church and of all believers on their way to the eternal glory reserved for them by God.

Blessed Virgin Mary!

The Ark of the Covenant

The ark of the covenant, that precious chest which contained the Ten Commandments written on stone by the finger of the Lord, was the visible sign of the presence of God in the midst of his people.[1] The ark had opened the waters of the Red Sea and had accompanied the people throughout the Exodus. After many trials and mishaps[2] it was enthroned in Jerusalem accompanied by great joy, seen as a promise of peace and stability, thanks to the divine protection the people had won back. The First Book of Chronicles glorified this event and gave it the dimensions of a grandiose public liturgy.[3] Of this long story, we read today a brief passage that lends itself to a transposition that can be applied to the feast of the Assumption of the Virgin Mary (1 Chr 15:3-4, 15-16; 16:1-2).[4]

David, who prefigured the Messiah who was to come, was the organizer and celebrant of this great liturgy. He made sure that all the rules were scrupulously observed: only the Levites were to carry the ark of God, "by means of poles laid on their shoulders."[5] It was the Levites who also provided the singers and musicians for this procession where nothing was left to chance. The role of the Levites was therefore paramount. By contrast, that of the priests was very low-key. It is true that at the time of this celebration there was as yet no temple. But it is doubtful that the author of this writing was concerned with historical truth. He wrote during the Exile. Worship was carried on in the synagogues without the offering of sacrifice, which could take place only in faraway Jerusalem. In this way the emphasis was placed on the worship of praise.

Curiously, the king himself exercised priestly powers: he offers himself, and has offered, "the holocaust and the sacrifices of communion"; then, when all is accomplished, "he blesses the people in the name of the Lord." Clearly we do not have here a description of a historical personage. No matter how great he may have been, the king was never in his lifetime a person of such stature. The author is projecting into the past the ideal of a King David such as was looked for on some future day.[6] Christians read this somewhat embellished story of the transfer of

the ark and saw in it the prefiguration of the cult that will be celebrated
in the heavenly Jerusalem. It is said, in fact, that Jeremiah hid the ark
in a place that was to remain secret "until God gathers his people together again and shows them mercy" (2 Macc 2:7). John, in Revelation,
has recorded this tradition (Rev 11:19).[7]

The ark of the covenant thus became in patristic writings an image of
Mary in whom the Word of God took flesh and who carried him in her
womb.[8]

> Today, the living and holy ark of the living God, the one whose womb car-
> ried her own Creator, rests in the Temple of the Lord, a Temple built not
> by the hand of man. David, the ancestor and relative of God, leaps with
> joy; the angels dance in chorus, the archangels applaud, and the powers
> of heaven sing of his glory.[9]

The realistic representation of the mystery of the assumption, as beautiful as it is,[10] always turns out to be somewhat disappointing, even ambiguous. We must go beyond the merely visible and understand that the
reality of the mystery will always remain impossible to express in words
or with the paintings of even the most gifted painters or most inspired
iconographers. The truest language of all is that of images, of poetry and
mysticism. When the Litanies of the Blessed Virgin call her "Mother of
the Savior," "Throne of Wisdom," "Most Sacred Dwelling Place," "Ark
of the New Covenant," they are expressing much more than literal
descriptions, and rightly so.[11] All these different titles given to Mary com-
plement each other's meaning. In particular, they show how one can proclaim her the "Ark of the Covenant" without hyperbole.

> Filled with grace and glory,
> Living Ark
> Borne toward the City of God,
> Come to meet Jesus;
> He whom you received into your dwelling place
> Welcomes you now into the Father's presence.
> *The Church, rejoicing, celebrates your passing,*
> *Alleluia, alleluia!*
> First among the redeemed,
> Victorious presence in the midst of strife!
> Mother of the Lord, humble and yet full of power,
> Your prayers are ever heard throughout the ages.
> Mary, source of our joy,
> You enter into the joy of God.[12]

Once again the liturgy shows remarkable discernment in choosing a
passage for the Assumption of the Virgin Mary that at first might seem

surprising: the transfer of the ark of the covenant to Jerusalem. It is a festive season for the Church because the Mother of God is bringing the Church to the dwelling of God, where each of us is called to take our place one day along with Mary. When the Church celebrates the "Queen of all the saints raised to heaven,"[13] it celebrates the glory of God and his Son, through and in whom we all hope to share, like Mary, in the eternal joy of the redeemed.

> *Let us go up to the place of your rest,*
> *you and the ark of your holiness*
>
> Behold, we heard of it in Ephrathah;
> we found it in the fields of Jaar.
> Let us enter into his dwelling,
> let us worship at his footstool.
> Advance, O Lord, to your resting place,
> you and the ark of your majesty.
> May your priests be clothed with justice;
> let your faithful ones shout merrily for joy.
> For the sake of David your servant,
> reject not the plea of your anointed . . .
> For the Lord has chosen Zion;
> he prefers her for his dwelling.
> "Zion is my resting place forever;
> in her will I dwell, for I prefer her."
> (Ps 132:6-10, 13-14)

Death Is Swallowed Up in Victory

The "resurrection of the flesh"—that is to say, of the human being in his or her totality, body, soul, and mind—is at the heart of the gospel and the Creed. It is a truth that has caused many to stumble, even among Christians. Some find the conjecture of an afterlife totally senseless, and think only of enjoying the pleasures of this life as much as they can. Others will admit that there is some sort of afterlife or reincarnation[14] of what one could call the soul or the spirit, but not of the body, which has become dust. Still others cannot accept that everything just disappears at death—it seems so meaningless and unjust—and they hold onto the notion that there must be "something" out there after death, but will not go so far as to say what. Paul devotes an entire chapter of his First Letter to the Corinthians[15] to this subject, for, he says, "And if Christ has not been raised, then empty [too] is our preaching; empty, too, your faith."[16] We read the conclusion of this line of thought at the Mass of the evening on August 14 (1 Cor 15:54-57).[17]

The problem with the dogma of resurrection is the body—how can it live again? In what form? With what characteristics? These questions and others of the same type defy our imagination. We can only attempt to answer them with analogies.

"What you sow is not brought to life unless it dies. And what you sow is not the body that is to be but a bare kernel of wheat, perhaps, or some other kind" (1 Cor 15:36-37). "So also is the resurrection of the dead" (1 Cor 15:42). There are no adequate words to speak of the selfsame identity of the mortal body and the body that will rise again. All we can do is affirm that the body will rise, using expressions that are admittedly paradoxical but nonetheless evocative of the future reality: "It is sown a natural body; it is raised a spiritual body. If there is a natural body, there is also a spiritual one" (1 Cor 15:44). In his conclusion, Paul says the same thing in different terms: "For this which is corruptible must clothe itself with incorruptibility, and this which is mortal must clothe itself with immortality." Reason, if not the imagination, is more satisfied by this final biblical image of putting on clothing. "Putting on immortality," like clothing "yourselves with Christ" (Gal 3:27) or putting on "the new self" (Col 3:10), implies a real transformation of one's being that keeps its deepest identity. This transformation has nothing to do with a disguise or a mere change in surface appearance.[18] It is the glory of the resurrected Christ that one will put on: "He will change our lowly body to conform with his glorified body . . . " (Phil 3:21). "Then the word that is written will come about:[19] 'Death swallowed up in [the] victory' " of Christ, "the firstborn from the dead" (Col 1:18).

Thinking of this brings a song of triumph to Paul's lips, and he even taunts death: "Where, O death, is your victory? Where, O death, is your sting?" (1 Cor 15:55).[20] This fearful enemy that Paul apostrophizes will lay everyone low one day, and no one reacts casually to the approach of his own death. No matter how painful the perspective of dying is, and the last struggle of our earthly life, the assurance of final victory keeps the Christian from losing heart. From now on we can proclaim that God, "even when we were dead in our transgressions, brought us to life in Christ . . . raised us up with him, and seated us with him in the heavens in Christ Jesus" (Eph 2:5-6). Is this assumption overweening boldness on our part, or perhaps presumptuous? Absolutely not! For "the sting of death is sin, and the power of sin is the law." In Christ and through him, God has already liberated us from both. He "even when we were dead in our transgressions, [he] brought us to life with Christ" (Eph 2:5).

This liberation from sin frees us from the direst consequences of death—which is the result of sin—and that is the loss of friendship with God. On the contrary, death with Christ is a passage, a Pasch, toward eternal union with God.

Similarly, we are freed from what in the Law (any law) defined sins without providing the strength to avoid them.[21] From now on we live under the rule of liberating love and the Spirit, is poured out in our hearts and allows us to love as we are loved (Rom 7–8). Mary, "full of grace," kept free from sin (the "sting" of death), has been "clothed in immortality" as soon as she had ended her earthly existence. "The elevation of her body and spirit to heavenly glory" foreshadows our own destiny.[22]

> When your days came to an end in the heart of the corruptible world, I showed my power to you in a vision; now that you are leaving this life, I shall show myself to you face to face . . .
>
> Your body is mine; I hold in my hands the depths of the earth, and no one can take anything from my grasp. Entrust your body to me; have I not, myself, entrusted my divinity to your womb? You are going to contemplate the glory of my Father, with the eyes of your soul all full of God; you are going to contemplate the glory of his only Son, with the eyes of your body without stain; you are going to contemplate the glory of the thrice-holy Spirit with the eyes of your immaculate spirit.[23]

"Let us give thanks to God who gives us victory through Jesus Christ our Lord."

Blessed Among All Women, the Mother of the Lord!

The very brief Gospel of the Mass for the Vigil of the Assumption was, in the sixth century, the one that the Roman liturgy had chosen for the day consecrated to the celebration of the Mother of God.[24] The passage chosen recalls the reason why the Church venerates in Mary, "blessed among women,"[25] the perfect image of the disciple who has already reached heavenly glory (Luke 11:27-28).

The scenario of this Gospel is extremely vivid. A woman in the crowd who heard Jesus speaking could not contain her enthusiasm and called out "Blessed is the womb that carried you and the breasts at which you nursed." Typically Jewish,[26] this spontaneous outburst expresses a feeling of admiration that many other people feel, especially women and mothers, and they have expressed it in similar terms on other occasions: "What good luck she had, the one who had such a son! How I would like to have a son like him!" It is not jealousy being expressed here—far from it. When she expresses herself like this, a woman has rather a feeling of spontaneous maternal affection for the son whom she admires so; she feels friendship for his mother. If Mary had been in the crowd that day when the woman cried out her admiration, like any mother whose child is praised, she must have stolen a discreet look at her son, a look of tenderness, and then closed her eyes, while perhaps a song, a lullaby, arose within her:

> My God, sleeping and weak in my arms,
> My child all warm on my beating heart,
> I adore in my arms and I rock, all astonished,
> The miracle that you, O God, have given me.
> Sons, O my God, I had none.
> Virgin that I am, in my humble state,
> What joy, budding in me, would have been born?
> But you, Almighty One, gave me this joy.
> What should I give back to you, I upon whom
> Your grace fell? O God, I smile to myself,
> For I too, small and limited as I am,
> I had a grace and I gave it to you.
> You have no mouth, O God,
> To speak to the lost people down here . . .
> Your mouth of milk turned to my breast,
> O my son, I gave it to you.[27]

And at that moment, Jesus answered by declaring "Rather, blessed are those who hear the word of God and observe it." He did not spurn the praise of his mother who, inspired by the Holy Spirit, had herself cried out "From now on will all ages call me blessed."[28] Nor did he try to prevent Mary from feeling pride. The handmaiden of the Lord who was chosen by God, her Savior,[29] took no personal glory in the amazing grace that was bestowed upon her. She never, deep within her heart, lost sight of the fact that everything had been given her by the One who had done marvels for her: "Holy is his name!"[30] It is to all of us that Jesus addressed his words, and to his disciples of today as well as those of yesterday. By themselves blood ties are useless; becoming a disciple through baptism and accepting the word with joy and enthusiasm do not mean much either. What is necessary is to hear the word and to keep it (Luke 8:11-15). Otherwise one is "like a person who built a house on the ground without a foundation. When the river burst against it, it collapsed at once and was completely destroyed" (Luke 6:49).

Mary, the mother of Jesus, is the model of the true disciple. She heard the word of God addressed to her, and she believed (Luke 1:45). But, at the same time, she kept it in her heart (Luke 2:19, 51), and bent her will entirely to the will of God (Luke 1:39). This does not mean that she always saw clearly what she was to do (Luke 2:50) or just where her submission would take her. But she always conformed her own will to the will of God.

> Your best servant is he who is more attentive not to hearing from your mouth what he already wants to hear, but to wanting what he hears from you.[31]

All her life, Mary was, in a unique way, the one who welcomed and kept the Word. When the angel announces to her that she is going to conceive and bear a child to whom she will give the name of Jesus, the young maiden of Nazareth answers without hesitation: "Behold, I am the handmaid of the Lord. May it be done to me according to your word" (Luke 1:26-38). And in this way she became the mother of the Word of God who took flesh of her flesh. She brought him into this world and raised him until he was old enough to go about through cities and towns announcing the good news of salvation. From this day on the mother effaced herself before her Son so that the Word that she had kept within herself as long as was necessary could now be heard by the crowds who were pressing all around Jesus. But Mary did not stay at a distance. The Gospels have little to say about what she did during the years of the public ministry of her son. But what little they do have to say appears meaningful. Mary, who followed the Lord even to Calvary (John 19:25-27), was among the disciples when the Spirit came down upon them, marking the birth of the Church and the beginning of the proclamation of the Word to all the nations (Acts 1:14). That woman who once called the mother of the Lord blessed was more right than she could know.

> The Savior confirms magnificently the witness of this woman. Not only does he call blessed she to whom it was given to bring forth in her body the Word of God, but he also calls blessed all those who will try to conceive in a spiritual way this same Word, through hearing it in faith, by bringing it forth, by nourishing it, either in their heart or in the heart of their neighbor, and by keeping it through the practice of the good. For the Mother of God is already blessed, without doubt, for having, in time, given the Word the means through which to become incarnate, but she is even more blessed to have kept the Word forever in an eternal love.[32]

Because she clung so closely to the Word, the Mother of God had nothing perishable to leave behind on earth when the day came to leave this world. Untouched as she was by its stinging dart, she shared immediately in the victory of her Son over sin.

Her entrance into the holy City is a feast day that fills the Church with gladness, a greater gladness than accompanied the enthronement of the ark of the covenant in the City of David.

For all the faithful who hope to share with her in the inheritance of eternal life,[33] she is the Blessed Virgin Mary whom we never tire of praising in song, giving thanks to God who "gives us victory through Jesus Christ our Lord."

> She is blessed of God,
> The Virgin
> Docile to the breath of the Spirit,
> She is blessed of God!
> Behold the new Eve
> Brought up to the joys of paradise.
> She is blessed of God,
> The woman
> Who gave birth to the first-born,
> She is blessed of God!
> Everyone proclaims her:
> "Blessed" in her humility.
> She is blessed of God,
> The mother
> Who sees her Son die on the cross,
> She is blessed of God!
> Standing at Calvary,
> She ushers in the age of faith.
> She is blessed of God,
> The queen
> Who prays for us, poor sinners,
> She is blessed of God!
> Her glory carries us forth
> To the day promised by the Lord.[34]

Glory and Praise to God for Mary, Marvel of His Grace!

The Woman, the Child, and the Dragon

At the Mass of the Day for the Assumption of the Virgin Mary, the first reading, like that of the Vigil, is from the Book of Revelation. This particular passage was chosen because it reports a vision of a woman in a position of primary importance (Rev 11:19a; 12:1-6a, 10ab).[1]

"Then God's temple in heaven was opened, and the ark of the covenant could be seen in the temple." The ark of the covenant of the Lord, that box made of precious woods that contained the tablets of the Law, had disappeared long ago, during the destruction of the Temple of Solomon in 587 B.C.[2] But it was said that Jeremiah had hidden it in a place that was to remain secret until the end of time (2 Macc 2:5-8). The ark, which had been constructed according to the exact plans of God himself (Exod 25:1-40)—his "throne"[3]—was to have the same proportions as the dwelling-place of God in heaven. In the vision, reality overtakes image. The seer is therefore transported out of time and space. What had been up to this point invisible is now revealed to his eyes. The heavens open and he contemplates the accomplishing of all things in the history of salvation.[4]

And then "a great sign appeared in the sky, a woman clothed with the sun, with the moon under her feet, and on her head a crown of twelve stars." Whatever may be the precise meaning of each of these attributes, they are reminiscent of certain images used elsewhere by the prophets referring to the glory promised to Jerusalem and to the peoples of the last days.[5] Now, this woman who shone with all the brightness of the sun, the moon, and the stars is "in pain as she labored to give birth." Her labor pains seem to be prolonged.[6] This heavenly vision is related in a perhaps surprising way to earthly realities. Popular wisdom frequently uses the image of the woman in childbirth to describe creative acts that take time and cause unavoidable pain in order to be brought to full maturity. One general use of this image is found in Isaiah 66:8—

"Can a country be brought forth in one day?"[7] And Paul reminds the Galatians what it cost him personally to found their community: "My children, for who I am again in labor until Christ be formed in you!" (Gal 4:19). In order to encourage someone experiencing a severe trial that can only have a happy outcome, John (16:21) writes: "When a woman is in labor, she is in anguish because her hour has arrived; but when she has given birth to a child, she no longer remembers the pain because of her joy that a child has been born into the world." The image is used also in a negative way to deplore a failure and to express disappointment: "We conceived and writhed in pain, giving birth to wind" (Isa 26:18).

While the woman of Revelation labors in pain to give birth, "another sign appeared in the sky; it was a huge red dragon, with seven heads and ten horns; and on its heads were seven diadems." Both his appearance and his size were terrifying, and he carried the signs of his immense power and extraordinary military violence[8] with arrogance, displaying them in a frightful way by sweeping up a third of the stars with his tail and hurling them down to earth. This monster is only waiting for the child to be born in order to devour it. But the woman brings forth "a son, a male child, destined to rule all the nations with an iron rod": that is to say, with indomitable power and authority. "Her child was caught up to God and his throne." As for the woman, she "fled into the desert, where she had a place prepared by God," sheltered from all danger. But clearly, danger is still present as long as the dragon remains nearby, with all its power and all its fearsome destructiveness. We feel sure that there will still be some terrible battles, but the passage does not go into them;[9] it goes on immediately to the victorious outcome of these last combats, which are met with an almost liturgical acclamation: "Now have salvation and power come, / and the kingdom of our God / and the authority of his Anointed."[10]

Initially, the two images of the woman seem to contradict each other. In the first scene she appears peacefully installed in a state of glory, but next we see her in all the pain of childbirth and frightened by all the dangers that threaten her and the fruit of her womb, as soon as it is born. We might prefer the images to occur in the inverse order, with the woman first in danger and pain, and afterwards at peace and in a state of glory. But visions and logic do not go hand in hand. The one and same image has two facets to it, we might say, and perhaps we should not be in too much of a hurry to read into it an interpretation of an individual woman, let alone necessarily a symbol of the Virgin Mary, mother of the Savior.

It is true, however, that the title given to the child—ruler of all the nations—and the authority attributed to him—he will rule them with an iron rod—as well as his elevation "to God and his throne" tempt us to see in him the Savior that all the powers of evil have not been able to defeat. From his birth on, the child was threatened by death (Matt 2:13-18).

However, the similarities stop there. The rest reminds us more of the birth of Christ in the hearts of the faithful. It is painful because it is long and takes place in the midst of persecutions, and because the disciples must constantly confront the dangers of temptations in order to be born in the faith and to persevere in it.[11] From this point of view, the woman becomes a symbol of the Church, which is contemplated by the seer in the glory of God and at the same time in the midst of all its earthly battles. The Lord is there to help it in its exodus so that the powers of evil do not bear it a mortal wound.

Without gainsaying this primary meaning of the image of the woman, Christian tradition has always seen in it a symbol of the Virgin Mary, which certainly goes beyond the intention of the author of Revelation, but does not do it any violence or change its meaning in any way. For the Semitic mind, the individual is never separate from his group, for he or she is its representative member. Moreover, because of her role in relationship to her Son, the faithful, and the community, Mary is the image of the Church that is still giving painful birth to believers, and which is already in glory in heaven with God.

> Is she Mary, or the Church? Or should we perhaps say that the image slides imperceptibly from one to the other? It is at once the Church who brings forth souls in Christ, doing battle with the dragon, and then it becomes the Woman who brings into the world the male child who triumphs over his adversary—Mary, his mother according to the flesh.
>
> This double interpretation of the figure called the "Woman" is incontestably an instance of the subtlety of Hebrew thought, as modern exegetes readily acknowledge. Already in Genesis, the Woman represents the whole line of women in its lengthy development, with a pause now and then at certain individuals who stand out in hagiography. Each one plays a particular role that gives her the value of a "type."
>
> Once again the author of Revelation does not describe idealized categories but living persons who carry out, in time, the purposes of God. If we keep in mind this way of thinking, we will not be surprised to find in the writings of an author as imbued with this Jewish mentality as St. John this use of the realistic symbol so familiar to Jews, and which corresponds so faithfully to their conception of the God of sacred history. This being so, there is no cause to take exception with the tradition of Catholic exegesis in read-

ing into the texts correlations that never would have occurred to the author. As moved as he is by the glory of the incarnation, St. John does not hesitate to connect Mary in a number of places with the mystery of redemption.[12]

At the Mass of the Day for the Assumption of the Blessed Virgin Mary, we read this page taken from Revelation as a contemplation of the Virgin taken up to heaven. John's vision casts a bright light on the mystery being celebrated in the liturgy. The joy of the Virgin of Bethlehem is inseparable from the pain of the mother who watched her Son die on the cross at Calvary. She followed a path that led to the paschal climax quite similar to that of her Son. The feast of the Assumption celebrates the pasch of Mary, which foreshadows that of the Church.

> *The queen stands at your right hand*
> *arrayed in gold*
>
> Hear, O daughter and see; turn your ear,
>   forget your people and your father's house.
> So shall the king desire your beauty;
>   for he is your lord. . . .
> They are borne with gladness and joy;
>   they enter the palace of the king.
> (Ps 45:11-12, 16)

All Will Come to Life Again, but Each One in Proper Order

The liturgy of the Day of the Feast of the Assumption, like that of the Vigil, contains a selection from the First Letter of Paul to the Corinthians, which treats of the resurrection of Christ and of the faithful.[13] In this passage, the apostle once more uses to illustrate his teaching a scene from the last stage of the history of salvation (1 Cor 15:20-27).[14]

"But now Christ has been raised from the dead, the firstfruits of those who have fallen asleep." The resurrection of the Lord is an undeniable fact. Doubt on this score would deprive all faith of its very foundation and would make salvation illusory, for if everything is ended with death, life has no meaning: it ends in a tragic and absurd failure (1 Cor 15:14-19). But this is not the case, for Christ is risen from the dead, "firstfruits"[15] of those who have died, who have fallen asleep. The "firstfruits" are the sampling of the whole; to offer the firstfruits of a harvest was to offer symbolically the whole harvest.[16] Making a "deposit" or a "down payment" on something means that one is already the owner of what one will finish paying for.[17] From now on, our faith in the resurrection of Christ assures us not only that some day we will rise again with him, but it permits us to say that we have already risen with him.[18]

The capital importance of the resurrection of Christ is intimately tied to the parallelism between Adam and Christ. Adam is not simply the first in a long line of human beings; he is the "primordial man," the "firstfruits" of humanity in its totality. His death was in some way the death of all those descended from him: "For just as in Adam all die, so too in Christ shall all be brought to life." Christ, as the second Adam, is the "primordial man" of a new humanity. All those who belong to his line "will live again in him."[19] He has purified them of the original, inborn, and hereditary stain of sin—and its poisonous "sting"—that marks down each man for death (1 Cor 15:55). With Adam, all have been expelled from paradise, the original paradise where the "tree of life" grew (Gen 3:22, 24). By taking flesh of our flesh, the Son of God changed the situation radically. The earth into which all men are born and in which they die no longer leads to the abyss. Death is no longer an ending but a passage—a pasch—into eternal life, as it was for Christ and will be for us. Humanity will follow behind the new Adam who opened up the gates, and will enter into another paradise that was only prefigured by the first, earthly one. And so it is that "in Christ shall all be brought to life, but each one in proper order: [first] Christ the firstfruits; then, at his coming, those who belong to Christ."

"First," "then," and "in the proper order" are not to be understood in the sense of "first in time," "next in time," and "one by one," in the way we speak of the order in which a crowd of people go into a room, or the way tickets are distributed and places inside are taken. Other than the consideration that these divisions of time have no meaning in eternity,[20] what Paul is saying has an altogether different significance. The resurrection of Christ is "first" in that it has radical primacy in everything, and before everything. He is "the Resurrected," the one to whom life belongs, and who gives life. The rest of us will be "the resurrected," with and through him. All "will be brought to life . . . in [their] proper order," which is that of the redeemed.[21] "Then comes the end, when he hands over the kingdom to his God and Father, when he has destroyed every sovereignty and every authority and power."

This last act is that of the end of time. "In the beginning was the Word"; "All things came to be through him"; he was "made flesh."[22] During his life on earth, Jesus, as he said himself, neither said nor did anything of himself alone, independently. He carried out faithfully all that the Father, who sent him, ordered him to say and do.[23] Once his mission was accomplished, Christ, in the end, makes allegiance to his Father, but he does not disappear as if a new and totally different era were beginning with his last act.[24] Of course, in a profound sense, all is accomplished at the pasch of the Lord. But his victory still has to be played out in time among humanity; and this time it is not yet over. And his victory must still produce all its effects among humankind. Christ will continue to rule over earth, "until [God] has put all his enemies under his feet. The last enemy to be destroyed is death," which strikes every human being. When comes the resurrection of all, it will be the time when "every knee must bend, / of those in heaven and on earth and under the earth, / and every tongue confess that / Jesus Christ is Lord" (Phil 20:10-11).

Holy Is the Lord; He Raises Up the Humble

The Gospel of childhood found in Luke draws a parallel between the birth of Jesus and that of John the Baptist, i.e., the birth of the Precursor and that of the Savior. This very structure brings out, though not explicitly, the primacy of the Son of Mary over the son of Elizabeth and Zechariah, the "prophet of the Most High," who "will go before the Lord to prepare his ways."[25] The *Magnificat,* the Canticle of Mary, ends the cycle of annunciations and reveals all the greatness of the mystery. It is the act of thanksgiving of the Church for the marvels accomplished by God in favor of the Mother of his Son, for God's love "is from age to age to those who fear him." At the Mass of the Day on the feast of the Assumption, the liturgy focuses on this Canticle of Mary more than on the visitation itself (Luke 1:39-56).[26]

The angel of the annunciation says to Mary: "And behold, Elizabeth, your relative has also conceived a son in her old age; and this is the sixth month for her who was called barren; for nothing will be impossible for God" (Luke 1:36).[27] Then "Mary set out and traveled to the hill country in haste to a town of Judah." This was not because she doubted the word of the angel. She wanted to waste no time in sharing her relative's joy and perhaps help her in whatever way she might be needed. However this may be, the evangelist doesn't bother to tell us the name of the town in Judah where Mary hastened. He leaves the reader to mull over her haste: "How beautiful upon the mountains are the feet of him who brings glad tidings, announcing peace, bearing good news!" (Isa 52:7-10).

Virgin Mary,
bearer of joyous news,
you run over the mountains of Judah,
and at your passage creation awakes:
the One whom the universe cannot contain
dwells within you,
the old world makes ready for spring!
The root of Jesse will flower,
The tree of life will give its fruit!
Sing and rejoice, Virgin Mary,
The Lord has visited his people.
Elizabeth runs to meet her joy,
she greets you, full of grace.
Truth takes root in the earth,
and John leaps for joy.
Daughter of Abraham, Mother of the Messiah,
we call you blessed.[28]

Luke's Gospel of childhood is so structured as to bring out the subordination of the coming and vocation of John the Baptist to the manifestation and mission of Jesus. This already stands out clearly from the account of the two annunciations.[29] With subtlety and remarkable delicacy, the report of Mary's visit to Elizabeth is more explicit. When she enters the house of Zechariah, Mary greets her cousin. "When Elizabeth heard Mary's greeting, the infant leaped in her womb." It is a joy for every woman to feel the movements of the child she is bearing; it reassures her that the baby is alive and well. Some mothers like to think that these movements mean precise things, that they constitute a message or contain some omen.[30]

Elizabeth was sure that in her case the "leaping" of the child in her womb was because the baby had heard the words of greeting of Mary and was filled with joy. Because of this "sign," and inspired by the Holy Spirit, her eyes were opened to the mystery: "And how does this happen to me, that the mother of my Lord should come to me?" Elizabeth already speaks as her son will later, on the banks of the Jordan, when Jesus goes to John to be baptized: "I need to be baptized by you, and yet you are coming to me?" (Matt 3:14).[31]

> She looks at her and says: Oh! She says only: Oh! and bows her head,
> For she understood everything all at once, her womb moved for joy,
> And clasping her hands, her poor woman's hands, she murmured:
> *Unde hoc mihi?*
> And I feel that I am there, seeing everything.

And I see the corners of her poor mouth trembling, and the sudden tears,
Those tears from the depths of someone who is no longer young,
     as from a heart that is weak and giving out,
And that grimace that one makes when laughing and crying:
She is crying, but there is immeasurable joy in her eyes.
The mother of John the Baptist looks at the mother of my God![32]

Inspired by the Holy Spirit who fills her, Elizabeth penetrates even further into the mystery. Speaking to Mary, she cries out to her: "Most blessed are you among women, and blessed is the fruit of your womb." The evangelist even puts into her mouth words that Jesus will use later on when speaking of the blessedness of the true disciple, of which she is the perfect model:[33] "Blessed are you who believed that what was spoken to you by the Lord would be fulfilled."[34] In Mary, all the just of the Old and New Testaments—"the poor of the Lord"—can contemplate with joy and thanksgiving the accomplishment of all that was promised, the fulfillment of all their hopes.

> All of this can only be understood in the light of the motherhood of Mary. It is to fulfill her role as mother that she is given this faith in Christ; it is because the incarnation of the Son of God is accomplished in her that she is "blessed among women" (Luke 1:42); it is because she has been singled out to become the "mother of the Lord" (Luke 1:43) that she is found to be, even before the incarnation, the " favored one" (Luke 1:28). For this reason, she is the exemplar of the new humanity, without losing her place among the ancient people of God, since Jesus is to inherit, through her, the throne of David.[35]

In answer to the praise she received from Elizabeth, the Virgin responds with praise of God.[36] The Canticle attributed to her reveals the depths of her soul and her faith, and her perfect submission to the word of God and the mission entrusted to her. This song, full of biblical reminiscences, speaks of the humble servant of God as the ideal image of the poor, the beloved of God, already spoken of by the inspired composers of the psalms, who celebrated as no one has since, the love and faithfulness of God. Even as he promised our fathers, promised Abraham and his descendants forever.[37] The *Magnificat* bespeaks an exalted and very pure vision of God and of human beings and their relationship to God as revealed in the Gospels,[38] but expressed here in lyrical language, moreover in strictly classical form and with classical themes.[39] No one has had the same personal experience as Mary, yet the Church can use the words of this canticle for itself, for it can see the marvels that the Lord has done for the faithful throughout the ages. What he has done for the littlest among his own arouses feelings of marveling gratitude and unspeakable joy. Who among us is not conscious of having been chosen by God, acting first and out of sheer love? After Mary, "Most blessed [by God] among all women," the Church and all the faithful give thanks for all the graces received from God.

For all her humility, Mary sees herself clearly at the center of the history of salvation: "From now on will all ages call me blessed." But she does not remain in contemplation of herself; rather, she marvels at the works of God—"Holy is his name"—acting out of a love which "is from age to age / to those who fear him." In the same way, the Church adds its voice to Mary's and all the saints and angels, singing of the justice of God, "the power of his right arm"[40] which in so many ways manifests his unfailing faithfulness, his paradoxical power and his surprising choices: "He is mindful of his love, of the promises made to our fathers"; "He has raised the lowly to high places; the hungry he has given every good thing, while the rich he has sent empty away"; "He upholds" the weak and those who fall.[41]

> Elizabeth was full of admiration for Mary; Mary was full of admiration for God. She marvels at God's looking down upon his little and humble handmaid. Immediately her thought turns outward, away from her own particular case to consider the love that God bears for all those who are little and humble, poor, unfortunate, and oppressed. Her own case is, for her, only an example of that mercy which God bestows upon those who are in particular need of his help and his salvation. What he has done for Mary is therefore to be seen as a revelation of his gratuitous love, of his compassionate mercy. And it is this revelation that makes the heart of the mother of the Lord leap for joy, which fills her with feelings of gratitude and thanksgiving, which spill over into her *Magnificat*.[42]

The Church celebrates the feast of the Assumption of the Virgin Mary by contemplating, "in the heavens, a great sign": a woman, "the handmaid of the Lord," has given birth to "the ruler of all the nations," and is there, "clothed with the sun, with the moon under her feet, and on her head a crown of twelve stars" (First Reading).

In Mary we anticipate all that will happen when the end comes, when Christ "raised from the dead," "hands over the kingdom to his God and Father, when he has destroyed every sovereignty and every authority and power" (Second Reading).

Along with Mary, the community of the faithful gives thanks for the marvels accomplished by the love of God which "is from age to age to those who fear him" (Gospel).

Here is a case where we find verification of something that our hearts have so much trouble believing because of our bitter experiences: that a human being should be able to enter into his or her eternity without having to do penance for anything. But such a human being exists: Mary. She had not for a single moment of her life anything to repent, no periods of emptiness or sterility. She had no reason to blush for a single act of hers, there were no shadows in her life, no actions that fell into the abyss of the past without having shone with the eternal light upon everything that this life contains of moral choice. Such a life as this of Mary's ended with her return to the house of the Father. But should we even say that it "ended"? Clearly, whatever was transitory in her life fell into the power of death; but only so that all that was eternal in her could shine in the full light, the eternal light made up of all the little flames of each instant of her shining existence.[43]

Mary was raised in the glory of her Son, the firstfruits from among the dead, because she believed the word and accepted it with her total availability. God made her blessed beyond anything she could have imagined. She continues to sing eternally the canticle of thanksgiving that she sang the day she went to see her cousin Elizabeth. Her praise of God is so perfect that the Church never tires of using those words, blessed as it is, even now, with the joy of the Mother of God that every believer hopes to share in one day.

Like dawn rising from the shadows,
Arise in the joy of the beloved,
You who gave birth to the Light!
Shining brighter than the noonday sun,
Arise in the joy of the beloved,
You who bore the Savior of this world!
As beautiful as the lily among thorns,
Arise in the joy of the beloved,
You who are blest among all women!
O Blessed Virgin Mary.
For having received without trembling the Word,
When the angel blessed you from the Lord,
Today you know the greatest glory
And all our generations call you blessed.
For having waited in your deep faith
For the day when the Living One would return from Hell,
Today you know the greatest of all glories
And our generations call you blessed.[44]

The Triumph of the Cross

In the fourth century, at Jerusalem, a small relic of the cross of Christ was venerated. We have a witness to this in St. Cyril: "We can still see it among us today," he says in 348. And he goes on to add: "Due to little pieces having been taken by the crowd of believers," the wood of the cross "has been distributed in splinters all over the world."[1] Egeria,[2] who made a pilgrimage to Jerusalem between 383 and 384, tells us about a great feast day celebrated in September.

> They call dedication day the day on which the holy church which is on Golgotha, the one they call the Martyrium, was consecrated to God. The holy church which is at the Anastasis, on the site where the Lord rose after his passion, was also consecrated to God on the same day. The dedication of these churches is therefore celebrated with the greatest solemnity, for the cross of the Lord was discovered on that day. It was, in fact, established that on the day when these above-named churches were consecrated for the first time, the cross of the Lord had been found, so that in this manner the two events are celebrated on the same day, together, and with great solemnity.[3]

The two basilicas that Egeria speaks of had been consecrated in 335. The date varies between the twelfth and the thirteenth of September. But another witness from the same time gives more precise information.[4] On the thirteenth, the liturgy took place at the Anastasis, and on the following day, September 14, at the Martyrium. The liturgy reached its climax on that day with the solemn presentation of the cross for the veneration of the faithful, as on Good Friday. In this way the memory and the commemoration of the dedication of both churches became of secondary importance, and the great solemnity of the "exaltation" of the cross captured all the attention. But another feast day was known, celebrated on May 7, that commemorated a miraculous apparition of the cross, which was seen at Jerusalem in 351. The celebration of September 14 spread rapidly, first throughout the East, and then in the West.

Constantine the Great (274/288–337) had built a church at Rome, dedicated to the cross, on the site of the former residence of his mother, St.

Helena (ca. 255–ca. 330). It was called "Jerusalem" until the eleventh century, when it received the name of "Holy Cross of Jerusalem." According to a tradition first attested by St. Ambrose (339–397), St. Helena had discovered the cross of Christ during a pilgrimage to Jerusalem, and had brought back a piece of it to Rome, placing it in the new basilica. Whatever the truth of this, the cult of the cross was known at Rome by the fourth century, as we know from the existence of the basilica of Constantine.[5] But the feast of September 14 was not celebrated in the Latin liturgy before the seventh century,[6] whereas we know of a feast day that was celebrated on May 3 from the sixth century on, which commemorated the discovery of the cross, and which was set on that day, following a different tradition from the one we read of in Egeria. But on May 20, in 514, the Persians captured and laid waste Jerusalem, carrying off in their booty the relic of the cross. This catastrophe aroused great emotion in the entire Christian world and gave birth to a renewed devotion to the cross. When the emperor Heraclius (575–641) recovered the precious relic, the feast of May 3 celebrated the event and it was thenceforth called the "Invention (Discovery) of the Cross."[7] Both celebrations remained in the Roman Calendar until 1960. In that year Pope John XXIII suppressed the feast of May 3.[8] The Roman Calendar as issued by the Second Vatican Council made the feast of September 14 a solemnity that in some years falls on a Sunday.[9] By ratifying the suppression of a kind of redundancy, this reform restored its primacy to the feast of the Triumph of the Cross, according to the ancient tradition that had been preserved by the Eastern churches, which celebrate this feast with very great solemnity.

When the new Lectionary for the solemnity of the Triumph of the Cross was composed, there was a an enormous choice of texts to choose from. For the feast of May 3 there were five different Gospels, according to the choice of the various churches. The parable of the treasure hidden in a field (Matt 13:44-52) called to mind the discovery of the precious wood of the cross. The story of the resurrection of the son of the widow of Nain (Luke 7:11-15) and of Jesus' driving out of the demons (Luke 11:14-28) emphasized the miraculous power of the Lord's cross. A number of missals had kept the story of Jesus and Nicodemus in which the Lord refers to the bronze serpent in the desert (John 3:1-15). And finally, other missals preferred the Gospel text from John (12:31-36), where Jesus declares that once he is lifted up from earth, he will draw all humankind to him. As for the Roman liturgy for September 14, it had chosen the parable of the treasure (Matt 13:44-52) and an excerpt from the passage about Nicodemus (John 3:1-15).

For the second reading—there were at that time only two at each Mass—the choice was narrower: the "hymn" from the Letter of Paul to the Philippians (Phil 2:5-11), two excerpts from the Letter to the Galatians (not to reject the scandal of the cross) (Gal 5:10-12), and the cross as the only claim to honor of the apostle (Gal 6:12-14), and the passage from the Book of Wisdom that recalls how God saved the just man from the waters of the deluge, thanks to the wood of the ark (Wis 10:4).

In all this array of texts, the Lectionary published since Vatican II chose first the Gospel most attested by tradition and certainly the closest in affinity to the theme of the feast: "For God so loved the world that he gave his only Son" (John 3:13-17). This choice led to that of the first reading: the episode of the bronze serpent spoken of by Jesus (Num 21:4b-9). For the second reading, even though it was already read on Palm Sunday, they chose the hymn to Christ, who took upon himself the condition of slave, making himself obedient even to death, and "because of this" was raised up by God "above every name" (Phil 2:6-11).

> May our only pride
> be the cross of our Lord Jesus Christ.
> In him, we have salvation, life, and resurrection;
> through him we are saved and delivered.[10]

The Cross of Christ, Our Pride and Our Hope!

Look to Him and You Will Be Saved!

The snake has always aroused strange feelings of revulsion and instinctual fear; curiosity, too, mixed with a certain fascination. This reptile that crawls and curls up on itself, that can climb trees and slip into unseen hiding places with its sudden movements and lidless, fixed eyes, darting out when we least expect it and disappearing just as suddenly into brush or muddy water, has a reputation for formidable wisdom, allied to a unique ability to hide anywhere.[1] Because it crawls and is found in the sands of even the most arid of deserts, the snake has been seen as a damned creature, condemned to eat dust as its food.[2] This strange animal, so different from all the others, seems to typify the sort of unforeseen, sly, and deadly danger against which there is no way to protect oneself. It is often considered a kind of monstrous beast that talks in riddles and solves them all.[3] In Genesis, in the story of our origins, the Bible presents the serpent as the symbol of the prideful possession of the knowledge of good and evil that robbed Adam and Eve of their blessed innocence and set them against God.[4] But in mythology, the snake also symbolizes fertility and rebirth, the power of regeneration of the waters that are in the bowels of the earth.[5] Snake-charmers who manage to disarm the beasts and make them harmless, and even play with them, are considered sorcerers. If one is bitten by a serpent and remains unharmed, this is proof of magic or of some wondrous and exceptional divine protection.[6] All of these ideas underlie the reading from Numbers in this day's liturgy (Num 21:4b-9).

All peoples keep alive the memory of the event to which they trace their origins. It is recounted from generation to generation, the facts often embellished or given a meaning that was not originally possessed but discovered after the fact. The symbolic value that a particular event assumes often becomes its most important feature, the essence that is transmitted to posterity; and not without reason, for it is often due to this symbolism that even a small event can become, more than any other, the point of departure for a new era in history.[7] A case in point is the long wandering in the desert that brought the people of God, who had been freed from slavery in Egypt, into the Promised Land, and the Bible refers constantly to this wandering in the desert. But there is another reason, a deeper one, for the constant re-reading of this fundamental episode. In some sense Exodus is a parable of the history of salvation, a mirror in which believers of all epochs see the image of their repeated infidelities, a parable of God's conduct toward those who abandon him. He tries to bring them back to the right path by reminding them of their sins; he purifies them with trials and punishments; and at the first sign of their conversion, he forgives them and once again places his trust in them.[8] For this reason the reading of the Book of Exodus is highly profitable, even today.[9] Certain episodes of this archetypical story are not only full of meaning but also foreshadow later events. Among these is the story of the bronze serpent.

Once more the people had rebelled against God and Moses, this time in a particularly scandalous fashion, virulently, insolently, unjustly. They suspect God of having "brought them out of Egypt" in order to let them die in the desert. They forget all that God had done for them through Moses, his servant.[10] We can understand that their exhaustion and all the hazards of their journey had taken their toll on their morale,[11] but even so, nothing could justify this intolerable behavior on their part. God, so to speak, cannot put up with them any longer. He sends against his people "saraph serpents, which bit the people so that many of them died." The rebellious people understood that this calamity was not due to natural causes in an inhospitable place, but was the punishment of God. So they turned to Moses, saying "We have sinned, by complaining against the Lord and against you. Pray the LORD to take the serpents from us." So God told them to make a serpent and to set it up at the top of a pole. All who had been bitten had only to look at it and they were healed.

The use of a bronze serpent was undoubtedly a custom among desert peoples. It was used as protection from an evil charm.[12] According to popular belief at those times, evil could be cured with evil[13] or at least exorcised in some way with a representation of the source of the harm. In the present instance, however, there is no trace of magic, since it is God who tells them to make a serpent and mount it on a pole, and it is God who heals.[14]

> For when the dire venom of beasts came upon them
>   and they were dying from the bite of crooked serpents,
>   your anger endured not to the end.
> But, as a warning, for a short time they were terrorized,
>   though they had a sign of salvation,
>   to remind them of the precept of your law.
> For he who turned toward it was saved,
>   not by what he saw,
>   but by you, the savior of all.
> (Wis 16:5-7)

This way of understanding the episode of the bronze serpent—and, in a more general way, all the great events of Exodus—explains the consistent conduct of God. His "punishments" are in reality "benefactions" (Wis 16:2). For in fact their purpose is always to make the people aware of the gravity of their sin and its dire consequences, and to move them to conversion, to return with a sincere heart to the Lord who alone gives life and who is ready to forgive all their sins, even the most serious.[15] Later Christian interpretation of the episode of the bronze serpent, informed as it is with the decisive event of the elevation on the cross of the Savior of the world, is completely in keeping with traditional biblical interpretation. Following the Gospel of John (3:13-17),[16] from the apostolic age on, the Fathers of the Church have seen the image of Christ raised up on the cross in the serpent that Moses had lifted up on a pole.

> Moses answered them: "When one of you is bitten, let him come to the serpent up on the wooden pole and let him be full of hope, believing that this serpent, even though it is not alive, can give life, and at that very moment he will be saved." They did as they were told, and behold another example of the glory of Jesus: All is in him and for him.[17]

Christian interpretation is legitimately founded on the conviction that all of Scripture, "beginning with Moses and all the prophets," concerns Christ (Luke 24:27). And it is in this spirit that the liturgy chooses its scriptural texts. They even gain further meaning, which gives them a very concrete relevancy because of their closeness to the mystery being celebrated; and this mystery is itself illumined in turn by its celebration in the liturgy.[18]

> *Do not forget the works of the Lord.*
>
> Hearken, my people, to my teaching;
>   incline your ears to the words of my mouth
> I will open my mouth in a parable,
>   I will utter mysteries from of old.

While he slew them they sought him
 and inquired after God again,
Remembering that God was their rock
 and the Most High God, their redeemer.
But they flattered him with their mouths
 and lied to him with their tongues,
Though their hearts were not steadfast toward him,
 nor were they faithful to his covenant.
Yet he, being merciful, forgave their sin
 and destroyed them not;
Often he turned back his anger
 and let none of his wrath be roused.
(Ps 78:1, 34-38)

Glory Through the Cross for Christ and for Us

The Letter of Paul to the Philippians bears witness to his indomitable faith
and hope. He is in prison and has no idea of what the future holds for
him. But he is sure of one thing: whatever may be the outcome of his
trial, the cause of the gospel will be strengthened. Bolstered by this conviction, he exhorts his correspondents: far from losing courage, they
should continue bravely to fight the good fight, while preserving unity
in humility, in mutual service. Suddenly, his tone changes. The subject
changes and becomes a paean of praise. The hymn to Christ that the apostle recalls at this juncture was undoubtedly used in the liturgy of his day.
In a few verses, it speaks movingly of the journey undertaken by the Son
of God made man, who lowered himself even to death on the cross, and
who, "because of this," was raised by God his Father "above every
name." Here we see revealed the meaning of all the trials endured by
the Christians and by the Church, and we are assured that victory lies
at the end of our pasch, as it did at the end of the Lord's (Phil 2:6-11).[19]

 "Though he was in the form of God"—that is, God himself—Christ
Jesus died on a cross. How could that have happened? How is it that
he did not escape from those who wanted his death? Doesn't this ignominious death contradict all that we say about him and all that we believe? In any case, this death remains one of the most formidable of
stumbling blocks along the path to faith, for the sarcasms heard on Calvary have not ceased to be heard, and the faithful, at least on some occasions, can hardly escape some degree of uneasiness: "He trusted in God;
let him deliver him now if he wants him. For he said, 'I am the Son of
God'" (Matt 27:43). But the Church and Christian teaching have never
sought to diminish the horrendous nature of this scandal, even when

many consider it an unacceptable contradiction. On the contrary, the Church has always affirmed that Jesus of Nazareth, the Christ, is true God and true man; he truly died on the cross.[20] "He did not regard equality with God something to be grasped," although he certainly kept the "form of God"—that is, the divine nature. But he never was intent upon jealously keeping this right for himself or deriving glory from it; he did not consider being equal to God some sort of prize to fight for.[21] The journey and comportment of the New Adam are exactly the opposite of those of the first. In fact, the first Adam, who was but a man, wanted to usurp divine nature, something that was not his to begin with and never could be (Gen 3:5).[22]

Christ Jesus, "rather . . . emptied himself, taking the form of a slave": he "emptied" himself.[23] This does not mean that human beings who are created in the image of God (Gen 1:27) are nothing, or that the "human likeness" is something to be despised; it also does not mean—if such a thing were even imaginable—that the "form of God" is like an article of clothing that one puts on and takes off.[24] "The Son of God was born in the likeness of humankind and found human in appearance." Without losing anything of his divinity, he "became flesh" (John 1:14), "servant," even slave;[25] he renounced the appearance of his glorious divinity that Peter, James, and John glimpsed on the mountain of the transfiguration. But incarnation was only the first and necessary stage of the "emptying" that the Son of God freely consented to. "He humbled himself, becoming obedient to death, even death on a cross!" The eternal Son of God undergoes death, the bitter fruit of sin, and a death reserved for criminals! At such a sight, reason flounders and words fail: only silent adoration can express something of the feelings that well up from the depths of the heart, especially if one remembers that through baptism our flesh, with its passions and its selfish tendencies, was crucified with Christ "so that we might live in newness of life."[26]

For when Christ Jesus reached the depths of his "form of slave," "God greatly exalted him and bestowed on him the name that is above every name, that at the name of Jesus every knee should bend, of those in heaven and on earth and under the earth, and every tongue confess that Jesus Christ is Lord. . . ." There is a relationship of cause and effect between the humbling of the Servant and the glory of the Lord: it is because he was obedient even unto death that he was raised up. What is more, this "exaltation"—we should perhaps say "super-exaltation"[27]— can only come from God, for it goes beyond all human possibilities, as

well as all imaginings: it is without equal. Similarly, the name given to
the Lord was "above all names" because there exists no name that can
adequately express his dignity. What is true of God is true of him.

> I have called him by every name one can think of, but not one could ex-
> press his dignity. For how could one find a name commensurable with him
> who is above all names?[28]

To call Jesus "Lord" is, ultimately, the best way for his disciples to speak
of him. For in fact this title belongs to him alone and expresses his absolute transcendence and his role as the risen One seated at the right hand
of God.[29] The goal of all preaching is to bring all people to acknowledge
in Jesus, "obedient to death, even death on a cross," the Lord whom
God has "exalted him . . . above every name," the King of the universe.
To say, "Jesus, the Lord" is one of the most ancient expressions of faith,
certainly the most fundamental and the one that ensures salvation. "And
no one can say, 'Jesus is Lord,' except by the holy Spirit" (1 Cor 12:3);
"For, if you confess with your mouth that Jesus is Lord and believe in
your heart that God raised him from the dead, you will be saved" (Rom
10:9).

> Whosoever has believed in Christ, even though he be not yet sanctified
> and brought into the body of the Church, must nevertheless already call
> upon him in whom he has believed. For Christ has come to reconcile the
> world with God and to offer to the Father all those who have believed in
> him. Now, those whom he offers to the Father are received by the Holy
> Spirit in order that they may be sanctified and given their full lives as mem-
> bers of the heavenly Church of the first-born, and so that they may be in-
> cluded in the vitality and perfection of the entire body; they then merit to
> be called "the Church of God without spot or wrinkle." And thus, before
> arriving at this degree of perfection, they call upon the name of our Lord
> Jesus Christ, "the mediator between God and men"; and the Spirit of God
> having descended into their hearts, this same Spirit crying "Abba, Father"
> teaches them to invoke the name of the Father.[30]

The hymn of the Letter to the Philippians proclaims the paradoxical
glory—yet the only true one—of him who manifested the "humility of
God."[31] Through the cross of his humiliation and his glory, Christ Jesus
took over the leadership of humanity redeemed from the folly of Adam.
Deceived by the serpent, Adam had disobeyed, thinking that he could become like God. By obediently accepting death, "even death on a cross,"
"God greatly exalted" the new Adam. Through his pasch, he opened up
to all of humanity the path that reaches to God, and he reconciled the entire cosmos to the creator of heaven and earth and all that they contain.

Through his obedience even unto death, hanging upon the cross, he destroyed that ancient disobedience committed on a tree of wood. Because it is the Word of almighty God himself that in its invisible state is spread among us throughout the entire universe, embracing it in all its length and its width and its height and its depths—for it is by the Word of God that all things down here have been ordered and governed—the crucifixion of the Son of God took place in all these dimensions too when it marked the sign of the cross upon the universe. For when it became visible, it must have made clear the participation of this universe in his crucifixion, so as to show, thanks to its visible form, the action that it exerts on the visible, namely, that it is he who illumines the heights (that is to say, all that is in the heavens), and he who contains the depths (what is in the subterranean regions), he who stretches out the width, from the East where the sun rises to the West where it sets, and he who governs like a pilot the region of the North Star as well as the wide equator of the South, and he who brings together all those who are so dispersed to the knowledge of the Father.[32]

That the World Be Saved Through Christ Crucified

A careful reading reveals that the Fourth Gospel was preached for a long time before it was written down. This is apparent from the remarks the evangelist sprinkles throughout the text. One hears in them an echo of the commentaries of the homilies that John gave as he reported the words and "signs" of the Lord.[33] We find an instance of this in the reflections that Jesus' talk with Nicodemus gave rise to in the evangelist's mind. They have a significance that even when they are read out of context is in no way diminished—quite the contrary (John 3:13-17).

The mystery of the incarnation is truly central in the theology and spirituality of John. We must always start with this and end with this. Everything rests on the reality of the incarnation: the Word which "in the beginning . . . was with God," which "was God," through whom "all things came to be," without whom "nothing came to be," and who "became flesh" (John 1:1-4:14). John's Gospel constantly reminds us of this double reality of the divinity and the humanity of Christ, affirmed at once, and forcibly, in what is called the "prologue" to the Fourth Gospel (John 1:1-18).[34] Because he was indissolubly "Son of God" and "Son of Man,"[35] Jesus, as the sole true witness to the Father, shares his knowledge of the things of heaven, the divine secrets. He is "the way and the truth and the life" (John 14:6).[36] "No one has ever seen God. The only son, God, who is at the Father's side, has revealed him" (John 1:18). For John, to know God is to enter into communion with him, to share his life. The knowledge John speaks of is a grace, and not the fruit of intellectual activity. Basing himself on these fundamentals of faith, the evangelist carries forward the teaching that Jesus gave to Nicodemus (John 3:1-13), this time in a clearly paschal context.

By becoming man, the Word of God "gave power to become the children of God, to those who believe in his name" (John 1:12). Christians know this. They no longer ask, as did Nicodemus, "How can this happen?" (John 3:9). They have received baptism, the sacrament of rebirth; in the Eucharist they recognize the Body and Blood of Christ, food and drink for eternal life (John 6:53-54). Born from above, through water and the Spirit, they confidently expect to enter one day into the kingdom of God (John 3:3-7). Their fate is indeed in the hands of the "Son of Man," who alone has ascended to the heavens from whence he came: "the true light, which enlightens everyone, was coming into the world" (John 1:9).[37] But "just as Moses lifted up the serpent in the desert, so must the Son of Man be lifted up, so that everyone who believes in him may have eternal life." Seen in the light of Easter, the cross is not the gibbet on which Christ died but the throne of his glory. This is why John is always saying that Jesus was "lifted up" on the cross. This "lifting" allows us to recognize his true nature and his transcendent dignity: "When you lift up the Son of Man, then you will realize that I AM . . . " (John 8:28).[38] It is also at that moment that the Lord will draw all things to him: "And when I am lifted up from the earth, I will draw everyone to myself" (John 12:32). The passion of our Lord Jesus Christ according to John is written like a royal coronation, with Jesus' entry into Jerusalem as the first stage and the key to its interpretation.[39] With John, it is the triumphant cross that the Church contemplates on this festive day.

> O marvelous power of the cross! O ineffable glory of the passion! There we find the tribunal of the Lord, there the judgment of the world, there the power of the crucified! You have drawn all things to yourself, Lord, and when you stretched out your hands one whole day toward a people who did not believe in you and persisted in discrediting you, the whole world acquired the understanding to confess your majesty! . . .

> Your cross is the source of all blessings, the source of all graces; through it, from their weakness, the faithful receive strength, from shame, glory, from death, life. Now, in truth, when the array of sacrifices of the flesh have come to an end, the unique offering of your Body and your Blood swallows up all the differences between the victims; for you are the true Lamb of God who takes away the sins of the world, and you accomplish in yourself all the mysteries, so that all the peoples may form a single kingdom, just as all the victims gave way to one sole sacrifice.[40]

Those who, in the desert, looked up at the bronze serpent that Moses lifted up on a pole preserved their lives (Num 21:9). And now it is to Christ, "lifted up" on the glorious cross, that we must raise our eyes not to be saved from the disastrous effects of the bite of a desert serpent, but in order to have eternal life. It is a look of faith that is needed. A look of faith will recognize in the cross the sign of salvation, and in the one who is "lifted up" on this precious wood, the Savior of the world. And then will be fulfilled the words of the prophet Zechariah (Zech 12:10) quoted by John at the end of his account of the passion: "They will look upon him whom they have pierced" (John 19:37). At the same time, we will see in the cross of Christ the supreme proof of the infinite love of God, who "gave his only Son" so that everyone may have eternal life.[41] "God sent his son into the world that we might have life through him." The cross reveals that "God is love" (1 John 4:16).

The solemn celebration of the Triumph of the Cross does not deny the sufferings of the passion of Christ or the ignominy of his crucifixion; nor does it ignore the sins that were the cause of his death anymore than a theater drama's happy outcome leads the audience to forget the terrible moments it has witnessed during the play—quite the contrary.[42] But the more one realizes the gravity of sin, the greater appears the love of God who pardons all. More than anything, his mercy reveals his power that nothing can resist for very long, not even sin. So the cross becomes the trophy of his glorious victory, and that of his Son who, in order to carry out his mission of salvation and manifest to the world the infinite love of the Father, "humbled himself, becoming obedient to death, even death on a cross" (Phil 2:8).

This "almost 'irrational' manifestation of the love of God for humanity"[43] reveals another characteristic of the generosity of God, greater than anyone could ever have imagined. He does not impose himself. He did not send his Son into the world in order to establish his kingdom by force. Jesus said as much to Pilate: "If my kingdom did belong to this world, my attendants [would] be fighting to keep me from being handed over to the Jews" (John 18:36). God does not want submissive and fearful slaves whose masters enjoy an illusion of power but are secretly despised and always subliminally afraid of a revolt on the part of those who serve them. God offers, along with his love, blessing and life (Deut 30:19). The Triumphant Cross, when raised up over the world, illumines the path that leads to life and points the way to the gates of the kingdom. Its brilliance lights up those who are still on the way, who look to the Son of

Man, singing "Jesus Christ is Lord, to the glory of God the Father" (Phil 2:11).

> Through the Cross that killed the Son of the Father,
>> Blessed rootstock where the grape is harvested,
>>> Jesus Christ, we bless you.
> By the Cross that brings fire to the world,
>> Burning bush that reveals your love,
>>> Jesus Christ, we glorify you.
> By the Cross planted on Calvary,
>> Living branch that heals all sins,
>>> Victorious God, your Church acclaims you.
> By the Wood that sang the wedding song,
>> Of the living God espousing humanity,
>>> Jesus Christ, we bless you.
> By the Wood that raised up in full strength
>> The Son of Man who drew the whole world to him,
>>> Jesus Christ, we glorify you.
> By the Wood on which your priesthood was accomplished,
>> O great High Priest, immolated for our sins,
>>> Victorious God, your Church acclaims you.
> Holy tree, rising from the earth even to the heavens,
>> So that the God of Jacob be exalted,
>>> Jesus Christ, we bless you.
> Great Ark that saves us from the anger of God,
>> By rescuing us from the deluge, with Noah,
>>> Jesus Christ, we glorify you.
> Loving Wood that sweetens bitter waters
>> And makes waters gush from the rock,
>>> Victorious God, your Church acclaims you.[44]

NOVEMBER 1

All Saints

Communion with the Virgin Mary and the saints of heaven is an important part of present-day liturgy.[1] As early as the fourth century, the saints were commemorated in the Eucharistic Prayer. Their cult grew in all the rites from the fourth and fifth centuries on. At first commemoration was made of the martyrs of the local Church, then of others who were particularly famous. After the era of persecutions, saints who were not martyrs and ascetics were joined to the names of the martyrs.[2] Catalogues were drawn up that were intended to be universal. Even though they included names of saints who had not been martyred, these catalogues were called "martyrologies."[3] A feast of All the Saints is attested in the fifth century in certain Eastern Churches—Antioch and Edessa, among others—from where it reached Rome. It was celebrated on the first Sunday after Pentecost. But when Pope Gregory the Great (590–604) assigned the Ember Days of spring to this week, it was transferred to November 1.

On May 13, 610, Pope Boniface IV (608–615) transformed the Roman pantheon into a church, which he dedicated to Mary and the martyrs[4] and made this day the feast of All Saints. In 835 Pope Gregory IV (827–844) had the emperor of the West, Louis the Pius (814–840), promulgate a decree that fixed November 1 as the feast of All Saints.[5] From that time on, what had first been a local celebration in Rome and in a few Churches rapidly became a common solemnity throughout all of Latin Europe, and the feast of May 13 disappeared.

We have all known persons who, although often very humble, have given an authentic, admirable, and inspiring example of sanctity to those close to them. It is right and fitting to celebrate them by associating their memory with that of the saints who figure in the various martyrologies, as well as all the countless others that no such register could possibly contain, even if they were known. The popularity of the feast of All Saints must certainly stem from this.[6] This celebration also expresses the legitimate concern—recognized by the liturgy—of the faithful to obtain for themselves the intercession of all the saints, leaving not a single one out: "Father, all-powerful and ever-living God, today we rejoice in the holy men and women of every time and place. May their prayers bring us for-giveness and love.''[7] But this is not all. The liturgy celebrates the thrice-holy God who is contemplated in the heavenly Jerusalem, surrounded by all the elect sanctified by his grace. Each one is an individual and per-sonal success of salvation but can only reflect a tiny part of the infinite holiness of God. Without exhausting it, they give a better image of this holiness when taken all together. The adoration of God is at the center of the celebration of All Saints. On this festive day earthly liturgy is more explicitly than ever an echo of the heavenly liturgy (Rev 7:2-4, 9-14—First Reading).[8] It is a solemn act of thanksgiving to God who has made us his children, through and in his Son. At the same time, all the assem-bled Christians proclaim their hope: ''What we shall be has not yet been revealed''; but ''we do know that when it is revealed we shall be like him, for we shall see him as he is'' (1 John 3:2). There is only one way open to all who hope to join the saintly men and women of heaven who bear witness to this future reality, and that is the way of the Beatitudes proclaimed by Jesus on the mountain (Matt 5:1-12a).

''Their glory fills us with joy, and their communion with us in your Church gives us inspiration and strength'' (Preface); we walk ahead to-ward that full realization of the paschal mystery,[9] so that at last ''God may be all in all'' (1 Cor 15:28), in the assembled Mystical Body.

> They come in singing,
> the saved ones;
> immense fresco of joy,
> love with a thousand faces
> that form one image,
> in the light,
> the only icon of glory:
> Jesus Christ!
> *Praise to you,*
> *Lord of all the living!*
> You shared in their trials,
> in the power of your resurrection,
> they sing:
> You have purified them in your spilt blood,
> they are children of the Father and give you thanks:
> You have fed them with the bread of life;
> triumphant over death, they acclaim you:
> *Praise to you,*
> *Lord of all the living!*[10]

People of God, People of Saints

From All Nations, Races, Peoples, and Tongues

John wrote the Book of Revelation in order to share with the faithful the revelation he had received concerning what "must happen soon" (Rev 1:1).[1] But far from teaching some sort of indifference toward the present in favor of some future existence, this prophetic message, on the contrary, reveals all the importance and reality of the present. For it is here and now that what "must happen soon" is being prepared. For this reason it is urgent for us even now to commit ourselves to what happens today in order to be able to share in what tomorrow brings. The revelation of the full realization of the designs of God affords us a supernatural understanding of present times, inspires us with courage, and constantly revives the hope of the faithful.[2] The page that is read on the day of the feast is one of the most beautiful and the most comforting of the Book of Revelation (Rev 7:2-4, 9-14).

Two successive visions revealed to John the hidden face of the earthly stage of the coming of salvation and the accomplishment in heaven of God's plans. "Then I saw another angel come up from the east,[3] holding the seal of the living God. He cried out in a loud voice to the four angels who were given power to damage the land and the sea,[4] 'Do not damage the land or the sea or the trees until we imprint the seal on the foreheads of the servants of our God.' "[5] Present time is presented as a period of remission: judgment has been put off until later. But this respite does not mean that God will be late in rendering justice. Those who would be tempted to think so are asked to "be patient a little while longer until the number was filled of their fellow servants . . . " (Rev 6:10-11). Writing to the Christians of Ephesus, Paul says: "In him you also, who have heard the word of truth, the gospel of your salvation, and have believed in him, were sealed with the promised holy Spirit, which is the first installment of our inheritance toward redemption as God's possession, to the praise of his glory" (Eph 1:13-14); "And do not grieve the holy Spirit of God, with which you were sealed for the day of redemption" (Eph 4:30). This way of speaking of Christian baptism must have been common in apostolic times.[6] What is more, the sacrament that is nowadays called "confirmation" was first known by the name of "seal."[7] The time we live in is therefore a time of mission, of preaching the gospel to all the nations, a time of gathering together into the Church those who receive the One sent of God, and have become children of God (John 1:12) like those who have gone before them. Through faith and the sacraments of faith, all belong to God and to his people.[8]

The number of those marked by the seal is incalculable: "One hundred and forty-four thousand, [twelve thousand] marked from every tribe of the Israelites." These are symbolic numbers that evoke both plenitude and fulfillment:[9] no one will be forgotten or left out of those who belong to God; the time of respite will last as long as is necessary so that all might be gathered together in the unity of his people.[10] This gathering and this unity will not be fully realized until the end of time, in the Jerusalem that John saw descending from heaven (Rev 21:1), to welcome into it all the children of God now dispersed. What had been a dream has become an unimaginable reality: people "from every nation, race, people, and tongue" are assembled, of one spirit despite their diversity, and without the slightest discrimination.[11] John saw this assembly gathered together at the end of time. All "stood before the throne and before the Lamb, wearing white robes and holding palm branches in their hands."

The description of this liturgy might remind us of many similar scenes common when a crowd acclaims a hero whose triumph they are celebrating: formerly, during the games held at the circus and, more recently, at a stadium or on similar occasions. Here the reference is more likely to the feast of booths—*Sukkoth*,[12] which was a feast of great public rejoicing, when people held palm branches; at the period of the New Testament it had clear messianic overtones which pointed to the universal reign of God in the last days.[13] The oracle of the Book of Zechariah (14:16) was uppermost in people's minds: "All who are left of all the nations that came against Jerusalem shall come up year after year to worship the King, the Lord of hosts, and to celebrate the feast of Booths."[14] This is the vision that John is contemplating. It is told to him that all those people wearing white—the liturgical color—"have survived the time of great distress," and "have washed their robes and made them white in the blood of the Lamb." From the beginning of his Gospel, John has presented the coming of the Son of God made man as the beginning of a great decisive battle between the darkness and the light,[15] and the life and ministry of Jesus as a trial in court[16] that culminates in the passion. And then, paradoxically, appears the victory of the Lord whose kingdom "is not here" (John 18:36). Like him, Christians are on trial: "If the world hates you, realize that it hated me first. If you belonged to the world, the world would love its own; but because you do not belong to the world, and I have chosen you out of the world, the world hates you" (John 15:18-19). With Christ, they will know glory, so long as they pass through the "time of great distress" without losing their faith. Some of them have shed their blood in this battle. But it is through the blood that flowed from the side of Christ, who is the paschal Lamb none of whose bones were broken, that all have been "washed" (John 19:34-37). John has heard them proclaim: "Salvation comes from our God, who is seated on the throne, and from the Lamb."

This acclamation from those who "have survived the time of great distress" joins that of the angels who "stood around the throne" and singing, who prostrate themselves with their faces to the ground and "worshiped God": "Worthy is the Lamb that was slain to receive power and riches, wisdom and strength, honor and glory and blessing." The liturgy of the Church is celebrated in unison with that of heaven; it anticipates it and gets ready to participate in it some day:

> With their great company and all the angels
> we praise your glory
> as we cry out with one voice:
> Holy, holy, holy Lord, God of power and might,
> heaven and earth are full of your glory.
>   Hosanna in the highest.
> Blessed is he who comes in the name of the Lord.
>   Hosanna in the highest.[17]

The two scenes of John's visions take place on two levels, on earth and in heaven. But he goes back and forth between the two, for what is happening invisibly here on earth has its continuation in heaven. The earthly Church that is assembling bit by bit, progressively, and with great difficulty, through all sorts of obstacles, begins its climb up the mountain of the Lord. The liturgy provides stopping places along the way, during which the faithful, who are usually dispersed far and wide, can gather together on a regular basis, in visible assemblies, which, although imperfect and as yet remote from their heavenly ideal, are nevertheless meaningful images of the great gathering to come. These meetings of communities or local Churches take place in the presence of the angels, the Virgin Mary, the apostles, the saints of all ages. In communion with them, in the hope of that day when side by side with them we will be able, "freed from the corruption of sin and death, to sing your glory with every creature through Christ our Lord, through whom you give us everything that is good."[18]

> *Lord, this is the people that longs to see your face.*
>
> The LORD's are the earth and its fullness;
>   the world and those who dwell in it.
> For he founded it upon the seas
>   and established it upon the rivers.
> Who can ascend the mountain of the LORD?
>   or who may stand in his holy place?
> He whose hands are sinless, whose heart is clean,
>   who desires not what is vain. . . .
> He shall receive a blessing from the LORD,
>   a reward from God his savior.
> Such is the race that seeks for him,
>   that seeks for the face of the God of Jacob.
> (Ps 24:1-6)

See How Great a Love the Father Has Shown Us

The love God bears us is at the center of the theology, the teaching, and the spirituality of St. John. He clearly enjoys enumerating the signs and manifestations of this divine love so that everyone may become more aware of it. In his thinking, all we need is to keep this love in mind, and then we will naturally attach ourselves to God with all our hearts, we will live in the one spontaneous desire to please him in all things, and, as a consequence, we will obtain salvation. The text read today focuses once more on the goals pursued by God in his love: to make of us his own children (1 John 3:1-3).[19]

"See what love the Father has bestowed on us that we may be called the children of God. Yet so we are" (1 John 3:1). It was for this that the Word became flesh (John 1:12) and that God "gave his only Son" (John 3:16), that he "handed him over," as Paul says (Rom 8:32) and as we recall in the words used in the celebration of the Eucharist.[20] And the words "children of God" are not used lightly, but express the reality of what we actually are, that we "come to share in the divine nature" (2 Pet 1:4), children by grace, as the only Son is eternally and by nature.

But if the disciples are to be united, as "children of God" with Christ, the "only Son," this will take place in the face of total incomprehension on the part of the rest of the world, which has not acknowledged in Jesus the Word who is the true light come into the world, he through whom all has been made (John 1:9-10). Similarly, "The reason the world does not recognize us is that it never recognized the Son." This lack of recognition can lead to hatred, and even persecution, which should neither surprise nor discourage the faithful. Jesus had warned them: "If the world hates you, realize that it hated me first." . . . "If they persecuted me, they will also persecute you. . . . And they will do all these things to you on account of my name, because they do not know the one who sent me" (John 15:18, 20-21). Christians and the Church should not, of course, do anything to deliberately provoke any persecution, either in words or acts, but it would remain rather disturbing for either to enjoy to any considerable degree the favors of this world. If they did enjoy such favor, they might need to ask themselves how faithful an image of Christ their behavior is giving the world, how closely their lives mirror the precepts of the Gospel: "But [what] if salt loses its taste?" (Matt 5:13).[21] When the world curries favor with the Church and Christians, it is in order to assimilate them and dilute the full strength of the gospel teaching. Similarly, the Church and Christians have never been able to find favor with the world without having had to renounce, to a greater or lesser degree, the purity of the gospel. "They do not belong to the world . . ." (John 17:11, 14): Certainly this is uncomfortable position to be in. As Jesus was before them, the disciples will be misunderstood and even persecuted from all sides.

> A light illumines them that will never go out, a white flame burns above the little flock, a supernatural phosphorescence that lights a place through the shadows of history and pierces the cloud of fables and theories that would darken it. It is the ray of light and fire that the world which has gone astray has surrounded and crowned it with, until the end of time, a light given it by its enemies only to make it shine all the brighter, and cast darkness on those who speak ill of it—it is the halo of hatred that glows on the forehead of the Church of God.[22]

Jesus was the Son of God. But this was not so readily seen—far from it. Some said he was John the Baptist, others Elijah or Jeremiah or one of the prophets—in other words, a man among others, although entrusted with an exceptional mission. When Peter spoke up in the name of the disciples and declared "You are the Messiah, the Son of the living God," Jesus replied "Blessed are you, Simon son of Jonah. For flesh and blood has not revealed this to you, but my heavenly Father" (Matt 16:13-17). On another occasion he declared "When you lift up the Son of Man, then you will realize that I AM . . . " (John 8:28). Before his pasch—his death, resurrection, and his return to the Father—his true identity remained veiled, and any profession of faith as to who he was contained a risk of ambiguity. After Peter's splendid declaration at Caesarea Philippi, Jesus taught for the first time that he must suffer and be put to death in order to rise again. "Then Peter took him aside and began to rebuke him, 'God forbid, Lord! No such thing shall ever happen to you.' " Jesus reproved him sharply, because he was "thinking not as God does, but as human beings do" (Matt 16:22-23).[23] On the other hand, on Golgotha, "the centurion who stood facing him saw how he breathed his last [and] said, 'Truly this man was the Son of God!' " (Mark 13:39). But it is only when the Lord comes back at the end of days that he will appear to all eyes in the plenitude of his power and glory.[24]

At the same time as it reveals to all the heretofore hidden identity of the Son of God, his glorious return[25] will also make clear "what we are": sons and daughters of God—which is already a reality, but which "does not yet show clearly." On that day, "we will be like him because we will see him as he is." "To see God" is the hope of the believer, who strains toward God with all his strength: "As the hind longs for the running waters, so my soul longs for you, O God. Athirst is my soul for God, the living God. When shall I go and behold the face of God?" (Ps 42:2-3).[26] But the disciples knew that the majesty of God is so great that humans' eyes cannot tolerate such light. One day Moses said to the Lord, "Do not let me see your glory!" and God answered, "Here is a place near me where you shall station yourself on the rock. When my glory passes I will set you in the hollow of the rock and will cover you with my hand until I have passed by. Then I will remove my hand, so that you see my back; but my face is not to be seen" (Exod 33:18-23). When God revealed himself to Elijah on Mount Horeb, he "hid his face in his cloak" (1 Kgs 19:13).[27] Later on there was the Temple, where one could go to "seek his face" and, without dying from it, "gaze on the loveliness of the Lord" and "see his power and his glory."[28] And at last there was Christ, the Word of God made flesh. His words, accompanied by many "signs," revealed "the glory as of the Father's only son, full of grace and truth" (John 1:14).[29]

God made this Son "the firstborn among many brothers" (Rom 8:29). From that point on, all those who accept him can say along with Paul and the apostles that all of us, gazing on the Lord's glory with unveiled faces, "are being transformed into the same image from glory to glory, as from the Lord who is the spirit" (2 Cor 3:18), since through baptism, the sacrament of faith, "we were indeed buried with him . . . so that . . . we too might live in newness of life." "For if we have grown into union with him through a death like his, we shall also be united with him in the resurrection" (Rom 6:4-5). Then "just as we have borne the image of the earthly one, we shall also bear the image of the heavenly one" (1 Cor 15:49). "He will change our lowly body to conform with his glorified body by the power that enables him also to bring all things into subjection to himself" (Phil 3:21).

"Everyone who has this hope based on him makes himself pure, as he is pure" (1 John 3:3). One could say that such a believer becomes more and more every day what he really is—a "son of God." In concrete terms, this means that whoever "lives the truth" (John 3:21), behaves like "children of the light" (John 12:36), avoiding any contamination from the darkness. All this is as far removed as possible from some simply exterior purity that has nothing to do with the purity of Christ and of God. There is also no thought here of reward. Only one thing counts: interior purity, that transparency which allows the light of God to fill one's entire being.

> "God is the rock of my heart and my portion forever" (Ps 73:26). The heart of the psalmist is pure: he loves God without personal ambition and does not ask for any other reward. He who would ask God for rewards and intends to serve him for the sake of those rewards attaches more worth to what he hopes to gain than he does to him from whom he hopes to gain it. So is there in fact no reward? None, except for God himself. God's reward is God himself.[30]

The Good News of the Beatitudes

After Jesus had spent forty days and forty nights in the desert, he heard of the arrest of John the Baptist and went first to Galilee. But he did not stay there. Leaving Nazareth, he went to stay in Capernaum, on the shores of the Lake of Gennesaret, where he walked about and proclaimed: "Repent, for the kingdom of heaven is at hand." As he went he saw two brothers, Simon and Andrew, who were fishing: "Come after me and I will make you fishers of men." They obeyed without the slightest hesitation. A little farther on he saw two others, James and John. Jesus called to them. They immediately followed him, leaving their father Zebedee alone in the boat, with the nets they were getting ready. Jesus kept traveling, this time in their company, and he continued to preach throughout

Galilee, proclaiming the good news and healing many sick or possessed persons as he went. This was all that was needed for great crowds to gather about him, who had come from Galilee and the Ten Cities, Jerusalem, and Judea, and from across the Jordan. Jesus took them up onto the mountain, sat down, as a teacher does, and began to teach them.[31] This inaugural teaching constitutes the first of the main structures that characterize the Gospel According to Matthew.[32] Jesus began by proclaiming the Beatitudes (Matt 5:1-12a).[33]

Crowds gathered about Jesus, drawn by the miracles and the announcement that the kingdom of God was at hand. Jesus declared to them: "Blessed are the poor in spirit . . . they who mourn . . .the meek . . . they who hunger and thirst for righteousness . . . the merciful . . . the clean of heart . . . the peacemakers . . . they who are persecuted for the sake of righteousness. . . . Blessed are you when they insult you and persecute you and utter every kind of evil against you [falsely] because of me." Jesus is not giving his approval, so to speak, of poverty and suffering and all the trials known so well to his audience, whose lives were harsh and often filled with injustices. Any such meaning would be in flagrant contradiction with the constant teaching of Scripture, which is severe in its condemnation of all those who are responsible for such terrible wrongs: They are impious, for they are resisting the will of God, who wants just the opposite, and who gave the Law in order to guide humankind along the way of his will. If the crowds who heard these words for the first time had understood them in this sense, they would have hooted with derision. But, as we read in Matthew: "When Jesus finished these words, the crowds were astonished at his teaching, for he taught them as one having authority, and not as their scribes" (Matt 7:28-29). The intolerable scandal of such statements would only have increased over the centuries. In order to be taken seriously, the disciples would have done better to drop them from their teaching, instead of perpetuating the memory of these words through the years and making them the basis of the preaching of the Church. And if such had been Jesus' meaning, what are we to think of the innumerable men and women who in the name of the gospel have given their entire lives, individually or in groups or in religious communities, to combat poverty and misery, to work for a more just division of the goods and resources of this world, to work for a better world, founded on justice? And finally, what sort of wisdom would Jesus have shown if he had meant that it is enough to be poor and unhappy in order to be considered a friend of God, a saint?

Such teaching would only justify and reinforce organized social chaos, promoted to the level of religious ideology![34]

The truth of the matter is that, when he proclaimed the Beatitudes, Jesus was reaffirming solemnly that "the kingdom of heaven is at hand" and was urging the conversion of the heart that opens up the gates of this kingdom. The kingdom is at hand because he who was sent by God is present, and because, through him, those signs foretold by the prophets as portents of the advent of the Messiah are beginning to be seen: "The blind regain their sight, the lame walk, lepers are cleansed, the deaf hear, the dead are raised, and the poor have the good news proclaimed to them." Jesus will quote this oracle from the prophecies of Isaiah in response to a question from John the Baptist, who had sent word to him, asking: "Are you the one who is to come, or should we look for another?"[35] The first miracles performed by Jesus that drew great crowds of followers already made the approach of the kingdom felt. It is good news for the poor and those who are unhappy for any reason, for it becomes clear that God will not tarry to intervene effectively in their behalf. He is, in fact, their primary defender, their rightful defender, one might say, and the only one they can count on. It is not that the poor can claim personal merits lacking to others. But they do find themselves in a position of need, without the means to defend themselves, victims of the injustices in society and, often, of the conduct of the rich and powerful. This is sufficient; God looks no further. He knows perfectly well that no one is without sin, that the poor can behave as badly as any others, that they can be hard-hearted and unfair to their neighbor, and just as greedy as any others. But God nevertheless comes out on their side, *a priori*. Hearing that the kingdom of heaven is at hand could only sound to them like good news and make them appreciate their good fortune, their happiness. But Jesus calls them to conversion as well, so that they might become the prototypes, as it were, the models of the just in accordance with the gospel.[36]

"Blessed are the meek." Poverty and humility characterize the meek and the lowly—in the biblical and gospel sense of the word—whom the *Magnificat* also says are blessed, because God raises them up (Luke 1:52).[37] Those who have all they need usually have more trouble acquiring this humility; some of the well-to-do have for this reason chosen to renounce of their own free will their worldly goods and to live as the poor, among the poor: they are numerous in the history of the Church.

But with grace, the rich, too, can acquire lowliness of heart. And the opposite is true. The poor are by no means without greed, hardness of heart, and the desire to dominate. Both are in need of conversion. For the lowliness and humility of the gospel are for everyone the fundamental qualities of the disciples of Christ. Early catechesis understood this well.[38] The Book of Acts gives us a picture of the ideal Christian community, where the practice of communal property of wealth allows each to receive according to his or her needs.[39] This is an image of the kingdom of heaven promised to the poor and lowly.

"Blessed are they who mourn, for they will be comforted." Affliction from whatever source always leads to hardship. It can never bring happiness. It is a harsh trial because one is alone in facing up to it, even when people of good will show sympathy. Each of us knows this from personal experience, at the very least in feeling his or her helplessness to bring help to others in need. "I looked for sympathy, and there was none" (Ps 69:21). But those who weep have at least one consolation: God understands them and will not fail to console those who turn to him. The deep emotion that Jesus expressed to see the pain of his friends Martha and Mary, who had just lost their brother Lazarus, was perfectly natural. There is nothing surprising at all in the tears that came to his eyes; they attest to his delicacy of feeling and sensitivity (John 11:33-34). The Gospel also recounts that one day Jesus arrived at Nain at the time when "a man who had died was being carried out." He did not know this widow, whose only son had died. The Lord "was moved with pity for her and said to her, 'Do not weep.' " He then ordered the dead man to get up, and "Jesus gave him to his mother" (Luke 7:1-15). This story reveals God's ways with all of us. He cannot remain unmoved when he sees the tears of the poor, represented here by this widow who has lost her only support. If he was there at that exact moment, it is not due to mere chance. He will always bring consolation to those who weep, even if he does not always perform miracles, as he did for the widow of Nain.

"Blessed are they who hunger and thirst for righteousness . . . who are persecuted for the sake of righteousness . . . ." Blessed also are those who are insulted, persecuted, slandered for Christ's sake. The term "righteousness," which was unknown to Mark and used only once by Luke, occurs seven times in Matthew.[40] It means a number of things: real, sincere, and practical adherence to God's will, God's Law, and in particular, effectual charity toward one's neighbor—those who lack food, drink, clothing—and toward the stranger, the prisoner, the sick (Matt 25:31-46). To pursue this righteousness with all one's strength is to work alongside

God: To suffer for the sake of righteousness and for the sake of faith is to share in the sufferings of Christ, the Just One slandered, persecuted, put to death.[41] And, consequently, the pursuit of such righteousness is to belong already to the kingdom, where the wounds inflicted by the persecutors will become glorious stigmata. Seeking righteousness and seeking the kingdom go hand in hand. "All these things will be given you besides" (Matt 6:33). "Blessed are the peacemakers, for they will be called children of God." Peace is the messianic gift par excellence, brought by Christ to those whom God loves (Luke 2:14), restored to sinners who have been pardoned, and to the sick who have been healed;[42] peace is the most precious gift left by the Lord to his disciples (John 14:27-33). When he appeared to them, the risen Lord greeted them by saying, "Peace be with you," and in his greeting they recognized him.[43] But peace is the fruit of reconciliation, of heartfelt forgiveness, given quickly and without counting personal cost: "Not seven times but seventy-seven times" (Matt 18:22).[44] Christ entrusted to the Church and to each of us Christians according to our strengths "the ministry of reconciliation" (2 Cor 5:18). Christ's disciples must conduct themselves in all circumstances as heralds and messengers of peace: "As you enter a house, wish it peace. If the house is worthy, let your peace come upon it; if not, let your peace return to you" (Matt 10:12-13).[45] But with peace there are no half measures: it must be entirely restored if it has been lost, especially before the common celebration of the Eucharist. "If you bring your gift to the altar, and there recall that your brother has anything against you, leave your gift there at the altar, go first and be reconciled with your brother, and then come and offer your gift" (Matt 5:23). "Behold how good it is, and how pleasant, where brethren dwell at one!" (Ps 133:1).

"Blessed are the merciful, for they shall be shown mercy." Along with righteousness and faithfulness—or good faith[46]—mercy is one of the "weightier things of the Law" (Matt 23:23). It is indeed the supreme attribute of God because it makes manifest his infinite love. Mercy signifies a deep and limitless benevolence which God manifests by not condemning, but by forgiving. "For it is love that I desire, and not sacrifice," says the Lord (Hos 6:6). Matthew reports that Jesus quoted these holy verses twice: the first time, to explain his attitude toward sinners (Matt 9:13); the second time, in answer to those who were scandalized that the disciples who were passing through a field of wheat on the sabbath tore off the ears of wheat and ate them (Matt 12:8). The parable of the pitiless servant illustrates forcefully the absolute necessity, repeated several times, to show mercy (Matt 18:23-35): "If you forgive others their transgressions, your heavenly Father will forgive you. But if you do not forgive others, neither will your Father forgive your transgressions" (Matt 6:14-15); "The measure with which you measure will be measured out to you." We must imitate God, conduct ourselves like him, and not behave with pusillanimity. To do good without expecting anything in return is to act like a child of God, who is the merciful Father (Luke 6:36-38). To show mercy does not betray weakness, quite the contrary. God forgives because he is the Almighty, and we must have something of his power in order to be able to pardon. Far from minimizing or ignoring the reality of sin, mercy bears witness to its gravity and calls attention to it. Only pardon can free from sin. And finally, pardon goes hand in hand with personal commitment against sin, its causes and its consequences. God gave an example of this: he "handed over" his own Son who took upon himself the sins of the world.

"Blessed are the clean of heart, for they will see God." In the Bible and everyday speech the "heart" meant the hidden center and deepest part of the individual.[47] It is in the heart that decisions are made, that there is true freedom of choice; it is in the heart that conversions take place, that the person recognizes the truth of speech, feelings, and commitments. The heart is "clean" when, in all simplicity, it welcomes the Holy Spirit and Christ.[48] This kind of transparent purity, a sort of clarity in harmony with God's own, goes far beyond purity understood in the narrower, merely moralistic sense. This particular Beatitude sums up, as it were, all the others, and expresses likeness and conformity to Christ. For Christ is the sole and perfect exemplar of the clean-hearted, the lowly, the one who hungers for righteousness, the merciful, the peacemaker, the persecuted, and slandered just, and for this reason he is the first exalted one of heaven. "Rejoice and be glad, for your reward will be great in heaven" if you become like him. For "each one of the Beatitudes becomes an appeal to actualize those conditions that lead to acceptance into the blessedness of the kingdom," "an urgent exhortation to possess those necessary qualities for sharing in the salvation offered by the gospel,"[49] "with the Virgin Mary, the blessed Mother of God, with the apostles and all the saints."[50]

Throughout the liturgy the Church celebrates the holiness of God the almighty Father, to whom belong "through Christ, with him and in him, in the unity of the Holy Spirit, all honor and all glory forever and ever." The Church proclaims the good news of salvation through Jesus, the Son of God made man, come into this world so that the light should shine in the darkness (John 1:4-5). "To those who did accept him he gave power to become children of God" (John 1:12). "[You] were sealed with the promised holy Spirit, which is the first installment of our inheritance toward redemption as God's possession, to the praise of his glory" (Eph 1:13-14).[51]

What we already are today, even though it cannot yet be clearly seen, the Church allows us to contemplate in the immense multitude from "every nation, race, people, and tongue," standing "before the throne and before the Lamb," that is, the multitude of our brothers and sisters, "the faithful of all the ages of history, sons and daughters of Abraham, as numerous as the stars of heaven, shining today with divine light."[52] The Church invites all the voices of the world to join their voices with theirs, to sing the praise of God whose holiness shines into infinity. Just as the countless stars, no matter what their size, shine with the brilliance of the sun, all those who are irradiated by the light of holiness become in God's heaven a multitude of brilliant rays of light reflecting Christ's glory. An incalculable number of these renewed creatures who are the work of the love of God and are all individuals different from one another appear day after day in the new heaven.

> Infinite Love! It would seem as if your marvels were complete, and that all that remains to do is to copy your works of old . . .
>
> And we do not perceive that your boundless activity is an infinite source of new thoughts, of new sufferings, new actions, new patriarchs, new prophets, new apostles, and new saints, who have no need to copy the lives and the writings of the others, but only to live in a state of perpetual abandonment to your secret designs.[53]

The brilliance of the saints comes from the same unique source of light that fills all of them. But no one of us shines with all the light by ourselves or keeps for ourselves that part of glory that we have received. On the contrary, we are happy to see our own light shine on the others, just as we joyfully and gratefully welcome the light we receive from them too. We never save ourselves alone, by our own efforts.

> We must not try to save our souls the way people save a treasure. . . .
> We must save our souls the way people lose a treasure. By spending it.
> We must save ourselves together. We must arrive all together in the heaven of our God. We must present ourselves together. We must not come to look for our God without each other. We must return all together to the house of our Father. We must also think a little about each other and work for each other. What might he say, if we arrived without each other?[54]

The earthly Church climbs toward the heavenly Jerusalem, singing the litanies of the saints. The multitude of the poor of heart, of the humble, those grievously afflicted and who cannot be comforted down here, those who hunger and thirst for holiness, the merciful, the clean of heart, the peacemakers, those persecuted for righteousness' sake, those who are insulted and slandered for Christ's sake and the sake of the gospel—all these men and women will never have their names written down in any other book than the Book of Life.[55] The words of the Lord sing in their hearts and encourage them to persevere in the face of all the hardships of their path: "Rejoice and be glad, for your reward is great in heaven."

> There, we will rest and we will see;
> we will see and we will love;
> we will love and we will praise.
> This will be the final day, which is without end.
> And what else could be our end
> But to arrive in the kingdom that is without end?[56]

All Souls—Commemoration of All the Faithful Departed

All Saints and All Souls have been commemorated together since earliest antiquity. It was, in fact, common funerary customs that gave rise to the cult, first of the martyrs and then of the other saints.[1] At a later period it was the feast of All Saints that led to the creation of the commemoration of All Souls,[2] itself belonging to an age-old tradition of praying for the dead, which in turn was based in ancient funerary practices, trust in the mercy of God, and faith in personal resurrection with Christ the Savior.[3]

In Rome, pagan burials often included the formal dedicating of offerings to the *manes*—the spirits—of the dead. This custom was widespread throughout the Roman provinces by the middle of the first century. At the same time, funerary inscriptions often included a wishful prayer—"May the earth lie lightly over you!"—which expressed not only the memory of the dead, but at the same time also tried, as it were, to exorcise the fear of death of the survivors, who hope that when it is their turn to die, others will remember them.[4] Initially, Christians buried their dead amongst pagans, and from force of habit used the traditional funerary epitaphs. The offerings to the *manes* gradually disappeared. A prayer for the repose of the person became the expressed wish, in the perspective of Easter. Sometimes the inscription asked the viewer to pray for the dead. Finally there appeared on the tombs prayers that included the phrases "in Christ"—*in Christo*—or the monogram of Christ.[5] But explicit prayers for the dead and their mention in the Eucharistic liturgy are numerous and attested to in remote antiquity.

The first witnesses to these prayers are found in two apocryphal writings.[6] The Acts of Paul and Thecla, which were probably written in Asia Minor between 160 and 180, report that Queen Tryphena had a dream. Her daughter, who had just died, asked her to pray to Thecla so that she might be admitted among the just.[7] In the Acts of John, another apocryphal writing that also originated in Asia Minor and dates from the middle of the second century, we see the apostle praying on a tomb on the third day after the death of the deceased. The story belongs to legend, but the interest of stories of this type lies not in the facts they relate, but in what they teach us about the customs and habits of the period in which they take place.[8] Tertullian (ca.160–ca. 225) reports that in North Africa, at least, in the second half of the second century, a liturgical prayer for the dead was already known. In one of his treatises he tells us that the dead person was "accompanied by the prayers of the priest" between his death and his burial.[9] Even though we can't be sure of the details, this must surely have been a prayer that was part of a liturgy—an "orison," as it used to be called—and not an act of private devotion. Elsewhere in Tertullian we find mention of a prayer at the death of a Christian, and again on the anniversary of his death.[10] Similarly, St. Cyprian, bishop of Carthage (d. 258), speaks more than once of the commemoration of the dead during the celebration of the Eucharist, which was forbidden to those who had broken the laws of the Church.[11]

From the fourth century on, there are numerous mentions of prayers for the dead. St. Cyril of Jerusalem (ca. 315–386), in a discussion of the Eucharistic Prayer in one of his catecheses, comes to the intercessions that follow the invocation of the Holy Spirit—the "epiclesis"—asking that the bread be made the Body of Christ, and the wine his Blood.

> We ask God for peace in brotherhood of the Churches, for harmony in the world, for the emperors, the armies and the allied powers, for the sick, the afflicted, and in a word, for all those in need of help we all pray together and we offer this victim.
>
> Next, we make mention of those who have fallen asleep, first the patriarchs, the prophets, the apostles, the martyrs, asking that God, thanks to their prayers and their intercessions, may accept our supplication.
>
> Next, we pray for the holy bishops and fathers who have fallen asleep, and, generally, for all those who have fallen asleep ahead of us, and we pray in their behalf, while here in the presence of the holy and awesome victim.[12]

Immediately afterwards, the bishop of Jerusalem attempts an explanation of the purpose of this prayer.

> I know a number of people who say: "What good does it do the souls who leave this world with or without sins that we make mention of them during the offering of the Eucharist?" Come now! If a king were to exile people who have offended him in some way, and their kinfolk were to come to the king and present him with a wreath, pleading for their condemned relative, would not that king grant them the reprieve they request? In the same way, we too, by presenting to God our supplications for those who have

fallen asleep, were they sinners, although we may not weave a wreath to present, we do offer the immolated Christ for our sins, making propitiation for them and for us to the God who loves men.[13]

St. John Chrysostom (ca. 347–407)[14] speaks in very much the same way. It is useless to lament because someone may have died in a state of sin.

> It would be better to help him, as much as possible, not with tears, but with prayers, supplications, and offerings.[15] These are not works of purely imaginary effect. It is not by mere chance that we make mention of the dead in the divine mysteries, and that we pray for them, by addressing our prayers to the Lamb offered on the altar, who took away the sins of the world; we do so for them to obtain some comfort. It is not for nothing that he who presides at the altar during the celebration of the holy mysteries proclaims: "For the sake of all those who have fallen asleep in Christ and for those who remember them."[16]

In 387, when St. Augustine was at Ostia, waiting to take ship with his mother and his brother, Monica fell seriously ill. Her sons were saddened at the thought that their mother might die on foreign ground. Monica, who perceived this, said to them: "Bury this body any place at all! Have no worries about it! All I ask of you is to remember me at the altar of the Lord, wherever you may be."[17] After recounting his mother's death, during which he closed his eyes, "in the ninth day of her illness, and in the fifty-third year of her life,"[18] St. Augustine remembers that he prayed "while we offered for her the sacrifice of our redemption before her remains, which were already placed near the tomb so that we could bury her in it according to local custom."[19]

The *Apostolic Constitutions*, a compilation of traditions and writings that were regarded as binding among Christians and were brought together in Antioch some time around 390, describe in detail how the prayers for the dead were organized.

> The third day after the death is observed with songs and prayers because of him who rose on the third day. In like manner, on the ninth day, remembering both the dead and their survivors. On the thirtieth day, according to ancient custom, we pray also, for thus did they do after the death of Moses (Deut 34:8). And again on the yearly anniversary of the death, in memory of the defunct. And we give of our worldly goods to the poor, in memory of the dead.[20]

What we have here is a Christianization of customs followed previously in pagan society that called for the families to get together on the third, the seventh, the ninth, and the fortieth days after the death of their relative, as well as on the anniversary of his birth, not his death. Christians kept the third and the ninth day, as well as the anniversary, but replaced the fortieth day with the thirtieth, and called the anniversary of death the *dies natalis*, the "day of birth" into eternity. The cult of the dead, which was very important in the Greco-Roman world, took the form, as well, of annual days of remembrance. In Rome these days took place February 13–22: This was the festival of the ancestors, called in Latin *parentalia*. These days of remembrance were undoubtedly full of pagan elements, but they did express a legitimate and praiseworthy gratitude toward ancestors; they also were observed in honor of other members of certain corporations. Christians could not continue to practice pagan rites that they observed before their conversion. But certainly nothing prevented them from showing their feelings of gratitude towards those who had gone before them—quite the contrary—and all the more so in the case of their fathers in the faith. In this spirit the feast of the "Chair of St. Peter at Rome" was instituted for February 22.[21] These diverse celebrations preserved a private, family feeling, in the broad sense of the term, or at least to a certain extent.

It was in the ninth century that the idea of a day of prayer for all the dead developed, similar to the day consecrated to the memory of all the saints.[22] It would appear that Amalarius of Metz (ca. 780–ca. 850), who played an important role in the Carolingian liturgical reform, was the first to call for the institution of this feast day.[23] But it was another hundred years before his wish was fulfilled. Many monasteries habitually commemorated the dead inscribed in their necrology or belonging to their suffrages. St. Odilo, the fifth abbot of Cluny (ca. 962–1049), prescribed that commemoration be made in all the monasteries of the Order of all the dead, both the known and the unknown, on the same day.[24] And for this celebration the day he chose was the day after All Saints.

> Just as in all the churches of Christendom, we celebrate on the first of November the feast of all the saints, in the same way we will celebrate, in our houses, the commemorative feast of all those who have died in the faith, from the beginning of the world until the end, in the following manner: On the above-mentioned day, after Chapter, the deacon and the cellarer will distribute alms of bread and wine to all the poor who come to the door, as is the custom on Holy Thursday. . . .
>
> In the evening, let all bells be rung, and Vespers will be sung for the dead. On the following day, after Matins, all the bells will be rung again, and Office will be said for them. Morning Mass will be celebrated in a solemn manner.

All the brothers must offer Mass in private and also celebrate publicly for the repose of the souls of all the faithful departed. Food will be distributed to twelve poor people.

In order that this decree be observed in perpetuity, we desire and we order that it should be observed not only here but also in all dependent houses; and if others follow our example, may they become for that reason participants in all our suffrages.

Just as we recall the memory of all Christians once a year, so also do we order and hold it most becoming for us to pray for all our brothers who serve in the army of the Lord under the Rule of St. Benedict, so that, through the mercy of God, we may make daily progress.[25]

This commemoration of all the faithful departed was first celebrated on November 2, 998. Pope Sylvester II (ca. 940–1003) gave his immediate approval to the abbot of Cluny's initiative, and his successors continued to favor the celebration of this feast in the numerous houses of the Order, which in turn contributed to its diffusion throughout the Latin Church. It was then only natural that the commemoration of all the faithful departed was included in the Roman Missal called for by the Council of Trent and published June 30, 1570, by Pope Pius V (1566–1572).

The way in which St. Odilo had prescribed that the feast of November 2 be celebrated remained unchanged right up to the liturgical reforms of Vatican II, with First Vespers of All Souls being sung the evening of All Saints. This is probably the origin of the strange custom of allowing all priests to celebrate three Masses on that day. For the monks who had participated in the community Eucharist of the morning, as well as the Mass that was celebrated in the late morning, also celebrated their own private Mass. But what is the most intriguing element in the decree of St. Odilo is that it expresses explicitly the meaning and the spirit of this commemoration of the dead. It is a continuation of the feast of All Saints. On November 1 we thank God for all those who have already been gathered to him; they are models for our contemplation, and we pray to them to intercede for us. This celebration cannot help but make clear to all the faithful that God's mercy is necessary in order to be saved. The contemplation of the heavenly Jerusalem where the saints "sing endlessly the praise of God" and to which "we travel on the road of truth"[26] leads naturally and spontaneously to the prayer for all the departed. Moreover, this commemoration encourages us to "make new progress every day," confessing the mercy of God and our own sins. And finally, the decree of St. Odilo brings to mind the ancient custom of distributing alms to the poor—the *refrigerium*[27]—when we pray for the dead.

They take heart
When they behold the face of God,
Those who ever sought peace.
Gather us together in the Spirit,
O Risen Lord,
Master of Life.
You know the Father:
Guide all those whom you love
Into his presence.
You live with the Father:
Keep all those whom you love
In your company.
And at the name of the Father
All those whom you love
Are born to live.[28]

In the Hope of Resurrection

The liturgical books do not contain a fixed liturgy for the commemoration of all the faithful departed as is the case for all the other major celebrations of the liturgical year.[1] The Missal offers a choice of three sets of prayers, each of which contains an opening antiphon, three prayers—for the beginning of the service, over the gifts, and after Communion—and an antiphon following Communion. There are also five Prefaces to choose from. Most importantly, there are no particular biblical texts prescribed for the readings, as there are on the other feast days. One is simply referred to the Lectionary's readings for the Masses for the Dead, which contain a large choice of texts: nine pages of the Old Testament;[2] twenty-four excerpts from the apostolic writings;[3] fifteen responsorial psalms;[4] eleven verses for the Alleluia;[5] and twenty-three texts for the Gospel reading.[6] Moreover, there are no directives as to how to structure the use of the texts: The celebrant is allowed great latitude in choosing, for each category, the scriptural texts that will form the structure of the Liturgy of the Word, which is therefore something of a surprise each time.[7] But the "Feast of the Dead" is less limited than any other to the liturgical celebration alone. Relatively few Christians have the leisure to attend Mass on November 2, which is not a holiday. But many, if not most, take time to honor the memory of the dead, at the very least by thinking of them or by paying a visit to the cemetery where they are buried. Cemeteries are at this time often filled with people who visit the tombs of loved ones, often bringing flowers. In this way people are influenced to do more than just think of their dead. These visits are often quite lengthy, as the living pray at the tombs of their families, their friends, and even acquaintances who are remembered particularly on that day. In this way, the first two days of November have become for most Christians, as well as for many of those who do not share our faith, a special time to commemorate the departed in one way or another.

The great number of biblical texts offered by the Lectionary constitute a veritable mine where we can find rich material for reflection on this day of the commemoration of all the faithful departed. Some of them may

even be read during the cemetery visit. There is no room here to go into
each of the biblical texts proposed by the readings for the Masses for the
Dead. Moreover, their richness and great diversity do not lend them to
being grouped according to theme. Any such attempt only reduces their
effectiveness, and is arbitrary at best. More importantly, this kind of log-
ical systematization of the biblical readings does not fit the nature and
the dynamics of the Liturgy of the Word in the Eucharistic celebration.[8]
And lastly, the texts of the Masses for the Dead are not meant to supply
all the necessary elements for a theology of death.[9] On the other hand,
even without looking at each of the readings of the Lectionary, we can
propose a few key ideas that can help guide each of us through the wealth
of material and draw greater benefit from it.

The Christian who today reads and meditates on Scripture does so, and
rightly, in light of the whole body of revelation and its historic progression, in the light also of his or her faith in Christ, and of the tradition
and teaching of the Church. This being so, no one will be tempted to
skip over the Old Testament on the pretext that it dates from distant times
and is the product of a culture that had as yet little to say about the problems that death poses, that are still hesitant about the idea of an afterlife
and what could possibly happen after death: in other words, ignoring
the Old Testament because the authors of these ancient writings and their
contemporaries did not have our faith. But actually it is striking how often
these early writings, elaborated over time, parallel our own thinking, even
though we benefit from the contributions of many thinkers laboring down
through the centuries and who had the benefit of later revelation. Moreover, these pages of the Bible offer a certain conception of humanity—a
certain anthropology—whose originality and value also characterize Christian thought, and are in fact its foundation.

Although the teaching of Jesus and the gospel represent considerable
progress in relation to these cultural and religious antecedents, they remain very much in the same vein. With the authority conferred by the
Lord upon those whom he chose, the preaching and catechesis of the
apostles took up and carried forward this teaching, whose deepest meaning was revealed by the resurrection of Christ, which made clear as well
its concrete implications for the way Christians should live. For the pasch
of Christ is the solid foundation of the Christian's way of looking at and
experiencing death, his or her relationship with the present-day world
and the world of the afterlife, the meaning of present time, and indeed
of every single thing. The pasch of Christ is the basis of Christian faith,

the first and last word. And as for the apostolic writings, they are not just some sort of treatise dealing more or less in abstractions outside of time; they all are based on the actual situation of a Christian community of real people and their problems, doubts, and questionings. Because of this, they remain astonishingly current, with a few necessary changes, and therefore always stimulating. Finally, they demonstrate how revelation can and must be constantly read in the light of everyday life and the thought of people of all races and cultures. In this way Scripture appears as a powerful and sure contribution to the progress of thought, offering always new perspectives and lighting up its way. This truth stands out clearly from the reading of the scriptural texts offered by the readings for the Masses for the Dead.

The Old Testament, which was written over some ten centuries before Christ, bears witness to human and religious thought that goes back much farther even than that. Many different influences contributed to its evolution: history with its uncertainties, contact with other cultures, progressive revelation. This is especially true in regard to questions about life and death.

Human Beings: Bodies Given the Breath of Life
In the Bible, human beings, along with all the other living creatures, are fashioned by God in the womb of woman, in the manner of a potter[10] or a weaver.[11] The vital element is found in the blood.[12] In humans there is a "spirit," a "breath" that comes from God. This spirit unifies this being of flesh and blood, who, thanks to this dynamic principle breathed into it by God, becomes a "person," a creature gifted with conscience. It is his or her spirit that enables a man or woman to express with their bodies what they are and what they are becoming in the depths of their being. In the Bible, the hidden seat of the person, the secret source of his or her feelings, impulses, and thoughts is found in the "heart" and the "loins."

The heart is the seat not only of love and hate, but also of desires and of joy, of regrets and sadness, irritation, courage, fear, discouragement, confidence, pride, intelligence, imagination, memory, worry, sincerity, falseness, and even skill in a craft or an art. It is therefore the principle of both good and bad acts, of virtue, and of sin. This is true also of the "loins," especially in the case of feelings marked by passion, and whatever generally has to do with force and violence,[13] both negative and positive. Genesis (2:1-23) teaches that the appearance of man on earth was due to the initiative of God: "God said: 'Let us make man in our image, after our likeness' . . . male and female he created them" (Gen 1:2-27). "At the time when the Lord God made the earth and the heavens . . . the Lord God formed man out of the clay of the ground and blew into his nostrils the breath of life, and so man became a living being" (Gen 2:4-7). It is also stated that man's capacity for reproduction came also from God: "Be fertile and multiply; fill the earth" (Gen 1:28). But this creative activity was not over on the seventh day, when God "rested . . . from all the work he had undertaken" (Gen 2:2). He continues to be creative, for every human being that is born on this earth holds his or her being and life from God: "Truly you have formed my inmost being; you knit me in my mother's womb" (Ps 139:13).

Moreover, and even more remarkably, the Bible immediately considers humans in their individual unity: They are beings of flesh and blood, animated by a breath of life. This conception is distinguished from the Greek conception and from others drawing on the Greek, that see humans as constituted of a soul *and* a body. We still speak this way today, even though we abjure dualism by immediately affirming the unity of the human being.[14] The Bible does not need to take such precautions, for at first glance and very obviously—so obviously that there is no need to say it — it sees humans in their unity.[15] What the Bible has to say on the subject of death and the afterlife is to be understood in this anthropological context.

The nine texts from the Old Testament chosen for the Masses for the Dead reflect several aspects of the mystery of death, such as it was understood by the people of the Bible over the course of the five centuries before the birth of Christ. We cannot ask them for more than they can give, nor for that matter look at them as some kind of synthesis of biblical thought, or as a picture hastily sketched of the evolution of biblical thought from the beginnings, or even after a certain date. Rather, these pages are the echo of all the inner searchings of the believers of this time, and of the answers that they were able to give to their questions with more or less confidence. What interests us is what they reveal of their reflections. For the questions preoccupying them already in those times are still around today. For this reason, it is useful to see how those people handled them back then, how far they got in seeking answers to these questions, which may or may not have satisfied both their reason and their faith in God.

What Happens to Humans When They Die?

The Book of Job frames with acuity and in strong language the problem of unjust and scandalous suffering, and of unmerited death.[16] It is familiar with the usual answer given to this agonizing question: "Sufferings are the punishment for sin." But it is not satisfied with this solution to the problem: At any rate, this answer flies in the face of the suffering and death of the innocent. With considerable boldness the author of Job shows us his hero who very directly turns to God to ask him for his reasons, and even to demand an accounting of his incomprehensible and shocking behavior (Job 14:1-3, 10-15).

"Man born from woman is short-lived and full of trouble, like a flower that springs up and fades, swift as a shadow that does not abide. Upon such a one will you cast your eyes so as to bring him into judgment before you"; "Oh, that you would hide me in the nether world and keep me sheltered till your wrath is past; would fix a time for me, and then remember me!" It is gratifying to find, in the Bible, a man who is otherwise exemplary who has the audacity to speak to God this boldly, without actually blaspheming. It happens so often to us to say: "Why did God do this to me?" But we say it with more timidity or, on the contrary, in a rebellious way that we are secretly ashamed of.

This is not Job's way, to stay mostly involved with himself, crushed by his suffering. He fights the despair that assails him. Like someone shipwrecked at night he strains to see the slightest flicker of light that pierces the blackness, that might offer some hope: "All the days of my drudgery I would wait, until my relief should come. You would call and I would answer you; you would esteem the work of your hands."

In the sixth poem, Job answers those who are tormenting him by telling him to stop fighting the way he does. He should acknowledge once and for all that he has been punished by God for his sins, and be finished with this interminable debate.[17] "How long will you vex my soul, grind me down with words? These ten times you have reviled me, have assailed me without shame! Be it indeed that I am at fault and that my fault remains with me. Even so, if you would vaunt yourselves against me and cast up to me my reproach, know then that God has dealt unfairly with me, and compassed me round with his net."[18] He goes on to describe the unbearable condition he has been put in, almost to the point of provocation. But afterwards, hope again bursts forth from him in a vibrant proclamation that arises in the depths of his pain but goes way beyond it:

Oh, would that my words were written down!
   Would that they were inscribed in a record:
That with an iron chisel and with lead
   they were cut in the rock forever!
But as for me, I know that my Vindicator lives,
   and that he will at last stand forth upon the dust;
Whom I myself shall see:
   my own eyes, not another's, shall behold him,
And from my flesh I shall see God;
   my inmost being is consumed with longing.
(Job 19:23-27a)

Finding Peace When All Is Unsure

As its name indicates, the Book of Lamentations is a collection of complaints in the midst of trial.[19] The readings for the Masses for the Dead offer an excerpt from the third poem which, if it were taken out its historical context and read in the liturgy of November 2, would be perfectly suited to the situation of those who are in deep mourning (Lam 3:17-26).

Overwhelmed by what has happened, one "forgets happiness," and knows no peace. All confidence has disappeared "with the hope that came from the Lord." Because one chews over one's problems forever, one lives in a perpetual state of bitterness. It is like a poison that burns in the soul. One no longer takes pleasure in anything, but loses strength and drags oneself through a life that has lost all meaning. Who has never had moments of such depression and spiritual aridity?

Our relatives and friends say to us at these times: "Stop going around in circles, shutting yourself off in your troubles that we understand well, but which will end up destroying you if you give into them." This may be good advice, but it is hard to follow. The author of the Book of Lamentations recounts how he succeeded, with great difficulty and only little by little, in pulling himself out of his deep despair.

My soul is deprived of peace,
   I have forgotten what happiness is;
I tell myself my future is lost,
   all that I hoped for from the LORD.
The thought of my homeless poverty
   is wormwood and gall;
Remembering it over and over
   leaves my soul downcast within me.
But I will call this to mind,
   as my reason to have hope:

> The favors of the LORD are not exhausted,
>   his mercies are not spent;
> They are renewed each morning,
>   so great is his faithfulness.
> My portion is the LORD, says my soul;
>   therefore will I hope in him.
> Good is the Lord to one who waits for him,
>   to the soul that seeks him;
> It is good to hope in silence
>   for the saving help of the LORD.
> (Lam 3:17-26)

He who can do this begins to live again and helps others with their own troubles.

The Lord Has Promised It: He Will Do Away with Death

The hope of the believer goes way beyond the expectation of a simple immediate consolation, as precious as that is. If he can pull himself up out of the painful and destructive depression that misfortune often inflicts, the believer is truly blessed if he can raise his eyes high enough to see afar off and attend to the words of the Lord God.

> On this mountain he will destroy
>   the veil that veils all peoples,
> The web that is woven over all the nations;
>   he will destroy death forever.
> The Lord GOD will wipe away
>   the tears from all faces;
> The reproach of his people he will remove
>   from the whole earth; for the LORD has
>   spoken.
>   On that day it will be said:
> "Behold our God, to whom we looked
>   to save us!
> This is the LORD for whom we looked;
>   let us rejoice and be glad that
>   he has saved us!"
> (Isa 25:7-9)

To hear words such as these in faith is to already lift oneself up and become, despite one's frailty, a witness to the good news of salvation, brought to all of us.

Yes, They Shall Awake to Life Eternal

When one approaches those who are grieving, one always feels helpless, not knowing what to say or do to comfort them. With all the best will in the world and no matter how sincere one is, whatever one tries to do seems derisory, and words seem empty. Silent presence often seems the best possible attitude, along with prayer, in order to leave room for God, who alone can say truly effective words, as he said to Daniel in his grief.

> At that time your people shall escape,
>   everyone who is found in the book.
> Many of those who sleep
>   in the dust of the earth shall awake;
> . . . The wise shall shine brightly
>   like the splendor of the firmament,
> And those who lead the many to justice
>   shall be like the stars forever.
> (Dan 12:1b-3)

The Church proclaims this text while commemorating and praying for the dead. It recalls that the last words of the prophecy of the Book of Daniel are taken up at the end of the parable of the good seed and the weeds: On the day of harvest, ''the righteous will shine like the sun in the kingdom of their Father'' (Matt 13:43).

They Were Thought to Be Utterly Destroyed, but They Are at Peace

The Second Book of the Martyrs of Israel was composed around 124 B.C. Like the First Book, it tells of the heroic fight the Jewish people put up to win back national autonomy and the freedom of worship that Antiochus Epiphanes IV (d. 163 B.C.) had tried to destroy.[20] We learn that Judas Maccabeus, the leader of Israel, ''took up a collection among all his soldiers, amounting to two thousand silver drachmas, which he sent to Jerusalem to provide for an expiatory sacrifice'' for the intention of the dead. The writer of the book comments that ''in doing this he acted in a very excellent and noble way, inasmuch as he had the resurrection of the dead in view; for if he were not expecting the fallen to rise again, it would have been useless and foolish to pray for them in death'' (2 Macc 12:43-46).

Putting up mausoleums and monuments to the memory of the dead, maintaining their tombs and keeping fresh flowers on them are worthwhile and praiseworthy acts that express the gratitude one has toward the dead, as well as the memories of them that one would like to keep alive. Praying for them and celebrating the liturgy of the dead are really acts of faith in the resurrection, so much a part of the liturgy of the dead. We turn with confidence to the Lord ''so that the dead may be freed from their sins.''

> . . . strengthen our hope that all our departed brothers and sisters
> will share in his resurrection,
> who lives and reigns with you and the Holy Spirit
> one God, for ever and ever.[21]

> Accept these gifts and receive our brothers and sisters into the glory of your
> Son, who is Lord for ever and ever.[22]

God Created Human Beings So That They Might Have Life

The Book of Wisdom was compiled under the reign of Emperor Augustus
(27 B.C.–14 A.D.) at the very earliest. It seems to have been put together
in Alexandria, a port city of Egypt where there was a large and prosper-
ous Jewish community.[23] From as early as the third century before Christ,
Alexandria had been a major intellectual center, with its famous library—
700,000 volumes around 50 B.C.![24]—and its museum, where some of the
most famous Greek sages taught. Within such a milieu and speaking
Greek, the Jewish community also experienced an intense and produc-
tive intellectual revival. It was here that somewhere between the second
and first centuries B.C. the Greek translation of the Bible—the Septuagint
—was composed. Also, an important and considerable body of Jewish
literature, written in Greek, came into being.[25] While it is true that the
Jewish community of Alexandria benefited from the surrounding culture,
it also had to face new currents of religious thought that created new problems and objections never before raised. It was no longer possible, as it
had been earlier, simply to maintain an attitude of superiority in the face
of pagan doctrines. Even while they lived in symbiotic relationship with
the surrounding cultural milieu, the Jewish community of Alexandria was
concerned with keeping its religious identity, its traditions, and its faith;
its leaders found themselves obliged to justify them, to elaborate what
one could call a credible apologia, a Wisdom that would be worthy of
respect on the part of the sages who were so influential at that time in
the city. This is the context in which faith in immortality took shape and
was further refined (Wis 2:1-4a, 22-23; 3:1-9).[26]

This situation reminds us of the present time, with many Christian communities existing like so many little islands in a world that does not share
their faith. Just as in antiquity, a number of Christians maintain that there
is nothing after death.

> "Brief and troublous is our lifetime;
>   neither is there any remedy for man's dying,
>   nor is anyone known to have come back from the nether world.

For haphazard were we born,
    and hereafter we shall be as though we had not been;
Because the breath in our nostrils is a smoke
    and reason is a spark at the beating of our hearts;
And when this is quenched, our body will be ashes
    and our spirit will be poured abroad like unresisting air . . . ."
These were their thoughts, but they erred;
    for their wickedness blinded them,
And they knew not the hidden counsels of God;
    neither did they count on a recompense of holiness
    nor discern the innocent souls' reward.
(Wis 2:1-5, 21-22)

The only answer possible is the affirmation of one's faith.

For God formed man to be imperishable;
    the image of his own nature he made him . . . .
But the souls of the just are in the hand of God,
    and no torment shall touch them. . . .
For if before men, indeed, they be punished,
    yet is their hope full of immortality;
Chastised a little, they shall be greatly blessed,
    because God tried them
    and found them worthy of himself.
As gold in the furnace, he proved them,
    and as sacrificial offerings he took them to himself.
In the time of their visitation they shall shine. . . .
Those who trust in him shall understand truth,
    and the faithful shall abide with him in love;
Because grace and mercy are with his holy ones,
    and his care is with his elect.
(Wis 2:23; 3:1-4, 9)

Lastly, we must not forget that it is the quality of the life, not its length in years, that counts in the eyes of God.

But the just man, though he die early, shall be at rest.
For the age that is honorable comes not with the passing of time,
    nor can it be measured in terms of years.
Rather, understanding is the hoary crown for men,
    and an unsullied life, the attainment of old age.
(Wis 4:7-9)

Pray the Psalms, Even in Grief and Trouble

There is really only one "prayerbook" that never wears out: the psalms. The fact alone that they have been used constantly down through so many centuries proves it. The Jewish faith has used them, and so has the

Church. We never tire of the psalms, and despite the fact that a little effort is needed to understand their literary genres, their particular poetical forms, their symbolism and imagery, the more one prays them, the more one gets out of them. In the Psalter, a collection of inspired prayers, we sometimes find ourselves down to small details no matter where we may be in our spiritual journey. This is because the psalms are cries from the human heart, speaking boldly to God with a sincerity and frankness that we might not otherwise permit ourselves if left to our own devices. But at the same time, even though the psalms speak for us just as we are and wherever we are, sometimes on the verge of despair or even close to rebellion against God, they are still so full of faith and trust in the Lord that they help us through all the crises and pain. We are sometimes surprised at how much they can help us to get up again and rise above ourselves, to breathe again, with the breath of the Spirit.[27]

> Put an end to my affliction and my suffering,
>   and take away all my sins.
> (Ps 25:18)

> Once I said in my anguish,
>   "I am cut off from your sight";
> Yet you heard the sound of my pleading
>   when I cried out to you.
> (Ps 31:23)

> The LORD is close to the brokenhearted;
>   and those who are crushed in spirit he saves.
> (Ps 34:19)

> For he knows how we are formed;
>   he remembers that we are dust.
> Man's days are like those of grass;
>   like a flower of the field he blooms;
> The wind sweeps over him and he is gone,
>   and his place knows him no more.
> But the kindness of the LORD is from eternity
>   to eternity toward those who fear him.
> (Ps 103:14-17a)

> I remember the days of old;
>   I meditate on all your doings,
>   the works of your hands I ponder.
> I stretch out my hands to you;
>   my soul thirsts for you like parched land.
> May your good spirit guide me
>   on level ground.

For your name's sake, O LORD, preserve me;
    in your justice free me from distress.
(Ps 143:5-6, 10-11)

Those who say the Office, even if infrequently, know the healing power of the psalms, and the responsorial psalm said or sung after the first reading of every Eucharistic celebration has also taught us this power. The choice of psalms selected for the Masses for the Dead is a remarkable example of it, for how many feelings invade us on the occasion of death or when we commemorate the dead! The psalms are always there to help us express all these feelings face to face with God, in a true dialogue with him, as we join our voices to others' who have prayed the Psalter.[28]

The Gospels

The Gospels, written between 64–69 (for Mark) and the end of the first century (John) are both divergent and concordant witnesses to the person of Jesus and his mystery, his teaching in words and in acts. But they do not present themselves as neutral testimonies, as "just the facts." Each one of the evangelists was a literary author. Each picked and chose among the various sources of information at his disposal—personal memories, oral tradition and otherwise—in order to write, under the inspiration of the Spirit, what seemed to him personally most important to pass down, based on his experience and in view of the catechesis of those for whom he wrote.[29] More than anything else, the Gospels are the proclamation of the good news of Jesus Christ, the Son of God, the Savior. Their whole purpose, and they reveal this so clearly, is to inspire and strengthen faith. The very heart of the gospel is the message of the pasch of Christ—his death, resurrection, and glorification at the right hand of the Father—and this message throws decisive light on the mystery of the life and death of human beings.

Jesus, the Good News of Happiness for All

The desire for happiness lies deep in everyone's heart. But life, in a multitude of ways, often seems to militate against this universal aspiration. Does this mean that man is accursed, condemned to seek in vain what he most desires, condemned to know only unhappiness or, at best, small joys that soon become cruel disappointments? Some of us have arrived at an attitude of generalized pessimism, sometimes held as a philosophy of life. But everyone of us, sooner or later, is shocked by some personal trial or loss into the temptation to despair. All seems lost, life itself seems pointless, and it seems as if there is no future worth living for, as if the sun had sunk forever into the ocean. But even if the Bible itself sometimes expresses such somber feelings,[30] and the psalms in particular give free rein to cries of the deepest human pain, the Bible is still full of the certitude that our hope will not be disappointed, and that there will come a day when all will know the happiness brought by the Messiah promised by God from the beginning.

When Jesus manifests himself, it will be a message of joy and happiness that he proclaims to all those whose lives seemed hopelessly unhappy: the poor, the sorrowing, those who hunger and thirst for righteousness, those who are persecuted, insulted, and slandered. "Rejoice and be glad, for your reward will be great in heaven" (Matt 5:1-12a).[31]

He summons all those "who labor and are burdened" to come to him for rest, and he gives thanks to his Father who reveals to them the secrets of his kingdom, which are "hidden . . . from the wise and the learned" (Matt 11:25-28).[32]

He will be their guide himself, for he is the good shepherd who knows each one of his own by name and wants to gather them all together to him (John 10:14-16).[33]

Even more, he is himself "the way and the truth and the life." If he has left this world, it is to prepare for us a place in the house of his Father (John 14:1-6).[34]

So the hope of happiness is not illusory. It remains deeply within the human heart because it was put there by God, who made man so that he might have life. And God has not changed his mind. Now, in his love, "he gave his only son, so that everyone who believes in him might not perish but might have eternal life" which was never lost. Yes, John insists, "For God did not send his Son into the world to condemn the world, but that the world might be saved through him" (John 3:16-17).[35]

And still people die.

Jesus, Face to Face with His Agony and Death

Like everyone else, Jesus was often confronted with death, which struck inexorably those whom he knew. He knew that death would not have the last word since he had come into the world in order to bring an end to its power by taking upon himself the sins of humanity. But death still remained a painful trial, a difficult step on the way to eternal life. Jesus was just as deeply moved by the reality of death as he was by the suffering and sickness that he saw around him. The Gospels contain two episodes that illustrate this.

One day, as he drew near to the village of Nain, "a man who had died was being carried out, the only son of his mother, and she was a widow." No one spoke to him or asked anything of him, but the Lord was "moved with pity for her. He stepped forward and touched the coffin." He commanded the young man to get up. "The dead man sat up and began to speak, and Jesus gave him to his mother" (Luke 7:12-15).[36]

At the death of his friend Lazarus, Jesus was affectionately reproached by Martha for not having come to her village sooner: "Lord, if you had been here, my brother would never have died." Distressed at the tears and pain of this woman, Jesus "became perturbed and deeply troubled." When he got to the tomb where Lazarus had lain "for four days" and from which Jesus was to make him rise, he began to weep (John 11:17-45).[37]

Jesus knew that the hour of his death would also be the hour of his glorification, and the source of salvation for all those that the Father had given him (John 17:1-3, 24-26). When all was accomplished, "bowing his head, he handed over his spirit" (John 19:30). And "when the centurion who stood facing him saw how he breathed his last he said 'Truly this man was the Son of God!'" (Mark 15:39). Yet when Jesus actually came to die, he was plunged into indescribable anguish. He needed to draw on all that bound him to the will of his Father in order to abandon himself to him. "*Abba*, Father, all things are possible to you. Take this cup away from me, but not what I will but what you will" (Mark 14:36).

So it does not mean that one lacks faith or hope or that one has been abandoned by God to be deeply affected by the death of those one loves, or filled with anguish at the thought of one's own death. When Jesus took this human anxiety and pain upon himself, he transfigured them. From now on every one of us can call on the human experience of the Son of God to find the grace to face the pangs of death without losing heart.

> In a sense, then, fear is nevertheless the daughter of God, redeemed on the night of Good Friday. Fear is not pretty to see—oh, no!—sometimes scorned, sometimes cursed, disowned by all. . . . And yet let us not be mistaken, it is at the bedside of every dying person, and it intercedes for man.[38]

From Death to Life, With and Through Jesus

Jesus said to the crowd, "For this is the will of my Father, that everyone who sees the Son and believes in him may have eternal life, and I shall raise him [on] the last day" (John 6:40); "Whoever hears my word and believes in the one who sent me has eternal life and will not come to condemnation, but has passed from death to life" (John 5:24-29); "Amen, Amen, I say to you, unless a grain of wheat falls to the ground and dies, it remains just a grain of wheat; but if it dies, it produces much fruit" (John 12:24-26).

Jesus himself had to go into a lengthy explanation of Scripture for the two disciples at Emmaus in order to make them understand, "beginning with Moses and all the prophets," that the Anointed One had to suffer his passion to "enter into his glory" (Luke 24:13-35).[39] The criminal crucified at the same time as Jesus had surely not spent much time studying Scripture. But he understood that Jesus was a holy man and that he could count on him, even while the others were mocking him. On the same day as Jesus, and with him, he passed from death on a cross to heaven (Luke 23:33-34, 39-46, 50, 52-53). Whoever shares in the sufferings of the crucified Lord or renounces the goods of this world "for [Christ's] sake and for the sake of the gospel . . . receive[s] a hundred times more now in this present age . . . and eternal life in the age to come" (Mark 10:28-30).

The Viaticum of the Journey, Pledge of Eternal Life

Whether short or long, a human life is an exodus strewn with perilous temptations, as were the lives of our fathers. Being faithful day after day leads to lassitude and dullness, but we must stay awake with our lamps lit (Matt 25:1-13).[40] Zeal in carrying out the humble work of every day that the master of the house has assigned to us carries the risk of going stale (Luke 12:35-38, 40). The sacrament of the Body and Blood of Christ is the food that strengthens us and makes it possible for us to continue our journey. It rekindles in us the desire the see the Day of the Lord. And it allows us already to take part in the banquet of the kingdom: "Happy are those who are called to his supper." "Whoever eats this bread will live forever" (John 6:51-58).[41] But the Eucharist is also the sacrament of brotherly love, on which we shall be judged (Matt 25:31-46).[42]

The Gospels proposed by the Lectionary for the Masses for the Dead proclaim a certain number of essential truths revealed both in words and in acts by the Lord. It is not uncommon for us not to want to hear them, at least at first, because when we are still in a state of shock at some great loss, we feel that we are incapable of observing them. We may find ourselves complaining or thinking as the disciples did when Jesus spoke about eating his flesh and drinking his blood: "This saying is hard; who can accept it?'' (John 6:60). Let us hope that we too can surmount our first reaction of revulsion and make our profession of faith in the words of Peter: "Master, to whom shall we go? You have the words of eternal life" (John 6:68).

The Acts of the Apostles have passed down to us a few examples of the "first proclamation of the Lord, called the *kerygma.*''[43]

The Apostolic Letters are circumstantial writings addressed to particular communities in order to strengthen them and guide the faith of those first believers in the gospel. The choice of subject as well as the manner of their explanation depended, then, on the concrete needs of their catechesis and the questions that a particular Church had raised.

The Book of Revelation belongs to an entirely different literary genre, that of revelations and prophecy. It affords us a glimpse of the end of days and the accomplishing of all things in the heavenly Jerusalem.

The readings for the Masses for the Dead are from each of these three types of writings: one from the Book of Acts, seven from the Letter of Paul to the Romans, four from his First Letter to the Corinthians, two excerpts from the Second Letter to the Corinthians, one from the Letter to the Philippians, one from the First Letter to the Thessalonians, and one from the Second Letter to Timothy.

The First Letter of Peter also supplies a text; the First Letter of John, three; and the Book of Revelation, three.

Each one of these twenty-four texts takes up the central message of the preaching of the apostles while emphasizing one or more particular points, sometimes giving more concrete consequences of the basics of faith as proclaimed by the apostles.

> This man God raised [on] the third day. . . . He is the one appointed by God as judge of the living and the dead. To him all the prophets bear witness, that everyone who believes in him will receive forgiveness of sins through his name (Acts 10:34-43).[44]

> Christ died for our sins in accordance with the scriptures . . . he was buried . . . he was raised on the third day in accordance with the scriptures. . . . Therefore, whether it be I or they, so we preach and so you believe (1 Cor 15:1-5, 11).[45]

> It is Christ [Jesus] who died, rather, was raised, who also is at the right hand of God, who indeed intercedes for us. . . . [neither] height, nor depth, nor any other creature will be able to separate us from the love of God in Christ Jesus our Lord (Rom 8:34-35, 37-39).

> For we know that if our earthly dwelling, a tent, should be destroyed, we have a building from God, a dwelling not made with hands, eternal in heaven (2 Cor 5:1, 6-10).

> Blessed are the dead who die in the Lord from now on . . . let them find
> rest from their labors, for their works accompany them (Rev 14:13).

Keep Your Eyes on What Is Invisible

The death of someone close to us can be so overwhelming that we lose
our bearings. Paul must have experienced this, for he wrote to the Thessalonians: "We do not want you to be unaware, brothers, about those
who have fallen asleep, so that you may not grieve like the rest, who
have no hope. For if we believe that Jesus died and rose, so too will God,
through Jesus, bring with him those who have fallen asleep . . . Thus
we shall always be with the Lord. Therefore, console one another with
these words" (1 Thess 4:13-14, 17d-18).[46]

> If for this life only we have hoped in Christ, we are the most pitiable people
> of all. But now Christ has been raised from the dead, the firstfruits of those
> who have fallen asleep (1 Cor 15:19-20).[47]

> None of us lives for oneself, and no one dies for oneself. For if we live,
> we live for the Lord, and if we die, we die for the Lord; so then, whether
> we live or die, we are the Lord's. For this is why Christ died and came
> to life, that he might be Lord of both the dead and the living (Rom 14:7-9,
> 10b-12).

> For just as in Adam all die, so too in Christ shall all be brought to life, but
> each one in proper order: Christ the firstfruits; then, at his coming, those
> who belong to Christ; then comes the end, when he hands over the king-
> dom to his God and Father, when he has destroyed every sovereignty and
> every authority and power. For he must reign until he has put all his ene-
> mies under his feet (1 Cor 15:22-24, 26b-27a).

> For the trumpet will sound, the dead will be raised incorruptible, and we
> shall be changed (1 Cor 15:52b).[48]

> So that as sin reigned in death, grace also may reign in justification for eternal
> life through Jesus Christ our Lord (Rom 5:21).

Remember Jesus Christ, raised from the dead, a descendant of David . . .

> If we have died with him,
>   we shall also live with him;
> if we persevere
>   we shall also reign with him.
> (2 Tim 2:8-13)[49]

Tomorrow There Will Appear What Already Is

"For Christ, while we were still helpless, yet died at the appointed time
for the ungodly." "We were reconciled with him by the death of his
Son. . . . Indeed if, while we were enemies, we were reconciled to God

through the death of his Son, how much more, once reconciled, will we be saved by his life,'' he who poured out his blood so that we might be justified (Rom 5:6-10). ''Beloved, we are God's children now. . . . We do know that when it is revealed we shall be like him, for we shall see him as he is'' (1 John 3:1-2).[50] In other words, what happened to Christ will happen to us. And then we shall see in the full light of day what we know now only by faith: We live even now as the Lord lives, and because he lives. Put another way: ''For if we have grown into union with him through a death like his, we shall also be united with him in the resurrection.'' This passage through death with Christ took place at baptism (Rom 6:5).[51] ''But our citizenship is in heaven, and from it we also await a savior, the Lord Jesus Christ. He will change our lowly body to conform with his glorified body by the power that enables him to bring all things into subjection to himself'' (Phil 3:20-21).[52]

This radical change in our situation, which made us sons and daughters in the Son and heirs along with him, requires us to become responsible. We must let ourselves be ''led by the Spirit of God'' (Rom 8:14-17).[53] The sign of this will be if we love one another, ''because love is of God,'' who has ''loved us and sent his Son as expiation for our sins'' (1 John 4, 7-10).[54] ''We know that we have passed from death to life because we love our brothers. . . . Children, let us love not in word or speech but in deed and truth.'' And then ''this is how we shall know that we belong to the truth and reassure our hearts before him . . . for God is greater than our hearts and knows everything'' (1 John 3:14, 16-20). The present time then is a time of childbirth. ''For creation waits with eager anticipation the revelation of the children of God. . . . We know that all creation is groaning in labor pains even until now; and not only that, but we ourselves, who have the firstfruits of the Spirit, we also groan within ourselves as we wait for adoption, the redemption of our bodies'' (Rom 8:18-23).[55]

In the Book of Revelation, John recounts that he saw the new heaven and the new earth. ''I saw the dead, the great and the lowly, standing before the throne, and scrolls were opened. Then another scroll was opened, the book of life. The dead were judged according to their deeds, by what was written in the scrolls. . . . Then Death and Hades were thrown into the pool of fire'' (Rev 20:11-15). And then ''I also saw the holy city, the new Jerusalem, coming down out of heaven, from God, prepared as a bride adorned for her husband. I heard a loud voice from the throne saying, 'Behold, God's dwelling is with the human race. He will dwell with them [as their God]. He will wipe every tear from their eyes, and there shall be no more death or mourning. . . . The victor will inherit these gifts, and I shall be his God, he will be my son' '' (Rev 21:1-5a, 6b-7).[56]

> Blessed be the God and Father of our Lord Jesus Christ, who in his great mercy gave us a new birth to a living hope through the resurrection of Jesus Christ from the dead, to an inheritance that is imperishable, undefiled, and unfading, kept in heaven for you who by the power of God are safeguarded through faith, to a salvation that is ready to be revealed in the final time. In this you rejoice, although now for a little while you may have to suffer through various trials, so that the genuineness of your faith, more precious than gold that is perishable even though tested by fire, may prove to be for praise, glory, and honor at the revelation of Jesus Christ. Although you have not seen him you love him; even though you do not see him now yet believe in him, you rejoice with an indescribable and glorious joy . . . . (1 Pet 1:3-8)[57]

Each of us remembers persons he has known or loved, to whom he is bound by gratitude: relatives and friends who have died, and whom one faithfully keeps alive in one's memory. This "cult" of the dead is expressed in many different ways: funerary monuments or memorials, photographs displayed prominently in one's home, the celebration of the anniversary of the birth or death of the loved one.

From earliest antiquity the Church has commemorated in the very heart of the Eucharistic celebration those who have left this world, all those whose goodness is known only to God. In her prayers for all the faithful departed, the Church says to God:

> In baptism he (she) died with Christ:
> may he (she) also share his resurrection,
> when Christ will raise our mortal bodies
> and make them like his own in glory.[58]

Since the tenth century, on the day after the feast of All Saints—All Souls Day—we commemorate all the faithful departed. This celebration, which is often anticipated the evening before, is one of the most popular of the liturgical year. A day of remembering and of gratitude expressed in prayer, the first day of November sets us squarely before the mystery—or the enigma—of death, which inexorably strikes down every person born into this world.

On the subject of death, Christians have as many questions as anyone else. To know that every life, from the very start, is destined for death cannot help but make us feel less than sure of ourselves, no matter how familiar with death we may be. We may even find ourselves in rebellion when death appears up close. It may be better tolerated after a long and fulfilled life, unless, of course, we view our lives as being of unbearable pain. But death strikes blindly, at any age, even—absurdly—little children, as well as men and women who seem to have great futures before them, who asked only to be allowed to live, who gave great promise and had not finished their life's work. And why? None of us is untouched by these agonizing questions. A few are led to doubt the very existence of God himself. Believers are sorely tried as well. Nothing is more normal: The Bible is full of instances of this anguished doubting. But at the same time, from earliest antiquity, it has also spoken, timidly at first, and then with more assurance, of an afterlife: a mysterious other world, another life impossible to imagine, and, finally, of resurrection. With the gospel, this hope becomes firmer, not because thought on this subject has progressed to the point of being convincing but because of one fact: Jesus, the Christ, is risen.

This event does not concern only the one who died on a cross after a few years of doing good on earth (Acts 10:38), and indirectly, those who acknowledge him as their Master and Lord, as is the case with the "immortal glory" of an ancestor or a person that is reflected in some way in us. "The firstborn of the dead" (Col 1:18), the risen Christ is the new Adam of a new humanity. Through his death he destroyed death. From now on, through him, with him, and in him, death is a passage, a pasch toward eternal life. Like him and through him, the dead will rise again with transformed bodies. All those who are resting in cemeteries where we go as pilgrims on November 1, the great crowd of nameless ones whose bodies are hidden in the earth, all will rise one day and will see God with their eyes of flesh (Job 19:27). This is our faith and our hope, proclaimed at funerals and in the annual celebration of the commemoration of all the faithful departed. It takes for granted the prayer of the Church for all those who have gone before us, whom we remember.

All this does not mean that all our questions have been laid to rest. They continue to distress us, and on certain days and in some circumstances, they distress us with unbearable intensity. Torn between conflicting feelings, we almost might—and sometimes actually do—give up. At these times we must remember the agony of Jesus and his cry on the cross: "My God, my God, why have you forsaken me?"[59] God took upon himself all the anguish of humankind up to and including the Innocent One scandalously condemned to an ignominious death. But he died with absolute trust in God: "Father, into your hands I commend my spirit" (Luke 23:46). Repeating two verses from the psalms that seem to apply to him,[60] Jesus gives witness with his own death to the truth and solidity of the hope of believers down the ages expressed by the psalmist when he said, addressing God: " . . . You will not abandon my soul to the nether world, nor will you suffer your faithful one to undergo corruption" (Ps 16:10). This conviction is founded on the experience of the love of God, which is revealed from the beginning, and which has never failed. "To love someone is to say: You will never die."[61] And that is precisely what God said to man when he created him (Gen 2:17). Nothing has ever made him go back on his promise.

> Even when he disobeyed you and lost your friendship
> you did not abandon him to the power of death,
> but helped all men to seek and find you.
> Again and again you offered a covenant to man,
> and through the prophets taught him to hope for salvation.
> Father, you so loved the world
> that in the fullness of time you sent your only Son to be our Savior. . . .
> In fulfillment of your will
> he gave himself up to death;
> but by rising from the dead,
> he destroyed death and restored life.[62]

To sum up, this faith alone allows us not to be overcome by sadness like those "who have no hope" (1 Thess 4:13). The liturgy of the dead even allows us to "mix our whys" with the praise of those who see the Lord face to face and who acknowledge in him the God who makes a mockery of death.[63]

> God, you reveal your light
> to those who pass in the night;
> blessed are you
> for the eyes that open today
> upon the new earth:
> they find you, O living God!
>
> *Glory to you, Lord,*
> *Light of the kingdom!*
>
> You reveal your face to them
> after the Exodus and the cloud;
> blessed are you
> for the eyes in which dances a gleam
> of the Easter dawn:
> They contemplate you, O living God!

Glory to you, Lord,
Light of the kingdom!

You show them your presence
and the joy of the saved;
blessed are you
for the dead who find peace
in the joy of your Nuptials:
They are your glory, O living God!

Glory to you, Lord,
Light of the kingdom!

You draw them to your mystery
with the strength of the Spirit;
blessed are you
for the bodies where life arises
until the eternal Dawn:
They rise again, O living God!

Glory to you, Lord,
Light of the kingdom![64]

Dedication of the Basilica of the Lateran

The Basilica of the Lateran is the cathedral of the diocese of Rome; the pope is its bishop. It gets its name from the domain of the Laterani family on the Celian Hill, which passed into the hands of Fausta, the wife of Constantine I.[1]

The Edict of Milan (313) put an end to the period of persecutions and made Christianity a kind of state religion.[2] The Christians then began the restoration of their revered places of worship and also built new ones, often with the help of imperial largesse. Emperor Constantine (d. 337) gave the palace of the Lateran to the Church, and on the site of the former barracks of the imperial guard he built a basilica that Pope Sylvester I (314–335) dedicated to the Holy Savior on November 9, 324. Damaged during several earthquakes—in the fourth century and especially in the tenth—it was almost entirely rebuilt by Sergius III (904–911). The domain of the Lateran was devastated by a fire in 1308 and again in 1361.[3] The basilica was severely damaged. Consecrated by Pope Benedict XIII in 1726, it was under constant reconstruction and restoration, the last time in 1938, when the flooring was redone.

Even before the construction of the basilica, a baptistery had been built on the ruins of ancient volcanic springs. Rebuilt by Sixtus III (432–440), its patron was St. John the Baptist, who from the twelfth century on, was the second titular patron saint of the basilica. Afterward St. John the Evangelist was also associated with the basilica, which is the reason it is often called "St. John Lateran." As for the palace, it was the residence of the bishop of Rome continuously until 1304. In that year Pope Benedict XI was forced to leave Rome by dangerous acts of sedition that threatened his safety. His successors took up residence in Avignon until 1377.[4] During this entire period the palace of the Lateran lay abandoned, and Pope Nicholas V (1447–1455) transferred the general offices of the Church to the Vatican. But the Basilica of the Lateran has always remained the cathedral of the pope, the bishop of Rome.[5] This is the origin of the importance accorded the annual celebration of its dedication.

In every diocese the cathedral is the symbol—one might be tempted to say the sacrament—of the unity of the local Church gathered around its bishop, its defender, and through him their unity with the other Churches that form the *Catholica*. This is why the anniversary of the dedication of the cathedral is celebrated as a solemn feast day throughout the diocese.[6] But the bishop who has his seat in Rome[7] has the ministry of the charity and unity of the entire Church, as well as that of his own diocese. His cathedral therefore is a symbol of much more than the Church of Rome.[8] Celebrating the anniversary of the cathedral that is the mother of all others founded down through the ages is to celebrate the Lord, who founded his Church in order to gather together in unity, under the crozier of Peter and his successors, all the children of God, wherever they may live.

> God our Father,
> from living stones, your chosen people,
> you built an eternal temple to your Church,
> so that your faithful people may continue to grow
> into the new and eternal Jerusalem.[9]

The Dwelling Places Where God Gathers His People

A Source of Living Waters Gushing from the Sanctuary

As a priest, Ezekiel's whole life was bound to the Temple. Deeply imbued with the sense of the holiness of God, he was zealous for the respect due this sacred place of God's presence and for the purity of the cult that was centered in it. When the sanctuary of the Lord was profaned by the armies of Nebuchadnezzar who besieged the city in 597 B.C., he was deeply distressed. Carried off into exile in Babylon, it was on the banks of the Kebar canal that he received his mission as a prophet.[1] For a long time he meditated in silence on the tragic events at Jerusalem. The glory of the Lord was deserted, the Temple profaned. But if God had punished the sins of his people, he had nonetheless not abandoned them. God's presence was his sanctuary in the land of exile. After this severe purification, he will establish a new covenant.[2] In 587 B.C. Ezekiel learned that the second taking of Jerusalem ended with the total destruction of the venerated Temple. With this catastrophe, all seemed lost.[3] But God announced to his priest and prophet that there would soon be a miraculous restoration of his people.[4] He will bring them back to their country and will live once again in their midst,[5] in a reconstructed Temple.[6] The text of the vision of which we read the essential part on this feast day begins with the spiritual meaning of the Temple in the heavenly Jerusalem (Ezek 47:1-2, 8-9, 12).[7]

"On the tenth day of the month beginning the twenty-fifth year of our exile, fourteen years after the city was taken," Ezekiel was taken in a vision to the top of a mountain from which he contemplated Jerusalem being rebuilt (Ezek 40:1-2).[8] A mysterious surveyor appears to the prophet. He shows him around the Temple, giving the measurements in detail,[9] and dictating to him precise rituals that are to be followed (Ezek 40:5–46:24). At the end of this guided tour, the prophet is led back to the entrance of the Temple, and there he has an extraordinary vision: "waters flowing out from beneath the threshold of the Temple toward the east."

This stream that keeps increasing in volume makes salt waters fresh, allows animals to live and multiply, and makes the earth so fertile that wonderful fruit trees grow on its banks. Each month they bear different fruit, and their leaves have healing properties. The stream becomes a mighty river and flows down into the Dead Sea—well-named, since its extremely salty waters allow no animal or vegetable life—and it sweetens its waters too.

This vision, taken in its context, expresses better than many a discourse addressed to reason the true significance of the Temple, and after it, our churches. The profanation of any sanctuary causes great distress to all believers. Its destruction or closing has always been a form of persecution that is deeply felt.[10] Its reconstruction and reopening fill them with hope and joy. But the presence of God in the midst of his people does not depend on the existence of a sanctuary. When they cannot go up to his House, he comes to them in their desert exile. It even happens that such a period of persecution and loss can lead to a greater depth of spiritual life, as was the case for this people in exile, and to renewal in the future.[11] This was Ezekiel's commitment. Overwhelmed as he was by the sack of Jerusalem and the destruction of the Temple, his eyes were finally opened to a radiant future brought about by the purification of suffering. The new city that he contemplates is called "The Lord is here" (Ezek 48:35). He sees fulfilled the promise: "Thus the nations shall know that it is I, the Lord, who make Israel holy, when my sanctuary shall be set up among them forever" (Ezek 37:28). The Temple is the holy of holies (Ezek 43:12) that nothing profane can sully (Ezek 43:12), and from it flows an inexhaustible source of life.

In the Temple of Solomon there was, to the right of the altar, a great tank of water used in the cult for purifications, called the "Sea of Bronze."[12] This tank did not figure in the Temple of Ezekiel's vision: From now on, it is a living water that gushes out near the altar, and it purifies and enriches all the country around. This is in accomplishment of the promise:

> I will sprinkle clean water upon you to cleanse you of all your impurities, and from all your idols I will cleanse you. I will give you a new heart and place a new spirit within you, taking from your bodies your stony hearts and giving you natural hearts. I will put my spirit within you and make you live by my statutes, careful to observe my decrees. You shall live in the land I gave your fathers; you shall be my people, and I will be your God (Ezek 36:25-28).[13]

It is the picture of a new creation.

> Who can, from paradise,
>   Contemplate the splendors
> Of marvelous construction,
>   Of ingenious planning?
> Spacious for the inhabitants,
>   With luminous dwellings.
> Its perfumed fountains
>   Pour out delight,
> But, come amongst us,
>   They begin to lose their fragrance,
> Having taken on, in quenching our thirst,
>   Something of our earthly scents.
> For this supreme Will
>   For whom all is easy
> Has collected the fountain waters
>   That flow from paradise,
> And holds them on earth
>   As if in channels
> So that at his call alone
>   They might flow down to us.
> And again in his clouds
>   He gathers up the waters
> To spread them abroad in the air
>   According to his own good Will.[14]

Without water, the gift of the heavens, there is no life. Living water is everywhere, but especially in arid lands, a natural and particularly powerful symbol of every form of natural and supernatural life.[15] The just man "is like a tree planted near running water, that yields its fruit in due season, and whose leaves never fade" (Ps 1:3). In the New Testament, water symbolizes the bath of rebirth[16] and the Spirit given for the remission of sins (John 7:39). And lastly, Jesus is the source of running water that purifies and regenerates whoever comes to him,[17] the Temple where the river flows that gives life to the new Jerusalem.[18]

> *How lovely is your dwelling place, Lord, mighty God!*
>
> My soul yearns and pines
>   for the courts of the LORD.
> My heart and my flesh
>   cry out for the living God.
> Even the sparrow finds a home,
>   and the swallow a nest
>   in which she puts her young—

Your altars, O LORD of hosts,
   my king and my God!
Happy they who dwell in your house!
   continually they praise you.
Happy the men whose strength you are!

———————————

They go from strength to strength . . .

———————————

I had rather one day in your courts
   than a thousand elsewhere;
I had rather lie at the threshold of the house of my God
   than dwell in the tents of the wicked.
(Ps 84:3-6a, 8a, 11)

"You Are the House That God Is Building"

"To construct" and "construction" are words commonly used to designate the action of producing a work of any kind and the result of this action. Etymologically, "construct" (from *construere*) means to put up or raise while putting together different elements, according to a master plan, and resulting in a single piece of cohesive work. The opposite, "destruct," means to "knock down." So it is not surprising that the Bible speaks of God, the creator of the universe and all that is in it, as the one who, more than any other, has the power to "construct" as well as to "overthrow" even the most solid and resistant structures. This vocabulary is particularly apt for describing the action of the Lord who chose to make a people and bring them together into one organic unity.[19] These are words that Paul likes to use when speaking of the Church and the Christian communities. An example is the text read on this feast day (1 Cor 3:9b-11, 16-17).[20]

"For we are God's co-workers; you are God's field, God's building. . . . Do you not know that you are the temple of God, and that the spirit of God dwells in you?" This construction is built on Christ as its foundation. The idea is familiar to Paul.

> [You are] members of the household of God, built upon the foundation of the apostles and prophets, with Christ Jesus himself as the capstone. Through him the whole structure is held together and grows into a temple sacred in the Lord; in him you also are being built together into a dwelling place of God in the Spirit (Eph 2:20-22).

He uses the same image of construction when he speaks of the Church as the body of Christ:

> We should grow in every way into him who is the head, Christ, from whom the whole body, joined and held together by every supporting ligament, with the proper functioning of each part, brings about the body's growth and builds itself up in love (Eph 4:16).

The apostle considers the consequences of this teaching on several levels: the unity that must reign in the community (1 Cor 1:13), the moral conduct of the Christian (1 Cor 6:15-19), the various gifts and functions in the Church (1 Cor 12:12-30), and the conduct and zeal of the apostles.[21] God is the master builder of this construction. He designs the plans and directs the work. He is the only one to have at his disposal all the means—the graces—that allow his project to be carried out. And finally, he chooses his workers, he gives each one his task, according to his possibilities and the gifts he has received.

"According to the grace of God given to me, like a wise master builder I laid a foundation" (1 Cor 3:10). Paul's role was not to draw up plans for his construction in an architect's studio. He worked out in the field to lay the foundations of a new Church. But as soon as his preaching had led to the formation of a small community, he made sure that it had the necessary minimum of organization, and then he left to begin elsewhere, entrusting the elders and other persons in charge with the new community's welfare.

He habitually revisited the communities that he had founded, and he wrote to the Churches that he had established in order to offer encouragement, handle problems as they arose, and, when necessary, correct various abuses or deviations. But he knew that he would not always be there to supervise his foundations. And so he made every effort to see that each community was able to oversee itself. The Book of Acts has preserved the account of Paul's last meeting with the elders of the Church of Ephesus, which he was destined never to see again. The words that he wrote to them from Miletus, saying goodbye, give us an idea of his feelings toward the leaders of the communities he had established, and his trust in them to take up full responsibility for their flock, with the grace of God.

> "So be vigilant and remember that for three years, night and day, I unceasingly admonished each of you with tears. And now I commend you to God and to that gracious word of his that can build you up and give you the inheritance among all who are consecrated. . . ." When he finished speaking, [Paul] knelt down and prayed with them all (Acts 20:31-32, 36).[22]

"According to the grace of God given to me, like a wise master builder I laid a foundation, and another is building upon it. But each one must be careful how he builds upon it, for no one can lay a foundation other than the one that is there, namely, Jesus Christ" (1 Cor 3:10-11). Just as he was himself sent by the Father, Jesus sent the apostles whom he had chosen to continue his mission (John 20:21). With them as a foundation, the "one, holy, catholic" Church is also "apostolic," as the Creed says. But the apostles also, during their lifetimes, put others in charge of various ministries in the Christian communities, to be leaders, to continue to instruct the faithful in fidelity to the gospel, and to keep them in unity. Sometimes it happened that the Spirit took the initiative to appoint these co-workers of the apostles.[23] More often, the Spirit drew attention to various sisters and brothers of the community by granting them special gifts for their mutual service.[24] This diversity of gifts and functions is indispensable for the building up of the Church and for its life as the body of Christ (1 Cor 12:12-30). Down through the centuries the Spirit has continued to grace the faithful with various new Gifts.[25] And under its action the Church has been provided with the ministries it has needed throughout the history of its development,[26] for its teaching and apostolate; the Church has always been able to call upon the good will and sense of responsibility of the people of God, in all domains, especially catechesis.[27] Whatever the form of their ministry, whether it be exercised full- or part-time, each must heed the warning of Paul: "But each one must be careful how he builds upon it." Similarly, we must not be misled into excessive veneration and gratitude for any worker for the gospel, no matter how legitimate. There is only one capstone of the Church and its faith: the Lord Jesus Christ.[28]

"Do you not know that you are the temple of God, and that the Spirit of God dwells in you? If anyone destroys God's temple, God will destroy that person; for the temple of God, which you are, is holy" (1 Cor 3:16-17). This reminder of the supreme dignity of the Christian invites us all to examine our personal conduct and our relations with others. Baptism remakes every Christian anew, a consecrated sanctuary in which the Spirit dwells.

> If then you were raised with Christ, seek what is above, where Christ is seated at the right hand of God. Think of what is above, not of what is on earth . . . [and] put on the new self, which is being renewed, for knowledge, in the image of its creator (Col 3:1-10).[29]

Whoever is truly conscious of this transformation due to divine grace will flee all that could sully, profane, or even destroy the temple of God that he or she has become. As for those who exercise a ministry or some other charge within the Church, they must constantly examine themselves to verify whether they are remaining truly faithful to the mission they have received, and to its objectives. They must help their sisters and brothers to build themselves up into true temples of God, founded on Christ. This they cannot do unless they forget themselves and remain attentive to the voice of the Spirit.

> Let no one deceive himself. If any one among you considers himself wise in this age, let him become a fool, so as to become wise. For the wisdom of this world is foolishness in the eyes of God. . . . So let no one boast about human beings, for everything belongs to you, Paul or Apollo or Kephas, or the world or life or death, or the present or the future: all belong to you, and you to Christ, and Christ to God.[30]

Jesus, the Holy Sanctuary of the Presence of God

All four evangelists have recorded Jesus' astounding action of one day at the Temple of Jerusalem. He made himself a whip out of some rope, and he drove out of the holy precincts the buyers and sellers and the money changers, turning over their tables. Matthew, Mark, and Luke place this episode shortly after Jesus' triumphal entry into Jerusalem.[31] In this context, this action of Jesus appears as the reaction of a prophet devoured by zeal for the house of God, as well as an extraordinary manifestation of the authority that he assumes over everything, even over the Temple.[32] By recording this episode between the story of Jesus' first "sign" at Cana in Galilee[33] and that of his conversation with Nicodemus,[34] John emphasizes the importance of the revelation that this episode brings. It is, in fact, a "sign" and not just an interesting and somewhat shocking story. By the same token, this page of the Gospel throws considerable light on the mystery celebrated on the feast day we are discussing here (John 2:13-22).[35]

"Since the Passover of the Jews was near, Jesus went up to Jerusalem." This seemingly unimportant detail at once suggests to the reader who is familiar with John's writings the paschal import of the "sign" that Jesus will carry out in the Temple, and, in a more general way, its relationship— which becomes explicit in the rest of the episode—with his last pasch.[36] This story must be understood as it was written, in the light of Easter faith.[37] It is important as well to be aware of the great respect, the veneration even, that Jesus felt for the Temple. His invective against the purely formal worship of some of those present bears witness to this (Matt 23:16-22), as does his faithful attendance at the Temple of Jerusalem for the great pilgrimage feasts. The Temple was also the locus of many of his great teachings. His behavior with the dealers and money changers is a clear manifestation of his devotion to the holy place. He could not tolerate the trafficking in his Father's house, even when some of it was necessary for the needs of the cult.[38] The disciples do not seem astonished at this virulent action of Jesus, devoured with zeal for the honor of God. A phrase from Scripture occurs to them: "Because zeal for your house consumes me" (Ps 69:10).[39] The verb is actually in the future tense in the Hebrew, which has been seen as foretelling Jesus' future condemnation.[40] But the meaning of this episode is actually much deeper.

Jesus' action calls into question his authority, the right he had to behave in such a way. "What sign can you show us for doing this?" Formulated in these terms, the question betrays a negative attitude; it is even a thinly veiled accusation that he has overstepped his authority. Jesus refuses to let himself be caught, by not answering.[41] John makes only brief mention of this debate that was no longer current when he wrote his Gospel. But he does think it important for Christians to fully grasp the meaning of this "sign" of Jesus at the Temple. Commenting on it, he recalls other words of Christ, enigmatic at the time: "Destroy this temple and in three days I will raise it up."[42] Obviously, Jesus was not claiming that in three days he could materially reconstruct the vast architectural complex of the Temple of Jerusalem.[43] For what would have been the purpose of such an action? It would have had no more meaning than for Jesus to have thrown himself down from the pinnacle of the Temple, as Satan had suggested to him in the desert, and indeed, Jesus did nothing of the kind.[44] It was for the benefit of others that Jesus performed his miracles, and not for his own glory. Every one of those miracles was a manifestation of the mercy of God, a proclamation of the good news of salvation, and only secondarily a "sign" that revealed the secret of who he was and of his glory, the ushering in of messianic times.[45]

The prophets had always longed for a truly holy Temple, forever purified of every defilement, a stable sanctuary of the presence of God, a place of worship in spirit and truth, a center for the study of the Law, a house of God where salvation would flow in abundance, and where the glory of the Lord would be revealed to all nations.[46] Jesus is the realization of this dream that always looked to the future, to the end of time. "But he was speaking about the temple of his body." The meaning of Jesus' words was not clear to the disciples until they recalled them in the light of the his resurrection. Jesus had made a promise before leaving this world to go to the Father: "The Advocate, the holy Spirit that the Father will send in my name—he will teach you everything and remind you of all that [I] told you" (John 14:26). The Father and the Spirit dwell in Jesus as God had never dwelt in any of the holiest of sanctuaries. In the heavenly city there is no temple, for "its temple is the Lord God almighty and the Lamb" (Rev 21:22). But the body of Christ is also the Church, headed by the risen Lord: "Like living stones, let yourself be built into a spiritual house to be a holy priesthood to offer spiritual sacrifices acceptable to God . . . " (1 Pet 2:5). This Temple is from now on the place of the divine presence and of the gathering of believers who worship God in spirit and in truth.

> Hearing Jesus announce the new sanctuary, the reader of the Gospel remembers his proclamation in the Temple during the feast of Sukkoth: "Let anyone who thirsts come to me and drink. Whoever believes in me, as scripture says: 'Rivers of living water will flow' " (John 7:37-38). They also remember the witness of the evangelist at Calvary who saw blood flowing from Jesus' pierced side, then water (John 19:34-35). Clearly, Jesus was the Temple foretold by the prophets (Ezek 47:1-12). Immediately a number of texts of St. John receive their full meaning. The body of Jesus, his flesh, is the dwelling place of the glory of God; upon Jesus the angels climb up and down, as in that awesome place where Jacob once had seen God; on him the Spirit eternally rests; Jesus has been consecrated by the Father, so that the Father is in him and he in the Father; wherever the Father makes his name to dwell, there, in this sanctuary, the adoring faithful will be gathered together and all will be consummated in unity; all will take part in the holiness of the Temple, for "we will come to him and make our dwelling with him" (John 14:23). The new sanctuary foretold by Jesus is his risen body, a body from which flow abundant streams of living water (Rev 21:22).[47]

The Basilica of the Lateran is the cathedral of the diocese of Rome, and the pope is its bishop. The celebration of the anniversary of its dedication expresses the communion of each Church and local community with the Church founded by the apostles Peter and Paul, with the pope as the head of the college of bishops, which presides over the charity of all the Churches throughout the world.

It is a feast day of the Lord, who is the capstone that creates unity out of the diversity of materials that went into the construction of each one of these communities, each with its own characteristics and personality.

The Basilica of the Lateran was built shortly after peace and security were granted to the Church, which had suffered from long persecutions. From then on, many places of worship were constructed and the number of Christian communities multiplied; the Church put down roots and grew throughout the world. Whether they were great monuments or humble, unpretentious structures, they were all given the name—church —of a higher reality, of which they were the symbols: the Church, the true Temple of the presence of God, source of the godly life that bears the abundant fruits of holiness.

No matter how legitimate our veneration for these consecrated temples may be, bearing witness as they do to the faith of those who built them, we must never make cult objects out of them. The gold decorations may darken, and the most venerable of sanctuaries, perhaps the work of an entire generation of believers, may become worn out and dilapidated; poverty will never have any brilliant outward show. What really counts, and constitutes the real beauty any of us can aspire to, is sincere piety and the evangelical life of those who worship at these sanctuaries.

> Beloved brethren, today we celebrate in joy the anniversary of this church, with the grace of Christ. But it is we who must be the temple of God, his true and living temple . . .
>
> Therefore, if we want to celebrate with joy the anniversary of a church, we must not destroy within ourselves, with bad actions, these living temples of God. And I say this so that all of you may understand: Every time we come into church, we must prepare our souls, so that they may be as beautiful as we want our church to be.
>
> Do you want to find a shining basilica? Then do not soil your soul with the uncleanness of sin. If you want the basilica to be brightly lit, and God also wants it to be, then may the light of good works shine in you, and the one who is in heaven will be glorified. Just as you enter into your church, so also does God enter into your souls, as he himself said: "I will live with them and move among them" (2 Cor 6:16).[48]

By emphasizing the people of God and the assembly as subjects of the liturgy, Vatican Council II gave new life to the most traditional, the deepest and most concrete meaning of the sign of the Temple. It is the assembly that, in a manner of speaking, consecrates the churches and makes of them holy places.[49] A Christian community can live without possessing or using such places, but it cannot exist in the absence of the assembly.[50] When all things have finally been accomplished in the heavenly Jerusalem, there will be no more Temple—only the numberless assembly of the elect, the body of Christ, singing endlessly of the glory of God.

> Jerusalem, O holy city,
> blessed vision of peace,
> you who raise your towers in the sky,
> built of living stones,

and crowned by thousands of angels
like a bride's retinue.
Worked with hammers,
the smooth, polished stones
are put into their place
by the hand of the craftsman,
set up to be forever
the holy Temple of the Lord.[51]

The Immaculate Conception of the Virgin Mary

The Church has always proclaimed the unique holiness of Mary, "full of grace," whom the power of the Most High overshadowed so that she might become through the action of the Holy Spirit, the Mother of the Son of God (Luke 1:28-35). Perfect "handmaiden of the Lord," Mary was faithful all her life to the word of God. This unfailing faithfulness made the Mother of God, "blessed among women," the only creature who has never sinned. But does this exceptional holiness imply that the Mother of God was preserved from the stain of original sin, which marks all the children of men partners from birth in the sin of Adam? This question was raised in the fifth century, during controversies over the need and the role of grace for the practice of virtue. According to the doctrine of Pelagius, a monk originally from Britain (ca. 354–d. after 418), Adam's sin was a bad example for all of us, but nothing more. Therefore every person, given freedom by God, can choose to conduct him- or herself differently from his distant ancestor. According to this theory, divine grace is not really necessary for virtue and salvation but is merely a help from God given to bolster the free will of every one of us.[1] St. Augustine (354–430), who has been called the "Doctor of Grace," vigorously fought this doctrine, known as Pelagianism.[2] Augustine teaches that every person born into this world is marked by the stain of Adam's sin. It is precisely for this reason that the Church confers baptism, and everyone acknowledges the necessity of this sacrament.[3]

For St. Augustine, the transmission of original sin takes place through human reproduction. Only Jesus escaped this inheritance, because he was "conceived by the holy Spirit," as the *Creed* says, and not through the ordinary laws of human nature. This was not true of Mary's conception and birth. This is why Augustine could not accept the idea that she had been preserved from original sin. Augustine's authority carried great weight in the development of Western theology. St. Bernard (1090–1153), who wrote so poetically of the Virgin Mary, followed Augustine's teaching, as did St. Thomas Aquinas (ca. 1225–1274), as well as the great Doctors of scholastic theology, such as St. Bonaventure (ca. 1217–1274) and St. Albert the Great (ca. 1200–1280). But this whole controversy over original sin was not known in the East, which was not greatly influenced by the thinking of St. Augustine. A hymn of St. Andrew of Crete (ca. 660–740) shows that in the Monastery of St. Sabas, near Jerusalem, they celebrated a feast on December 9 in honor of the Virgin Mary, known even today under the name of the "Conception of St. Anne." It does not celebrate exactly the same thing as the feast of the Immaculate Conception of the Virgin Mary, but rather addresses the circumstances of her birth, as recounted in the apocryphal writing known as the Proto-Gospel of James, written somewhere around the middle of the second century.[4] Although it does not discuss any exemption from original sin that Mary might have enjoyed, this feast day emphasized the purity of the conception of the Mother of God. It spread rapidly throughout the East, and then gradually began to be observed in the West, in Naples in the ninth century, and in Sicily in the tenth.

Elsewhere, three ninth-century liturgical calendars mention a feast of the "Conception of Mary," celebrated in Ireland on May 3 or 4. The exact meaning of this feast day remains uncertain, for lack of extant liturgical texts. In England, two other liturgical calendars show that in the eleventh century this feast was celebrated on December 8 in Benedictine monasteries. We also know of two liturgical texts from a Mass in honor of the "Conception of Mary."[5] This feast had its enthusiastic supporters, such as Elsinus, abbot of Ramsey (1080–1087) and Eadmer (ca. 1060–ca. 1128), monk, disciple, and biographer of St. Anselm, bishop of Canterbury (ca. 1033–1109), who wrote a treatise on the conception of Mary. But there were also those who opposed this feast day on the grounds that it was not in conformity with the tradition of the Church and doctrinally questionable. This did not prevent it from spreading rapidly in the West. In the twelfth century it became the practice in Normandy, where it met with such enthusiasm that it was called the "feast day of the Normans," and, at the same time, it began to be celebrated in Lyons, the primatial Church of the Gauls, despite the opposition of St. Bernard. In a letter written to the canons of this city between 1137 and 1138, he speaks of the "presumptuous novelty, mother of audacity, sister of superstition, daughter of irresponsibility" of this doctrine.[6] However, the abbot of Clairvaux ends by saying that he is willing to submit to the judgment of the Church of Rome if it sees otherwise. The acceptance of this feast day by the majority of Franciscans in 1263 was all the more influential in that one of them, Duns Scotus (ca. 1265–1308), who taught successively in Oxford, Paris, and Cologne, showed with his legendary subtlety of thought that the objections to this doctrine were not insurmountable, and that there were good reasons to proclaim the freedom from original sin granted to Mary. In the meantime the celebration of this feast spread into Belgium, Spain, Italy, several monasteries in Germany, and rapidly throughout all of France.

All this controversy might have ended with the Council of Basel-Ferraro (1431–1442) which published on September 17, 1439, a decree on the privilege of the immaculate conception of the Mother of God, and instituted for the whole Church a feast day to be celebrated on the following December 8, and to be known as the feast of the "Conception of the Virgin Mary," and for which John of Segovia (d. 1463) composed the liturgy.[7] But the impact of these decisions was weakened by the successive metamorphoses that this Council went through.[8] Pope Sixtus IV (1471–1484) approved this feast in 1476 and promulgated, for its celebration, a new liturgy composed by the Franciscan Leonard of Nogarolis,[9] while in 1480 another Franciscan, Bernardin of Bustis, composed yet a third.

But a few years later the pope was constrained to intervene to put an end to controversies that were troubling some of the faithful. Both those who were for and those who were against treated each other as heretics. The pope imposed silence on both, "since the matter has not yet been decided by the Roman Church and the Apostolic See."[10] During the fifth session of the Council of Trent, on June 17, 1546, a similar attitude was adopted: "This holy Council declares that it does not intend to include the blessed and immaculate Virgin Mary, the Mother of God, in this decree relative to original sin, but it does pronounce that the constitutions of Pope Sixtus IV, of blessed memory, must be observed, namely, that the opinions of both sides must be respected."[11] But the Fathers had requested that one liturgy only be chosen for the feast. Pope Pius V (1566–1572) selected the oldest, composed by John of Segovia, which was an adaptation of that of the Nativity of the Virgin Mary, and he published it in the *Roman Missal*.[12]

Pope Alexander VII made a clearer pronouncement than his predecessors on the privilege of the immaculate conception of Mary. On December 8, 1661, he published a papal bull in which he affirmed explicitly that "Mary, in consideration of the merits of Jesus Christ her son, the Redeemer of humankind, was preserved intact from the stain of original sin.'' He supported his affirmation with the *consensus* of the Christian people. The number of those who celebrate the feast of her conception had done nothing but increase, "to the point where almost all Catholics had adopted it."[13] Pope Clement XI (1700–1721) decreed in 1708 that the universal Church should celebrate the feast of the "Conception of the Immaculate Virgin." So faith in the absolute purity of the Mother of God was progressively imposed on the conscience of the Church. In this evolution, the faithful played a primary role.

The Christian people has almost instinctively grasped the mystery, despite the opposite opinion of a number of theologians, even from among the most eminent. On their side, the popes exercised their ministry of discernment, acknowledging, with prudent slowness, the rightness of popular opinion.[14] Finally, Pope Pius IX (1846–1878), after consulting widely with Catholic bishops all around the world,[15] solemnly defined the dogma of the Immaculate Conception in a papal bull of December 8, 1854.[16]

> For the honor of the holy and indivisible Trinity, for the honor of the Virgin Mary, Mother of God, for the exaltation of the Catholic faith and the growth of the Christian religion, by the authority of our Lord Jesus Christ, of the blessed Apostles Peter and Paul, and our own, we declare, pronounce, and define that the doctrine which holds that the blessed Virgin Mary was, from the first instant of her conception, by a singular grace and favor of Jesus Christ, Savior of humankind, preserved free of all stain of original sin, is a doctrine revealed by God, and that it must therefore be firmly and constantly believed by all the faithful.[17]

It was nine years before the new liturgy that was promised actually was promulgated. It was truly new, but followed that of Leonard of Nogarolis for the opening prayer and the Communion antiphon. The two readings of the Mass were taken respectively from the Book of Proverbs (Prov 8:22-35, the praise Wisdom gives herself)[18] and the Gospel According to Luke (Luke 1:26-28, the angel's greeting to Mary). Our present liturgy is distinguished from the preceding one by the choices of biblical readings, of which there are three. The first is the page from Genesis called the "Proto-Gospel" (Gen 3:9-15, 20) because, coming immediately after the story of the fall of Adam and Eve, it is the first declaration of salvation through the victory of a woman—a new Eve—who will crush the head of the serpent. Afterwards comes the thanksgiving of Paul to God, the Father of our Lord Jesus Christ, he who "has blessed us in Christ with every spiritual blessing . . . as he chose us in him, before the foundation of the world, to be holy and without blemish before him" (Eph 1:3-

6, 11-12). Mary is the perfect model of this vocation of all the faithful to sanctity, since God preserved her from all stain of sin. The passage of the annunciation was kept, but this time in its entirety (Luke 1:28-42). Elsewhere, the Missal of Paul VI contains a Preface and a proper text for the Eucharistic Prayer.

> You allowed no stain of Adam's sin
> to touch the Virgin Mary.
> Full of grace, she was to be a worthy mother of your Son,
> your sign of favor to the Church at its beginning,
> and the promise of its perfection as the bride of Christ,
>   radiant in beauty.
> Purest of virgins, she was to bring forth your Son,
> the innocent lamb who takes away our sins.
> You chose her from all women to be our advocate with you
> and our pattern of holiness.[19]

As unique as is Mary's privilege, it does not mean that she is a creature who does not belong to this world, to our common humanity; on the contrary. Preserved from sin from the first instant of her conception, the Mother of God is the Woman, "the mother of all the living " (Gen 3:20), just as God willed her to be on the day of creation.

> Because she was to become the mother of the Lord, Mary saw herself set free all her life long, from alpha to omega, from the power of evil, which we all unknowingly are exposed to because we belong, historically, to this "world." Without ceasing to be human, since sin does not define human nature, the Virgin is "deconditioned" in relation to the enslavement to sin that is inherent in our human condition. This is because of the role that God reserves for her in the economy of love: The one who is to give her flesh and blood to the Lord must be freed from all other control but that of the Lord. This is what we mean by her "Immaculate Conception."[20]

Mary: Full of Grace, New Eve, Mother of the Living

Salvation Is First Proclaimed Immediately After the Fall

In the form of a simple story rich in images, the Book of Genesis teaches us some profound and subtle truths on the subject of sin and its entry into the world, despite the fact that God had created man and woman in a state of sanctity: "In his image, in the divine image he created him."[1] The sages of Israel had long meditated on the human condition, on the nature of sin, and the conduct of God toward sinners. There was nothing theoretical in their thinking; it was based on the historical experience of the relations between the Lord and his people. When the Israelites tried to live outside of the Law that had been given them, they knew nothing but misfortune. But God did not abandon them in this sad state. He gave them assurances even when he punished them for their sins: In his eyes, the future still remained open, and forgiveness was always offered. This is the way of God. He created human beings to share his life with him, and the happiness that he enjoyed fully. Nothing could make him change his mind; he never had a share in the breaking-off of relations between him and his people brought about by the unfaithfulness of his creatures. The very first proclamation of salvation dates from the original fall from grace. This is what the liturgy of the feast of the Immaculate Conception of the Virgin Mary teaches us (Gen 3:9-15, 20).[2]

Whatever concrete form it may take, sin is an act of rebellion on the part of the creature, who decides he or she can lead his or her own life, and determine what is right and what is wrong, without reference to God. It is a truly senseless thing to do, almost suicidal, in a way. For it is tantamount to cutting oneself off from the source of life and being. The story of the Book of Genesis expresses this in a particularly thought-provoking manner. Man was living with God in a climate of trusting familiarity: Now he is afraid of him. He becomes aware that he is naked, his nudity being a symbol of his profound poverty and lack of protection against all the forces of destruction that up until then he had been secure from.[3] "Who told you that you were naked? You have eaten, then, from the tree of which I had forbidden you to eat!'' By speaking thus to Adam, he wants him to become aware of the seriousness of his sin, and give him the chance to beg his forgiveness. But Adam tries to deny his responsibility, even going so far as to blame God, in a manner of speaking, for what had happened: ''The woman whom you put here with me—she gave me fruit from the tree, and so I ate it.'' The loss of communion with God sets his creatures against each other, despite their common lot, as we see in the sudden aggression of the man against the woman whom he had first greeted with marveling joy, saying: ''This one, at last, is bone of my bones, and flesh of my flesh'' (Gen 2:23). As for the woman, she also tries to deny her responsibility: ''The serpent tricked me into it, so I ate it.'' Here we are at the very root of the evil that has entered into the world. So God, who has had nothing to say in response to the pitiful explanations of Adam and Eve, turns with severity to the serpent: ''Because you have done this, you shall be banned from all the animals and from all the wild creatures. On your belly shall you crawl, and dirt shall you eat all the days of your life.'' This is a condemnation without appeal of the one through whom sin entered into the world.

There are a number of reasons for the choice of the serpent, this sinister animal so unlike all the others, to stand for that evil being who led the woman into temptation and inveigled her into eating the fruit of the forbidden tree.[4] Still, his identity remains mysterious, for the author of the story of the fall gives us no information at all about him. The only text of the Old Testament that speaks of him is in the Book of Wisdom (Wis 2:24): '' . . . By the envy of the devil, death entered the world.'' Similarly, John's Gospel tells us that Jesus said, about those who do not listen to his words: ''You belong to your father the devil'' (John 8:44). On the other hand, the Book of Revelation is more explicit about the ''huge dragon, the ancient serpent, who is called the Devil and Satan, who deceived the whole world'' (Rev 12:9). This is in line with the whole tradition of patristic thinking on the fall: The instigator of original sin is the devil, that creature of God who is the cause of all the evils that have befallen humanity and who even now lays pitfalls for it and tries to turn it against God.[5] The author of the story calls upon popular imagery to describe the curse that befell the serpent: The fact that he crawls on his belly and seems to eat the dust of the earth, which its presence in the desert seems to mean, is because God so willed it and condemned him to live this way. However this may be, from this point on, there is open and merciless hostility between the tempter and the woman he deceived, between him and the descendants of the "mother of the living." This battle that began thus in the very beginning of days will prove to be violent: The serpent will remain dangerous, and will continue to try to make as much mischief as he can. But he will finally be vanquished by the offspring of the woman.[6]

The term "offspring" can be interpreted in either the singular or the plural sense.[7] The literary context of the story invites us to understand that the author had in mind an individual person, sent by God, who will fight out a decisive battle with the serpent, and triumph over him.

> In this history, individuals play the most important roles: Adam, Noah, Abraham, Isaac, Jacob, Joseph, etc. When God blesses the individual, this blessing is reflected upon the group or the people. . . . What is more, the author of the oracle was familiar with the hope of a Messiah, the expectation of the one the peoples will all obey (Gen 49:10), the one through whom Jacob overcomes all his foes (Num 24:19).[8]

But we are left with another question: Who, among the offspring of the woman, will vanquish the serpent? The Hebrew does not give us precise information: In fact, it uses a neuter pronoun. The Greek translates it with a masculine one, interpreting the text to mean that the serpent will be crushed by a son of the woman. But St. Jerome's (ca. 342–420) Latin translates the Hebrew neuter with a feminine pronoun.[9] He carries one step forward the messianic perspective of the Greek translation. It is a daughter of the woman, a new Eve, who will crush the head of the serpent.[10] This interpretation undoubtedly goes farther than the intention of the original author. But he does say that she who was called until then the woman—*ishah*—because she was taken from the man—*ish*—(Gen 2:22-23), receives a new name—*Hawwah* (Eve)—meaning "the living woman," because thanks to her, and despite her sin, life continues. Christian tradition has interpreted this text in the light of later revelation and the coming of the Lord. It has never suggested that this was the meaning the author of Genesis had in mind, but it has seen in this "mother of all the living" the one who was to give life to the Living One above all others, the new Adam, who vanquished the ancient serpent, sin, and death.

> Eve was a virgin, without corruption: When she conceived the word of the serpent, she gave birth to disobedience and death. But the Virgin Mary conceived faith and joy when the angel Gabriel announced to her the good news that the Spirit of the Lord would come upon her, and the power of the Most High would cover her with its shadow, and that for this reason the holy Being who was to be born of her would be the Son of God; and

she answered: "May it be done to me according to your word." And so there was born of her the one of whom Scripture speaks, the one through whom God destroys the serpent along with the men and angels who resemble him, and delivers from death those who do penance for their sins and believe in him.[11]

Faith teaches that human beings were created by God "in his image," in a state of friendship and familiarity with their Creator. But experience shows that humans are born wounded in their will, which instead of leading them to turn spontaneously toward God induces them into sin. On the other hand, history bears witness that God has not abandoned his creatures: On the contrary, he has never ceased calling them back to himself, showing himself ever ready to forgive them at the first sign of repentance. These are fundamental questions that try to understand the world and human condition, to find the path of one's proper vocation, and finally to discover something of the mystery of God himself. The inspired sages of Israel meditated at great length on these questions. In order to throw some light on them we must go back to the very origins of humankind. Man's friendship and closeness with God were disturbed even from that moment on, because the man and the woman, tempted by the serpent, rejected their condition as creatures, which alone ensured their happiness. They let themselves be persuaded by the serpent that if they were to assert their independence from God they would enjoy an autonomy full of promises. But in fact they cut themselves off from the source of life which came from God. And so they found themselves naked, exposed to all the dangers of a now hostile environment, and defenseless in the face of all the attacks of evil in all its forms. The harmony that had reigned between them gave way to a state of war that is illustrated clearly by the drama of Cain who killed his own brother, Abel.

But the hope of salvation also has its roots in what happened in the very beginning. From that very moment, and for the first time, God promised to restore the original order that was disturbed by sin. He announced that from among the offspring of the woman, known henceforth as Eve, the "mother of the living," there would appear one who would vanquish the "ancient serpent" who was responsible for original sin. A second Adam would come, the leader of a new humanity, born of another woman, who would crush the head of the serpent. This is the first proclamation of the good news of salvation, whose nature was still unclear; it is called the "proto-gospel."

Christian tradition has seen in Jesus the new Adam, and goes on from there to develop a whole theory of sin and the salvation brought by

Christic.[12] It has also seen in Mary, the mother of the Savior, the new Eve, whose coming was announced after the fall. For these reasons this text of the Book of Genesis was chosen for the feast of the Immaculate Conception. It helps to throw light on the mystery being celebrated, giving it a place in the mystery of redemption.

> *Sing to the Lord a new song,*
> *for he has done wondrous deeds.*

> Sing to the LORD a new song,
>   for he has done wondrous deeds;
> His right hand has won victory for him,
>   his holy arm.
> The LORD has made his salvation known:
>   in the sight of all the nations he has revealed his justice.
> He has remembered his kindness and his faithfulness
>   toward the house of Israel.
> All the ends of the earth have seen
>   the salvation by our God.
> Sing joyfully to the LORD, all you lands . . .
>   sing joyfully before the king, the LORD.
> (Ps 98:1-4a, 6b)

God Has Filled Us with Grace, Chosen Us, Predestined Us

God's plan for our salvation, the mystery that was decided upon from all eternity, hidden throughout the centuries, realized in Jesus Christ, and now revealed to those who believe, is taking place in the life of the Church. This is the subject of the Letter of Paul to the Ephesians.[13] It begins with a solemn thanksgiving in liturgical style addressed to the Father for the work he has accomplished for the sake of the faithful through his Son.[14] The excerpt read today applies in a very particular way to the Virgin Mary who was chosen before the creation of the world to be holy and blameless in the sight of God (Eph 1:3-6, 11-12).

"Blessed be the God and Father of our Lord Jesus Christ, who has blessed us in Christ with every spiritual blessing in the heavens!" The tone of the entire letter is set in this vibrant act of thanksgiving.[15] With an enthusiasm that he can barely restrain, the apostle celebrates the working out of salvation, which follows a strictly Trinitarian pattern: Everything comes from the Father who is "in heaven," through Jesus Christ, his Son, in the Holy Spirit. But everything also returns to the Father, "for the praise of the glory of his grace that he granted us in the beloved."[16] He gives a clear idea of what this plan of the Father was, in a series of striking statements: "[God] chose us in him, before the foundation of the world, to be holy and without blemish before him. In love he destined us for adoption to himself through Jesus Christ, in accord with the favor of his will. . . ." It would be hard to find a clearer expression of the truth that the initiative for salvation comes from the Father, from his love. Similarly, the role of Christ is emphasized: He was part of the decision along with the Father, and it was "in him" and "through him" that the Father "administers everything according to his will and counsel." We seem to hear echoes of John: "He was in the beginning with God. And all things came to be through him, and without him nothing came to be" (John 1:2-3).

The first stage of the accomplishment of God's plan was the election of Israel, the people set apart that God chose for himself.[17]

In the Letter to the Romans, Paul enumerates the privileges of the people to whom he belongs: "They are Israelites; theirs the adoption, the glory, the covenants, the giving of the law, the worship, and the promises . . . the patriarchs." Israel was chosen to receive and transmit to the world the hope in the coming of the Messiah: " . . . and from them, according to the flesh, is the Messiah. God who is over all be blessed forever" (Rom 9:4-5). Everything that is said in this text of capital importance holds true, eminently, in the case of the Virgin Mary. If every one of us was chosen "before the foundation of the world," how much more so she who was to be the Mother of the Savior, whom God had, from all eternity, intended to send as the Savior of the world. In this sense she is the first of the creatures whom God has chosen.[18] In her son, Jesus Christ, she was filled to overflowing with the blessing of the Spirit: "Virgin without compare, mirror of the holiness of God, dwelling place of the Holy Spirit, ark of the new covenant, queen of patriarchs, of the prophets, of the apostles, of all the saints."[19] She is the perfect model of all those whom God has chosen in his love to be "holy and without reproach in his eyes," those who have put their hope "in Christ, for the praise of the glory" of the Father.

"The Lord Is With You, Mary, Full of Grace"

The Gospel of the annunciation of the Lord is a page of revelation on the origin and nature of Jesus, born of the Virgin Mary. It is in the context of the nativity of the Lord that we can best grasp the full meaning and intent of Luke, who wrote it with the greatest of care.[20] We read it again on March 25, when we perhaps place greater emphasis on the way in which the "servant of the Lord" welcomed the words that were spoken to her by the angel,[21] without getting too far away from its deepest meaning. On the feast of the Immaculate Conception we look particularly at the holiness of Mary (Luke 1:26-38).[22]

The story of the annunciation is written in the form of a dialogue between the angel Gabriel who "was sent from God to a town of Galilee called Nazareth, to a virgin" by the name of Mary. This is the classic literary genre in the Old Testament for proclamations of extraordinary births[23] or the calling of certain prophets.[24] Its use here suggests that we are at the place where the two covenants meet and separate. But what is most striking is the place given in this annunciation to the child who is to be born. This gospel concerns directly the birth of the one whom she must call Jesus, "because he will save his people from their sins" (Matt 1:21). This is why we speak of the annunciation of the Lord.[25] Everything the story tells us about the Virgin Mary must be understood in reference to her son, who gives the true measure of her greatness and of the singular grace given her by God. The story takes place in a quiet atmosphere. At the same time, the way the angel approaches the young girl of Nazareth and the whole tone of the dialogue express the great respect of the messenger sent by God for the girl whose house he enters. He begins by greeting her, not in the usual way in Israel—by saying "Peace" (*Shalom*)—but using the Greek expression, *Kaire* ("Rejoice" [JB]). But this is precisely how in the Greek translation of the Bible, the *Septuagint*, the prophets addressed the "Daughter of Zion" when they were announcing the approaching coming of the Messiah: "Shout for joy, O daughter Zion, sing joyfully, O Israel! Be glad and exult with all your heart, O daughter Jerusalem!" (Zeph 3:14);[26] "Fear not, O land! exult and rejoice! For the Lord has done great things" (Joel 3:21); "Rejoice heartily, O daughter Zion, shout for joy, O daughter Jerusalem! See, your king shall come to you" (Zech 9:9).[27] More than any other, and the first of all, Mary should rejoice, for, as the angel says to her, "The Lord is with you." We are reminded of the prophecy of the Book of Isaiah: "The virgin shall be with child, and bear a son, and shall name him Immanuel" ("God is with us").[28] So Mary is at the very heart of the accomplishment of all that was promised, and at the same time she appears as the perfect prefigurement of the people of God who have been "highly favored" by the Lord.

The angel also says that she is "full of grace" [JB], a phrase that expresses how fully God dwells in her, she who is filled with holiness.[29] There are no obstacles in her to the action of the Holy Spirit and to the "power of the Most High" who is going to "overshadow" her, under its protection.[30] The Spirit will make her, a virgin, the mother of the Son of God, for "nothing is impossible with God."[31] And the scene ends with Mary's acquiescence: "Behold, I am the handmaid of the Lord. May it be done to me according to your word."

> Her way of saying yes not only sums up and anticipates all the yeses of humanity, who have died or are yet to be born, but it represents such a profound consecration of self that, contrasted with us and with those who are called saints because they have given themselves so passionately to God, Mary is entirely summed up in her yes, to which there are no afterthoughts at all. She will never take her yes back; on the contrary, she will only give it more depth, from the visitation to the nativity, from the visit to the Temple to the hidden life at Nazareth, from Cana to Calvary, from the Upper Room to the last encounter. Day after day, she "heard the word of God and kept it," so that at the hour of her death there was nothing in her but a pure offering.[32]

From before the creation of the world, God had chosen Mary, a young girl from Nazareth, to be the mother of his beloved Son, Jesus, the Savior of the world. He wanted her holy and without blemish in his eyes, "full of grace," like no other of his creatures. The new Eve, "younger than sin, younger than the race she sprang from,"[33] escaped the bite of the ancient serpent, the instigator of original sin. This is the faith of the Church when it celebrates the solemnity of the Immaculate Conception of the Virgin Mary. "She is not only the first among creatures, she is a unique creature, infinitely unique, infinitely rare."[34]

But it is to God and his Christ that we raise our adoration and thanksgiving in the Christian assembly, when we contemplate in Mary the first of the redeemed, the image of the Church that the Lord has wanted "that he might present to himself the church in splendor, without spot or wrinkle or any such thing, that she might be holy and without blemish" (Eph 5:27).

> Behold the dawn before the day,
> Behold the virgin mother,
> The woman promised from all ages.
> She has built her home
> In the wishes of the Father.
> No fear, no refusal,
> Comes to trouble the work of grace,
> Her heart is full of unspeakable waiting.
> She offers to God the silence
> Where the Word dwells.

Under the answering look
The new times leapt within her,
The mysterious advent of the kingdom to be born.
The Spirit overshadows her
And gently keeps her.
Here is the unwed spouse,
Mary the servant and the queen,
Who bears in secret the salvation
 of the world.
The Blood of Christ redeems her
But she is its source.[35]

In the Margins of a Travel Diary

Sometimes we say of a trip that we take all the time, "I know it by heart" or "I could do it with my eyes closed." This means that from force of habit there are no more surprises. On this trip with all its familiar landmarks we no longer pay any attention to the signs that may point out difficulties or dangers or that require us to be patient: We know them all. We know also that the monotony of the long straight roads carries a risk of falling asleep. Everything has been thought of: rest stops where we can relax a while, service stations where we can refuel. There is never any change in this routine, except for days when one may be particularly tired or when traffic is unusually heavy or something unforeseen happens. It may happen that we go through the liturgical year in the same routine way. The stages along the way, always the same, are so well known to us: Sundays, those brief pauses that we regularly observe or that we may allow ourselves to skip for a variety of reasons, especially during that long monotonous stretch of Ordinary Time. On the other hand, we may be more scrupulous about observing the major feasts like Christmas, Easter, Pentecost, the Assumption, All Saints Day, and perhaps a few others. We tend to wake up somewhat during Lent, or at least we try. But in general, we find ourselves saying, like Qoheleth (Eccl 1:2-11), that "A liturgical year begins on the first Sunday of Advent and ends on the Saturday of the Thirty-fourth week in Ordinary Time; the next day we begin the new liturgical year, which will be identical, even though we call it by a different letter. But whether it is Year A, Year B, or Year C, there is really nothing new from one liturgical year to another: a perpetual return to the beginning, with no surprises in store." However, when we take the time to attentively go over the three years of the liturgical cycle, such a judgment—or prejudice—soon reveals itself as baseless.

A Surprising Long-Distance Hike

Going through the liturgical year reminds one of a long hike, offering so much more variety and pleasure than a highway that is by definition a place from which all natural charm has been systematically removed.

This trail has well-marked distance markers, but it allows and even favors a great freedom. Every Sunday and every feast day we gather together to hear the word that the Church has chosen to share with us. The homily reminds us that this word is being enacted every day, today as well. But Scripture is so rich that we can find something new in it every time we hear it. We can also make ourselves a little store of it with which to nourish ourselves during the week.

Every liturgical celebration, no matter how dynamic, always has some moments when one can do some self-examining, express oneself openly to God, or remain silent and simply savor what the Lord is saying or see how one "shapes up" in relation to what is being asked. But we can also simply stay quietly in the presence of the Lord because we do not know what to think or say. On the highway it is forbidden to stop and dangerous to slow down in order to get a better look at some beautiful scenery, and the slightest distraction can be fatal. But on the long journey of the liturgical year we can do all those things. It is important to remain attentive to the word and to the Spirit and not to let our minds wander down distracting alleys and dead-end streets. We should remain alert. But there is room for a good deal of personal freedom here. One's personal maturity and degree of spiritual development also come into play. If we consider the liturgical books alone, every Year A is the same, as are Year B and Year C. But each one of us knows from experience that when we actually live through these years, for better or worse, they are not the same at all. There is always something new to see that we missed on an earlier journey through the same landscape—we missed something marvelous because we were not in the right frame of mind to appreciate it. This often happens when we do the same old familiar route for the hundredth time or when we suddenly see something in a lovely landscape that we've been looking at for years. Sometimes we are shocked, and justifiably so, when we hear tourists who are distracted or in a hurry say: "It's always the same thing" or, even worse, "I already saw it last year" when the guide points something out to them. And while it is always a good idea to prepare a trip ahead of time, we perhaps draw the most benefit from a long trip by sharing our discoveries with others who have been there with us.

The Liturgy and Its Paths Through the Bible
As we hear Scripture proclaimed throughout the liturgical year, we are struck by the fact that a certain number of texts are repeated more than

once in the same year. To give just two examples: the story of the annunciation of the Lord (Luke 1:26-38) that is read on the Fourth Sunday
of Advent in Year B, as well as on March 25 and December 8; and the
episode of the transfiguration that is read on the Second Sunday of Lent
and on August 6.[1] What is more, except for Ordinary Time when one
Gospel is read continuously from one Sunday to the next, the liturgy
draws on several different books of the Bible from one week to the next.[2]
And, with the noteworthy exception of Advent and Lent, what is perhaps even more confusing, the second reading, taken from the apostolic
writings, was not chosen because it "fits" in with the theme of the first
reading. Clearly the liturgy has its own particular way of reading Scripture, which is quite different from what might be called "studious" reading and that other kind of reading we call *lectio divina*. We have here three
levels of reading the Bible that are apparently independent from one
another.

Studious reading of the Bible is like any other when we read an entire
book sequentially, from the first to the last page.[3] This way we follow
the development of the author's thought and the story line, paragraph
by paragraph. It may happen that an interruption makes us forget what
we had been reading, forcing us to go back in the text and sometimes
even re-read the book from the beginning. It is certainly possible, especially in the case of a book that develops one particular subject, to take
a given passage and quote it in another context dealing with the same
subject. This is done all the time in order to illustrate or define one's
thought, by borrowing from an author who has said, better than we ever
could, exactly what we wish to express. But not all books "read like a
novel." They often demand an effort of attention in order to follow the
thought of the author's cultural background, vocabulary, and even the
more general context of the author's thought. In these cases it becomes
necessary to begin with an introduction,[4] and one's reading will bear more
fruit if the edition one is reading contains good footnotes.[5] Such notes
will invariably explain how the author is using a particular word, the
meaning of a given concept, etc. They may also send the reader to other
parts of the book or other works of the same period. It is not unusual
to do this sort of studious reading with a pencil in hand, in order to underline certain passages or to make some personal notations.

We have today some very good translations that favor this studious
reading of the Bible, but none of them claim to be perfect or the only good
one. It may happen that for a particular passage the Hebrew or Greek

reading is not sure, or that there are several plausible ways to interpret it, given that there is no punctuation, no division into paragraphs or chapters. It is always difficult to go from one language to another, and it carries some risks. It is impossible to transmit all the nuances of meaning of a word or expression, the grammatical construction, or even just the sound of the words in our ear. The translator has to make choices. Usually, modern translations of the Bible give explanations of these choices in the footnotes, pointing out other possible translations, pointing out important nuances of meaning with the help of a glossary or a brief explanation, etc. But it is often useful to use more than one translation and compare the two.[6]

This kind of reading can be hard work, truly studious, for instance, when one tries to find the meaning and semantic evolution of a particular word or expression. One has to consult several books at the same time. A commentary is often useful. For this sort of work one needs a whole collection of books besides the Bible, and it helps to have the help, at least at the beginning, of a specialist in such study, an exegete. We will immediately find out that such an effort is well worth the trouble, not only for a better understanding of the particular text—this is our first goal—but also to benefit from our study in order to get more, personally, from our reading of the Bible—and this is our ultimate purpose. For it is essential first to understand as much as possible of the text itself, objectively, one might say. For it is the Word of God, and must be accepted as is. Without this first, laborious stage, the reading of the Bible can become overly subjective. Carried to the extreme, this can lead us to read into it what isn't there, seeking support for one's own intuitions, answers to personal questions that are not there in the text, etc. So it behooves us to be prudent when we approach a text to find out "what it means to me," when that means looking for the thoughts and feelings that its reading calls forth in us.[7]

Lectio divina is certainly to be distinguished from the above studious reading of the Bible, but the line of demarcation between the two is not so clear. It is easy to go back and forth between the two without noticing it and, indeed, this is the goal of the Christian who studies Scripture. Studious reading—exegesis—does not necessarily require faith. One can study the Bible as if it were just any text to find out its meaning without seeing it as the Word of God,[8] whereas *lectio divina* is always an act of faith. In it we savor the text from a spiritual perspective, nourished by the Word of God. We do so in an atmosphere of prayer and contemplation. It can be done in a group, but in that case there must be enough time for silence. More normally, this kind of reading is done in solitude, face to face with God, attentive to the Holy Spirit. This is not to say that we no longer pay attention to the literal meaning of a text, quite the contrary: *Lectio divina* is based on it and must never lose sight of it lest we get lost in excessive subjectivity and the mirages of the imagination. This is why the use of a commentary is helpful. One useful way to do this kind of reading is to keep the Bible open to a particular passage and to have next to it, easy to consult, a commentary by one of the Fathers of the Church or another spiritual writer.[9] But each of us has to find the best method for him or herself, making sure, however, that it is a valid approach. The connection between this spiritual reading of the Bible and the more studious kind of reading is obvious and must not be lost sight of.[10]

"Liturgical reading" is again different from the other two types in several ways. First of all, the texts have been chosen by the Church, read out loud by a reader, and assigned to particular celebrations in the Lectionary. Instead of focusing on just one book of the Bible on Sundays and feast days, we read a passage from the Old Testament, an excerpt from the apostolic writings, and lastly a portion from the Gospel.[11] It is often hard to see the reasons behind the choices, e.g., why there are certain excerpts selected from their context, and why such and such a sequence has been chosen for the liturgical year. The rhythm of the service does not leave much time for thought on these questions, as in studious reading or for meditation on the text as in *lectio divina,* for as soon as they have been read, the Lectionary is closed. It is true that we sing or recite a responsorial psalm after the first reading, which helps us interiorize it, make it our own, and turn toward God in a moment of prayer after, sometimes, a moment of silence. But it is sung by a soloist, and only a few verses at that, to which we respond with the refrain. The homily follows the reading of the Gospel, but again we are listening to words. Moreover, if this reading has some relationship with the first two, it is only in passing, and we sometimes wish that it would clearly respond to one or the other. And we cannot expect an explanation or a chance to ask questions. For all these reasons, the readings from the Bible during liturgical celebrations are often disconcerting for the faithful and leave them unsatisfied.

In order to understand this "liturgical reading" and benefit from it, it is important to leave certain prejudices behind, in particular the perceived need to hear only those passages that transmit ideas or some immediately practical teaching. The purpose of the liturgy is not to teach either Church doctrine or spirituality. It is the celebration of a mystery that we all share in, here and now, thanks to visible acts and our own participation. The proclamation of Scripture is a part of the liturgical celebration. The texts are chosen, taken out of their context, and ordered so as to shed light upon the meaning of the liturgical season or feast day, to help each of us to enter personally and within the Church into the celebration of the mystery. Of course, the liturgy does have great teaching and catechetical value, but only as a sacramental action, that is to say, with the use of efficacious signs, among which the proclamation of the Word of God holds an important, but not separate, place. So the liturgical reading of a text has a distinctly different perspective from that of either the studious reading or the *lectio divina*. Even when, as in Ordinary Time, the reading of the Bible is more or less sequential—a Gospel reading, and then a text from the apostolic writings,[12]—it does not purport to have us read an entire book of the Bible for its own sake, as we might do alone or in a study group.

It is also true that the biblical passages read during a liturgical celebration may be taken out of their original literary context, but they are inserted into a new context, that of the liturgy being celebrated within a given community at a given time. Any number of outside events, such as an anniversary, the profession of faith of a group of youngsters, a jubilee, the arrival of a new parish priest, the feast day of the community's patron saint, a disaster of some sort—all these, and others like them, can qualify the nature of the celebration, and are, loosely speaking, elements of the liturgical context. None of these circumstantial elements take away from the primary meaning of the texts read, but they can broaden the dimensions of the mystery, which in turn can give unexpected new meaning to the human event. In such a case, the same page from Scripture can take on another precise meaning depending on the liturgical context in which it is proclaimed. It is a question of emphasizing one or other aspect of its contents.[13] Thus there is no real conflict between the liturgical reading of Scripture and the others; on the contrary. The three ways of reading the Bible are closely related, but in a distinct hierarchy.[14]

The studious reading is fundamental; it will always be the indispensable point of departure—we must always come back to it. We cannot construct anything that is not based on the primary and objective meaning of the text. Any reading of the Bible that would lose such contact would quickly deteriorate, whether we are aware of it or not, and the texts would lend themselves to being manipulated or turned into plays on words, with the Bible used to illustrate anything at all, or its opposite! Still, this care to stay in close contact with the primary meaning of the text has nothing in common with the sort of fundamentalism that sees nothing in Scripture but the strictly literal meaning, and refuses to take into account the literary genre of the work or the intentions of the author, and misses the deepest meaning of the text altogether.[15] To get as close as possible to that deeper meaning, we need to see, also, how the particular text was progressively understood in tradition: The Bible itself has never ceased re-reading earlier stories, oracles, and past events in the light of later experiences and revelations. One of the best known and most meaningful example concerns the Exodus. Re-reading the story of the flight from Egypt and the forty years of wandering in the desert has led us to see that this fundamental event foreshadowed and prefigured what was going to happen later on, what God was to accomplish in present times. Every liberation of a people where God took the initiative recalls the first Exodus, which bore within itself the promise of an ultimate liberation under the leadership of a new Moses, whom Israel was expecting and yearning for. So it is no longer possible to read any of the passages referring to the flight from Egypt without reference to its later interpretation. Again and again Jesus used this traditional way of interpreting the Scriptures, and he revealed in so doing the fullness of their meaning. The story of the pilgrims of Emmaus is the most telling example: "Then beginning with Moses and all the prophets, he interpreted to them what referred to him in all the scriptures" (Luke 24:27).[16] This is why the Church has always read Scripture this way, without, of course, claiming that every detail refers to Christ.[17]

Lectio divina should be seen in the same perspective, for while the liturgical reading uses this train of thought for its celebrations, *lectio divina* benefits from its consequences. The Scriptures that we hear at Mass are accomplished, here and now, in the celebration of the mystery. And, again, this "liturgical" reading rests squarely on its studious reading.

The homily clearly is not, and should not be, an exegetical explanation of the texts read, even if sometimes it may be necessary to explain the meaning of a certain word or recall or point out briefly what may be indispensable for the understanding of the Word, to clear up or avoid certain ambiguities. But whoever gives the homily should have taken the time to look seriously—even laboriously—at the texts. And those who take part in the celebration will benefit much more from it if they have also taken the trouble to become familiar with the Bible, even doing some studious reading inasmuch as they can. At the very least they should avoid remaining in doubt as to the meaning of a certain word of text, either finding the answers to their questions on their own or by asking for help from someone competent. To do so is to take the Word of God and the liturgy seriously.[18] The Gospels tell us several times that the disciples asked Jesus to explain his words.[19]

Hearing the biblical texts proclaimed during the liturgy points us in the direction of *lectio divina*, which in turn requires us to return again and again to the studious reading of the Bible. It is for this reason that the liturgy can be considered a kind of crossroads for the various ways of reading the Scriptures, and opens the way to each.

Journeys for Today and Traditions of the Church

Today, as at any time during its history, one can speak of the eternal Church. Founded on and by Christ, its unique capstone,[20] one amid the diversity of communities that constitute it, holy by the grace of the Spirit of holiness, open to all who are called by the Father and who, in faith, receive baptism for the forgiveness of sins (Matt 28:19), the Church offers the promise of eternal life (Matt 16:18). But to speak of an eternal liturgy is ambiguous, even false, if we are speaking of any one liturgy—for example, Roman liturgy—and even more so if we mean a particular ritual, for instance, the Mass, or a given sacrament.

We must not forget that the liturgy evolved over time and is still evolving. Our bits of information from the first few centuries of the life of the Church are precious, but they are fragmentary and indirect. Starting with the fourth century, our sources become more numerous and more precise. From the fifth century on, we begin to see taking shape the great liturgical families that historians classify in two groups: the Syrian and the Alexandrian. Within each, different rites are distinguished: Assyro-Chaldean, Syro-Malabar, Syro-Antiochian, Maronite, Byzantine, Armenian, Coptic, and Ethiopian. Despite their common origins, they all have their distinct character, beginning with their language.

The liturgies of the West gave up Greek for Latin toward the middle of the fourth century and were quite diverse until the eighth century, with the Church of Rome exerting no particular influence on the others. It was Charlemagne (ca. 742–814), king of the Franks in 768, then emperor of the West in 800, who imposed the exclusive use of Roman liturgical books throughout his kingdom in place of all others that had been in use until then. This decision reflected his politics of unification and cohesion. It was not until the time of St. Gregory VII (1073–1085) that liturgical homogeneity became an ecclesiological principle: This was the first great liturgical reform in the West. From then on, the popes claimed the right to make liturgical decisions for all the Churches.

The other great liturgical reform took place at the Council of Trent.[21] During the twenty-fifth session (December 3–4, 1563), it was decreed that a "new" Missal was to be published. Pope St. Pius V (1566–1572) did so four years later, on July 14, 1570, when he promulgated the *Roman Missal (Missale Romanum)*. Despite the desires of some to go even further in the revision of the liturgical books, matters rested there for three more centuries of stability in the liturgy.[22]

The liturgical reform of modern times was begun by Pius X (1903–1914) and continued by Benedict XV (1914–1922). This is why the title of the Roman Missal in use during the period before Vatican Council II said: "Following the decree of the Council of Trent edited by order of St. Pius V, revised by the other pontiffs, reformed by Pius X and published by the authority of Benedict XV."[23] It was therefore a dated Missal, as was the one of Paul VI (April 6, 1969). None of them claimed to be an "eternal Missal."[24] Not all the reforms have been so in depth as that of the Council of Trent or of Vatican II, four centuries later. But like the Church, the liturgy will always need reforming.[25] It often happens, moreover, that the most important changes are not the most spectacular. In any case, the reforms of liturgical structures and the publication of new books do not constitute an end in themselves.

> It is the goal of this most sacred Council to intensify the daily growth of Catholics in Christian living; to make more responsive to the requirements of our times those Church observances which are open to adaptation; to nurture whatever can contribute to the unity of all who believe in Christ; and to strengthen those aspects of the Church which can help summon all of [humankind] into her embrace.[26]

And finally, the best of reforms that are decreed, and the best thought-out books can do nothing to further the objectives of those who had worked for the reforms if the means to reform are not used. It sometimes takes years—history tells us so—for the fruits of liturgical reform to ripen. But the evolution of the liturgy, its progress as well as its decline, also depends on a number of other factors: the state of contemporary theology, the knowledge and importance of Scripture, the missionary activity and apostolic zeal of the ecclesial entities, and the fervor and spiritual dynamism of the faithful. Liturgical evolution also depends on the evolution of Christian doctrine, and in fact, facilitates it.[27]

The opposite is true, too: The liturgy contributes greatly to the life of the Church in every domain, for if it "does not exhaust the entire activity of the Church" and of Christians, it is "the summit toward which the activity of the Church is directed; at the same time, it is the fount from which all the Church's power flows."[28]

On October 11, 1962, Pope John XXIII (1958–1963) declared: "The lights spread by this Council will be a source of spiritual enrichment for the Church. After having found new energy in it, she will look fearlessly towards the future."[29] And Pope Paul VI (1963–1978) celebrated its ending on December 7, 1965, with these words: "The entire Council can be summed up in this religious conclusion: It is nothing but a friendly and pressing call to humanity to find once more, through the path of fraternal love, this God of whom it was said: To depart from him is to perish; to turn to him is to rise again; to dwell in him is to be unshakable; to return to him is to be reborn; to live in him, is to live."[30]

May we live every liturgical year and every liturgy in this spirit, joining our praise to that of all the saints of heaven and earth!

We praise you, O Lord!
We acclaim you: you are Lord!
Yours, O Eternal Father,
is the hymn of the universe.

Before you the archangels lie prostrate,
the angels and the spirits of heaven;
they give you thanks;
they adore and they sing:

Holy, holy, holy is the Lord,
God of the Universe;
heaven and earth
are full of your glory.

The apostles glorify you,
the prophets proclaim you,
the martyrs bear witness to you;
the Church all over the world
proclaims and acknowledges you.

O God, we adore you:
Father infinitely holy,
eternal and beloved Father,
Spirit of power and of peace.

Christ, the Son of the Living God,
the Lord of glory,
you did not fear to take flesh
in the body of a virgin
to free captive humanity.

By your victory over death,
you opened up to all who believe
the gates of the kingdom;
you rule at the right hand of the Father;
you will come again in judgment.

Show yourself as friend and defender
of all, saved by your blood:
bring them with all your saints
into your glory and your light.[31]

NOTES

Introduction—Page 1

1. Vol. 1: Advent, Christmas, Epiphany; vol. 2: Lent; vol. 3: Easter Triduum and the Easter Season; vol. 4: Ordinary Time, Year A; vol. 5: Ordinary Time, Year B; vol. 6: Ordinary Time, Year C.

2. Christmas; Holy Family; Mary, Mother of God; Epiphany; and Baptism of the Lord, which is between the time of Christmas-Epiphany and Ordinary Time (vol. 1); Passion Sunday, Paschal Triduum, Ascension and Pentecost (vol. 3).

3. Every year, Ordinary Time is divided into two periods: from the Monday following the Sunday after Epiphany or following the Baptism of the Lord to Ash Wednesday; then, from the Monday after Pentecost to the Saturday before the First Sunday of Advent. The number of weeks and Sundays varies from year to year in each period. Besides this, all the available Mass texts (thirty-four for weekdays, thirty-three for Sundays) are not used every year. See *Days of the Lord* 4:12, "The Detailed Account of Sundays."

4. The *Ordo lectionum missae*, 2nd ed., nos. 164–172, pp. 93–96, groups them separately after the series of Sundays in Ordinary Time (nos. 64–162, pp. 45–88) under the title *Sollemnitates Domini tempore "per annum" occurrentes* ("Solemnities of the Lord Occurring in Ordinary Time").

5. On the one hand, the celebration of these three solemnities is not linked to a fixed Sunday or week. On the other hand, they form a contrast with Ordinary Time, "during which the liturgy does not celebrate any particular aspect of the mystery of Christ, but rather commemorates the fullness of the mystery of Christ itself, especially on Sunday" (*Universal Norms of the Liturgical Year*, no. 43).

6. In the calendar of the Liturgical Year, one speaks of the "Temporal Cycle" and "Sanctoral Cycle," two terms that belong exclusively to the technical vocabulary of the liturgy.

The Temporal Cycle designates the succession of the celebrations that structure the various liturgical "times," from the First Sunday of Advent to Saturday of the Thirty-fourth Week in Ordinary Time. Because Christmas does not always occur on the same day of the week, the date of the beginning of Advent varies from year to year. In order to establish the liturgical calendar of every year, the (movable) date of Easter must be taken into consideration. (See *Days of the Lord* 1:9–11.)

The Sanctoral Cycle—so called because it concerns the celebration of saints' feasts—is a perpetual calendar: every year, the feasts fall on the same dates.

7. In countries where the Assumption and All Saints are holy days of obligation, these feasts carry the same obligation of attendance as a Sunday, even if they fall on a weekday.

8. See *Days of the Lord* 1:1–19.

Trinity Sunday—Pages 5–7

1. This preface is found in the *Gelasian Sacramentary*, a liturgical book that goes back to the eighth century and contains all that priests needed to celebrate the "holy mysteries"

(*sacramenta*): what are now called the opening prayer, the prayer over the gifts, the prayer after communion, prefaces, canon. Sacramentaries are the ancestors of missals.

2. Before the liturgical reform of Vatican II, the preface of the Trinity was used on all Sundays after Pentecost.

3. The Mass is the work of Alcuin, abbot of St. Martin of Tours (796–804). The feast is first attested in Liège, Belgium, at the time of Bishop Stephen (903–920).

4. Preface of the Trinity. It repeats the articles of the Nicaea-Constantinople Creed that is sung at Sunday Mass.

5. St. Ambrose, bishop of Milan (339–397), *Des sacrements*, bk. 6, 2:5-6, 8, Sources chrétiennes, 25bis (Paris: Cerf, 1961) 141. This teaching is addressed to neophytes.

6. "Through our Lord Jesus Christ, your Son, who lives and reigns with you and the Holy Spirit" (when the prayer is addressed to the Father); "he who reigns with you and the Holy Spirit" (when the prayer is addressed to the Father with mention of the Son at the end); "you who live with the Father and the Holy Spirit" (when the prayer is addressed to the Son).

7. See C. Vagaggini, "La perspective christologique et trinitaire dans la liturgie," *Initiation théologique à la liturgie*, adapted from the Italian by Ph. Rouillard (Bruges: Apostolat liturgique—Paris: Société liturgique, 1959) 146–172.

8. See C. Vagaggini, "Deux points de vue sur la Trinité: Le point de vue du Nouveau Testament et la Tradition primitive," *Initiation*, 135–145.

9. We must recognize that this emphasis on the Trinitarian faith—one God in three Persons, Father, Son, and Holy Spirit—is far from superfluous today. For if Christ holds a great place in Christians' consciousness, for many, the perception of the Father and the Spirit as distinct persons remains rather vague. It seems that, for them, "God" is an idea, an abstraction, in the philosophical mode. According to recent surveys, a large percentage of Christians do not consider Christ as the true Son of God become human. As for the Holy Spirit . . .

10. St. Athanasius, bishop of Alexandria (ca. 295–373), *Lettres à Sérapion*, Sources chrétiennes 15 (Paris: Cerf, 1947) 133–134.

TRINITY SUNDAY, YEAR A—Pages 8–16

1. "I am who am": by saying this to Moses, God refused to reveal his identity ("My name is none of your business; do what I say"). These words have also been understood as the affirmation of the transcendence of God in contrast to the idols: "I am the one who is." Lastly, one can also understand: "I am who I shall be," that is to say, "My actions in the world will make clear who I am." To tell the truth, these interpretations do not exclude one another. See Henri de Lubac, *Sur les chemins de Dieu*, Traditions chrétiennes (Paris: Cerf, 1983) 163–164; "Yahweh" in *Vocabulaire de théologie biblique* (Paris: Cerf, 1970) cols. 1387–1390; "Yahvé" in *Dictionnaire encyclopédique de la Bible* (Paris: Cerf, 1987) 1347–1350; the notes of the *Bible de Jérusalem*, editio major (Paris: Cerf, rev. 1973), and the *Traduction oecuménique de la Bible*, edition intégrale (Paris: Cerf, rev. 1988).

The Lectionary usually translates it "The Lord," a translation of the Hebrew *Adonai*, which the Jews used in order not to pronounce the divine name. To avoid all risk of distraction, when the vowels were placed in the Hebrew text of the Bible, the Jews punctuated "Yahweh" (which was not pronounced) with the vowels of Adonai (which was said instead). Not knowing about this, some read as if the written vowels corresponded to the consonants of "Yahweh" with the resulting barbarism "Jehovah."

2. The root of the Hebrew word *rahum*, which means "tender," designates the bowels: God is he who has a heart, feelings coming from the innermost part of himself. But this

kindness does not make him a pliable, easygoing being because of simplicity, naivete or fear of conflict. It is founded on a strong love without complacency or weakness toward evil.

3. Num 14:18; Deut 7:8-10; Neh 9:17; Pss 86:15; 145:8; Jer 32:18; Joel 2:13; Nah 1:3.

4. Isa 54; Jer 2-3; Ezek 16; Hos 1-2.

5. S. Ben Chorin, *Le judaïsme en prière: La liturgie de la synagogue*, Patrimoines (Paris: Cerf, 1984) 136. These *middot* are taken from Exod 34:6-7. Depending on the way the text is divided, the resulting list varies in length. The usual list contains thirteen "measures." Islam also has a list of attributes or names of God, ninety-nine in number (the one hundredth is unknown). The first two are "The Clement," "The Merciful," and the ninety-ninth "The Patient." See L. Gardet, *L'Islam: Religion et communauté*, Foi vivante 127 (Paris: Desclée de Brouwer, 1970) 64-65; *Dire Dieu*, by Jewish, Christian, and Muslim writers, Ecrivains croyants (Paris: Univers Media, 1978) 24-26.

6. S. Ben Chorin, *Le judaïsme en prière*, 150. The week that separates New Year's Day (Rosh Hashanah) from Yom Kippur.

7. Matt 6:9; Mark 14:36; Luke 11:2; Rom 8:15; Gal 4:6.

8. See H. de Lubac, *Sur les chemins de Dieu*, Foi vivante 22 (Paris: Aubier, 1966), particularly, "De l'ineffabilité de Dieu," 140-146, and "Postface," 241-257.

9. Hymns attributed to Gregory Nazianzen (329-389), *La Liturgie des Heures*, Office des Lectures, mercredi I and III.

10. *Le psautier: Version oecuménique, texte liturgique* (Paris: Cerf 1977) AT 41, pp. 321-323.

11. We are accustomed to name first the Father, then the Son, and, in the third place, the Holy Spirit. In Scripture, and more explicitly in the ancient patristic tradition, the Trinitarian scheme kept by the liturgy goes from Christ to the Father in the Spirit. See C. Vagaggini, "La liturgie et la dialectique christologique et trinitaire du salut: A Patre per Christum in Spiritu ad Patrem," *Initiation*, 1:135-174.

12. The Second Letter to the Corinthians is usually dated 57-58.

13. Rom 5:5; 8:1-17; 1 Cor 6:11; Eph 4:4-7.

14. St. Gregory Nazianzen (329-389), "Discours" ("Cinquième discours théologique") 31:26, Sources chrétiennes 250 (Paris: Cerf, 1978) 327.

15. The "proofs" of the existence of God have a twofold objective: to demonstrate that far from being contrary to reason, the existence of God fully satisfies reason. These proofs aim at convincing the hearers not to reject this existence as irrational, presenting it as "probable," that is, firmly supported by reason. To say, like Voltaire in *Satires: Les cabales*, "The universe puzzles me and I cannot conceive / That this clock runs and has no clock maker" means that the universe cannot be understood without a principle that explains its order and its regular functioning. But the concrete existence of a personal and transcendent God is of another order. It can be known only because God revealed himself and only in the faith that welcomes this revelation.

16. Nothing shows this better than the testimony of those who call themselves atheists. See Ch. Chabanis, *Dieu existe-t-il? Non répondent P. Anquetil, R. Aron, Ch. Boulle, etc.* (twenty personalities from different circles) (Paris: Fayard, 1973).

17. Ch. Chabanis, "Entretien avec Dieu," *Dieu existe-t-il?*, 407-408.

18. Paul's letters contain several lists of vices and types of behavior incompatible with the Christian condition: Rom 1:29-31; 13:13; 1 Cor 5:10-11; 6:9-10; Gal 5:19-21; Eph 4:31; 5:3-5; Col 3:5-8; 1 Tim 1:9-10; 6:4-5; 2 Tim 3:2-5; Titus 3:3. Each time, there is a mention of what, in one way or another, is contrary to charity, fellowship, peace, but here, as in 2 Cor 12:20, with a particular insistence.

19. Phil 3:1; 4:4-5; 1 Thess 5:16.

20. This exhortation is found in the conclusion of several apostolic letters: Rom 16:16; 1 Cor 16:20; 1 Thess 5:26; 1 Pet 5:14.

21. During the assembly, one can exchange a "sign of peace" only with one's close neigh-

bors. But this peace extends by ripples to reach those who are farther and even those who are not present at the celebration. Therefore, this gesture is not trivial, and it be would wrong to give a "false peace."

22. St. Bernard (1090–1153), *Sermons sur le Cantique des Cantiques*, 8:2, *oeuvres mystiques de saint Bernard*, trans. A. Béguin (Paris: Seuil, 1967) 133.

23. Paul applies this principle to the Church, with its many members: 1 Cor 12:12-30.

24. This passage from John's Gospel is an excerpt from personal reflections—homily-like—made by the apostle after the story of the conversation between Jesus and Nicodemus (John 3:1-5). From verse 16 on, the form is no longer that of dialogue. The verbs are in the third person and in the past tense. The terminology and the expressions used attest to a well-developed faith. Lastly, the style is akin to a rhythmic prose suggesting that of the "Prologue" of the Fourth Gospel (John 1:1-18).

25. The New Testament often speaks of the fact that Christ, "given up" for our salvation, is the supreme manifestation of God's love: John 13:1; 15:13; Rom 5:8-9; 8:32, 39; Gal 2:20; Eph 5:2, 25; Phil 2:8; 1 John 3:16; 4:7-21.

"Given up" is used to refer to the death of Christ in the words of institution: "This is my body which will be given up for you. . . . This is the cup of my blood . . . shed for you and for all." See Luke 22:19; 1 Cor 11:24.

26. This story is read during the Easter Vigil and, under a shorter form, on the Second Sunday in Lent, Year B. See *Days of the Lord* 2:83–84; 3:46–49.

27. In the catacombs, more than twenty representations of the sacrifice of Isaac have been discovered. Among these, the most remarkable, because of its early date, is in the Catacombs of Priscilla in Rome. On the date of the "Greek Chapel" where it is located, see *Days of the Lord* 5:350, n. 25.

28. R. Le Déaut, *La nuit pascale: Essai sur la signification de la Pâque juive àpartir du Targûm d'Exode XII, 42*, Analecta biblica 22 (Rome: Institut biblique pontifical, 1963) 208.

On the meaning of the word "Targum," see *Days of the Lord* 3:314, n. 17.

29. It is passion, tainted with selfishness, although the fact is denied—one loves for oneself and expects to have the right to be loved in return—which seeks to impose itself. It can go so far as to lead to murder or suicide for revenge or through despair or resentment. This does not mean that one can or should remain indifferent to the other's response: it is normal to suffer when one is not loved as one loves. One day, Jesus wept because his own were not responding to his expectation (Luke 19:41).

30. For many persons today, the drama is that no one loves them or no longer loves them; they feel that nobody loves them. One of the gravest duties and responsibilities of believers is to be present to these unloved ones, as efficient and credible witnesses—in acts and not only in words—of the love of God offered to all.

31. Henri Lacordaire, "Soixante-douzième conférence de Notre- Dame de Paris," *oeuvres* (Paris: Poussièlgue, 1893) 6:198.

32. Gal 4:4; Eph 1:10.

33. Office of Trinity Sunday, antiphons of the Canticle of Mary, *La Liturgie des Heures*, 3:6, 18.

TRINITY SUNDAY, YEAR B—Pages 17–27

1. In particular, *Pastoral Constitution on the Church in the Modern World (Gaudium et Spes)* nos. 4, 11; *Decree on Ecumenism (Unitatis Reintegratio)* no. 4; *Decree on the Ministry and Life of Priests (Presbyterorum Ordinis)* no. 69; *The Documents of Vatican II*, ed. Walter M. Abbott, S.J. (New York: Herder and Herder, 1966) 201, 209, 347–350, 543–546, 552–554.

2. This excerpt, at the end of the first discourse attributed to Moses, belongs to an ensemble made up of fragments from diverse sources.

The style of Deuteronomy is at once doctrinal and friendly, as is fitting when one wants to communicate to others strong, deeply personal convictions.

See F. Garcia-Lopez, "Le Deutéronome," *Cahiers Evangile* 63 (1988).

3. Certain chapters of Genesis were probably written at the time of Solomon (ca. 970–931 B.C.), that is, about three centuries after the Exodus, and are based on previous oral traditions. Other chapters, the first for example, were written only after the Exile.

4. See Ps 96:4-5.

5. See Isa 40:19-29; 41:21-29; 44:6-20.

6. Pss 2; 3; 4; 7; 9; 12; 13; 17; 22; 28; 30; 31; 35; 38; 41; 54; 55; 56; 59; 64; 69; 70; 73; 74; 77; 80; 83; 86; 88; 94; 102; 107; 109; 129; 140; 142; 143.

7. Vatican II, *Church in the Modern World*, nos. 4, 11.

8. See Rom 8:26; 2 Cor 12:4.

9. For Paul, not to have known Christ according to the flesh does not constitute a disadvantage for the believer (2 Cor 5:16). On the other hand, he strongly insists on the experience of the Holy Spirit, which manifests itself in the Church and believers' hearts. One often hears of the "rediscovery" of the Spirit in our time, as if it had been more or less forgotten. Such a statement should be qualified and its underpinnings closely examined. It also would be fitting to question whether to speak more of the Holy Spirit really means that one rediscovers it. What Vatican II says about it in numerous passages is quite traditional and was never forgotten. See "Table analytique," *Concile oecuménique Vatican II* (Paris: Centurion, 1967) 814–816. The liturgy, in particular, always very explicitly kept the memory of the Holy Spirit: doxology of the introductory verse at the Hours of the Office and at the end of each psalm, Gloria and Credo, invocation (epiclesis) and conclusion of the Canon at Mass. The great rites like the blessing of the holy oils and baptismal water and ordinations are accompanied by a solemn invocation of the Holy Spirit. Theology and spirituality books should also come under scrutiny. Lastly, one should take into account the expressions and the aids of "popular" piety: hymns, novenas, etc. This being said, it remains that the Holy Spirit has taken a more explicit place in many persons' consciousness—and we could not be happier about it; however, we should remember that any spiritual progress needs constant stimulation and education.

10. Matt 3:16-17; Mark 1:10-11; Luke 3:21-22; John 1:32-34. Paul goes so far as to say, "The Lord is the Spirit" (2 Cor 3:17-18). By this, he means that the Lord's action is inseparable from the Spirit's; the Spirit is present and acts where Christ is present and acts.

11. Matt 4:1; 12:28; Mark 1:12; Luke 4:14, 18; 10:21; John 3:34.

12. J. Mouroux, "Remarques sur la foi dans saint Paul," *Revue apologétique* 65 (1937) 293–294.

13. See W. Marchel, *Dieu Père dans le Nouveau Testament*, Lire la Bible 67 (Paris: Cerf, 1966).

14. B. M. Chevignard, *La doctrine spirituelle de l'Evangile*, Foi vivante 4 (Paris: Cerf, 1965) 74.

15. See Ch. Perrot, "L'Epître aux Romains," *Cahiers Evangile* 65 (1988) 43.

16. People have always uttered "every kind of evil . . . [falsely]" (Matt 5:12) against Christians. The object of these calumnies varies with time and place. But they most often come down to accusing Christ's disciples of disturbing the established order, of collaborating, consciously or not, with those who, for a variety of reasons, seek to destabilize society.

17. Simeon the New Theologian (d. 1022), *Hymnes*, 44:406-414, 425-433, Sources chrétiennes 196 (Paris: Cerf, 1973) 99–101.

18. See H. Roux, *L'Evangile du Royaume* (Geneva: Labor et fides, 1956) 293–295; S. de Dietrich, *"Mais moi je vous dis"*: *Commentaire de l'Evangile de Matthieu* (Neuchâtel: Delachaux et Niestlé, 1965) 184–187; "Lecture de l'Evangile selon saint Matthieu," *Cahiers Evangile* 9 (1974) 6–8.

19. This is the only appearance to the Eleven recorded in Matthew's Gospel. As "the first day of the week was dawning," the women who had come to the tomb were commis-

sioned by the risen Christ to announce this appointment, "Go tell my brothers to go to Galilee, and there they will see me" (28:10).

20. See J. Dupont, "L'évangile de saint Matthieu: Quelques clés de lecture," *Communautés et liturgies* 57 (1975) 9–11.

21. The "Name" designates the very person. See *Vocabulaire de théologie biblique*, cols. 827–832; *Dictionnaire encyclopédique de la Bible*, 903–904; the notes of the *Bible de Jérusalem* and of the *Traduction oecuménique de la Bible*.

22. Prophets had evoked the universal vocation of the Israel of the last times: see Isa 60:1-5; Ezek 36:23; 39:7; etc. See "Universalisme" in *Dictionnaire encyclopédique de la Bible*, 1291–1293.

23. During his ministry, Jesus addressed first of all "the lost sheep of the house of Israel" (Matt 10:5-6), although he did not refuse to welcome pagans who came to him; see Matt 8:8-13; 15:21-28; Mark 7:24-30; Luke 7:1-10.

24. Acts 2:38, 41; 8:12-13, 16, 36, 38; 10:47-48; 16:15, 33; 18:8; 19:5; 22:16; Rom 6:3-11; 1 Cor 1:13-17; 12:13; 15:29; Gal 3:27; Eph 4:5; Col 2:12; 1 Pet 3:21.

25. See "Baptême" in *Vocabulaire de théologie biblique*, cols. 110–115, and in *Dictionnaire encyclopédique de la Bible*, 182–186.

26. Matt 3:3-6; Mark 1:4; Luke 3:3; John 1:25-33.

27. Acts 1:5; 8:16; 11:16; 13:24; 18:25; 19:3-4.

28. This is undoubtedly the meaning of the expression "baptism in the name of Jesus Christ" that is not the formula of Christian baptism (Acts 2:38; 8:16; 10:48; 19:5; 22:16). See the *Bible de Jérusalem*, 1574, n. *k*, and the *Traduction oecuménique de la Bible*, 2621, n. *t*.

29. W. Trilling, "Les traits essentiels de l'Eglise du Christ," *Assemblées du Seigneur*, 1st series, no. 53 (Bruges: Publications de Saint-André, 1964) 26.

30. Today, this triple immersion is still signified by the triple pouring of water on the head of the person being baptized.

31. See Dupont, "L'Evangile de saint Matthieu," 21-25.

32. This first announcement of the gospel is called the "kerygma" (from the Greek, meaning "proclamation," "message," derived from *kerux*, a word that designates the herald whose duty was to officially proclaim the news). The kerygma, which is properly the work of evangelization, is therefore distinct from the catechesis given to those who have received the good news and have been converted.

Today, much is said about the need for a "new" or a "second" evangelization in countries formerly evangelized but returned to a practical paganism. Although he has already been announced ("first evangelization"), Jesus Christ is no longer known or recognized as the Lord by a great number of inhabitants, even by the majority of them; he must be announced anew ("second evangelization"). It is even necessary to proclaim the good news from scratch when addressing not only non-Christians settled today as immigrants in countries traditionally Christian, but also to those who, in great numbers and despite their baptism, live outside the Christian community, like immigrants from inside. Concretely, where the gospel had been received—even if poorly practiced—the Church had to catechize believers. Relying on their baptism, it constantly repeated to them, "Become what you are." Insofar as it speaks, as it must, to baptized persons who do not have or no longer have faith, the time for the kerygma has come back.

33. Vatican II, *Constitution on the Sacred Liturgy (Sacrosanctum Concilium)* no. 9, 155.

34. Vatican II, *Church in the Modern World*, no. 40:2.

35. Commission Francophone Cistercienne, *La nuit, le jour* (Paris: Desclée-Cerf, 1973) 107 (Fiche de chant L LH 114).

TRINITY SUNDAY, YEAR C—Pages 28–35

1. The Book of Job (ch. 28) underlines the unfathomable character of wisdom. In the Book of Sirach, wisdom, identified with the Law revealed by God, is a good reserved for

Israel where it dwells (Sir 24:3-10). The Book of Wisdom personifies wisdom in a eulogy that is the crowning stage of preceding reflections.

2. See "Sagesse" in *Vocabulaire de théologie biblique*, cols. 1170–1177, and in *Dictionnaire encyclopédique de la Bible*, 1153–1155; J. N. Aletti-M. Gilbert, "La Sagesse et Jésus Christ," *Cahiers Evangile* 32 (1980); P. Bonnard, *La Sagesse en personne annoncée et venue, Jésus Christ*, Lectio divina 44 (Paris: Cerf, 1965).

3. See A. Gelin, "Le chant de l'Infante (Pr 8, 22-31)," *Bible et vie chrétienne* 7 (1954) 89–95; J. Alonso-Diaz, "La Sagesse aux côtés de Dieu (Pr 8, 22-33)," *Assemblées du Seigneur*, 2nd series, no. 31 (Paris: Publications de Saint-André—Cerf, 1973) 30-35.

4. The Hebrew term—*kanab*—can mean "to beget" or "to create." "The man had relations with his wife Eve, and she conceived and bore Cain, saying, '*I have produced* a man with the help of the Lord' " (Gen 4:1); "Truly you *formed* my inmost being / you knit me in my mother's womb" (Ps 139:13).

5. A. Gelin, "Le chant de l'Infante," 91, n. 3.

6. Thus, the liturgy has recourse to these texts to suggest the Virgin Mary present in God's thought before the creation within her capacity as mother of the Savior: Prov 8:22-31 is read at the Mass of the Presentation of Mary on November 21. In a still more obvious and immediate way, what the Bible says about personified Wisdom is applied to Christ and to the Holy Spirit. This does not mean that these texts directly speak of them. But these texts are rightly applied to them because, in all truth, Christ and the Spirit are Wisdom, not only personified, but in person.

7. Gen 1:1-2:4; Job 38:4-11; Pss 24:1-2; 104:5-6.

8. The two images are not coherent. But why should they be? A. Gelin, "Le chant de l'Infante" 93, n. 3, has resolved this contradiction by appealing to "the Greek version of Aquila." This translation of the Old Testament into Greek can be dated from the years 128–129. It is characterized by this: for each Hebrew word there is a Greek word; it is called a "tracing-paper translation." See *Dictionnaire encyclopédique de la Bible*, 1306-1307. In this version, one reads the Hebrew root *hamun* ("child," "infant") instead of *hamon* ("master artisan"). The image would then be that of a father who speaks to his child, marveling at what is in the process of being realized. This is only a hypothetical translation.

9. Sydney Carter, "I Danced in the Morning" ("Lord of the Dance"), *Worship* (Chicago: GIA Publications, 1986) no. 636.

10. The doctrinal part of the Letter to the Romans (1:16-11:36) first considers the condition of all persons—Jews and pagans—under the domination of sin (1:18-4:25), then salvation through faith in Jesus Christ and Christian life in the Spirit (5:12-8:39). Between the two developments, a brief passage acts as a hinge (5:1-11); the reading for this Sunday is excerpted from it (Rom 5:5b-11 is read at the Mass of the Sacred Heart, Year C).

On the Letter to the Romans, see the introduction of the *Traduction oecuménique de la Bible*, 2691-2697; Perrot, "L'épître aux Romains." Ample excerpts from this letter are read from the Ninth to the Twenty-fourth Sunday in Ordinary Time, Year A, *Days of the Lord* 4:81-192.

11. Paul spoke several times of this period in his life and of his zeal for God: 2 Cor 11:22; Gal 1:13-14. See also Acts 22:3; 26:4-5.

12. Acts 9:1-19; 22:4-16; 26:12-18.

13. The same can be said of the priestly and religious vocations to which one remains attached, and also of the commitment of Christian marriage.

14. Rom 3:21-30; Phil 3:9.

15. Bede the Venerable (ca. 672-735), *Homélie 12 pour la Vigile de Pentecôte, Lectures chrétiennes pour notre temps* (Abbaye d'Orval, 1971) (Fiche O 26).

16. To persuade someone that his or her situation is hopeless, that he or she is abandoned by all, is a particularly cruel form of psychological torture. It is to seek to reduce a human being to nothing by destroying what can give that person the strength to withstand ill treatments and gain the upper hand.

17. Rom 8:21; 1 Cor 15:19.

18. Rom 5:8; Eph 2:4; 1 John 3:1; 4:4, 8, 12, 16, 19.

19. Ruysbroeck the Admirable (1293–1381), *Les sept degrés de l'amour spirituel, Oeuvres*, trans. Benedictines of Saint-Paul de Wisques (Brussels—Paris: Vromant, 1922) 1:248–249.

20. See A. Lion, *Lire saint Jean*, Lire la Bible 32 (Paris: Cerf, 1972); A. Jaubert, ''Lecture de l'évangile selon saint Jean,'' *Cahiers Evangile* 17 (1976); A. Jaubert, *Approches de l'évangile de Jean*, Parole de Dieu (Paris: Seuil, 1976); C. Mollat, *Le quatrième évangile* (Geneva: Labor et fides, 1988); the introductions of the *Bible de Jérusalem*, 1523–1526, and the *Traduction oecuménique de la Bible*, 2535–2544.

21. John 20:31. This verse, which belongs to the conclusion of John's Gospel, added by an unknown author, perfectly expresses the intention of the evangelist. See *Days of the Lord* 3:321, n. 2.

22. All the writings of the New Testament prove this work of reflection on Jesus' words and actions. The Gospels do not present Jesus in the raw, in the way of neutral records containing objective information, without any attempt at understanding causes and circumstances. For their part, the apostles' letters, in particular Paul's and the Letter to the Hebrews, like the discourses reported in the Acts of the Apostles, beginning with the very first one on Pentecost (2:14-36), show that the first announcement of the gospel—the ''kerygma''— (see *Days of the Lord* 3:331, n. 2) was, from the beginning, complemented by catechetical and theological developments.

23. Matt 26:75; Mark 14:72; Luke 22:60; 24:6, 8; John 2:22; 14:26; 15:26; 16:12-15.

24. St. John of the Cross, *Ascent of Mount Carmel*, trans. and ed. E. Allison Peers (Garden City, N.Y.: Image Books, 1958) 201.

25. Judaism and Catholicism are habitually classified among ''the religions of the Book.'' One must be clear about the meaning of this expression. Effectively, the Bible is the primary source of revelation for Jews and Christians, but this is because it is the living word of the living God.

See Vatican II, *Dogmatic Constitution on Divine Revelation (Dei Verbum)*, nos. 7–10.

26. Whatever may be the case for a hypothetical Gospel according to Matthew first written in Aramaic (Jesus' tongue), we know the words and the teaching of Jesus through the Greek language.

27. Any translation is a challenging task, especially when the two languages do not belong to the same family, which was the case. Besides, the Greek cultural universe was foreign to that of the Jews, particularly from the religious viewpoint. It was necessary to fashion not only an appropriate vocabulary but, to a certain extent, a Christian-Greek language derived from what was commonly spoken in the Mediterranean world (called the *koine*, ''common language'').

28. The words ''preachers'' and ''theologians'' include all those who, in one way or another, study Scripture and ponder the Lord's teaching in order to share with others the fruit of their research. Matthew's Gospel alludes to them when it mentions the scribes ''instructed in the kingdom of heaven'' bringing from their ''storeroom both the new and the old'' (13:52-53). See J. Dupont, ''L'évangile de saint Matthieu,'' 40.

29. William of St.-Thierry (ca. 1085–1148), *Le miroir de la foi*, Sources chrétiennes 301 (Paris: Cerf, 1982) 139.

30. J. Mouroux, *Je crois en toi*, Foi vivante 3 (Paris: Cerf, 1965) 82.

31. ''My teaching is not my own but is from the one who sent me'' (John 7:16); ''I did not speak on my own, but the Father who sent me commanded me what to say and speak'' (John 12:49); ''The words that I speak to you I do not speak on my own. The Father who dwells in me is doing his works'' (John 14:10).

32. See John 14:1-21.

33. St.Augustine (354–430), *Traité sur saint Jean*, quoted in H. Tissot, *Les Pères vous parlent de l'Evangile* (Bruges: Apostolat liturgique, 1954) 1:526.

34. Commission Francophone Cistercienne, *Tropaires des dimanches*, Le livre d'Heures d'En-Calcat (Dourgne, 1980) 48 (Fiche de chant U LH 86).

35. In a certain way, their faith is without dogma. What distinguishes them from persons of diverse religions who believe in God is, at the most, moral standards or forms of worship. They see themselves as Christians because they were born at such and such a time, in such and such a milieu. Their mentality is characterized by a sort of false ecumenism that ignores any kind of really important difference.

36. J. Thomas, "Actualité de la Trinité," *Assemblées du Seigneur*, 2nd series, no. 31 (Paris: Publications de Saint-André—Cerf, 1973) 66.

37. Creed of Nicaea-Constantinople.

38. See Leonardo Boff, *Trinité, société et libération*, Théologies de la libération (Paris: Cerf, 1990).

39. Commission Francophone Cistercienne, *La nuit, le jour, 108*.

The Body and Blood of Christ—Pages 38-40

1. In the countries where this solemnity is observed as a holy day, it is celebrated on the Thursday after Trinity Sunday.

2. St. Augustine, *Commentaire sur le psaume 98*, ed. J.-P. Migne, *Patrologie latine* 37, col. 1254c.

3. As early as the third century, the reserved Eucharist was placed in a vase in the shape of a dove; later on, in a small structure in the shape of a tower; finally, in a tabernacle. See "Colombe eucharistique" and "Tabernacle" in F. Cabrol—H. Leclercq, *Dictionnaire d'archéologie chrétienne et de liturgie*, vol. 3/2 (Paris: Letouzey, 1924) cols. 2231-2234; vol. 15/2 (1953) cols. 1945-1947.

4. In the ninth century, a sharp controversy pitted two monks of the Benedictine abbey of Corbie in Northern France, Paschasius Radbertus (d. 865) and Ratramnus (d. after 868). The first insisted on an extreme Eucharistic symbolism; the other affirmed a pure and simple identity between the Eucharist and the historical Christ, thus paving the way for grave and shocking misunderstandings.

There was a second round in the controversy in the eleventh century when Berengar, archdeacon of Angers and "master of the schools" in Tours (ca. 1010–1088), taught that the Eucharist was only the symbol of the body of Christ. Lanfranc (1005–1089), born in Pavia, monk, then prior of the abbey of Bec, abbot of Saint-Etienne in Caen, and finally archbishop of Canterbury, vigorously opposed Berengar, whose doctrine was condemned by several councils. At the Council of Rome (1079), he signed a profession of faith acknowledging that "the bread and the wine placed on the altar are, by the mystery of the holy prayer and by the words of our Redeemer, substantially changed into the flesh, true and vivifying, and into the blood of our Lord Jesus Christ, and that after the consecration, they are the true body and the true blood of Christ." G. Dumeige, *La foi catholique: Textes doctrinaux du magistère de l'Eglise* (Paris: Orante, 1961) 403.

5. Ibid., 411, 414-415.

6. From the Greek *hagios* ("holy") and *scopein* ("to see"), "a means of seeing holy things."

7. Another expression of this devotion was the desire to see the host after the consecration. The first document relative to this elevation is a prescription of Eudes de Sully, bishop of Paris (1196–1208). The elevation of the chalice came later: it is mentioned in the course of the thirteenth century.

8. The texts of the Mass attached to the pontifical bull were composed by St. Thomas Aquinas (1228–1274). The entrance antiphon, the opening prayer, the prayer over the gifts, and the prayer after Communion are still those in the present-day missal.

9. The triumphal, even triumphalist, character of this procession was the more obvious as the majority of those in the cortège were unable to see the Blessed Sacrament. This was the reason most people preferred to stand on the route of the procession.

10. These constraints consisted mainly in restrictions imposed on traffic, especially in cities, in a certain number of streets.

11. In 1959, the Congregation of Rites published a reminder that the Corpus Christi procession was a "pious exercise" left to bishops' discretion, and not a liturgical rite prescribed by Roman law.

12. Christians must witness to their faith without fear, but humbly, without arrogance and still less in a way that can appear aggressive.

13. See R. Cabié, "The Adoration of the Blessed Sacrament," A. G. Martimort, *The Church at Prayer, II: The Eucharist* (Collegeville, Minn.: The Liturgical Press, 1986) 245–253; "Corpus Christi," ibid., IV, 103–105; A. Adam, *La liturgie aujourd'hui: Précis de liturgie catholique,* Mysteria 1 (Paris: Brepols, 1989) 290; R. Gantoy, "L'adoration du Saint-Sacrement: Origine et évolution," *Carmel* 25 (1981) 4–8.

14. Preface of the solemnity.

BODY AND BLOOD OF CHRIST, YEAR A—Pages 41–48

1. This is the interpretation followed especially by the prophets of the period before the Exile, like Hosea (2:16) and Jeremiah (2:2).

2. In fact, the two types of readings are not that clear-cut. Recalling the marvels of Exodus and exhorting to conversion usually go hand in hand. Thus, for instance, Pss 78 and 105.

3. The "actualization" liturgists speak of—in accordance with biblical tradition and by appealing, like it, to the notion of "memorial"—consists neither in pretending to render present events that cannot be reproduced in an identical manner, nor in going back to the past that cannot be repeated, either by an effort of imagination or by recourse to magical rites that mimic what one evokes. Situated in time, no event of salvation is ever reproduced exactly as it was. But its author is God who transcends time. As a consequence, "actualization" in worship and liturgy has for its immediate object this intervention of God who saves here and now, like yesterday and tomorrow. Thus, the risen Christ no longer dies. But each time we commemorate his passion and resurrection as he told us to do, we participate, by faith and through "signs," in this death and this resurrection that took place once for all, but whose fruits are ripening for us today.

4. When they saw this for the first time, they "asked one another, 'What is this?' for they did not know what it was" (Exod 16:15).

5. The manna is mentioned several times in the Old Testament: Exod 16 (the principal text); Num 11:7-9; Josh 5:12; Neh 9:20; Pss 78:23-31; 105:40.; Wis 15:20-29. The New Testament, in its turn, gives an important place to the manna, albeit with different interpretations: Matt 4:4; Luke 4:4; John 6:31-58; 1 Cor 10:3; 2 Cor 8:15; Rev 2:17. These Christian interpretations of the manna can be understood only in reference to Jewish traditions and rabbinical midrash. On the meaning of the word "midrash," see *Days of the Lord* 1:340, n. 9. See "Manne" in *Vocabulaire de théologie biblique,* cols. 708–710, and in *Dictionnaire encyclopédique de la Bible,* 781–782.

6. Exod 16:4; Num 11:4-6; 21:4-5; Deut 29:4-5.

7. Nerses Snorhali (1102–1173), *Jésus Fils unique de Dieu,* Sources chrétiennes 203 (Paris: Cerf, 1973) 64–65.

8. In connection with the disorders in the assemblies, Paul reminds the Corinthians of what the Lord did "on the night he was handed over" (1 Cor 11:23-26). The text read to-

day is part of the long development on the question of the use of meats bought on the market that had come from sacrifices offered in pagan temples (1 Cor 8:1–11:1). Idols are nothing. Knowing this, the faithful may consume this meat without any scruple, but they must see to it that this freedom does not scandalize the "weak," who could mistake this for a sort of worship of false gods. Having specified these points to which he will come back later (1 Cor 10:19-32), Paul writes, "Avoid idolatry" (1 Cor 10:14). It is at this point that he speaks of the Eucharist (today's text).

9. "Real" is opposed to "moral": Christ and the believer are truly one. We find the same type of argumentation and the same realism when Paul speaks of fornication: "Do you not know that your bodies are members of Christ? Shall I then take Christ's members and make them the members of a prostitute? Of course not! [Or] do you not know that anyone who joins himself to a prostitute becomes one body with her? For 'the two' it says, 'will become one flesh.' But whoever is joined to the Lord becomes one spirit with him" (1 Cor 6:15-17). See the Second Sunday in Ordinary Time, Year B, *Days of the Lord* 5:14–17.

10. Rom 12:5; 1 Cor 6:15; 10:17; 12:13, 27; Eph 1:23; 3:6; 4:4-6, 12, 16; 5:23, 30; Col 1:18, 24; 2:17, 19; 3:15.

11. Equivalent terms are found in Eucharistic Prayers I, III, and IV at the epiclesis after the consecration.

12. Vatican II, *Dogmatic constitution on the Church*, nos. 3, 11, 26; *Constitution on the Sacred Liturgy*, nos.10, 47; *Dogmatic Constitution on Divine Revelation*, no. 26; and so on, *Documents of Vatican II*.

13. *La doctrine des Douze Apôtres or Didachè* (1st c.) 9:4, Sources chrétiennes 248 (Paris: Cerf 1978) 177. See *Days of the Lord* 3:245.

14. Patrice de La Tour du Pin, *Une somme de poésie: III. Le jeu de l'homme devant Dieu* (Paris: Gallimard, 1983) 284–285.

15. Except for some verses, chapter 6 of John's Gospel is read in its entirety from the Seventeenth to the Twenty-first Sunday in Ordinary Time, Year B, *Days of the Lord* 5:155–157.

16. Seventeenth Sunday in Ordinary Time, ibid., 160–163.

17. In Christian terminology, "given" means "handed over." Besides, in the New Testament, "for," when applied to Jesus, usually indicates the redemptive value of his death and resurrection: Mark 14:24; Luke 22:19; John 10:11, 15; Rom 5:6; 1 Cor 11:24; 15:3. The Nicene Creed says "For our sake he was crucified under Pontius Pilate / he suffered, died, and was buried."

18. John has recourse to realistic terms difficult to translate. He does not use the ordinary word for "eat" (*esthiein* or *phagein*), but that which literally means "chew," "munch." Instead of saying "body" (*soma*), a word that designates the person in its totality and its unity, although evoked under its physical aspect, he says "flesh" (*sarx*), which directly refers to what can be seen and touched, grasped and reached immediately and physically. Now, at the time John was writing, the Eucharistic body of Christ was commonly called *soma*. The recourse to an unusual wording reveals the author's intention to oppose every temptation to false spiritualization. The same intention appears in the way John says in 1:14, "and the Word became flesh" (*sarx egeneto*).

Sarx also connotes what is fragile, precarious in humanity, what makes it weak and vulnerable. The word designating the dead body, the corpse, is *ptoma*.

19. The blood poured out is the symbol of life. See *Days of the Lord* 5:186.

20. John uses the verb "remain" to express the relations that unite the Father and the Son, as well as the disciples with the Father and the Son, through the Spirit: 15:4-7; 17:21-23; 1 John 2:24; 3:24; 4:13, 16.

21. St. Ignatius of Antioch (d. ca. 110), *Lettre aux Ephésiens*, 20:2, Sources chrétiennes 10 (Paris: Cerf, 1951) 91.

22. St. Irenaeus (ca. 135–202), *Contre les hérésies*, IV, 18:5, Sources chrétiennes 100bis (Paris: Cerf, 1965) 613.

23. Acclamation after the consecration, no.1.

24. This rock was always providentially there when the people were in need of water. It was said that it accompanied the people (1 Cor 10:4).

25. P. de La Tour du Pin, *Une somme de poésie: III*, 295–296 (Fiche de chant M 16).

BODY AND BLOOD OF CHRIST, YEAR B—Pages 49–55

1. See "Alliance" in *Vocabulaire de théologie biblique*, cols. 28–38, and *Dictionnaire encyclopédique de la Bible*, 35–38. The primitive meaning of the Hebrew term—*berit*—seems to be "in-between." The covenant creates a relation of solidarity between the two partners.

2. Gen 6:18; 9:9-17.

3. Gen 15:18; 17:2-21.

4. The final redaction of the Book of Exodus—and of the other books of the Pentateuch—includes traditions coming from diverse circles and different times. See the introductions and notes in the *Bible de Jérusalem* and the *Traduction oecuménique de la Bible*; C. Wiéner, "Le Livre de l'Exode," *Cahiers Evangile* 54 (1985). But the question of the sources and literary traditions of the Pentateuch is seriously debated today. See *Le Pentateuque en question*, ed. A. de Pury, Le monde de la Bible (Geneva: Labor et fides, 1989).

5. The *Bible de Jérusalem* calls this ensemble of laws "The Code of the Covenant." Its prescriptions suppose a settled and agricultural people. What we have is legislation after the Exodus, inserted in order to stress these prescriptions' connection with the Ten Commandments.

6. See Ph. Rouillard, "La lecture de l'Ecriture dans la liturgie juive et les traditions occidentales," *Paroisse et liturgie* 5 (1969) 483–487; R. Gantoy, "L'assemblée dans l'économie du salut," *Assemblées du Seigneur*, 2nd series, no. 1 (Paris: Publications de Saint-André—Cerf, 1962) 67–70.

7. R. Draï, *La traversée du désert: L'invention de la responsabilité*, L'espace du politique (Paris: Fayard, 1988) 113, thinks that Moses sensed some unexpressed reservations in the promise of the people; he wrote down "the words and ordinances of the LORD" in order to forestall any debates concerning the terms agreed upon. The text does not specify on what these "words" were written. Later on, it will be said that they were written on stone tablets, and in God's handwriting (Exod 32:15-16; 34:1).

8. See also Deut 27:2; 1 Kgs 18:31-32.

9. These cultic forms have become so foreign to us that we risk being unable to perceive their meaning; they may even appear quite barbaric. However, we are familiar today in ordinary life with customs that correspond to the same intentions. To offer somebody a present that is going to belong to the person as his or her own is a gesture of homage. On the other hand, when we bring friends a dish or a drink, they must immediately share it with the donor, for it is a gesture of communion. In both cases, what is offered must be of good quality, even if it is a modest gift; one does not offer faded flowers or a cake one wants to get rid of because it is a mess (see Lev 1:1, 10; 3:1, 6).

See "Sacrifice" in *Vocabulaire de théologie biblique*, cols. 1163–1170, and *Dictionnaire encyclopédique de la Bible*, 1148–1151.

10. This is what explains the prohibition of eating "flesh with its lifeblood" (Gen 9:5) "since the life of every living body is its blood" (Lev 17:14). Hence, the still current expressions we use today: "to shed the blood of someone" for "to take his or her life"; "to give an account of someone's blood" for "to answer for his or her life"; and so forth.

See "Sang" in *Vocabulaire de théologie biblique*, cols. 1192–1196, and *Dictionnaire encyclopédique de la Bible*, 1168; *Days of the Lord* 5:186.

11. C. Bourgin, "La nouvelle alliance dans le sang du Christ (He 9)," *Assemblées du Seigneur*, 2nd series, no. 32 (Paris: Publications de Saint-André—Cerf, 1971) 43.

12. See *Days of the Lord* 5:244-245.

13. The *Bible de Jérusalem* and the *Traduction oecuménique de la Bible* translate "blessings that were to come" instead of "good things that have come to be."

14. See *Days of the Lord* 3:350, n. 3.

15. See description in Num 29:7-11; Lev 16. See also "Expiations, Jour des" in *Dictionnaire encyclopédique de la Bible*, 461-463.

16. See Heb 7:25; 9:24.

17. See Heb 10:4-10 with the quotation of Psalm 40:7-9. This passage from Hebrews is read on the Fourth Sunday of Advent, Year C, and the feast of the Annunciation.

18. Pius XII, pope (1939-1958), encyclical *Mediator Dei* (November 20, 1947), Introduction, in *La documentation catholique* 45 (1948) col. 195.

19. To these three testimonies we must add Paul's. In 1 Cor 11:23, he limits himself to what is called "the institution of the Eucharist." This remarkable convergence proves that we have here a tradition "received from the Lord" (1 Cor 11:23). The First Letter to the Corinthians, which probably goes back to the year 53, antedates the written Gospels.

John's Gospel records the last meal of the Lord (13:1-30) but does not mention the blessings over the bread and wine. See *Days of the Lord* 3:19-22. On the other hand, he recounts Jesus' long discourse (13:31-16:33) and his prayer pronounced in conclusion (ch. 17), which are not found in the other Gospels, although there is an echo of them in Luke's Gospel (22:24-34).

20. The three Gospels place this last meal "on the first day of the Feast of Unleavened Bread" (Matt 26:17; Mark 14:12; Luke 22:7); whereas, according to John's chronology, Jesus died at the moment when the lambs were immolated in the Temple for the solemn day of Passover (18:28; 19:31). Leaving aside these questions of calendar (see A. Jaubert, *La date de la Cène: Calendrier biblique et liturgie chrétienne*, Etudes bibliques [Paris: Gabalda, 1975]), it remains true that the Lord's last meal is situated in the perspective of the Covenant (Paul and the Synoptics).

21. A "man . . . carrying a jar of water" must have been easy to spot; ordinarily, it was the women's task to draw water from the fountain.

22. According to the Greek text, Jesus told the disciples to ask, "Where is *my* guest room?"

23. Similarly, Jesus sent "two of his disciples" to Bethphage, saying to them, "Go into the village opposite you, and immediately on entering it, you will find a colt tethered on which no one has ever sat. Untie it and bring it here. If anyone should say to you, 'Why are you doing this?' reply, 'The Master has need of it and will send it back here at once.' " That time also, everything happened as Jesus had told (Mark 11:1-6: Passion Sunday, Year B).

24. We could see here a prophecy in action, Jesus in some way representing his death. See J. Dupont, " 'Ceci est mon corps,' 'ceci est mon sang,' " *Etudes sur les Evangiles synoptiques*, I (Louvain: University Press—Peters, 1985) 188-189; A. Descamps and collaborators, *L'Eucharistie: Symbole et réalité* (Gembloux-Paris: Duculot, 1970) 71-86.

25. The blood is indeed life. Besides, the covenant in blood refers us to Moses' sprinkling the people with blood at the conclusion of the Covenant at Sinai (Exod 24:3-8, first reading).

26. Compare with the other tradition represented by Paul (1 Cor 11:23-26) and Luke (22:15-20); the rites of the bread and the cup are separated by the interval of the meal.

27. Fr. Varillon, *L'humilité de Dieu* (Paris: Centurion, 1974) 156-157.

28. P. Emmanuel, *Evangéliaire*, Livre de vie (Paris: Seuil, 1961) 157.

29. P. de La Tour du Pin, *Une somme de poésie: III*, 244-245.

BODY AND BLOOD OF CHRIST, YEAR C—Pages 56-65

1. With Psalm 76:3 ("In Salem is his abode / his dwelling is in Zion"), the Jewish tradition identified Salem with Jerusalem. St. Jerome (ca. 347-420) first adopted this hypothe-

sis, then rejected it and reproached the other Fathers for following it. See "Salem" in *Dictionnaire encyclopédique de la Bible*, 1159.

2. The Letter to the Hebrews—and it alone among the New Testament writings—mentions Melchizedek nine times in relation to the priesthood of Christ: 5:6, 10; 6:20; 7:1, 3, 10, 11, 15, 17.

3. Look with favor on these offerings
   and accept them as once you accepted
   the gifts of your servant Abel,
   the sacrifice of Abraham, our father in faith,
   and the bread and wine offered by your priest Melchizedek.

4. See the introductions to the Book of Genesis and the notes in the *Bible de Jérusalem* and the *Traduction oecuménique de la Bible*; "Abraham" in *Vocabulaire de théologie biblique*, cols.3–7, and *Dictionnaire encyclopédique de la Bible*, 8–9; M. Collin, "Abraham," *Cahiers Evangile* 56 (1986).

5. See R. Martin-Achard, *Actualité d'Abraham* (Neuchâtel: Delachaux et Niestlé, 1969).

6. See G. Von Rad, *La Genèse* (Geneva: Labor et fides, 1968) 174.

7. Gen 9:25; 27:33; 48:18.

8. Gen 1:27-28; 12:2-3; 28:3-4; Ps 67:2-3.

9. Gen 24:48; Exod 18:10; Deut 8:10; 1 Sam 25:32, 39.

10. Num 6:22; Deut 27:14-26; Pss 103:1-2; 144:1; Dan 2:19-23.

11. Luke 1:68; 2 Cor 1:3; Eph 1:3; 1 Pet 1:3.

12. It is the first time that the Bible mentions a priest.

13. See above, n. 2.

14. St. Hilary of Poitiers (ca. 315–367), *Traité des mystères*, bk. 1:1, Sources chrétiennes 19 (Paris: Cerf, 1947) 73–75.

15. Heb 9:15; 12:24.

16. He speaks of it twice in his First Letter to the Corinthians: 10:16-21 (see the second reading for the Body and Blood of Christ, Year A, above); 11:23-26 (text read on Holy Thursday; see *Days of the Lord* 3:18–19). See n. 19 in Body and Blood of Christ, Year B.

17. Matt 26:26; Mark 14:22; Luke 22:14-21; 1 Cor 11:23.

18. See Matt 26:28; Mark 10:45; 14:24; Luke 22:20; the notes of the *Bible de Jérusalem* and the *Traduction oecuménique de la Bible* on these texts.

19. *Traduction oecuménique de la Bible*, 163, n. a.
This kind of rubric belongs to the oral teaching of the laws called Mishnah, later set down in writing in the Talmud. See "Mishnah" and "Talmud" in *Dictionnaire encyclopédique de la Bible*, 848–849.

20. See 1 Cor 10:16-17 (the Body and Blood of Christ, Year A, above).

21. St. John Chrysostom (ca. 350–407), *Homélie 24 sur la Première lettre aux Corinthiens*, 5, in A. Hamman, *La messe: Liturgies anciennes et textes liturgiques*, Lettres chrétiennes 9 (Paris: Grasset, 1964) 179–180.

22. Matt 14:13-21 (Eighteenth Sunday in Ordinary Time, Year A, *Days of the Lord* 4:145–147); Matt 15:32-38; Mark 6:34-44; 8:1-10 (Saturday of the Fifth Week in Ordinary Time); John 6:5-13 (Seventeenth Sunday in Ordinary Time, Year B, *Days of the Lord* 5:160–164).

23. Matthew and Mark have two accounts of this miracle.

24. The miracle of the multiplication of the loaves resembles that of the manna in the desert after the Exodus. But it was not Moses who accomplished it; it was God who caused this food to come down from heaven, a food unknown until then (Exod 16:1-36).

25. Matt 16:9-10; Mark 8:18-21; John 6:15.

26. The Greek verb *lalein* ("to speak") has in Luke a quasi-technical meaning. It is used in reference to the prophets and Jesus who speak the very word of God, that is, who transmit his revelation.

27. In the fabric of Luke's Gospel, the episode is placed after the return of the Twelve sent on a mission (Luke 9:1-6, 10-11). It is followed by Peter's confession, the first prediction of the passion, and the words on the conditions of discipleship (9:18-26), the transfiguration (9:28-36), the healing of a boy with a demon (9:37-43), the second prediction of the passion (9:43-45), the teaching concerning the greatest in the kingdom (9:46-48), and the use of Jesus' name (9:49-50). This whole section is suffused by an aura of crisis. Indeed, immediately afterwards, Luke says that Jesus "resolutely determined to journey to Jerusalem," where he was to be delivered to death (9:51). It is therefore necessary to take sides for or against him (9:20, 26). This literary framework must not be forgotten. However, it is in the liturgical context of today's feast that this gospel passage is read.

28. See *Days of the Lord* 3:111–115.

29. This is found in the other evangelists also, in particular John because of the long discourse following the working of the "sign" (ch. 6), but for other reasons.

See Sr. Jeanne d'Arc, *Les pèlerins d'Emmaus*, Lire la Bible 47 (Paris: Cerf, 1977). She ponders the parallelism between this meal and the multiplication of the loaves of which Luke's Gospel, in contrast with Matthew's and Mark's, has only one account. The bread broken at Emmaus could very well be, for the believers who know where to find the true bread of life, a key to understanding the miracle worked by Jesus in order to feed the crowd that had followed him into the desert.

30. In the course of their recent mission, the Twelve had experienced that they could travel without taking anything along for the trip—neither bread nor money—counting on the possibility that perhaps after several refusals, they would find a hospitable house (Luke 9:1-6). But Jesus had not prepared them to feel themselves responsible for providing the food needed by those who might follow them to "a deserted place."

31. Those who became believers because of Peter's discourse after he had cured the crippled beggar sitting at "the Beautiful Gate" of the Temple, were also "[about] five thousand" (Acts 4:4). Is it mere coincidence?

32. Mark says "in squares" (*The Jerusalem Bible*), "by ranks" (*par rangées*, *Traduction oecuménique de la Bible*) of hundreds and fifties. Beyond the details of translation, the impression produced is that of a very orderly crowd.

33. One thinks of the assembly in the desert after the Exodus: Exod 18.21, 25; Num 11:14; Deut 1:15.

34. Literally, "Make them recline on couches [as in festive banquets] by tablefuls of fifty."

35. St. Justin Martyr (ca. 100–165), *Première apologie*, 67, in A. Hamman, *La philosophie passe au Christ*, Littératures chrétiennes 3 (Paris: Editions de Paris, 1958) 94–95.

36. See *Days of the Lord* 5:350, n.25.

37. The evangelists speak of twelve (Matt 14:20; Mark 6:43; Luke 9:17; John 6:13) or seven baskets (Matt 15:37; Mark 8:8). These two numbers are symbolic: seven is the perfect number and the number of deacons assigned to serve at the tables of Christians converted from paganism (Acts 6:2-6); twelve evokes the number of the apostles entrusted with distributing the multiplied bread to the people.

38. St. Ambrose (339–397), *Traité sur L'Evangile de Luc*, VI:84, Sources chrétiennes 45bis (Paris: Cerf, 1971) 259.

39. Ibid., 86–87, p. 260.

40. G. Bessière, *Le feu qui rafraîchit*, Epiphanie (Paris: Cerf, 1978) 95–96. The phrase between quotation marks is taken from E. Bloch, *Le Principe Espérance* (Paris: Gallimard, 1970) 1:28.

41. See *Days of the Lord* 3:4.

42. The narrative of the washing of the feet from John's Gospel (13:1-15) is read. See *Days of the Lord* 3:19–22.

43. St. Cyril of Jerusalem (ca. 315–386), *Catéchèses mystagogiques*, V:20–21, Sources chrétiennes 126 (Paris: Cerf, 1966) 171–173.

Mystagogy (from the Greek *mustes*, "initiate," and *agein*, "to lead") is the initiation into mysteries. In Christian terminology, the word designates the theological and symbolical exposition of the liturgical rites of initiation, in particular those of baptism and the Eucharist.

Sacred Heart of Jesus—Pages 66–68

1. See "L'exemple d'une mystique: Sainte Gertrude et la spiritualité liturgique," in C. Vagaggini, *Initiation théologique à la liturgie*, adapted from the Italian by R. Gantoy (Bruges—Paris: Biblica, 1963) 2:206–239.

2. This movement originated in the Netherlands under the impulse of Geert de Groote (1340–1394) and his disciples, the Brethren of the Common Life, who after his death formed the Canonical Congregation of Windesheim to which Thomas à Kempis (1379 or 1380–1471), the author of the famous *Imitation of Christ*, belonged. The movement had for its object the reform of the clergy and faithful by returning to the simple and accessible sources of the gospel.

3. Margaret Mary Alacoque also urged Christians to devote the first Friday of each month to the worship of the Sacred Heart and the institution of "Holy Hours" of prayer and adoration on the day before.

4. Encyclical *Annum sacrum* (May 25, 1899), in *Lettres apostoliques de Léon XIII: Encycliques, brefs etc., Texte latin avec traduction française en regard* (Paris: Bonne Presse, n.d.) 6:24–37.

5. Encyclical *Miserentissimus Redemptor*, on the reparation owed by all to the Sacred Heart of Jesus (May 8, 1928), *La documentation catholique* 19 (1928) cols. 1283–1294.

6. Encyclical *Haurietis aquas* (May 15, 1956), ibid. 53 (1956) cols. 709–742.

7. A Mass granted in 1765 to Poland and Portugal by Clement XIII (1758–1769); a second Mass granted to Venice, Austria, and Spain by Pius VI (1775–1799); a third one in 1856, when the feast was extended to the whole Church by Pius IX (1846–1878); finally, a fourth one, composed by order of Pius XI (1922–1939). On the history of the devotion to the Sacred Heart and the liturgy of the feast, see A. G. Martimort, *The Church at Prayer: The Liturgy and Time*, IV:105–106; A. Adam, *La liturgie aujourd'hui*, 292–293.

8. One may choose the ancient wording for the opening prayer:
   Father,
   we have wounded the heart of Jesus your Son,
   but he brings us forgiveness and grace.
   Help us to prove our grateful love
   and make amends for our sins.

9. The two readings of the formulary of Pius XI (Eph 3:8-12, 14-19; John 19:31-37) have been kept for Year B, but Hos 11:1, 3-4, 8c-9 has been added. In Year A, we read Deut 7:6-11; 1 John 4:7-16; Matt 11:25-30. In Year C, we read Ezek 34:11-16; Rom 5:5b-11; Luke 15:5-7.

SACRED HEART, YEAR A—Pages 69–76

1. The Hebrew term used here, *segulah*, belongs to the juridical vocabulary that designates private property (1 Chr 29:3).

2. Gen 2:24; Deut 21:11; Jer 13:11.

3. What is said here reworks in a significant way what is read in an ancient text: "I, the LORD, your God, am a jealous God, inflicting punishment for their fathers' wickedness on the children of those who hate me, down to the third and fourth generation; but bestowing

mercy down to the thousandth generation on the children of those who love me and keep my commandments'' (Exod 20:5-6). If the steadfastness of the faithfulness and love of God is expressed in identical terms, there is no longer any mention of chastisement of the fathers' sins inflicted on their children and grandchildren, but mention of an immediate response that strikes only the guilty party.

4. R. Tagore, *Poèmes de Kabir* (Paris: N.R.F., Gallimard, 1922) 96.

Kabir (ca. 1440-1518), a simple and unlettered Indian weaver, elaborated a mystical philosophy. His words and songs were collected by his disciples. He preached union and concord. His thought inspired Nanak (1469-1539), who refused the Brahmanic castes and preached universal brotherhood and sisterhood. He founded the religious sect of the Sikhs, which today forms a community of some twelve million spread throughout all of India. The men are recognized by their turbans, their carefully combed and rolled beards, their steel bracelets, and the knives they wear in their belts. Women enjoy equal status with men.

5. The verb ''love'': 74 times out of 159 in the whole New Testament (44 in the Gospel, 27 in the First Letter, 3 in the Second and 1 in the Third). The noun ''love'': 28 times out of 63 in the whole New Testament (7 in the Gospel, 18 in the First Letter, 3 in the Second).

6. See the preceding paragraph.

7. We must understand correctly what ''supernatural'' means. One often imagines some sort of quality simply added to what is—and remains—natural or, on the contrary, disfiguring it. In reality, supernatural means ''what concerns grace, the order of the divine.'' Agape is the love inspired by divine grace and going farther than the limits accessible to human love—''natural'' love—even the purest and the loftiest. In other terms, agape is love, but carried to its perfection because it comes from God and leads to God. Thus, one says that life is ''supernatural'' when, through grace, it has become a participation in divine life.

8. ''Define'' means to determine, by a simple formula, the ensemble of characteristics that distinguish a thing or a person from all others.

9. ''Quality'' is here understood in its etymological sense: what makes a thing or a person such as it is (from the Latin *qualis*, ''such''). In this sense, the quality can be what we call a defect, an infirmity, etc.

10. See above, Trinity Sunday, Year A, n. 5, on the names of God in Islam.

11. For example, Jer 3:12; Pss 103; 145:8-9. See ''Miséricorde'' and ''Tendresse'' in *Vocabulaire de théologie biblique*, cols. 766-769, 1284-1285; ''Miséricorde'' in *Dictionnaire encyclopédique de la Bible*, 847.

12. St. Augustine, *Commentaire de la Première épître de saint Jean*, IX:9, Sources chrétiennes 75 (Paris: Cerf, 1973) 168.

13. ''Know'' is also the verb used by John when he speaks of the relation between Jesus and his Father: 7:29; 8:19, 32, 55; 10:15; 14:7, 17; 17:25; 1 John 2:4, 14; 4:6; 5:20.

14. ''Remain'' occurs 68 times in John's writings out of 116 times in the whole New Testament and is used most often to express the reciprocal inhabitation of the Father and the Son (14:10-11; 15:10), the habitation of the Father and the Son (15:4-7; 1 John 3:24; 4:16) in believers, who themselves are in the Son (6:56; 15:4-7, 9, 10; 1 John 2:6, 27-28) and in the Father (17:21, 23; 1 John 1:24; 3:24; 4:16).

15. Djalal Al-Din Al-Rumi (1207-1273), ''Ode 426,'' *Odes mystiques* (Paris: Klinksieck, 1973) 168.

This Persian poet, born in Iran, left his country at the time of the Mongolian invasion (1230). After having studied in Syria, he taught theology in Konya (formerly Iconium) in Turkey. Besides an exposition of the doctrine of Sufism and a mystical treatise, he wrote two collections of poems, among which is one of quatrains (the *Odes*).

16. The New Testament abundantly teaches this. Love is proved by acts: toward God, the criterion is the observance of the commandments; toward neighbors, what we do or omit to do (Matt 25:31-46).

17. This text is also proclaimed on the Fourteenth Sunday in Ordinary Time, Year A. See *Days of the Lord* 4:116–118.

In the plan of Matthew's Gospel, the hymn of jubilation and the call of Jesus are inserted after the lamentation over the cities of Galilee that remained unrepentant despite the Lord's preaching and working miracles in their midst (11:20-24). In Luke's Gospel (10:21-22), on the contrary, Jesus "rejoiced [in] the Holy Spirit" after having heard the seventy-two disciples report to him the marvelous success of their mission (10:17-20). The same words thus illuminate two different situations. Enshrined in the context of the liturgical celebration of the Sacred Heart of Jesus, they set its meaning in relief.

18. The word translated as "childlike"—*nepioi* in Greek—corresponds to a Hebrew word that would be better rendered by "simple." This word is pejorative in the Book of Proverbs, where it designates the foolish, the people without intelligence who commit all sorts of blunders (7:7; 9:4, 6; 14:18; 19:25; 22:3; 27:12; etc.). In the psalms, on the contrary, the simple are praised because they form the enviable category of the weak without pride who are the beneficiaries of divine benevolence. In particular, God gives them the deep intelligence of things heavenly: "The decree of the LORD is trustworthy / giving wisdom to the simple" (Ps 19:8). Their condition is not any more meritorious than that of others, but for no other reason than their weakness, God is their special protector: "The LORD keeps the little ones; / I was brought low, and he saved me" (Ps 116:6).

19. Cardinal G. Danneels, "Exégèse et service de l'Eglise aujourd'hui," *A cause de l'Evangile: Etudes sur les Synoptiques et les Actes offertes au P. Jacques Dupont, à l'occasion de son 70ème anniversaire*, Lectio divina 123 (Paris: Publications de Saint-André—Cerf, 1985) 8, 14.

20. In the context of Matthew's Gospel, one cannot help but compare these words with what Jesus said about the scribes and Pharisees of his time, who loaded heavy burdens on other people's backs (Matt 23:4). See J. Dupont, *Les Béatitudes: II, La Bonne Nouvelle*, Etudes bibliques (Paris: Gabalda, 1969) 203.

21. St. John Chrysostom, *Homélie 38 sur Saint Matthieu*, in H. Tissot, *Les Pères vous parlent de l'Evangile* (Bruges: Apostolat liturgique, 1955) 2:430-431.

22. D. Rimaud, in *Missel noté de l'assemblée* (Paris: Brepols—Cerf—Chalet—Levain, 1990) 220 (Fiche de chant G 297).

SACRED HEART, YEAR B—Pages 77–88

1. The prophets who wrote down their oracles are called writer-prophets. The first of them is Amos who exercised his ministry in the southern kingdom. Hosea exercised his in the northern kingdom roughly at the same time, around 750 before our era. The New Testament quotes the Book of Hosea seventeen times. But his influence is not measured only by the number of explicit quotations and the use of the same images. It is far deeper. See the introduction of the *Traduction oecuménique de la Bible*, 1105-1111; J. Asurmendi, "Amos et Osée," *Cahiers Evangile* 64 (1988).

2. Hosea's thought especially marked Jeremiah a century later and the Deuteronomists; it perhaps also influenced the author of the Song of Songs in the third century before our era.

3. Hosea is the main actor in his story. On God's order, he married "a harlot wife," possibly a "sacred prostitute" connected with a Canaanite sanctuary. His painful conjugal adventures became symbolic actions that revealed the behavior and treasons of the people.

4. We must correctly understand the meaning of these biblical anthropomorphisms. They do not come down to purely and simply attributing to God human passions—even the vilest and crassest—as was customary in mythology where we see gods and goddesses tearing one another apart, slaves to impulses of all kinds—particularly sexual—that led them to use their superhuman powers to satisfy their passions. The realism of biblical anthropomorphisms does not in the least negate God's holiness, but shows that God is not impervious

to the feelings we know. Is there any reason to be surprised when we know that humankind was created in God's image?

5. See H. Van Den Bussche, "La ballade de l'amour méconnu," *Bible et vie chrétienne* 41 (1961) 18–34; P.-M. Guillaume, "La conversion de Dieu," *Assemblées du Seigneur*, 2nd series, no. 32 (Paris: Publications de Saint-André—Cerf, 1971) 82–86.

6. Hos 12:10, 14; 13:4.

7. Exod 4:22; Jer 2:1-9.

8. H. Capieu, *Demeures* (Paris: Mercure de France, 1963) 75–76.

9. It is under this twofold condition that we may correctly have recourse to anthropomorphisms to speak of God (see above, n. 4). Anyhow, it is more exact to begin with God before speaking of humans and to say, for example, that God is living, free, loving, etc., and that we, being made in his image, are participating in these divine qualities and benefit in our limited measure by life, freedom, capacity for love, etc., which have in God their source and infinite perfection. It is by contemplating God that we can have a true idea of what are and must be life, freedom, love, etc.

10. The letter is divided into two nearly equal parts, easy to distinguish: chapters 1–3, 4–6. (See the bibliographical references in *Days of the Lord* 5:344, n. 2.)

11. The letter begins with a long thanksgiving (1:3-14), followed by a prayer that exalts Christ, ruler of the universe and head of the Church (1:15-23); and the whole first part ends with a kind of hymn that sings the boundless love of Christ (3:14-19) and ends with a doxology (3:20-21). The climate is truly that of a celebration.

12. See *Days of the Lord* 3:315, n. 26.

13. Sometimes, one says that creatures are nothing. We must understand what is meant: they are nothing in comparison with God; they would be nothing if God had not given them being and was not maintaining them in existence. Understood in the absolute sense, "nothing" does not honor God.

14. This invocation repeats that at the beginning of the same letter (Eph 1:17-19). See Ascension, Year A, *Days of the Lord* 3:210-211.

15. Rom 13:14; Gal 3:27.

16. Rom 6:3-11; 1 Cor 1:13; Gal 2:20; Eph 2:5-6; 4:24; Phil 1:21; Col 2:12; 3:9.

17. See above, feast of the Sacred Heart, Year A, n. 18.

18. P. de La Tour du Pin, *Une somme de poésie: I, Le jeu de l'homme en lui-même* (Paris: Gallimard, 1981) 177.

19. John 13:23-30; 18:15; 19:25-27, 35.

20. "Now Jesus did many other signs in the presence of [his] disciples that are not written in this book. But these are written that you may [come to] believe that Jesus is the Messiah, the Son of God, and that through this belief you may have life in his name" (20:30-31).

It is thus that tradition has understood the evangelist's words from the very beginning: "There are also many other things that Jesus did, but if these were to be described individually, I do not think the whole world would contain the books that would be written" (John 21:25).

On this chapter 21, considered an appendix added later on by John himself or, more probably, by a disciple, see *Days of the Lord* 3:321, n. 2; *Traduction oecuménique de la Bible*, 2604, n. t.

21. See the introductions of the *Bible de Jérusalem*, 1523–1526, and the *Traduction oecuménique de la Bible*, 2535–2544; *Dictionnaire encyclopédique de la Bible*, 646–651; A. Lion, *Lire saint Jean*; D. Mollat, *Saint Jean maître spirituel* (Paris: Beauchesne, 1976).

22. See *Days of the Lord* 3:28-33.

23. The Sabbath begins on the day before at sunset; so do all other festive days.

24. See I. de la Potterie, "La Passion selon saint Jean," *La Passion selon les quatre évangiles*, Lire la Bible 55 (Paris: Cerf, 1981) 65–87. This is a reprint of an article published in *Assem-

blées du Seigneur, 2nd series, no. 21 (Paris: Publications de Saint-André—Cerf, 1969) 21-34; de la Potterie, *La passion de Jésus Christ selon l'Evangile de Jean,* Lire la Bible 73 (Paris: Cerf, 1986).

25. Deut 21:22-23; John 18:28; Gal 3:13.

26. Mark 15:27-32; Luke 23:35-37.

27. Second reading of the Fifth Sunday in Lent, Year B. See *Days of the Lord* 2:155-156.

28. Gospel of the Second Sunday in Ordinary Time, Year A. See *Days of the Lord* 4:24-27.

29. Gospel of the Second Sunday in Ordinary Time, Year B. See *Days of the Lord* 5:17-21.

30. See *Days of the Lord* 3:24-26.

The comparison with this text could be facilitated by the fact that the Aramean word designating "the lamb" can also mean "the servant." See Jaubert, *Approches de l'Evangile de Jean,* 146: "Between the image of the lamb and that of the Suffering Servant of Isaiah, an association of ideas is likely," but questioned.

31. Second reading of the Third Sunday of Easter, Year A. See *Days of the Lord* 3:109-110.

32. See "Agneau de Dieu" in *Vocabulaire de théologie biblique,* cols. 26-28, and in *Dictionnaire encyclopédique de la Bible,* 22-23.

33. Rev 5:8, 12, 13; 6:1, 16; 7:9, 10, 14, 17; 8:1; 12:11; 13:8; 14:1, 4 (twice), 10; 15:3; 17:14 (twice); 19:7, 9; 21:9, 14, 22, 23, 27; 22:1, 3.

34. John 13:1; Rev 7:14-16.

35. It is possible to see in this act the coup de grace given by one of the soldiers who still had doubts about the rapid death of the crucified, which also amazed Pilate (Mark 15:44). Or else a last gesture of cruelty against the body of a condemned man who kept a perfect and impressive dignity to the end.

36. Gospel of the Vigil Mass of Pentecost. See *Days of the Lord* 3:264-267.

37. Gospel of the Second Sunday in Ordinary Time, Year A. See *Days of the Lord* 4:24-26.

38. Gospel of the Third Sunday in Lent, Year A. See *Days of the Lord* 2:109-117.

39. See above, Corpus Christi, Year B, commentary on the first reading.

40. Nerses Snorhali (1102-1173), *Jésus Fils unique du Père,* Sources chrétiennes 203 (Paris: Cerf, 1973) 186.

41. The Book of Zechariah is made from the oracles of two prophets: Zechariah (1-8) and another whose name is unknown (9-14). This second part must have been written shortly after 312 before our era, whereas the first one dates back to the years 520-518. See the introductions of the *Bible de Jérusalem,* 1089-1090, and the *Traduction oecuménique de la Bible,* 1235-1240; "Zacharie, Livre de" in *Dictionnaire encyclopédique de la Bible,* 1358-1360.

42. In the narrative of the entrance into Jerusalem before the passion, Matthew (21:5) and John (12:15) quote a text of Zechariah (9:9):

> See, your king shall come to you;
> a just savior is he,
> Meek, and riding on an ass,
> on a colt, the foal of an ass.

See Passion Sunday, Years A and B, and the first reading of the Fourteenth Sunday in Ordinary Time, Year A.

43. Zeph 2:3; 3:11-13; Isa 49:13; 57:15; 61:1-2; 66:2; Pss 22:27; 69:33-34.

44. Zech 11:4-17; 13:7-9.

45. Isa 42:1-8; 49:1-6; 50:4-11; 52:13-15. These poems are read on the Baptism of the Lord, Year A; the Second Sunday in Ordinary Time, Year A; Passion Sunday; Good Friday. See *Days of the Lord* 1:296-297; 2:221-222; 3:24-26; 4:22-23.

46. Zech 12:10-13:1 is read on the Twelfth Sunday in Ordinary Time, Year C. See *Days of the Lord* 6:94-95.

47. The episode remained deeply stamped in the memory of the people of God, and it is often recalled when biblical authors evoked the realization of the promises: Isa 43:20; 44:3; 48:21; 49:10; Ezek 47:1-12. Similarly in the New Testament: 1 Cor 10:4.

48. In the New Testament, the word "hour" designates the turn taken by salvation history at the death and resurrection of Jesus, the prelude to his return at the end of time: Matt 24:36, 44, 50; 25:13; Mark 13:32; Luke 12:19-20; 1 John 2:18; Rev 3:3, 10; 9:15; 14:7, 15. In John's Gospel, this theme is especially developed with expressions such as "the hour is coming," "the hour has come": 2:4; 4:21, 23; 5:25, 28; 7:30; 8:20; 12:23, 27; 13:1; 16:2, 4, 21, 25, 32; 17:1; 19:27. See "Heure" in *Dictionnaire de théologie biblique*, cols. 537-539.

49. Commission Francophone Cistercienne, *La nuit, le jour*, 96 (Fiche de chant I 132).

SACRED HEART, YEAR C—Pages 89-97

1. "You shall declare before the Lᴏʀᴅ, your God, 'My father was a wandering Aramean' " (Deut 26:5).

2. See "Pasteur et troupeau" in *Vocabulaire de théologie biblique*, 198-199.

3. It occupies the whole of chapter 34, that is, 31 verses. The context is that of the Exile. It is said that God "tends his flock," "rescue[s]" and "gather[s]" the sheep, "seek[s] out" "the lost" and "bind[s] up" "the injured." The New Testament takes its inspiration from this text: Matt 9:36; Mark 6:34; Luke 15:3-7; John 10.

4. With the difference of a few verses (34:11-12, 15-17), this text is read on the Thirty-fourth Sunday in Ordinary Time (Christ the King), Year A. See *Days of the Lord* 4:264-265. In the Book of Ezekiel, God's conduct is presented as a reaction against the misdeeds of the "shepherds of Israel," unfaithful to their mission and severely condemned (34:1-10). Similarly, it is said that God is going to "judge between one sheep and another, between rams and goats" (34:17-22). Finally comes the announcement of a shepherd according to the heart of God (34:23-31). Only the central part of the oracle is kept here, but this in no way does violence to the text or distorts its meaning. On the contrary, the context of the feast of the Sacred Heart and the connection with the words of Jesus reported in the day's Gospel (Luke 15:3-7) explain the meaning of this prediction of the personal intervention of God on which the prophet insists, and show it to be realized in the Lord's ministry. In any case, this is the way one must make a synoptic reading of prophecies and gospel. The prophetic announcements shed light on what happens to Jesus and the Church. Conversely, these realizations allow us to understand what the ancient oracles were announcing. See *Days of the Lord* 5:209-210 and n. 23.

5. Ezek 34:11-16.

6. Gen 29:9; 30:29, 31, 36, 38, 40; 37:2; Exod 2:16; 3:1; 1 Sam 16:11.

7. 1 Chr 27:29-31 (Luke 15:15; John 10:12); Zech 11:12; Gen 30:28-43.

God entrusted this task to Moses first, then to Joshua, then to the judges and the kings: 2 Sam 5:2; 24:17; Ps 78:70-71; Ezek 34:6-31. They often disappointed him and abused his trust, whence the prophets' very bitter reproaches: Jer 23:1-2; 50:6; Ezek 34:1-10; Isa 56:11; Zech 11:4-17.

8. See *Days of the Lord* 5:147.

9. This no doubt is harking back to the Exodus and the march in the desert. That period was marked by strife and uncertainty. The entrance into the Promised Land and the settlement there were laborious. But now, under the protection of the Lord, the flock has nothing to fear (Ps 23); it is going to enjoy the rich pastures that are allotted to it.

10. St. Gregory of Nyssa (ca. 335-395), *Homélie sur le Cantique des cantiques*, 2, in *Liturgies des Heures*, IV, 323.

11. This is not only because of the value of each sheep, especially for the owner of a large flock. It is enough to have met a shepherd once to realize how attached this person may become—in a sentimental way one could say—to each of the sheep that for him or her is unique and distinct from all others. See *Days of the Lord* 3:334, n. 18.

12. *The Jerusalem Bible* (London: Darton, Longman, and Todd, 1966).

13. Eucharistic Prayer IV, which exactly sums up Paul's teaching in the first part of his Letter to the Romans (1:18–3:20).

14. On Paul's Letter to the Romans, see *Days of the Lord* 4:81–83. This letter is read from the Ninth to the Twenty-fourth Sunday in Ordinary Time, Year A.

Rom 5:5-11 is also the second reading on Trinity Sunday, Year C (see above), and the Eleventh Sunday in Ordinary Time, Year A. See *Days of the Lord* 4:95–96.

15. This is what Fr. Maximilian Kolbe did when, at the age of forty-seven, in the concentration camp of Auschwitz, he offered to take the place of the father of a family condemned to starve to death in a cell. Fr. Kolbe, who died August 14, 1941, was canonized by Pope John-Paul II on October 10, 1982.

16. St. Gertrude (1255–1302), *Révélations*, quoted by A. Hamon, *Histoire de la dévotion au Sacré-Coeur* (Paris: Beauchesne, 1925) 2:150.

17. St. Philip Neri (1515–1595), in M. Jouhandeau, *Saint Philippe Néri* (Paris: Plon, 1957) 68.

18. Luke's chapter 15 records three parables that illustrate God's mercy: that of today, that of the lost coin (8–10), and that of the prodigal son (11–32). This chapter is read in its entirety on the Twenty-Fourth Sunday in Ordinary Time, Year C. See *Days of the Lord* 6:210–214.

See the analysis of this whole chapter in J. Dupont, "Réjouissez-vous avec moi," *Assemblées du Seigneur*, 2nd series, no. 55 (Paris: Publications de Saint-André—Cerf, 1974) 70–79. In Luke's Gospel, these three parables are placed in a polemical context. Some are murmuring against Jesus and reproaching him with his attitude toward sinners; they find it scandalous that he welcomes them and goes so far as to take meals with them. The Gospels attest that such criticisms were often leveled against Jesus: Matt 9:9-13; Mark 2:13-17; Luke 5:27-32; 19:1-10. Jesus answered that he was sent "to the lost sheep of the house of Israel" (Matt 15:24).

On the feast of the Sacred Heart, the parable of the lost sheep is not read in this polemical context but in that of the liturgical celebration of the day. See above, n. 4.

19. See J. Dupont, *Pourquoi les paraboles? La méthode parabolique de Jésus,* Lire la Bible 46 (Paris: Cerf, 1977) 105–111.

20. City dwellers will identify more readily with the woman who has lost a coin (Luke 15:8-10) or with the father whose son comes back home after straying (Luke 15:11-32). But they can understand what the loss of one sheep represents for a shepherd or the loss of one cow for a farmer or, in certain regions, the loss of one goose or one duck or a swarm of bees or any domestic animal. No owner takes this lightly. See above, n. 11.

21. It would be inappropriate to blame the shepherd for leaving the rest of the flock "in the desert" (Matthew [18:12] says, "in the hills"). To raise such an objection would be to demonstrate a total ignorance of the normal behavior of any shepherd who never leaves the flock without making sure it is safe; this is so obvious that the parable does not have to specify it. At any rate, the characteristic of a parable is to go to the essential; it can omit details and, sometimes, tolerate some exaggeration and even some unlikelihood to make a point.

22. The woman acts in the same way when she finds the lost coin (Luke 15:9). As for the father of the prodigal son, he orders a great feast to be prepared to celebrate his younger son's return. His only sadness is seeing his older son scandalized and resentful by these festivities that he does not understand and in which he refuses to participate (Luke 15:22-24, 28-32).

23. Ezek 34:11-16, first reading.

24. F. Mauriac, *Journal* (Paris: Grasset, 1934) 1:131. This was said concerning a criminal woman rejected by all, but who had implored God's pardon.

25. When one suffers in one member, the whole attention concentrates on it, and one says "my leg," "my arm," "my tooth."

26. Ch. Péguy, *Le porche de la deuxième vertu, Oeuvres poétiques complètes* (Paris: Bibliothèque de la Pléiade, N.R.F., Gallimard, 1957) 575–576.

27. C. Geffré, *Un espace pour Dieu* (Paris: Cerf, 1971) 59.

28. See J. Dupont, "Les implications christologiques de la parabole de la brebis perdue," *Jésus aux origines de la christologie* (Gembloux: Duculot, 1974). Reprinted in *Etudes sur les Evangiles synoptiques* by the same author, Bibliotheca Ephemeridum theologicarum lovaniensium LXX-B (Louvain: University Press, 1985) 2:647–666.

29. Commission Francophone Cistercienne, *Guetteur de l'aube* (Paris: Desclée, 1976) 70.

30. The same is true for the development of faith and for theology; a council gives "witness and voice to the faith of the whole People of God gathered together by Christ." *Pastoral Constitution on the Church in the Modern World (Gaudium et Spes)*, no. 3, *The Documents of Vatican II*, 200–201.

31. The adage *Lex orandi, lex credendi* ("The rule of prayer is the rule of faith") states this reciprocal relation between faith and its expression in prayer, in liturgy. We could also express it by saying, "Show me how you pray (and celebrate) and I shall tell you how you believe; as your faith is, so must be your prayer and liturgy."

32. More recently, we witnessed this legitimate and necessary interaction between the local Churches and the people of God, on the one hand, and those responsible for the ultimate discernment, on the other, at work during the period which prepared Vatican II. Then one was hearing talk of "experiments" done under the guidance and responsibility of bishops, religious superiors, even "experts" specifically assigned to the task by the higher-ups in charge of liturgical reform, in particular for the regulation of Eucharistic concelebration and for the elaboration of a new structure of the Liturgy of the Hours. The term "experiment" is probably not the most adequate to describe what was thus accomplished: R. Gantoy, "L'expérience en liturgie," *Communautés et liturgies* 49 (1967) 203–204; Gantoy, "Au-delà de la créativité: Perspectives d'avenir," ibid. 54 (1972) 504–514; Gantoy, "Les chantiers de la prière: A propos d'un Directoire pour l'Office," ibid. 60 (1978) 45–56.

33. Thus, the feast of Christ the King. See *Days of the Lord* 4:256–264.

34. K. Rahner, "Coeur" in *Encyclopédie de la foi*, ed. H. Fries, Cogitatio fidei 15 (Paris: Cerf, 1965) 1:202.

The Sanctoral Cycle—Pages 99–102

1. See above, Introduction, n. 6.

2. Promulgated on March 21, 1969.

3. St. Joseph (March 19), Annunciation (March 25), Birth of St. John (June 24), Sts. Peter and Paul (June 29), Assumption (August 15), All Saints (November 1), Immaculate Conception (December 8).

4. Conversion of St. Paul (January 25), Presentation of the Lord (February 2), Chair of St. Peter (February 22), St. Mark (April 25), Sts. Philip and James (May 3), St. Matthias (May 14), Visitation (May 31), St. Thomas (July 3), St. James (July 25), Transfiguration (August 6), St. Lawrence (August 10), St. Bartholomew (August 24), Birth of Mary (September 8), Triumph of the Cross (September 14), St. Matthew (September 21), St. Luke (October 18), Sts. Simon and Jude (October 28), St. Andrew (November 30), St. John (December 27), Holy Innocents (December 28).

5. The obligatory memorials must be celebrated everywhere; the others are left to the free choice of everyone. But no memorial is ever celebrated on a Sunday. Besides, the obligatory memorials that fall in Lent become optional, and the others cannot be celebrated that year.

6. The solemnity of the Immaculate Conception is always during Advent: when December 8 is a Sunday, the celebration is delayed until Monday. The same is true of St. Joseph and the Annunciation, which always fall during Lent. But if March 19 or March 25 falls during Holy Week or Easter Week, the celebration of the feast is transferred to the second week of Easter. Thus in 1989, the solemnity of St. Joseph was celebrated on April 4, and that of the Annunciation on April 3. This latter feast is most often transferred: it will be celebrated on April 7 in 1997, on April 8 in 2002, on April 4 in 2005, on March 31 in 2008.

7. Vatican II, Constitution on the Sacred Liturgy (*Sacrosanctum Concilium*), no. 106, *Documents of Vatican II.*

8. Eucharistic Prayer II.

9. Eucharistic Prayer III.

10. Eucharistic Prayer IV.

11. Ignatius of Antioch (d. 110), *Lettre aux Romains*, salutation, Sources chrétiennes 10, p. 125.

12. The anniversary of the cathedral and other consecrated churches is written into the calendar of each diocese.

13. Before Vatican II, the Mass was always that listed in the calendar for that day; the sanctoral cycle then contained 346 names. On other days, outside Advent and in the time between Septuagesima and Easter, the formulary of the Sunday Mass was repeated during the week.

14. See A.-G. Martimort, *L'Eglise en prière* (Paris: Desclée, 1983) 142–143; P. Jounel, *Le renouveaudu culte des saints dans la liturgie romaine* (Rome: Ed. Liturgiche, 1986); Adam, *La liturgie aujourd'hui*, 298–299.

15. On the origins, historical development, and theology of the veneration of the saints, see Martimort, ibid. 124–125; Adam, ibid. 296–300.

16. There is deviation or deformation when the veneration of the saints excessively dwells on the miraculous or does not lead to God, to whom alone adoration is due and who remains the unique source of all graces. The reform of the Sanctoral Cycle effected by Vatican II precisely had as its objective to maximize the true nature of the veneration of saints. On the one hand, a certain number of saints whose historicity was in doubt were erased from the calendar. On the other hand, priority was restored to the celebration of the mystery of salvation that unfolds in the liturgical seasons (see above, n. 14).

17. Preface of Holy Men and Women, I.

18. Preface of Holy Men and Women, II.

February 2, The Presentation of the Lord—Pages 103–105

1. M. L. McClure and C. L. Feltoe, trans., *The Pilgrimage of Etheria*, Translations of Christian Literature, Series 3, Liturgical Texts (Ann Arbor, Mich: University Microfilms International, 1978) 56.

Egeria (sometimes Etheria) was a highborn Spanish or Gallic woman, quite probably a nun, who between 381 and 384 made a long pilgrimage to Egypt and the Holy Land, particularly to Sinai and Jerusalem. Her book, written in Latin, was discovered in 1884 in a convent in Arezzo, Italy; it is a precious document because of the precise descriptions she gives of the places she visited and the liturgies she took part in.

The *anastasis* (Greek for "resurrection") was the name given to the complex of sanctuaries around Golgotha and tomb of Christ, built on Constantine's orders, beginning in 326. Enclosed within a vast rotunda, it is still preserved in its original form and dimensions in spite of destruction and numerous restorations. "The mysteries" designate the celebration of the Eucharist (the Mass).

2. The holy places always attracted many pilgrims. But pilgrims were particularly numerous after the Constantinian peace (313), and even more so after the journey made in 326 by the Empress Helena, the mother of Constantine (306-337). See "Pélerinage," *Dictionnaire d'archéologie chrétienne et de liturgie*, vol. 14/1, cols. 65-176.

3. The feasts in question are principally feasts that celebrate events of Christ's life localized in sanctuaries to which people came: thus the Nativity of the Lord (see *Days of the Lord* 1:192), Passion Sunday (see *Days of the Lord* 2:210-211).

4. See *Days of the Lord* 1:192; 340, n. 1.

Eastern Churches to this day celebrate the Manifestation (this is the meaning of the Greek word *epiphania*) in the flesh on January 6.

The celebration described in Egeria's journal took place on February 15.

5. [TRANSLATOR'S NOTE: The Law does not prescribe anywhere that any child, including first-born males, should be presented in the Temple. It does state that first-born males, human or animal, belong to God (Exod 13:2; 22:28-29; Deut 15:19). If the animal is a sacrificial animal, it is to be sacrificed; if not, it is to be redeemed or destroyed (Exod 34:19-20). The child is redeemed (Exod 34:19-20). In a later law the price was set at five shekels of silver (Num 18:15-17). Many exegetes believe Luke thought the redemption of the child required his being brought to the Temple; others think he had 1 Sam 1:24-28 in mind when he wrote this episode.]

6. The Law did not prescribe that the purification in the Temple should take place on exactly the fortieth day.

7. For most people, this name concentrated attention on a secondary aspect of the celebration, the use of candles blessed beforehand (the blessing was adopted only from the tenth century on in the Germanic countries, and, in Rome, it is not attested before the twelfth century). However, this rite of light is significant. The Canticle of Simeon hailed Jesus, calling him "a light for revelation to the Gentiles" (Luke 2:32). From this viewpoint, the popular term *chandeleur*—Candlemas—was very fitting.

8. The change of name was introduced by the Roman Calendar (*Calendarium romanum*) promulgated on February 14, 1969, by Pope Paul VI.

9. This antiphon may be replaced with another appropriate song.

10. *Liturgie monastique des Heures*, Abbaye de Clervaux, 1981, 1311 (Fiche de chant V LH 125).

THE PRESENTATION: GOING TO MEET THE AWAITED ONE—
Pages 106-118

1. The book—3 chapters, 55 verses—is composed of six discourses in the form of dialogue (1:2-5; 1:6-2:9; 2:10-16; 2:17-3:5; 3:6-12; 3:13-21). It ends with a general exhortation to observe the Law and the promise of Elijah's return (3:22-24). It is usually accepted that the book was written ca. 400 B.C. (480–460 according to the *Traduction oecuménique de la Bible*). The author's true name is unknown. The book was called Malachi because the word *mal'aki* ("my messenger," 3:1) was taken for a proper name.

This prophetic writing is particularly interesting because it has a new viewpoint on the nations. Later on it was given a pronounced messianic meaning and Jesus was seen as the messenger the prophet announced.

See the introductions of the *Bible de Jérusalem*, p.1090, and the *Traduction oecuménique de la Bible*, 1261; "Malachie" and "Malachie, Livre" in *Dictionnaire encyclopédique de la Bible*, 772. See also *Days of the Lord* 4:236-237; 6:304-305.

2. It is enough to think of the harsh disappointments that followed, for instance, the end of World War II, the liberation of occupied countries, the overthrow of oppressive re-

gimes, or, in the Church, those that marked the aftermath of Vatican II. Some came to think that the struggles for liberty were useless, to say that the Council reforms had destabilized the Church; whereas others were in danger of getting discouraged or could only dream of returning to the situation prior to the Council.

3. It is the subject of the Book of Job. See also Pss 37 and 73; Hab 1:1-2; the Book of Jonah.

4. As early as the eighth century B.C., the coming of the "Day of the Lord" was announced as a blessing for the just, those who observed the prescriptions of the Covenant, but as a fearsome event for the impious, for the nations hostile to the people of God: Isa 2:6-22; Ezek 7:7-27; Joel 1:15; 2:1-17; Amos 2:13-16; 3:1-12; 5:18-20; Zeph 1:7, 14-15.

5. The exegetical study of this text as we have it shows that there were later additions. But it is clear that in its present state, the text distinguishes two stages and two persons.

6. Some have identified the messenger with the author himself; others, with Nehemiah, who shortly before had inaugurated the reform of the worship and religious institutions of Israel. Still others have spoken of Elijah, the prophet taken up into heaven (2 Kgs 2:11), because a certain tradition held that his return was to be the preliminary sign of the advent of the Lord at the end of time (2 Kgs 2:11; Sir 48:10; Mal 3:24; Matt 17:1-13; Luke 1:17).

7. People gave importance to this text when John and Jesus appeared: Matt 11:14; 16:14; 17:10-12; Mark 6:15; 8:28; 9:11-13; Luke 9:19; John 1:21, 25.

8. Every reform has this twofold objective; it was that of Ezra, for example (Ezra 8:17-30)

9. Djalal Al-Din Al Rumi, called "Mawlana" ("our master"), (1207–1273), in L'Esprit dit: "Viens," introduction and presentation of the texts by R. Cabié and J.-P. Bagot, Langage des hommes/Parole de Dieu 3 (Paris: Cerf—Droguet et Ardant, 1975) 104–105.

Djalal Al-Din Al Rumi, a Muslim mystic who lived in Anatolia (the part of Turkey that comprises Asia Minor), was the founder of the order of the mawlanis, better known as the "Whirling Dervishes."

Khadir (or Khezr) is the name given to a mysterious personage who represents the spiritual master par excellence.

10. Mark 1:2; John 1:23.

11. Matt 21:12-17; Mark 11:15-17; Luke 19:45-46; John 2:13-17.

12. First reading.

13. On the Letter to the Hebrews, see Days of the Lord 5:303–304.

14. Rom 7:13-14; 1 Cor 15:56.

15. See above, p. 84.

16. The devil is the one who destroys, who exterminates: Wis 2:24; 1 Cor 5:5; 10:10; John 8:44.

17. James Hamilton Charlesworth, ed. and trans., The Odes of Solomon; The Syriac Texts, Texts and Translations 13, Pseudepigrapha Series 7 (Missoula, Mont.: Scholars Press, 1977) 145–146, Ode 42.

These "odes," discovered in 1909 in a Syriac manuscript, must have been written in the first third of the second century.

18. Gal 3:16, 29.

19. John of Fécamp (ca. 990–1078), Confession théologique, II:6, in Lectures chrétiennes pour notre temps (Paris: Orval, 1973) Fiche G 1.

20. This doctrine is developed at length in the Letter to the Hebrews: 4:14–10:31.

21. St. Paulinus of Nola (353–431), Lettre 38, in Lectures chrétiennes pour notre temps, Fiche F 47.

22. Announcement of the birth of John to Zechariah (1:5-25); announcement of the birth of Jesus to Mary (1:26-38); Mary's visit to her cousin Elizabeth, the mother of the Baptist (1:39-56); John's birth and circumcision (1:57-80); Jesus' birth and circumcision (2:1-21); presentation of Jesus in the Temple (2:22-40); Jesus at twelve in the Temple among the doctors of the Law (2:41-52).

23. Among other traits, commentators have noted the parallelism between the stories directly concerning Jesus and those concerning John, who is always placed in relation to the one he is announcing: the insistent reference to prophecies; the place of the two women, Elizabeth and especially Mary.

See R. Laurentin, *Structure et théologie de Luc 1-2*, Etudes bibliques (Paris: Gabalda, 1957); R. Laurentin, *Les évangiles de Noël* (Paris: Desclée, 1985); L. Monloubou, *Lire aujourd'hui les évangiles de l'enfance*, Croire aujourd'hui (Paris: Sénevé, 1971); C. Perrot, "Les récits de l'enfance de Jésus, Mt 1-2, Lc 1-2," *Cahiers Evangile* 18 (1976).

24. This Gospel is also that of the feast of the Holy Family, Year B. See *Days of the Lord* 1:233-236.

25. The purification of the new mother was to take place forty days after the birth of a boy and eighty days after the birth of a girl. The ritual prescribed the holocaust of a lamb and the offering of a pigeon or a turtledove. If the woman was poor, the lamb could be replaced by a second pigeon or turtledove (Lev 12:1-8). Until recently, the *Roman Ritual* had a ceremony of "churching" to celebrate the happy return of the mother into the community.

In commemoration of the tenth plague of Egypt, which had not struck the Hebrews (Exod 12:29), every first-born if it was a male, whether human or animal, was consecrated to the Lord (Exod 13:2) and was to be "redeemed" by an offering made to the Lord (Exod 13:12-13, 15; 34:20; Num 18:15-16).

26. The present name of the feast—called Purification of the Virgin Mary before the liturgical reform of Vatican II—does justice to this fact.

27. Jesus was circumcised on the eighth day, as the Law prescribed (Gen 17:12; Lev 12:3). The Synoptic Gospels, in particular, stress that the Lord manifested great respect for the prescriptions of the Law. Thus, for instance, Matt 5:17-20; 17:24-27; Mark 1:44; Luke 17:14.

28. Vatican II, *Dogmatic Constitution on the Church (Lumen Gentium)*, no. 62, in *The Documents of Vatican II*, p. 92.

29. Ibid., no. 67, p. 95.

30. For instance, Isa 42:6; 49:6.

31. See, for example, *Days of the Lord* 6:71-73, 115-117.

32. Matt 10:34-37; Luke 12:51-53; John 1:11; 3:19-21.

33. Isa 8:8, 14-15; 28:15.

34. Matt 21:42; Acts 4:11; Rom 9:32-33; 1 Pet 2:7. The same ambivalence is also found concerning Simon, to whom Jesus gave the name of Peter because on this rock he would build his church (Matt 16:18); however, Peter could become "an obstacle" for Jesus himself (Matt 16:23).

35. See also Eph 6:17; Rev 1:1, 16; 19:15.

36. The sword Simeon speaks of does not refer to the sufferings of Mary's heart during the Passion of Jesus. See *Days of the Lord* 1:234-235.

37. Origen (ca. 185-254), *Homélies sur saint Luc*, XV: 1, 5, Sources chrétiennes 87 (Paris: Cerf, 1962) 233-235, 237.

38. In his Gospel, as in the Acts of the Apostles, Luke gives an important place to women.

According to the Law (Deut 19:15), two witnesses were required to attest the veracity of a statement. The New Testament mentions this prescription several times: Matt 18:16; 26:60-61; John 8:17; 2 Cor 13:1; 1 Tim 5:19.

Some commentators thought that this man and woman represented the whole of humankind—"male and female he created them" (Gen 1:27)—coming to meet the Lord. If Luke intended to suggest this, he did it in a mightily discreet way.

39. Commission Francophone Cistercienne, *Prière au fil des heures*, Vivante liturgie 99 (Paris: Publications de Saint-André—Centurion, 1982) 180.

40. John 1:14, 51; 2:18-21; 4:19-23; 7:37-39; Rev 21:22.

41. Antiphon of the Canticle of Mary.

42. On this theme, see O. Clément, *Anachroniques* (Paris: Desclée de Brouwer, 1990) 265–266. The following remarks are largely inspired by this speech of the author at the Catholic University of Louvain (Louvain-la-Neuve, Belgium) on February 2, 1989, when the author received the insignia of Doctor *honoris causa*, pp. 259–266.

43. Ambrose (339–397), *Traité sur l'Evangile de saint Luc*, II:59, p. 99.

See Ch. Combaz, *Eloge de l'âge dans un monde jeune et bronzé* (Paris: Laffont, 1989).

44. See *Days of the Lord* 3:315, n. 26.

45. See *Days of the Lord* 1:288–293.

46. Commission Francophone Cistercienne, *Guetteur de l'aube*, 142; *Hymnaire de la liturgie des Heures* (Paris: Cerf—Chalet—Levain, 1990) 220 (Fiche de chant V 253).

Joseph, Husband of Mary—Pages 119–121

1. The Martyrology is a liturgical book that lists, for every day of the year, the saints whose feasts are celebrated or memorialized.

2. Their various authors are influenced by one another.

3. Frequently associated with that of "foster father of Jesus."

4. A.-G. Martimort, *The Church at Prayer: The Liturgy and Time* IV (Collegeville, Minn.: The Liturgical Press, 1986) 143–144.

5. See *Days of the Lord* 1:7–9.

6. Ibid., 5–7.

7. The devotion to various saints was in fact localized at first. Vatican II formulated the following principle for the revision of the calendar of saints' feasts: "Lest the feasts of the saints, however, take precedence over the feasts which commemorate the very mysteries of salvation, many of them should be left to be celebrated by a particular Church or nation or community; only those should be extended to the universal Church which commemorate saints who are truly of universal significance" (*Constitution on the Sacred Liturgy*, No. 111, *The Documents of Vatican II*, p.170. See also *Days of the Lord* 1:16–17.

8. It is mentioned in the Symbol of St. Epiphanius (ca. 374). The Council of Ephesus in 431 declared anathema whoever would deny that Mary is the Mother of God (A. Dumeige, *La foi catholique: Textes doctrinaux du magistère de l'Eglise* [Paris: Orante, 1961], nos. 5, 295).

The prayer *Sub tuum praesidium* goes back to the fourth century: "We fly to your protection, O holy Mother of God. Do not reject our prayers in our needs, but deliver us always from all danger, O glorious and blessed Virgin."

9. Joseph is, of course, represented on icons of the nativity (but never in the foreground) wondering about Mary's motherhood, the secret of which the angel reveals to him in a dream. Later on he would be represented in the paintings of the flight into Egypt. Even the apocryphal gospels of the infancy are very reserved concerning Joseph. The only true exception is the *Story of Joseph the Carpenter*, probably written in Egypt in the fourth century. It portrays Jesus, on Mount Carmel, narrating the life of his foster father: widowed at eighty-nine years of age, he marries Mary two years later and dies between Jesus and Mary at the age of 111; his soul is taken up into heaven and his intact body awaits the Lord's return. These details and some others—borrowed from the *Proto-Gospel of James*, probably written in Egypt also at the beginning of the second century—were hardly calculated to inspire piety and to serve as a basis for liturgical veneration. See "Apocryphes du N. T." in *Dictionnaire encyclopédique de la Bible*, 113–130.

10. Gospel of March 19 and of the Fourth Sunday of Advent, Year A. See *Days of the Lord* 1:142–143.

11. Gospel of the Holy Family, Year A. See *Days of the Lord* 1:225–228.

12. Optional Gospel for March 19 and Gospel of the Holy Family, Year C. See *Days of the Lord* 1:239–241.

13. Neither Hebrew nor biblical Greek allows any distinction between "carpenter" and "cabinetmaker." Carpenters-cabinetmakers are mentioned several times in the Old Testament, along with masons or stonecutters, especially in the context of the building, repairing, or rebuilding of the Temple. In a village or a small town, the carpenter-cabinetmaker must have been an artisan to whom people had recourse in a variety of circumstances, who knew everybody and was known by everybody, who entered all houses.

14. The Gospels do not speak of the death—the "Dormition" as the Eastern Christians say—of the Virgin Mary either. Probably under the influence of the apocryphal writings (see above, n. 9), iconographic traditions have represented Joseph as an old man. But there is no basis for this viewpoint.

15. Commission Francophone Cistercienne, *La nuit, le jour,* 143.

BLESSED ARE THE FAITHFUL SERVANTS—Pages 122–132

1. See "David" in *Vocabulaire de théologie biblique*, cols. 247–250, and in *Dictionnaire encyclopédique de la Bible*, 332–333

2. This oracle is also read (2 Sam 7:1-5, 8-11, 16) on the Fourth Sunday of Advent, Year B (see *Days of the Lord* 1:146–148) and at the morning Mass of December 24.

3. The oracle of Nathan is, as it were, the prologue of the great history of the succession to the throne of David (2 Sam 9–20; 1 Kgs 1–2). But through constant rereading, people understood that it announced another David unlike any other king, and they kept alive the hope of his coming: Hos 3:5; Isa 11:11-12; Jer 23:5-6; Ezek 34:23-31; 37:24-28.

4. Ps 89:31-36.

5. Ps 132:11.

6. Augustine (354–430), *Commentaire du psaume 131, Oeuvres complètes* (Paris: Vivès, 1871) 15:639–640. In the Latin Psalter that Augustine quotes, verse 39b of Psalm 89 reads, *distulisti Christum tuum.* The verb *differre* literally means "to put off," which can also be understood as "to reject." Augustine chose the first meaning; modern translations, for instance the *Jerusalem Bible*, read, "[you] raged at your anointed."

7. See "Justice" in *Vocabulaire de théologie biblique*, cols. 636–645, and in *Dictionnaire encyclopédique de la Bible*, 707–709.

8. Rom 1:16–4:25. On this letter, see R. Baulès, *L'évangile, Puissance de Dieu*, Lectio divina 53 (Paris: Cerf, 1968); F. Leenhardt, *L'Epître de saint Paul aux Romains* (Geneva: Delachaux—Labor et fides, 1981); S. Lyonnet, *Le message de l'épître aux Romains*, Lire la Bible 28 (Paris: Cerf, 1969); H. Ponsot, *Une introduction à la lettre aux Romains*, Initiations (Paris: Cerf, 1988); Ch. Perrot, "L'Epître aux Romains," *Cahiers Evangile* 65 (1988). Ample excerpts from this letter are read from the Ninth to the Twenty-fourth Sunday in Ordinary Time, Year A. See *Days of the Lord* 4:81–192.

9. See the "Chronological Table" of the *Jerusalem Bible*. Some people say that Abraham lived according to the Law before the Law. In the same vein, sometimes people say that certain persons who live righteous lives are Christians without knowing it, although they do not know the gospel or Christ or even explicitly deny these. This way of speaking is suspect, to say the least. Christ is, it is true, the unique Savior of all human beings in the world. But he alone can discern in a sovereign manner those who belong to him or those in whom he recognizes himself. No one can limit his liberality or impose ways or conditions on his grace. On Judgment Day, there will be a good number of surprises (Matt 25:31-46). Besides, certain ways of speaking betray an annexationist mentality (everything that is good is Christian), even if it is unconscious.

10. Certain Semites of the western regions were in the habit of immolating the first-born child in cases of calamity. Abraham came from the East where such practice was unknown. When the Bible speaks of these sacrifices, it calls them the "abominable practice of the nations." See 2 Kgs 16:3; 21:6; 23:10; Jer 7:30-31; Mic 6:7. "I never commanded them, nor did it even enter my mind that they should practice such abominations" (Jer 32:35). In fact, the Law prohibited murder (Exod 20:13). If it proclaimed that the first-born belonged to the Lord, this recognition of God's property was to be expressed by an offering made to the sanctuary, and not by the sacrifice of the child.

11. Luke (3:23-38), who also gives a genealogy of Jesus, goes back from Joseph to Adam, "the son of God."

12. Matt 1:1-25. The whole of chapter 1 is read at the Vigil Mass on December 24. See Days of the Lord 1:197-199.

13. This Gospel is also read on the Fourth Sunday of Advent, Year A. See Days of the Lord 1:142-145. The liturgical context is not the same in both cases. On March 19, we are invited to look more closely at the personality and vocation of Joseph.

14. See Days of the Lord 1:142-143.

15. Preface of the feast of St. Joseph.

16. See "Justice de l'homme" in Vocabulaire de théologie biblique, cols. 642-643, and in Dictionnaire encyclopédique de la Bible, 708-709.

17. Preface of Holy Men and Women I.

18. J. Guitton, La Vierge Marie, Livre de vie (Paris: Editions Montaigne, 1949) 52.

19. Such questions arise because of an amalgam of the narratives of Matthew and Luke. Then the events succeed one another in the following manner: annunciation to Mary, who immediately set out on her way to her cousin Elizabeth, with whom she remained about three months (Luke 1:26-48). At this point, people imagine that Joseph noticed, like everybody else, that Mary was pregnant and that this discovery troubled him; an angel was sent to calm his inner turmoil. Nothing of all this was recorded by Matthew (Luke does not mention any announcement to Joseph). We must guard against fusing two Gospels—or four—into one narrative of the "life of Jesus." Each one must be taken in itself. See Days of the Lord 6:348, n. 43.

20. Commission Francophone Cistercienne, Guetteur de l'aube (Fiche de chant W LH 196).

21. L. Deiss, La liturgie des Heures, 2:1283 (Fiche de chant W 68).

This silence caused certain persons to imagine that Joseph—portrayed as an old man (see above, n. 14)—died, at the latest, about twelve years after the birth of the Savior because it was necessary to take into account the episode of the pilgrimage to the Temple made by Jesus and his parents (Luke 2:41-51). But there is no certain information on this subject in the Gospels. The remark of the folk of Nazareth who say when speaking of Jesus, "Is he not the carpenter's son?" (Matt 13:55; Mark 6:3) is not conclusive. It can be understood to mean that Joseph was still there, along with other relatives of Jesus; but it can also be understood to mean that Joseph was already dead, because in villages the memory of family connections is very long.

23. Matt 1:20; 2:13, 19, 22.

24. Although less frequent than in the Old Testament, dreams are not lacking in the New. Besides Joseph's case, we have those of Peter (Acts 2:17); Paul (Acts 16:9-10; 23:11; 27:23). See "Songes" in Vocabulaire de théologie biblique, cols. 1245-1247. Certain mystics relate that they received revelations in dreams, although they usually say "in ecstasy," that is, in a state in which one is taken out of oneself and the sensible world.

25. Gen 15:12-21; 20:3-6; 28:11-12; 37:5-11; 46:2-4.

26. Bernardine of Siena, Homélie sur saint Joseph, in La liturgie des Heures, 2:1262.

27. This oracle is read at the Vigil Mass of Pentecost. See Days of the Lord 3:260-262.

28. Luke 2:40, 52, 51.

29. This same passage from Luke's Gospel, plus the two missing verses (2:41-52), is read on the feast of the Holy Family, Year C. See *Days of the Lord* 1:238-241. See J. Dupont, "Jésus à douze ans (Lc 2, 41-52)," *Assemblées du Seigneur*, 1st series, No. 14 (Bruges: Publications de Saint-André, 1961) 25-43.

We notice in this passage a few themes that will recur in the rest of Luke's Gospel: the Temple, Jerusalem, the "three days," the necessity—"it was necessary"—in which Jesus found himself accomplishing his Father's will, the incomprehension of the people around him, the connection of the two verbs "seek" and "find." Some of these allusions bring to mind the slow journeying toward the paschal faith described in chapter 24.

30. Luke 3:21-22; 4:1-30.

In the Acts of the Apostles (1:21-22), Luke relates that Peter proposed finding a replacement for Judas in the group of the Twelve: "Therefore, it is necessary that one of the men who accompanied us the whole time the Lord Jesus came and went among us, beginning from the baptism of John until the day on which he was taken up from us, become with us a witness to his resurrection."

31. Nowadays, it is at the age of thirteen and one day that a youth becomes a *Bar Mitzvah* ("son of the Law," that is, obliged to observe the commandments). In most communities, this rite of passage is celebrated in a ceremony that takes place in the synagogue. Boys step up on the platform to chant the scriptural text they have learned and rehearsed for a long time; they pronounce a prayer and a profession of faith. The rite of passage for girls is called *Bat Mitzvah*. See A. Vincent, *Le judaisme*, Bibliothèque catholique des sciences religieuses (Paris: Bloud et Gay, 1932) 203-204.

32. Luke 19:47; 21:37-38.

33. Religious iconography often represented the scene in this manner, which is similar to the way it showed young Samuel left in the service of the temple in Shiloh (1 Sam 3:1-21). See *Days of the Lord* 5:11-14.

34. At that time, the roads were not safe, as is shown by the parable of the Good Samaritan (Luke 10:29-37). This is why people traveled in groups.

35. The Greek word—*teknon*—used here is a diminutive. It suggests a translation such as "my boy."

36. There is another frequent but less exact translation: "I must be about my Father's business."

37. This verse, omitted on the feast of St. Joseph, is read on the feast of the Holy Family, Year C. See *Days of the Lord* 1:241.

38. Also Luke 9:44; 18:32-33.

39. Luke 9:45; 18:34.

40. Gospel of the Twenty-third Sunday in Ordinary Time, Year C. See *Days of the Lord* 6:200-205.

41. Preface of the feast of St. Joseph.

42. Commission Francophone Cistercienne, *Sur la trace de Dieu* (Paris: Desclée, 1979) 110 (Fiche de chant W 118).

Annunciation of the Lord—Pages 133-134

1. This formulation does not always use the same terms, but the meaning is rigorously the same.

2. On the origin of the feast of the Nativity of the Lord, see *Days of the Lord* 1:191-192.

3. Indeed, the Council of Toledo speaks of this feast because of the difficulty in celebrating it during Lent; therefore, the feast already existed.

The same difficulty persists today. March 25 falls quite often during Holy Week (e.g., in 2002, 2005), sometimes during Easter Week (e.g., in 2008). The Annunciation is then delayed until Monday of the Second Week of Easter.

4. The tale is told of Spanish monks who, having stopped at Cluny, asked Abbot Odilo (962–1049) to secretly celebrate the feast of the Annunciation on December 18, according to their custom.

5. There is a detailed study in F. Cabrol and H. Leclercq, *Dictionnaire d'archéologie chrétienne et de liturgie*, vol. 1/2, cols. 2241–2255.

6. One habitually says that the date of March 25 (conception of Jesus) was fixed in relation to the date of his birth on December 25 (nine months later). This is not evident, for the date of Christmas was not fixed from the first. In the East, Christmas is celebrated on January 6; whereas, in the West, around the fourth century, the birth was separated from the manifestation of the Lord. Certain authors think that March 25 was the date of both the death of Christ and his conception. In this case, it is Christmas that depends upon the Annunciation. See F. Cabrol and H. Leclercq, *Dictionnaire d'archéologie chrétienne et de liturgie*, cols. 2247–2249.

7. Ps 40:8; Heb 10:7.

8. Prayer over the Gifts.

9. Opening Prayer.

10. See Prayer after Communion.

11. Preface of the feast.

THE GOOD NEWS OF THE INCARNATION ANNOUNCED TO MARY—
Pages 135–143

1. This prophecy is also proclaimed on the Fourth Sunday of Advent, Year A. See *Days of the Lord* 1:139–140.

2. It is the alliance with the redoubtable Assyria, whose demands were soon to prove disastrous on the political and religious planes.

3. On the twofold translation "the young woman" (according to the Hebrew text) or "the virgin" (according to the Greek text and the Vulgate, the Latin translation of the Bible by St. Jerome [ca. 347–420]), see *Days of the Lord* 1:326, n. 3.

4. Fourth Sunday of Advent, Year C. See *Days of the Lord* 1:15–57. The words "she who is to give birth" indeed bring to mind Isaiah's prophecy.

5. Fourth Sunday of Advent, Year A. See *Days of the Lord* 1:142–143.

6. The meaning of a scriptural text is said to be "plenary" when it encompasses these successive enrichments. This development of the primary meaning is homogeneous, without break, because the same God speaks through the prophets and the events of salvation history. "This plan of revelation is realized by deeds and words having an inner unity: the deeds wrought by God in the history of salvation manifest and confirm the teaching and realities signified by the words, while the words proclaim the deeds and clarify the mystery contained in them." *Dogmatic Constitution on Divine Revelation* (*Dei Verbum*), no. 2, *Documents of Vatican II*.

7. See *Days of the Lord* 5:244–245. From the Twenty-seventh to the Thirty-third Sunday in Ordinary Time, Year B, seven excerpts from the Letter to the Hebrews are read: ibid., 249–251, 259, 268–269, 275–277, 284–286, 291–292, 303–304.

8. The same text, minus one verse (Heb 10:5-10), is read on the Fourth Sunday of Advent, Year C. See *Days of the Lord* 1:160–161.

9. Psalm 119 abundantly repeats this throughout its 176 verses.

10. Psalm 40:7 is quoted here according to the Greek version, which says "body" where the Hebrew says "ears."

11. Eucharistic Prayer IV. The other Eucharistic prayers use equivalent terms.

12. "Introduction to the Letter to the Hebrews," *Traduction oecuménique de la Bible.*

13. See also Matt 11:27; John 7:29; 10:15; 17:25-26.

14. Luke 4:16-21.

15. This text is read on the Fifth Sunday of Lent, Year B. See *Days of the Lord* 2:155-156.

16. Augustine (354-430), *Homélie sur le Psaume 122,2,* in *Les plus belles homélies de saint Augustin sur les psaumes,* chosen and presented by G. Humeau (Paris: Beauchesne, 1947) 415.

17. This Gospel is also read on the Fourth Sunday of Advent, Year B. See *Days of the Lord* 1:148-154.

18. Luke's Gospel does not say that Mary was only engaged to Joseph. She was "betrothed," which means that she was officially his bride, even though she had not yet been solemnly brought into her husband's house at the time of the celebration of the wedding, which preceded the consummation of the marriage. See Deut 22:23-24; Gen 29:27; Judg 14:12; Tob 9:7.

19. Gabriel means "man of God" or "strength of God." This angel appears for the first time in the Book of Daniel (8:16; 9:21), where he acts as interpreter. He is charged with announcing the divine interventions for the salvation of humankind, and more particularly the advent of the Messiah. See X. Léon-Dufour, "Gabriel," *Dictionnaire du Nouveau Testament* (Paris: Seuil, 1975) 272.

20. The aura of joy that suffuses this announcement evokes that of the messianic times the prophets speak of. See Zeph 3:14; Joel 2:21; Zech 9:9.

21. 2 Sam 7:12; Isa 7:10-14 (first reading); 9:5-6; Pss 89:36-38; 132.

22. This conception is announced in a stereotyped formula found in other announcements of miraculous motherhood: Gen 16:11; 17:19; Judg 13:5-7; Isa 7:14. See P. Claudel, "Les maternités miraculeuses," *Assemblées du Seigneur,* 1st series, No. 6 (Bruges: Publications de Saint-André, 1965) 58-73.

23. Heavenly announcements are habitually accompanied by a sign: Judg 6:36-40; Isa 7:10, 16.

24. Virginity was very important for the young woman given in marriage (Gen 24:16; Exod 22:15-16; Lev 21:13-15; Deut 22:13-29; Judg 19.24). Jeremiah renounced marriage, but in order to announce in a symbolic manner imminent punishment: women and children would be massacred (Jer 16:1-4). However, one can cite the cases of women who voluntarily remained widows: Judith (8:4-8), Anna (Luke 2:37). Lastly, the Essenes, whose influence on Judaism around 100 B.C. was considerable, observed continence. It seems, however, that the motivation was more one of legal purity than of asceticism. See "Virginité" in *Vocabulaire de théologie biblique,* cols. 1366-1370.

25. Pius IX (1846-1878), *Bulle Ineffabilis Deus,* December 8, 1854, defined the Immaculate Conception of Mary as a dogma of faith. Dumeige, *La foi catholique,* p. 238.

26. Certain writers—in particular St. Bernard in an admirable text—have dramatized the *fiat* of Mary by showing heaven and earth anxiously waiting for her decision. See *Days of the Lord* 1:152-153 and 174 (Bernard's text).

27. P. Emmanuel, *Sophia* (Paris: Seuil, 1973) 186.

28. As the name indicates, a martyrology was first a catalogue or list of martyrs whose memory or cult was celebrated in various Churches, usually on the anniversary of their death called *dies natalis,* "birthday" (in heaven). Afterwards, other feasts were mentioned. The first *Roman Martyrology* was published in 1584 by Pope Gregory XIII (1572-1585). It was often revised; its last Latin edition was in 1956. After the publication of the *Roman Calendar* (*Calendarium romanum*) in 1969, a new revision is in the offing, a considerable work now in progress. But certain monasteries have made an adaptation of the old martyrology for local use. Among those that have been published: E. Andry, *Martyrologe romain: Adaptation française et monastique,* 2 vols. (Solesmes, 1972). In a more immediately and generally practi-

cal perspective: A. Vinel, *Le livre des prénoms selon le nouveau calendrier* (Paris: Albin Michel, 1972). Finally, let us mention the *liste des saints et saintes de Dieu reconnus par l'Eglise*, reprinted every year in *L'agenda du chrétien* (Paris: Brepols) 37–41. See Adam, *La liturgie aujourd'hui*, 54 and 300.

29. The Gospels, Acts, and the apostolic letters show that the person of Jesus—his mystery—and his teaching were progressively understood, thanks to the decisive light of his pasch, the central event of salvation, the radiant core of the Christian faith. Taking its point of departure there, attention finally turned to the years that preceded the public manifestation of the Lord. Then the "Infancy Narratives" of Matthew and Luke took form. They certainly owe a great deal to Mary who kept in her heart the vivid memory of those events (Luke 2:51). This is what explains the rich doctrinal and theological content of these passages; they have nothing in common with anecdotal stories, intended to be edifying, such as those found in apocryphal gospels. See above, feast of St. Joseph, n. 9.

30. See above, introduction to the Annunciation.

31. P. de La Tour du Pin, *Une somme de poésie: III*, 288 (Fiche de chant P 72).

Birth of John the Baptist—Pages 144–145

1. See "Jean Baptiste" in *Vocabulaire de théologie biblique*, cols. 583–585, and "Jean" in *Dictionnaire encyclopédique de la Bible*, 642–643.

2. Acts 10:37; 11:16; 13:24-25; 18:25; 19:1-5.

3. See *Days of the Lord* 1:191–192.

4. See "Jean Baptiste" in *Dictionnaire d'archéologie chrétienne et de liturgie*, vol. 7/2, cols. 2174–2184.

5. Ibid., cols. 2171–2174.

6. In Rome, Christmas was substituted for the pagan celebration of the victory of the sun over darkness at the time of the year when days are again lengthening (see *Days of the Lord* 1:19). It is possible that the traditional bonfires on June 24 are also a survival of a feast celebrating the sun at its zenith.

7. Eucharistic Prayer IV.

FORERUNNER OF THE LORD, MESSENGER OF JOY—Pages 146–153

1. The introduction to the Book of Jeremiah (1:1-3) does tell us that Jeremiah was the "son of Hilkiah, of a priestly family in Anathoth, in the land of Benjamin," that his calling took place in the thirteenth year of the reign of Josiah (therefore in 627 B.C.), that he also exercised his ministry during the reign of Jehoiakim (609-598) and until "the fifth month of the eleventh year" of that of Zedekiah "until the downfall and exile of Jerusalem" (587), that is to say, some forty years in all.

2. This text is read on the Fifth Sunday in Ordinary Time, Year C. See *Days of the Lord* 6:35–36.

3. Fifteenth Sunday in Ordinary Time, Year B, ibid., 5:137–139.

4. St. John carefully noted the time of his encounter with Jesus, pointed out to him by the Baptist, on the banks of the Jordan: "It was about four in the afternoon" (John 1:39).

5. In fact, Jeremiah would have to pronounce oracles concerning the nations that God used to accomplish his plans.

Paul on the way to Damascus would receive a mission in terms quite similar, but it would be to announce the gospel. Paul would see in the conversion of the pagans a message of God addressed to Israel; he hoped that this conversion, arousing "jealousy," would lead Israel to be converted to the Lord (Acts 13:47; 26:17; Rom 11:11; Gal 1:15-16).

6. Jeremiah was very different from Isaiah and Amos, for instance. They never questioned their vocations and seemed much surer of themselves and their missions (Isa 6:8; Amos 7:15).

7. Jer 15:10-11; 20:14-18. Ps 22 corresponds well to what Jeremiah's life was, full of anguish and dangers. In spite of it all, Jeremiah remained strongly attached to God and faithful to the mission he had received.

8. In the New Testament, the laying on of hands is used to confer the gift of the Spirit (Acts 8:17-19; 9:17), to heal (Acts 28:8), to "ordain" to a ministry (Acts 6:6), to accredit those sent on mission (Acts 13:3), and so forth. The celebration of every sacrament of the Church has a more or less solemn imposition of the hands; in certain sacraments, in particular ordination to the priesthood, the laying on of hands constitutes the principal gesture of the rite. See "Imposition des mains" in *Vocabulaire de théologie biblique*, cols. 569-570, and in *Dictionnaire encyclopédique de la Bible*, 612.

9. There is a striking contrast between the callings of Jeremiah and Isaiah. In a vision in the Temple, the latter volunteered to announce God's word. Then a seraph purified his lips with "an ember he had taken with tongs from the altar" (Isa 6:1-16). With Jeremiah, it was God himself who acted without intermediary. Besides, he acted with gentleness and tenderness.

10. Jer 1:8, 19; 2:3; 22:24; 28:11; 29:31; 37:17; 51:57.

11. Exod 4:10-17; Judg 6:15; 1 Sam 16:7-11; Jer 1:7; Ezek 2:1; Amos 7:14-15. Mary, Joseph, and the apostles were "poor." The history of the Church and the saints attests the same thing.

12. In the Book of Jeremiah, these verbs always have God for their subject: 12:14; 18:7-9; 22:6; 31:28; 42:10; 45:4.

13. See E. Cothenet, "Les épîtres de Pierre," *Cahiers Evangile* 47 (1984).

14. Nineteenth Sunday in Ordinary Time, Year C. See *Days of the Lord* 6:158-160.

15. Third Sunday of Easter, Year A. See *Days of the Lord* 3:111-114.

16. Acts 3:21-24; 10:43; 15:15-17; 2 Tim 3:16; 2 Pet 1:19-21.

17. In the Missal of Pius V, the Old Testament was read only during the week.

18. *Dogmatic Constitution on Divine Revelation (Dei Verbum)*, no. 4, *Documents of Vatican II*, 113.

19. These first four verses of Luke's book constitute a prologue of classical construction in which the author concisely makes explicit his purpose and his concern for accurate information.

20. A similar declaration is found at the end of John's Gospel (20:30-31).

21. Born ca. 74 B.C., Herod the Great reigned from 37 on. He died in the spring of the year 4 of our era, shortly before Passover. On this person, not to be confused with Herod Antipas (4-39), of whom the Gospels also speak, see *Days of the Lord* 1:341, n. 19, and *Dictionnaire encyclopédique de la Bible*, 580-581.

22. Gen 24:60; Ruth 4:11-13; 1 Sam 4:20; 2 Sam 18:18; Prov 17:6; Ps 128:3-5.

23. Gen 16:1; 17:15-19; 18:10-15; 21:1-7.

24. Each division or class of priests was on duty in the Temple for one week, by turns (2 Chr 23:8), after which everyone went home (Luke 1:23, 39-40).

25. This offering of incense was made every day, morning and evening, on the "altar of incense," which was placed in front of the holy of holies (Exod 30:7-8; 2 Chr 26:16-18). Only once a year, on the Day of Atonement (*Yom Kippur*), the high priest entered beyond the veil of the sanctuary with the censer (Lev 16:12-13).

26. Fear and distress are normal and habitual reactions to a supernatural manifestation. This fear is not really fright; it is what we might call sacred awe before the mystery. Besides, it gives rise to adoration and praise of God: Matt 9:8; Mark 4:41; Luke 1:29, 65; 2:9; 5:26; 7:16; 8:25; 24:37; Acts 5:5, 11; 19:17.

27. Luke 1:30; 2:10. When Jesus manifested himself to the disciples, he also said, ''Do not be afraid'' (Matt 14:27; Mark 6:50; Luke 5:10).

28. Dan 8:15-26; 9:21-27.

29. In the Bible, to give a name to someone is an act of authority. In the case of a child, it is the act by which the father recognizes the child. Consequently, God declared that he was taking possession of the child to be born. Besides, he gave him a name that indicated the meaning of his election. The neighbors and relatives of Zechariah and Elizabeth were surprised that the name given the child was not that of any of the family members (Luke 1:57-66).

30. ''Nazirites'' were persons who were bound by a vow to God, either for life or, more often, for a specified period. They were subjected to precise rules. In particular, they had to abstain from drinking wine and cutting their hair (Num 6:1-21; Amos 2:11-12; Judg 13:4-7, 14; 1 Sam 1:11). Paul made a Nazirite vow that ended in Cenchrae (Acts 18:18). He also joined four other ''Nazirites'' when accomplishing in the Temple the sacrifices required at the expiration of the vow (Acts 21:23-24, 26). See ''Nazir'' in *Dictionnaire encyclopédique de la Bible*, 894.

31. These traits mark a resemblance between John and Samuel (1 Sam 1:11).

32. Mal 3:23-24; Sir 48:10.

See R. Swaeles, ''Jésus nouvel Elie dans saint Luc,'' *Assemblées du Seigneur*, 1st series, No. 68 (Bruges: Publications de Saint-André, 1964) 41–66.

33. See P. Ternant, ''Repentez-vous et convertissez-vous!'' *Assemblées du Seigneur*, 1st series, No. 21 (Bruges: Publications de Saint-André, 1963) 50–79.

34. J. E. Frié, *La Liturgie des Heures*, 3:1121; also in *Hymnaire de la Liturgie des Heures* (Paris: Cerf—Chalet—Levain, 1989) 326 (Fiche de chant G 295-1).

35. Augustine (354–430), *Homélie pour la Nativité de Jean Baptiste, La Liturgie des Heures*, 3:1116.

36. R. Bruckberger, *L'histoire de Jésus Christ* (Paris: Grasset, 1965) 131.

37. See Laurentin, *Structure et théologie de Lc 1–2*; Ch. Perrot, ''Les récits de l'enfance de Jésus.''

38. Matt 11:11; Luke 7:28.

A MAN SENT FROM GOD: HIS NAME WAS JOHN—Pages 154–160

1. Isa 42:1-4; 49:1-7; 50:4-9; 52:13–53:12. Some exegetes include more verses in the first three poems.

See P. Grelot, *Les poèmes du Serviteur: De la lecture critique à l'herméneutique*, Lectio divina 103 (Paris: Cerf, 1981).

2. We think, for instance, of Jeremiah (1:5) or Paul (Gal 1:15).

3. This ''new name'' is probably the one Christ received after his resurrection; when this new name is communicated, it will cause us to participate in the glorious destiny of the Lord. See the notes of the *Bible de Jérusalem*, 1785, and of the *Traduction oecuménique de la Bible*, 3035.

4. Acts 2:14-30 (Peter on Pentecost Day); 7:1-53 (Stephen).

5. Acts 13:16-41. The ministry of Paul and Barnabas in Antioch in Pisidia was the most important moment of Paul's first missionary journey. His message having been rejected in the synagogue, he decided to turn to the pagans, conscious of obeying the Lord's order expressed by the prophet (Isa 49:6, first reading): ''I have made you a light to the Gentiles, that you may be an instrument of salvation to the ends of the earth'' (Acts 13:46-47). This scene evokes that of the preaching of Jesus in the synagogue in Nazareth. His fellow citizens not having accepted the good news, he departed for Capernaum (Luke 4:16-31).

See M. Gourgues, ''L'Evangile aux païens (Ac 13–18),'' *Cahiers Evangile* 67 (1989) 45–46.

6. This portrait of David is sketched from three scriptural texts: 2 Sam 7:4-16; Isa 44:28; Ps 89:21-22.

7. 1 Sam 16-24; 1 Kgs 1:1-2:11; 1 Chr 11-29.

The rereading and the meditation of the prophetic oracles played an important role in keeping alive and renewing again and again the hope for a new David: Isa 11:11-12; Jer 23:5-6; 33:15-16; Ezek 34:23-31; 37:24-28; Hos 3:5. Similarly, the prayer of the "Royal Psalms," later interpreted as messianic and, today in the Church, as applying to Christ: Pss 2; 18:32-51; 20; 21; 72; 89:1-5b, 20b-38; 110; 132 (27:1-6; 51:3-19).

See "David" in *Vocabulaire de théologie biblique*, cols. 247-250, and in *Dictionnaire encyclopédique de la Bible*, 332-333.

8. The Greek verb translated here by "has brought" can also mean "has raised." See the *Jerusalem Bible*, which says "raised up," n. *m*.

9. Matt 3:11; Mark 1:7; Luke 3:15-16; John 15:20-27.

10. Thomas Aquinas (1228-1274), *Leçons sur saint Jean*, 4, 1, in *Lectures pour chaque jour de l'année: Prière du temps présent* (Paris: Cerf—Desclée de Brouwer—Desclée et Cie—Mame, 1974) 742-743.

11. Announcement of the birth of John (1:5-25); announcement of the birth of Jesus (1:26-38), followed by the visit of Mary to Elizabeth, who rendered homage to the future mother of the Savior, saluted by John's leap in his mother's womb (1:39-41); birth and circumcision of John (1:57-79) with a brief note on his childhood (1:80); birth and circumcision of Jesus (2:1-21); presentation of Jesus in the Temple with the prophecies of Simeon and Anna (2:22-39); note on Jesus' childhood (2:40).

12. See for example Gen 25:24.

13. Jer 31:12-13; Isa 51:3; Zeph 3:14-17; Zach 9:9.

14. Luke 1:28, 44, 47; 2:10.

15. Exod 4:24-26; Lev 12:3. See "Circoncision" in *Vocabulaire de théologie biblique*, cols. 171-173, and in *Dictionnaire encyclopédique de la Bible*, 283-284.

16. In Luke's Gospel, amazement is the reaction of those who sense they are in the presence of the supernatural: 1:21, 63; 2:18, 33. See also Acts 2:7; 3:12; and so forth.

17. See n. 14 above.

18. Luke 5:26; 7:16; 8:25; 24:37.

19. "The hand of the Lord" symbolizes the divine intervention: Exod 7:4-5; Num 11:23; Deut 2:15.

20. Luke 4:26; 7:49; 8:25; 9:43.

21. See Luke 4:37; 6:17; 7:17; 9:7-9.

22. Luke twice uses equivalent terms about the growth of Jesus (2:40, 52). A similar formula appears concerning the childhood of Isaac (Gen 21:8), of Samson (Judg 13:24-25), of Samuel, the prophet who was charged with anointing David (1 Sam 3:19).

23. The question has been raised: Was John in contact with the community of the monks of Qumran during his stay in the desert?

Around 100 B.C. and afterwards, a rather numerous community of ascetics lived some 10 kilometers to the south of the present-day town of Jericho, near the Dead Sea. The imposing ruins of this monastery were excavated between 1951 and 1958, after the discovery of precious manuscripts (from April 1, 1947, on) in nearby caves. These manuscripts, about 600 in all, contain some copies of books of the Old Testament. They are kept in Jerusalem in a museum called the "Shrine of the Book."

Among other customs, the monks of Qumran practiced many ritual baths of purification. John's baptism was different from their baths because it was given only once. The literature relative to Qumran and the Dead Sea Scrolls is considerable. See "Qumrân, *Le monde de la Bible* 4 (1978); J. Pouilly, "Qumrân" and "Morte, Manuscrits de la mer" in *Dictionnaire encyclopédique de la Bible*, 1085-1088 and 859-861.

24. Matt 15:31; Mark 7:37.

25. Matt 3:3; Mark 1:3; John 1:23.

26. Emmanuel, *Evangéliaire*, 48–49.

27. Like the Magnificat of Mary (Luke 1:47-55) and the Nunc Dimittis of Simeon (Luke 2:29-31), the Benedictus of Zechariah is a hymn of faith and thanksgiving for the Christian community.

28. Christian piety has understood this well: iconography, the number of children named after John the Baptist, and the multitude of churches dedicated to him give abundant testimony of this.

29. J. Guitton, *Ce que je crois* (Paris: Grasset, 1971) 74.

30. Commission Francophone Cistercienne, *La nuit, le jour*, 145 (Fiche de chant W LH 160).

Peter and Paul, Apostles—Pages 161–163

1. It is called *Chronographer of 354* or *Philocalian Calendar*, after Furius Dionysius Philocalus, an artist who illuminated part of the document. It was a splendid manuscript adorned with rich illustrations. It was lost in the seventeenth century, but faithful copies exist that reproduce even the drawings of the original. Among other things, we find in it the days of burial (*depositio*) of the popes from 254 to 354, of the principal martyrs, and of the celebration in Rome of a certain number of Christian feasts. If such a calendar was established at that date, it is obviously because the celebration of these feasts had already been a custom for some time.

See N. Maurice Denis-Boulet, *Le calendrier chrétien*, Je sais-je crois 112 (Paris: Fayard, 1959) 52–55; Ph. Rouillard, "Les Apôtres Pierre et Paul dans la liturgie romaine," *Assemblées du Seigneur*, 1st series, No. 84 (Paris: Publications de Saint-André—Cerf, 1967) 7–13.

2. This celebration is now a feast, not a memorial.

3. The ancient Roman calendar had three divisions: the "kalends" (or "calends"), the first day of the month; the "ides," which fell on the fifteenth day in March, May, July, and October (months with thirty-one days) and on the thirteenth day in the other months (January, August, and December, which have thirty-one days; April, June, September, November, which have thirty days; and February which has twenty-eight or twenty-nine days); the "nones," which fell on the ninth day before the ides of a month. The counting of days was done backward in relation to the next division. The eighth day before the calends of March (which was written "VIII kal. martii") was therefore February 22.

4. It was the day of the "dear relatives" (*cara cognatio*), of the "dear departed ones" as we would say.

5. Such seats are still visible in certain catacombs.

6. Rouillard, "Les Apôtres Pierre et Paul," 8.

7. The word "catacombs" must not be understood in the modern sense. "At the catacombs" (*ad catacumbas*), means "in (or near) the cemetery."

Excavations done under the basilica of St. Peter between 1940 and 1949, then between 1953 and 1957, have confirmed the traditional data that placed Peter's tomb on Vatican Hill, over which a basilica had been built. These excavations have made it possible to verify that the altar erected by Clement VIII (1592–1605), on which the Pope still celebrates the Eucharist, rests on an altar consecrated by Callistus II (1119–1124), which in turn contains the altar erected by Gregory the Great (590–604), when he raised the level of the Constantinian basilica (4th c.). These altars are on top of a small structure situated in the middle of a rather vast ensemble that can be dated from the years 147–161 and was the object of work throughout the third century, work that testifies to uninterrupted veneration. According to tradition, Peter underwent martyrdom during the persecution started by Nero in 64.

See A. G. Martimort, "Vingt-cinq ans de travaux et de recherches sur la mort de saint

Pierre et sur sa sépulture," *Bulletin d'histoire ecclésiastique* 73 (1972), 73–101; same author, "A propos des reliques de saint Pierre," *Bulletin d'histoire ecclésiastique* 87 (1986), 92–111; J. Ruysschaert, "Les premiers siècles de la tombe de Pierre, une discussion dégagée d'une hypothèse," *Revue des archéologues et historiens d'art de Louvain* 8 (1975), 7–47; Martimort, "Pierre," *Catholicisme: Hier—Aujourd'hui—Demain*, vol. 2 (Paris: Letouzey, 1988) cols. 333–338.

8. According to tradition, the Ostian Way (*Via ostiense*) was the place of Paul's martyrdom. The basilica of Tre Fontane was built on the presumed spot of his beheading; the basilica of St.Paul on the location of his tomb.

9. Martimort, "Pierre," col. 337.

10. Sacramentaries are ancient liturgical books containing everything the priest needed to say Mass: prayers, prefaces, canon. They are the ancestors of today's altar missals.

11. However, on June 29, the three prayers of Mass (opening prayer, prayer over the gifts, and prayer after communion) mentioned the two apostles. On June 30, each of the prayers mentioning Paul was followed (under the same conclusion) by another prayer in which Peter was named.

12. Preface of the Solemnity of Sts. Peter and Paul.

PETER AND PAUL, PILLARS OF THE CHURCH—Pages 164–172

1. Acts 2:1-47; 4:32–5:11.

2. Matt 13:36; 17:25; Mark 2:1; 3:20; 7:17; 9:28, 33; 10:10; Luke 7:10.

3. Luke 22:8; John 20:3-8.

4. Matt 10:2; Mark 3:16; Luke 6:14; Acts 1:13.

5. John 20:3, 6; Acts 1:15-22; 2:14; 4:8; 8:14, 24; 15:7.

6. This gate was probably the one called the Corinthian Gate, at the east of the sanctuary. Through it, one passed from the court of the Gentiles to the court of the women.

7. Lev 21:18; 2 Sam 5:8.

8. Matt 9:1-7; Mark 2:1-12; Luke 5:12-25.

The following passages of Acts underscore the parallelism even more. The cure worked by Jesus aroused the indignation of scribes and Pharisees who heard him say to the paralytic, "Your sins are forgiven." While the beggar at "the Beautiful Gate" was clinging to the apostles after being cured and a crowd was gathering, Peter announced the resurrection of Christ and exhorted his hearers to be converted (Acts 3:11-26). This discourse caused the first intervention by the authorities. Peter and John were arrested and jailed. On the next day, they appeared before the Sanhedrin. They were questioned, "By what power or by what name have you done this?" Then they were ordered "not to speak or teach at all in the name of Jesus (Acts 4:1-22). But they, having gone back to the community and joined it in giving thanks to God (Acts 4:23-31), ignored the injunction and worked new miracles (Acts 5:12-16). Arrested again, and miraculously liberated from the prison into which they had been thrown (Acts 5:17-26), they resumed preaching in the Temple. They were seized and, but for Gamaliel's intervention, would have been put to death. They were beaten and, once more, ordered not to speak "in the name of Jesus" (Acts 5:27-42).

9. Matt 9:6; Mark 2:11; Luke 5:24.

10. Leo the Great, pope (440–461), *Sermon IV*, 91, 3, Sources chrétiennes 200 (Paris: Cerf, 1973) 233–235.

11. Acts 10:1–11:18.

12. Acts 15:1-35 (the "council" of Jerusalem); 2 Pet 3:15-16 (Paul's wisdom and the worth of his teaching).

13. Vatican II (October 11, 1962–December 7, 1965) has been in our own time a signal manifestation of God's power and of the decisive intervention of the Spirit that have opened the Church to a broader universality and have knocked down many a barrier, in spite of—today as yesterday—prejudice and reluctance. The acceptance of all languages in the lit-

urgy is the most spectacular proof of this. But we must not forget either the importance of the *Dogmatic Constitution on the Church* (*Lumen Gentium*) and the *Dogmatic Constitution on Divine Revelation* (*Dei Verbum*), the *Pastoral Constitution on the Church in the Modern World* (*Gaudium et Spes*), the *Decrees* on the Apostolate of the Laity (*Apostolicam actuositatem*) and on Ecumenism (*Unitatis Redintegratio*), the *Declarations* on Religious Freedom (*Dignitatis Humanae*) and on the Relationship of the Church with the Non-Christian Religions (*Nostra Aetate*). To these documents we must add significant gestures, such as the abolition of the reciprocal anathemas between the Catholic and Orthodox Churches (Paul VI and Athenagoras, December 7, 1965); John-Paul II's visits to Canterbury (May 29, 1982) and the Synagogue of Rome (April 13, 1986); his organizing the world day of prayer for peace in Assisi (October 27, 1986); his numerous trips that manifest, together with the pastoral care of all the Churches, the respect of Peter's successor for the original personality of each one of them and for the populations among which they are implanted.

14. Besides this recollection, we have three accounts of Paul's vocation. The first one is the detailed report of the facts (Acts 9:1-19). The other two are parts of discourses Paul pronounced in front of civil authorities in order to prove that he had not committed any crime. The first of these two speeches was delivered in Jerusalem before the cohort commander (Acts 22:4-21); the second, in Caesarea before King Agrippa (Acts 26:1-23).

15. See P. Bonnard, *L'Epître de saint Paul aux Galates*, Commentaire du Nouveau Testament 9 (Neuchâtel: Delachaux et Niestlé, 1972); E. Cothenet, "L'Epître aux Galates," *Cahiers Evangile* 34 (1980); Cothenet, *Chrétiens en conflit: L'Epître de Paul aux Galates*, Essais bibliques (Geneva: Labor et Fides, 1987); Cothenet, "L'Epître aux Galates: La liberté," *Lumière et Vie* 192 (1989).

16. The question of the proximate criterion of faith was often raised in the Church. This was the case, for instance, in the fourth and fifth centuries, at the time of the controversies on the respective roles of grace and human will in the practice of virtue. St. Augustine first thought that recourse to Scripture would resolve the stalemate. But he had to recognize that all were drawing their arguments from the same texts interpreted in opposite ways. After Augustine's death, Vincent of Lérins (d. before 450) believed he had found the solution in the principle he stated in the following manner: "What has been accepted everywhere, always and by all, is binding." But this was tantamount to making history the criterion of faith and negating the possibility of any evolution in dogmas. Finally, the Council of Orange (529), convoked by Cesarius, bishop of Arles from 503 to 543, promulgated a series of propositions on grace which Pope Felix III (526-530) had sent to the Council in virtue of his sovereign doctrinal authority. The *Dogmatic Constitution on Divine Revelation* (*Dei Verbum*) of Vatican II, promulgated by Paul VI on November 18, 1965, again addressed the question of the authentic transmission of revealed truth.

17. This reminds us of the vocation of Jeremiah (1:5) or of God's Servant in the Book of Isaiah (49:1).

18. This stay in Arabia is mentioned only here. Paul does not say why he went there or that he stayed there three years.

19. It is well known that the term "brother" can be understood as "relative"; it is the case here. We cannot detect any contempt for the other apostles in what Paul says. Later on, he contacted Peter and had the opportunity, among others, to verify that his preaching was in conformity with the common tradition of the Church (Acts 15:1-4; 1 Cor 15:3).

20. John Chrysostom (ca. 350-407), *Homélies sur saint Paul*, IV, 2, trans. P. Soler, *Les Pères dans la foi* (Paris: Desclée de Brouwer, 1980) 57.

21. Commission Francophone Cistercienne, *La nuit, le jour*, 148 (Fiche de chant W LH 178).

22. See "Pierre" in *Vocabulaire de théologie biblique*, cols. 996-998, in *Dictionnaire de spiritualité*, tome 12/2 (Paris: Beauchesne, 1986), and in *Dictionnaire encyclopédique de la Bible*, 1022-1024. See also R. Brown. K. Donfried, J. Reumann, eds. *Saint Pierre dans le Nouveau Testa-*

ment, Lectio divina (Paris: Cerf, 1974); "Pierre, pêcheur du lac, pêcheur d'hommes," *Le monde de la Bible* 27 (1983).

23. Chapter 21 (25 verses) of John's Gospel was added later to the text written by the evangelist. See *Days of the Lord* 3:321, n. 2. This conclusion is read almost entirely (John 21:1-19) on the Third Sunday of Easter, Year C. See ibid., 126–132.

24. We are reminded of the visit to the tomb on Easter Sunday. Peter and John ran together. Being swifter, John arrived first, saw, when bending down, that the body was not there, but he did not enter. He waited for Peter, who did enter the tomb and carefully examined the place. This story already marked the primacy of Peter over John, although the latter was called "the disciple whom Jesus loved" (John 20:1-19).

25. There is a striking contrast between this attitude of Peter and his presumptuous assurance when, pushing himself forward, he had said to Jesus, "Though all may have their faith in you shaken, mine will never be. . . . Even though I should have to die with you, I will not deny you" (Matt 26:33, 35).

26. According to the *Rule of St. Benedict,* the monk (or nun) who is professing his (or her) vows must sing three times in the middle of the choir, "Receive me, [Lord], as you have promised, and I shall live; do not disappoint me in my hope" (Ps 119:116, according to the text of the Vulgate: "Suscipe me, Domine, secundum eloquium tuum et vivam; et ne confundas me ab expectatione mea"). The triple repetition gives a particular weight to this formula of commitment. The same is true for Peter's triple protestation of love and for the words of investiture pronounced by the Lord three times.

27. "More than these" is said only after the first question. But the Fourth Gospel betrays a certain competition between Peter and John, "the disciple Jesus loved." John was called first, but Peter was the only one who received a "name of vocation" (see John 1:35-42). At the last Supper, Peter had recourse to John reclining close to Jesus, to ask for the traitor's name (John 13:23-26). During Jesus' trial, it was "the other disciple" who introduced Peter into the high priest's house (John 18:15-27). On Easter morning, it was Peter who first entered the empty tomb although John had arrived before him (John 20:2-8). After the miraculous catch of fish, it was John who recognized Jesus, but it was Peter who, jumping into the sea, first rejoined the risen One (John 21:7). Lastly, the question put to Jesus by Peter on what would become of John reveals the interest that the early community had concerning both of them (John 21:21-23).

28. This is what is shown by the allusion to his martyrdom (John 21:18-19).

29. Ignatius of Antioch (d. 110), *Lettre aux Romains, salutations,* Sources chrétiennes 10bis (Paris: Cerf, 1951) 125.

30. J. Colson, *L'épiscopat catholique: Collégialité et primauté dans les trois premiers siècles de l'Eglise,* Unam sanctam 43 (Paris: Cerf, 1963) 46.

See *Days of the Lord* 3:130-132 ("The Pastoral Ministry of Peter Under the 'Sign' of Love").

31. Innocent III, pope (1198–1216), *Sermon 21, Lectures chrétiennes pour notre temps,* Fiche No. 7 (Abbaye d'Orval, 1970).

32. See n. 7 above.

33. John 10:11; 1 Pet 5:4.

According to the *Acts of Peter,* an apocryphal work of the second century, a Greek fragment of which we possess, he was crucified upside down.

34. *Missale Gothicum* (edition L. C. Mohlberg) (Rome: Herder, 1958), No. 378, quoted by Ph. Rouillard, "Les Apôtres Pierre et Paul dans la liturgie romaine," *Assemblées du Seigneur,* 1st series, No. 84 (Paris: Publications de Saint-André—Cerf, 1967) 11-12. This *Missal,* called "Gothic," is of Gallic origin and goes back to the seventh or the eighth century.

PETER AND PAUL, MIRRORS OF THE CHURCH—Pages 173–183

1. Acts 4:1-22.
2. Acts 4:17-42.
3. Acts 6:8-7,60.
4. Acts 8:1b-40; 11:19-30. "It was in Antioch that the disciples were first called Christians" (Acts 11:26).
5. This first general persecution probably affected principally converts of Greek origin, while the others probably remained at least provisionally safe.
6. Before beginning the history of these events, the author of the Acts of the Apostles recounts the conversion of Saul, who became the apostle Paul, his preaching at Damascus and his first visit to Jerusalem (9:1-31); Peter's healing of Aeneas, a paralytic from Lydda (Lod) and of Tabitha whom he brings back to life (9:3-43) at Joppa (Jaffa); the baptism, after a vision, of the pagan Cornelius and his family (10:1-48), and the telling of this capital event to the community of Jerusalem (11:1-18).
7. Herod Agrippa I, the grandson of Herod the Great, was king of Judea and Samaria from 41 to 44. His policies favored Palestinian Judaism (see *Days of the Lord* 4:313, n. 15; 6:360, notes 37–38).

It is his successor, Herod Agrippa II (48–95), who was present when Paul was brought before Festus (Acts 25:1-26, 32).

See *Days of the Lord* 1:341, n. 19, n. 32., and the article "Hérode" in *Dictionnaire encyclopédique da la Bible* (Paris: Brepols, 1987) 580–581.

8. There are four different Jameses. The one called "James the Great" was the elder brother of John, whom Herod had beheaded between 41 and 44: A legend has him evangelizing Spain. James, the son of Alphaeus, is one of the Twelve. James, the son of Clopas and Mary (Mark 15:40; John 19:25), brother of Joseph (Matt 27:56; Mark 15:40) and of Jude (Jude 1), the "brother of the Lord" (Mark 6:3; Gal 1:19), played a prominent role in the community of Jerusalem (Acts 15:13; 21:18; 1 Cor 9:5; 15:7; Gal 2:12). He would have been the author of the epistle that bears his name (Jas). Lastly, there is James, the son of the Apostle Jude (Luke 6:16; Acts 1:13).
9. Although a precise date is not given, it must lie within fairly narrow limits: between 41 and 44 (n. 7). But in view of what follows (Acts 12:20-23), the date of 44 could be upheld.
10. Gen 15:13; Exod 1:11; 5:22-23; Num 20:15; Deut 25:6; Josh 24:4. Stephen's oration recalls this kind of slavery, God's ways in delivering the people (Acts 7:6-7, 17-36), and the promise of another prophet who will resemble Moses (Acts 7:37).
11. Without giving details, the Acts of the Apostles has already recounted that the apostles were once before delivered from prison by an angel (Acts 5:19-21). See also what happened to Paul and Silas. After having been beaten with rods, they are imprisoned by order of the *strategoi* (local rulers) of Philippi in Macedonia, who on the following morning set them free. Meantime, toward midnight, the prison is shaken by an earthquake and all the doors open wide. The jailkeeper, who thinks that the prisoners have escaped, wants to kill himself. But Paul prevents him, preaches the gospel to him, and baptizes him along with all his family (Acts 16:16-40).
12. Ps 2:1-2 is quoted in the prayer said by the community after Peter's first deliverance (Acts 4:23-30).
13. Reports of recourse to prayer are one of the characteristics of Luke's writing: Luke 3:21; 6:12; 9:28-29; 11:5-8; 18:1-14; 21:36; Acts 1:14; 2:42, 46; 6:4; 10:2.
14. Every Hour of the daily Office begins with this verse. See also: Ps 21:20; 29:11; 37:23; 39:14,18; 43:27; 45:2; 69:2, 6; 70:12; 79:3; 107:13; 113b:9-11; 117:14; 120:2; 123:8.
15. The angels are mysterious personages who intervene either to carry a divine message or to accomplish some action of which God is the author. The term used to designate them says nothing whatever about their nature, but only describes their function: messengers.

So saying "the angel," "an angel," "angels," or "the angels" are all one and the same thing. The proper names that they sometimes bear are really attributes of God, rather than descriptive of the angels themselves: "Gabriel" ("God is my strength"), "Raphael" ("God heals"), "Michael" ("Who is like God?"), etc.

See the article "Angels," in *Vocabulaire de théologie biblique* (Paris: Cerf, 1970) cols. 58–61; the article "angel," in *Dictionnaire encyclopédique de la Bible* (Paris: Brepols, 1987) 59–61. From a more particular point of view: C. Vaggini, "La liturgie et les anges," in *Initiation théologique à la liturgie*, vol. 1 (Bruges: Apostolat liturgique; Paris: Société liturgique) 1959, 233–245.

16. This translation is called the Septuagint because, according to legend, it was composed by seventy rabbis, each working in isolation, and who all came up with the same translation. The work, which was undoubtedly begun in the second century B.C., seems to have been finished—at least the most recent books—around the beginning of the first century A.D. The Septuagint was the basis for our modern translations of the Bible. See the article "Versions anciennes de la Bible," 3. "Versions grecques," in *Dictionnaire encyclopédique de la Bible* (Paris: Brepols, 1987) 1304–1306.

17. Ps 105:10 (Septuagint) says also: "He saves them from the hand of the oppressor, he redeems them from the hands of the enemy."

18. See J. Dupont, "Pierre délivré de prison" (Acts 12:1-11) in *Assemblées du Seigneur*, 1st series, no. 84 (Paris: Publications de St. André, Cerf, 1967) 16–17.

19. This ancient midrash comments on what is said in Exodus (12:43-51). It is quoted by J. Dupont, *art. cit.*, 23, based on the translation of R. Le Déaut, "La Nuit pascale. Essai sur la signification de la Pâque juive à partir du Targum d'Exode 12:42," *Analecta biblica* 22 (Rome, 1963) 352.

On the meaning of "midrash" and "targum," see *Days of the Lord* 1:340, n. 9, and 341, n. 17; 3:314, n. 17, and 326, n. 12.

20. See the introductions of the *Bible de Jérusalem*, 1622–1623 and those of the *T.O.B.* (édition intégrale, 1988) 2885–2887.

21. Paul is put in chains "like a criminal" (2 Tim 2:9); he asks Timothy not to be ashamed of him (2 Tim 1:8, 12, 16).

The verses (2 Tim 4) omitted concern Timothy. Paul asks him to come to him, along with Mark, because he is alone with Luke, and to bring him the cloak left at Troas at the house of Carpus, as well as the books ("especially the parchments"); he warns him about "Alexander the coppersmith" who has done him a great deal of harm. In verse 16 the only phrase kept is "everyone deserted me," omitting "At my first defense no one appeared on my behalf," and his forgiving of those who had left him in the crisis.

22. This text is also read on the Thirtieth Sunday in Ordinary Time, Year C: *Days of the Lord* 6:272–273.

23. Twenty-second Sunday of Ordinary Time, Year A: *Days of the Lord* 4:172–173.

24. This is what Vatican II recalled in several documents: The faithful constitute a holy priesthood in order to offer the spiritual sacrifice of their lives, and their witness to Christ (*Dogmatic Constitution on the Church: Lumen Gentium*, 10–11); the priesthood of the laity is exercised in their apostolate (Decree on the Apostolate of the Laity: *Apostolicam actuositatem*, 2): in *The Documents of Vatican II*, 26–29.

25. Certain sacrifices of the cult called for the pouring out of a liquid—oil, perfume, the blood of a victim—on the altar or on the ground: Exod 29:40-41; Num 15:5, 7; 28:7.

Paul knew that the death penalty for a Roman citizen was decapitation. His blood would truly be poured out, just as in the sacrifices that called for libations. He saw his death as a cult offering.

26. Phil 1:7, 12-17. See the introductions of the *Bible de Jérusalem*, 1620–1621, and of the *T.O.B.* (édition intégrale, 1988) 2834–2835; the article "Philippiens, Epître," in *Dictionnaire encyclopédique de la Bible* (Paris: Brepols, 1987) 1017–1018.

27. Paul was martyred during the persecution of Nero (64–68), probably in 67: The Letter to Timothy would date to the same time. As for the Letter to the Philippians, it dates to 56–57 if it was written during his first imprisonment in that city or from 61–62 if the imprisonment it speaks of took place somewhere else. See ibid. (preceding note).

28. Rom 13:12; 1 Cor 14:8; 2 Cor 10:3-4; Eph 6:10-20; Col 2:1; 1 Tim 1:18; 4:10, 6:12.

29. 1 Cor 9:24; Gal 2:2; Phil 3:12; Col 2:18.

30. The apostle is an athlete who fights and races for Christ: 1 Cor 9:24; 2 Tim 2:5.

31. See above, n. 21.

32. The letters of Paul are studded with doxologies of the same type, more or less developed: Rom 9:5; 11:33-36; Gal 1:5; Eph 3:21; Phil 4:20; 1 Tim 1:17.

33. St. John Chrysostom (ca. 350–407), *Deuxième homélie sur saint Paul*, in *Homélies sur saint Paul* (trans. P. Soler), Les Pères dans la foi (Paris: Desclée de Brouwer, 1980) 11:8, 41.

34. Matt 16:13–17:9; Mark 8:27–9:30; Luke 18–36.

35. This Gospel is also read on the Twenty-first Sunday in Ordinary Time, Year A: *Days of the Lord* 4:165–170.

36. 2 Kgs 2; Sir 48:10; Mal 3:23-24.

37. P. Ganne, *"Qui dites-vous que je suis?" Leçons sur le Christ*, texts collected and presented by L. Fraisse (Paris: Centurion, 1982) 30–31.

38. In Hebrew, "son of man" means primarily and quite simply "man." But the expression gradually acquired in the Bible, especially in the Book of Daniel and in Revelation, a somewhat mysterious meaning: It evoked an uncommon being belonging to the world of God, and finally it came to mean the Messiah; similarly, "gods," "sons of gods": Gen 6:1-4; 2 Sam 7:14; Job 1:6; Pss 28:1; 81:6-7; 88:7, 27-28.

See the article "Fils de Dieu" and "Fils de l'homme" in *Vocabulaire de théologie biblique* (Paris: Cerf, 1970) cols. 466–475, and in *Dictionnaire encyclopédique de la Bible* (Paris: Brepols, 1987) 477–482.

39. In Aramaic, *kepha* means a rock or boulder, not a loose stone. This surname was not translated in Paul's letters: 1 Cor 1:12; 15:5; Gal 1:18; 2:9, 11, 14. This was because neither in Greek (*petros/petra*) nor in Latin (*petrus/petra*) was the play on words possible, as it was in Aramaic (and is in French).

40. As in the Greek Bible (Septuagint) and the Aramaic translation (targum). At Qumran, on the other hand, it was said that this rock referred to the community. So we have here a witness to a double traditional interpretation—personal and communal—of the oracle taken up by the New Testament.

41. Acts 4:11; Eph 2:20; 1 Pet 2:7.

42. "Church" (*ekklēsia*) is a Greek word. In common usage, it designated first a convocation of the people, and then the place where this took place. In the Greek Bible, it translates the Hebrew words *gahal* and *edah* that, during the Exodus and after the Exile, meant the assembly of people convoked by God to hear his words: Deut 23:2-3; 31:30; Num 15:24; 16:3; Judg 21:10; Ezra 10:1; Neh 8:18.

43. Jesus says "my Church" the same way he says "my lambs" and "my sheep" (John 21:15, 16, 17).

44. "I will place the key of the House of David on his shoulder; when he opens, no one shall shut, when he shuts, no one shall open" (Isa 22:22). In Revelation (3:7), this text is applied to Christ.

45. Matt 24:45-51; 25:14-30; Luke 12:41-48; 16:10-12; 19:11-28; 1 Cor 4:1-2; 1 Tim 1:12.

46. Saint Augustine (354–430), *Sermon 295 pour la fête des saints Pierre et Paul*, in *La Liturgie des Heures*, vol. 3 (Paris: Cerf—Desclée—Brouwer—Mame, 1980) 1132.

47. "Just as Saint Peter and the other apostles constitute, through the institution of the Lord, a single apostolic college, similarly the Roman pontiff, successor of Peter, and the bishops who are the successors of the apostles form among themselves one entity" (Vati-

can II, *Dogmatic Constitution on the Church* [(*Lumen Gentium*]), n. 22, in *The Documents of Vatican II*, 42–44.

48. St. Benedict (ca. 480–547), *La Règle de saint Benoît* (trans. A. Dumas), chapter 27, "Comment l'abbé doit avoir soin des excommuniés" (Paris: Cerf, 1977) 84.

49. Ibid., chapter 64, "De l'institution de l'abbé," 127.

50. Ibid., 127–128.

51. Formula of promulgation by the pope of each conciliar text: "The entirety as well as each one of the points that have been edicted in this Constitution (or this Decree, this Declaration) have been pleasing to the Fathers of the Council. And we, by virtue of the apostolic power which we hold from Christ, in unity with the venerable Fathers, we do approve, order and decree them in the Holy Spirit, and we order that what has thus been established in Council be promulgated for the glory of God."

52. *Sacramentaire de Vérone*, no. 374, ed. Mohlberg (Rome: Herder, 1960). This sacramentary that was for a long time attributed to Leo the Great (440–461) must have been compiled, in fact, in the second half of the sixth century.

53. Commission Francophone Cistercienne, *Sur la trace de Dieu* (Paris: Desclée, 1979) 111; *Hymnaire de La Liturgie des Heures* (Paris: Cerf—Chalet—Levain, 1989) 232 (Fiche de chant W LH 211-b).

The Transfiguration of the Lord—Pages 184–185

1. Matt 4:1-11 (Year A); Mark 1:12-15 (Year B); Luke 4:1-13 (Year C): *Days of the Lord* 2:44–47; 52–55; 59–62.

2. Matt 17:1-9 (Year A); Mark 9:2-10 (Year B); Luke 9:28b-36 (Year C); ibid., 2:76-79; 86-87; 90-94.

3. September 14: see above, pp. 226–235.

4. Monasticism was born in Egypt around A.D. 250. It spread widely in the Sinai region from the beginning of the fourth century on. See P. Cousin, *Précis d'histoire monastique* (Paris: Bloud et Gay, 1956); A. Guillaumont, *Aux origines du monachisme chrétien*, Spiritualité orientale 30, Abbaye de Bellefontaine, Bégrolles en-Mauges, 1979; D. J. Chitty, *Et le désert devint une cité . . .* Spiritualité orientale 31, ibid., 1980; P. Deseille, *L'Evangile au désert*, L'échelle de Jacob (Paris: O.E.I.L.—YMCA-Press, 1985); I. Gobry, *Les moines en Occident*, tome 1, *De saint Antoine à Basile. Les origines orientales* (Paris: Fayard, 1985); G.-M. Oury, *Les moines*, Bibliothèque d'histoire du christianisme 13 (Paris: Desclée, 1987).

5. One can see even today a superb sixth or seventh century mosaic of the transfiguration in the monastery of St. Catherine in the Sinai, founded in 530 by the emperor Justinian (527–565).

In 1844, in the same monastery of St. Catherine, L. F. Tischendorf (1815–1874) discovered (in a wastepaper basket!) a papyrus containing the New Testament and almost the entire Old Testament, in Greek. This precious manuscript, which is usually dated to the fourth century is now preserved at the British Museum of London, under the name "Sinaiticus."

6. This is the famous "Jesus prayer": "Lord Jesus, Son of God, Savior, have mercy on me!"

This spirituality, born of the monastic tradition of Mount Sinai, was particularly fully developed in the Middle Ages in the monasteries of Mount Athos, under the influence of the holy monk Gregory Palamas (1296–1359), who became archbishop of Thessalonica in 1347. The name "hesychasmos" (from the Greek *hezychazein*, "to pacify oneself") has been given to this spiritual tradition. See J. Meyendorf, *Saint Gregoire Palamas et la mystique orthodoxe*, Maîtres spirituels 20 (Paris: Seuil, 1959).

7. Callixtus III (Alonso Borgia) was Spanish. Born at Jaliva (Valencia) in 1378, student, then preacher, at the University of Lerida, he was named canon of the cathedral of this city.

8. J.-B. Ferrères, "La Transfiguration de Notre Seigneur. Histoire de sa fête et de sa messe" in *Ephemerides theologicae lovanienses* 5 (1928), 632–643; J. Leclercq, *Pierre Le Vénérable*, Saint Wandrille, 1946.

9. *Days of the Lord* 3:34–35.

10. Entrance Antiphon.

11. Preface.

12. Prayer after Communion.

HOPING FOR THE DAY WHEN THE MORNING STAR WILL RISE—

Pages 186–199

1. Historically (Dan 7:19-22), the oracle takes place during a period of crisis, at a time when Antiochus Epiphanes IV (175–164 B.C.) who was pursuing a policy of enforced Hellenization, persecuted the Jews. He forbade them the practice of their religion and went so far as to profane their Temple (1 Macc 1:1-6:17; 2 Macc 4:1-9, 29). The oracle is addressed to those who live under this oppression: "Do not lose heart, but stand fast! The days of the terrible persecutor are numbered, because God himself, in whom you must put all your hope, is going to intervene to liberate you." So this is a veiled appeal to confidence and, at the same time, to resistance. See *Days of the Lord* 5:374, n. 8.

In its present form, the Book of Daniel must have been written in the time of Antiochus Epiphanes IV. In the Greek translation of the Bible (Septuagint) and in the Latin Bible (Vulgate) of St. Jerome, Daniel is the fourth of the great prophets. In the Jewish canon he is put among the hagiographers. See A. Lacocque, *Daniel et son temps* (Geneva: Labor et fides, 1983); the article "Daniel, Livre," in *Dictionnaire encyclopédique de la Bible* (Paris: Brepols, 1987) 327-330.

2. Every attempt at producing an actual pictorial representation of this scene is doomed to deterioration into the fantastic or the meaninglessly anecdotal; all such images have little in common with the majesty and the particularly allusive character of this account of visions that defy the imagination.

3. Dan 12:1; Exod 32:32-33; Isa 4:3; Mal 3:16; Pss 55:9; 68:29; 138:16; Luke 10:20; Rev 3:5; 17:8; 20:12, 15; 21:27.

4. The verses of this text selected by the liturgy omit verses 11 and 12 where sentence was pronounced: The persecuting empire, personified by Antiochus IV, is destroyed; the other kingdoms benefit from a "life reprieve" because they no longer represent a danger for the people of God.

5. The Greek translates: "Son of the Man."

6. See above, p. 362, n. 38.

7. In the Gospels, the expression "Son of Man" is found seventy times.

8. Mark 2:28; Luke 6:5.

9. Matt 9:6; Mark 2:10; Luke 5:24.

10. John 1:51; 3:14; 12:21, 34; 13:31.

11. Matt 24:27-44; Mark 13:24-32; Luke 21:25-27; Matt 26:64; Mark 14:62; Luke 22:69.

12. Matt 16:27; Mark 8:38; Luke 9:26; John 5:26-29.

13. P. Teilhard De Chardin, *Le Milieu divin. Essai de vie intérieure* (Paris: Seuil, 1957) 195-196.

14. There is general agreement today that this letter, placed under the patronage of St. Peter, was not written by him. It is later than the Letter of Jude, which dates to the years 80–90, and was written at a time when a collection of the letters of Paul had already been compiled; the author of this letter gives this collection an authority equal to that of Scripture (2 Pet 3:15-16). For this reason it is thought that 2 Pet was written between 80 and

180. It was already known in Egypt in the third century, but it was not admitted to the canon of Scripture until the fourth century in the West and in Asia Minor, and the fifth and sixth centuries in Syria and Constantinople (see *Days of the Lord* 3:321, n. 2).

See the introductions of *Bible de Jérusalem*, 1748, and the T.O.B. (édition intégrale, 1988) 2983–2986; the article "Pierre, Epîtres, in *Dictionnaire encyclopédique de la Bible* (Paris: Brepols, 1987) 1026.

This letter is used only four times in the Lectionary: on the feast of the Transfiguration; the Fourth Sunday in Advent, Year B (3:8-14) (*Days of the Lord* 1:77–78); Monday and Tuesday of the Ninth Week in Ordinary Time, even years (1:1-7; 3:12-15a, 17-18). This equates to 24 of the 61 verses in the letter. But the 21 verses of chapter 2 have to be left out of the count, for they constitute a virulent condemnation of the false doctors, a reading that could not be done in public today without getting into long explanations.

15. This phenomenon has acquired, today, considerable proportions. Contemporary gnosticism is nourished on orientalism; and what is peculiar in our modern scientific world—on the occult. See Cardinal G. Danneels, *Le Christ ou le Verseau. Lettre pastorale de Noël* 1990, in *La documentation catholique*, 88 (1991) 117–129.

16. St. Paul warns about the temptation that consists in crediting "legends," or "tales" wherever they may originate: 1 Tim 1:4; 4:7; 2 Tim 4:4; Titus 1:14.

17. The "we" employed in this text refers not only to Peter, but to all the apostles who witnessed with him the resurrection and the enthronment of the Lord in the glory of God.

18. Symbol of Nicaea-Constantinople.

19. References to the Scriptures are found throughout Acts and the apostolic letters: Acts 3:18-26; 7:1-52; 13:16-41; 28:23, etc.

20. The story of the encounter between Philip and Queen Candace is particularly significant. The meaning of the prophecy about the Servant of the Lord (Isa 53:7-8) remained obscure to this man who was coming back from Jerusalem, until the moment when the deacon told him that the prophet was speaking about Jesus. "Then Philip opened his mouth and, beginning with this scripture passage, he proclaimed Jesus to him" (Acts 8:26-39).

21. Vatican II, *Constitution of Dogma on Divine Revelation (Dei Verbum)*, no. 7, in *The Documents of Vatican II*, 114–115.

22. Rev 2:28; 22:16.

23. St. Bonaventure (1221-1274), *Breviloquium*, Prologue, in *La Liturgie des Heures* (Paris: Cerf—Desclée de Brouwer—Mame, 1980) vol. 1, 531-532.

24. Vatican II, *Constitution of Dogma on Divine Revelation*, no. 25, op. cit. (n. 21) 144.

25. Bossuet, "Sur la parole de Dieu. Sermon pour le Deuxième dimanche du Carême 1661," in *Oeuvres*, tome 3 (Paris: Firmin-Didot, 1879) 392.

26. See M. Coune, "Radieuse transfiguration," in *Assemblées du Seigneur*, 2nd series, no. 15 (Paris: Publications de Saint-André—Cerf, 1973) 47-50.

27. These three accounts are also read on the Second Sunday in Lent: Matt 17:1-9, Year A; Mark 9:2-10, Year B; Luke 9:28b-36, Year C. See *Days of the Lord* 2:76-79; 84-86; 90-92.

28. The liturgical readings have omitted these references. In fact, on the one hand they suppose that the preceding has just been read; on the other, although the mystery took place in time, it is celebrated in the "today" of the life of the Church and the faithful.

29. The liturgy maintains this relationship, but expresses it in another way: The feast of the Transfiguration (August 6) is celebrated forty days before the feast of the Triumph of the Cross (September 14).

30. Exod 24:12-17; 25:1-18; 32:7-15; 34:5, 29; 1 Kgs 19:1-18.

31. Dan 7:10 (First Reading); 10:7-16.

32. Some of the traditional elements in the apocalypses: the "voice" in the "cloud," the fear of the witnesses. See Gen 37:11; Dan 4:28; 8:26; 10:14; 12:4-9; Rev 1:3; 22:7, 9-10.

33. Matt 10:27; Luke 12:3.

34. P. Claudel, *Corona Benignitatis anni Dei*, "La Transfiguration" in *Oeuvres*. La Pléïade 125, N.R.F. (Paris: Gallimard, 1967) 450–451.

35. See, for instance, the "kingdom" parables (ch. 13), the ecclesial import of Jesus' teaching throughout chapters 16–18, and the long speech about the end of time (chs. 24–25).

36. There are at least 130 passages where Matthew refers to the Old Testament, and in 43 of these he gives explicit quotations. Moreover, the very character of this Gospel and the style and language of the author are full of semiticisms.

37. See *Cahiers Evangile* 9 (1874) 61–62.

38. Isa 2:2; 11:9; Dan 9:16.

39. Icons of the transfiguration always show Christ in glory, blessing with his right hand, while, like a new Moses, he holds in his left hand the scroll of the gospel that he has brought: M. Coune, art. cit. (n. 26) 61.

40. Peter says, "If you wish, I will make three tents here." These words may reveal not only his desire to install himself with Jesus, Moses, and Elijah in the beatitude of the transfiguration; it may also allude to the feast of Booths (*Sukkot*) with its messianic orientation that points to the definitive establishing of the kingdom of God. See *Days of the Lord* 3:356, notes 43 and 44.

41. Commission Francophone Cistercienne, *Sur la trace de Dieu* (Paris: Desclée, 1979) 89 (Fiche de chant I 280).

42. Mark 16:1-8. The final section of this Gospel (16:9-20) that speaks of the apparitions of the risen Christ was undoubtedly added at a later date. See notes of the *Bible de Jérusalem* (1479) and those of the *T.O.B.* (édition intégrale, 1988, 2435–2436); *Days of the Lord* 3:321, n. 2.

43. There are 324 verses prior to the episode of the transfiguration, and 326 after. On the structure of Mark's Gospel, see *Days of the Lord* 4:3-5.

44. E. Pousset, *Une représentation de l'Evangile selon saint Marc*, Toulouse, Source de vie (Paris: Desclée de Brouwer, 1978) 149–150.

45. Chromatius of Aquileia (d. 408), *Commentaire sur l'Evangile de la Transfiguration selon saint Matthieu*, 6 (trans. M. Coune) in *Transfigurance* XXVII (1976) 13.

46. Commission Francophone Cistercienne, *Sur la trace de Dieu* (Paris: Desclée, 1979) 89 (Fiche de chant I 280).

47. Matthew (16:28) says " . . . until they see the Son of Man coming in his kingdom." Mark (9:1) has " . . . until they see that the kingdom of God has come in power." So the perspective is that of the end of time.

48. Luke 22:69; Acts 2:36.

49. "After six days" say Matt 17:1 and Mark 9:2. See above, n. 28.

50. St. Ambrose (339–397), *Traité sur l'Evangile de saint Luc*, II, VII, 6, in Sources chrétiennes 52 (Paris: Cerf, 1958) 10–11. "The eighth day" means Sunday.

51. Luke 5:16; 6:12; 9:18; 11:1; 21:37; 22:39. See also 3:21; 23:34.

52. According to Luke, John holds a special place in the early community, alongside Peter. This is why he is named here before James: Luke 8:51; Acts 1:13; 3:1; 4:13.

53. Luke 21:27; 24:26; Acts 3:13; 22:11.

54. Luke 9:51–19:27. See the "scheme" of Luke's Gospel in *Days of the Lord* 6:2-6

55. Exod 13:22; Dan 7:13; Matt 24:30; 1 Thess 4:17; Rev 1:7; 14:14-16.

56. See the article "Nuée" in *Vocabulaire de théologie biblique* (Paris: Cerf, 1970) cols. 845–848.

57. Commission Francophone Cistercienne, *Sur la trace de Dieu* (Paris: Desclée, 1979) 89 (Fiche de chant I 280).

58. Sedulius, a Latin poet who wrote between 425 and 450. See *Dictionnaire encyclopédique du christianisme ancien*, vol. 2 (Paris: Cerf, 1990) 2258–2259: *Quicumque Christum quaeritis, oculos in altum tollite: illic licebit visere signum perennis gloriae.* This hymn used to be sung during the First Vespers of the Transfiguration, in the Roman Breviary.

59. The Fourth Gospel does not contain the episode of the transfiguration of the Lord.

But it does tell us that one day when Jesus was speaking of his passion and was clearly distressed, a voice came from the heavens, saying: "I have glorified it and will glorify it again" (John 12:27-30). Moreover, in John's Gospel the life of Jesus, from the first "sign" at Cana right up to the crucifixion, was a continual revelation of his glory.

60. St. Peter De Celle (1115-1183), abbot of Montier-la-Celle, near Troyes, and of Saint Rémi of Rheims, then bishop of Chartres, *Deuxième homélie sur la Transfiguration* (trans. M. Coune), in *Transfigurance* XXIII (1988) 15.

61. St. Cyril of Alexandria (ca. 380-444), *Homélie* 10 (trans. M. Coune), in *Transfigurance* VII (1974) 15.

The Assumption of the Blessed Virgin Mary—Pages 200-204

1. This was the case with the traditional funerary meals, for instance. See above, p. 161.

2. Inscriptions or graffiti on the tombs also expressed this belief.

3. A. G. Martimort, *The Church at Prayer. The Liturgy and Time* IV (Collegeville, Minn.: The Liturgical Press, 1983) 108-129; A. Adam, *La liturgie aujourd'hui. Précis de liturgie catholique*, Mysteria 1 (Paris: Brepols, 1989) 296-297; *Days of the Lord* 1:191-193.

4. Matt 1:1-2:23; Luke 1:5-2:52.

5. The apocryphal writings that concern Mary, such as the *Proto-Gospel of James* (2nd c.) speak only of her childhood, her marriage to Joseph, and her motherhood.

6. Latin and French text in *Prières de toujours* (Paris: Brepols, 1979) 30; French alone, with music (Fiche de chant V 66) in *Missel noté de l'assemblée* (Paris: Brepols—Cerf—Chalet—Levain, 1990) 340.

7. F. Mercenier, "La plus ancienne prière à la sainte Vierge," in *Questions liturgiques et paroissiales* 25 (1940) 33-36.

8. See *Days of the Lord* 1:318, n. 11.

9. G. Dumeige, *La foi catholique. Textes doctrinaux du magistère de l'Eglise* (Paris: Orante, 1961) 191.

10. See A. G. Martimort, art. cit. (n. 3 above) 130-143.

11. *Dictionnaire encyclopédique de la Bible* (Paris: Brepols) 116.

12. In the present state of excavation, no more precise date can be given than "between the end of the first century and the beginning of the third." See R. Laurentin, article "Marie," in *Catholicisme*, tome 8 (Paris: Letouzey et Ané, 1979) cols. 539-540.

13. Quoted ibid.

14. M. Bobichon, *Marie dans la nouvelle Liturgie de la parole*, tome 1, Pâque nouvelle (Lyon: Chalet, 1971) 110.

15. Purification (February 2), Apparitions at Lourdes (February 11), Annunciation (March 25), Visitation (July 2), Our Lady of Mount Carmel (July 16), Dedication of Saint Mary Major (August 5), Assumption (August 15), Immaculate Heart of Mary (August 22), Nativity of the Virgin Mary (September 8), The Holy Name of Mary (September 12), Our Lady of the Seven Sorrows (Friday in Passion Week and September 15), Our Lady of Mercy (September 24), Our Lady of the Rosary (October 7), the Maternity of the Blessed Virgin Mary (October 11), the Presentation (November 21), the Immaculate Conception (December 8). Besides these feasts that were to be celebrated universally, there were nine others proper to particular localities, and some of these were widely observed: the Espousals of the Virgin Mary (January 23), Our Lady of Good Counsel (April 26), Our Lady the Helper (May 24), Mary the Mediatrix (May 31), Our Lady of Perpetual Help (June 27), Our Lady of Loretto (December 10), Our Lady of the Miraculous Medal (November 27), Our Lady of the Expectation (December 18).

16. Papal bull *Ineffabilis Deus*, in Dumeige, *La foi catholique*, 238.

17. Dogmatic Constitution *Munificentissimus Deus*, ibid., 247.

18. Laurentin, op. cit. (n. 11), col. 110.

19. *Calendarium Romanum* (Vatican City: Vatican Polyglot Press, 1969).

20. From this time forward Marian feasts are relegated to one of three groups of greater to lesser solemnity. The most important are: the Annunciation (of the Lord); the Assumption, and the Immaculate Conception (which celebrate mysteries of the faith); Holy Mary, Mother of God according to the "definition" of the Council of Ephesus (it replaces the feast of the Maternity of the Virgin Mary instituted in 1931 by Pope Pius XI on the occasion of the fifteenth centenary of the Council of Ephesus—its new name is more explicit as to the real meaning of the feast). The second group comprises the two feasts of the Visitation and the Nativity of Mary. The third group consists of four "obligatory commemorations" and four "optional commemorations." The first four are Mary the Queen, Our Lady of Sorrows, Our Lady of the Rosary, and the Presentation of Mary in the Temple. The second four are Our Lady of Lourdes, the Immaculate Heart of Mary, Our Lady of Mount Carmel, and the Dedication of the Basilica of St. Mary Major. So we now have in the *General Roman Calendar* fifteen Marian celebrations instead of nineteen. And eight of them have been assigned less importance than previously, while of those, four are now optional.

21. Vatican II, *Dogmatic Constitution on the Church (Lumen Gentium)*, No. 55, in *The Documents of Vatican II*, 87.

22. Ibid., No. 61, 109.

23. Ibid., No. 56, 105–106.

24. Ibid., No. 68, 115.

25. Eucharistic Prayer II.

26. Eucharistic Prayer III.

27. Eucharistic Prayer IV.

28. According to the numbering of our present-day Bibles. (In the Vulgate, which followed the old Missals and the liturgy before the Council: 24:23-31).

29. The liturgy for this Mass was promulgated after the dogma of the assumption was defined on November 1, 1950. Until then an excerpt from Sirach was read: "Wisdom had set up her tent in Jacob, where she distributes her gifts" (Sir 24:7-15 [24:11-13, 15-20 in the Vulgate], and the gospel of Martha and Mary (Luke 10:38-42).

30. Mass of the Day, opening prayer.

THE ASSUMPTION: BLESSED VIRGIN MARY—Pages 205–212

1. See the articles "Arche d'alliance" and "Arche," in *Vocabulaire de théologie biblique* (Paris: Cerf, 1970) cols. 84–87, and in *Dictionnaire encyclopédique de la Bible* (Paris: Brepols, 1987) 131–133.

2. The ark was taken by the Philistines and wandered from one refuge to another for a period of time (1 Sam 4:1-7:1; 2 Sam 6:1-12).

3. According to 2 Sam 6:1-23, this transferral was the cause of a great popular celebration of a somewhat profane nature.

4. This story is no less than 72 verses long (1 Chr 15:1-16, 43). What we in fact have here is a re-reading of the event and of a theological development, rather than a historical account. The author sees the transferral of the ark as it might have happened in a nation of priests and a holy people not led astray by sin. He sees David as a model king, and he makes Jerusalem out to be the sacred place where the people are gathered together once more around the Law of God. In this way the transferral of the ark becomes a parable proclaiming the realization of the ideal according to the will of God, and encourages the people of the time of the author to work toward this as a goal.

5. Deut 10:8-9; Num 4:1-16; 1 Chr 15:2-15. The bars made it possible to carry the precious coffer without touching it. It would cost one dearly to touch it. See 2 Sam 6:6-7.

6. The author attenuates or skips entirely over the shocking details and episodes that could alter David's image. An example is the dance of David before the ark, which scandalized a number of witnesses, and in particular Mikal, the daughter of Saul (2 Sam 6:20; 1 Chr 15:29).

7. First reading of the Mass of the Day.

8. This is not really exegesis. The Fathers do not claim that the texts from Scripture about the ark should be understood as pertaining to the Virgin Mary. But they found in the ark a very eloquent image, not without some objective foundation, in that Mary was the receptacle of the Word of God.

9. St. John Damascene (675-754), Deuxième homélie pour la Dormition, in Lectures chrétiennes pour notre temps (Abbaye d'Orval, 1978) Fiche M 42.

10. This does not in any way deny the value of the paintings or icons of the assumption, which are not only remarkable for their beauty and their inspiration but are also valuable sources of prayer and contemplation.

11. "Litanies of the Holy Virgin," in Prières de toujours (Paris: Brepols, 1979) 136-139.

12. Commission Francophone Cistercienne, Sur la trace de Dieu, 103 (Fiche de chant V 242).

13. "Litanies de la Sainte Vierge," op. cit. (n. 11), 138.

14. See Cardinal G. Danneels, Au-delà de la mort. Réincarnation et résurrection. Message de Pâques (Malines: Presses de l'archevêché, 1991).

15. 1 Cor 15:1-58.

16. 1 Cor 15:14, 17. The community addressed by St. Paul was particularly vital but also turbulent, for everything led to arguments. This was due to the fact that in that cosmopolitan town the most diverse religious and philosophical trends of thought were current, and they favored certain syncretist tendencies that sometimes affected Christians too.

Generous excerpts from 1 Cor are read from the Fourth to the Eighth Sunday of Year A, from the Second to the Sixth Sunday of Year B, and from the Second to the Eighth Sunday of Year C: Days of the Lord 4, 5, 6.

17. 1 Cor 15:54-58 was already briefly discussed in Days of the Lord 6:62.

18. E. Haulotte, "Symbolique du vêtement," in Assemblées de Seigneur, 1st series, no. 43 (Bruges: Publications de Saint-André, 1964) 49-75.

19. Isa 25:8, quoted freely.

20. Another freely-quoted passage from Scripture (Hos 13:14). See J. Galot, "Midrash sur la mort! (1 Cor 15:54c-57)," in Revue biblique 79 (1972) 161-188.

21. Rom 5:12-21; 7:7; 9:14.

22. These are the proper terms of the dogmatic definition of 1950: Dumeige, La foi catholique, 247.

23. St. Germain (Patriarch of Constantinople, 715-730), Sermon 3 pour la Dormition de la Sainte Vierge, in Lectures mariales du Bréviaire cistercien (Abbaye d'Orval, 1968) 58.

24. This feast, celebrated originally January 1, and then August 15, was of a general nature. This is probably the reason why this Gospel remained in the Missal of Pius V for the celebrations of the Virgin that did not have their own liturgy (Common of the Virgin).

25. Luke 1:42; Gospel of the Mass of the Day.

26. Other examples: Luke 10:23; 23:29; Matt 13:16.

27. M. Noël, "Berceuse de la Mère de Dieu," in Rosaire des joies (Paris: Stock, 1933) 47-48.

28. Magnificat (Luke 1:48): Gospel of the Mass of the Day.

29. Luke 1:48: ibid.

30. Luke 1:49: ibid.

31. St. Augustine (354-430), Les Confessions, livre X, 26, 31, in Oeuvres de saint Augustin, Bibliothèque augustinienne, vol. 14 (Paris: Desclée de Brouwer, 1962) 209.

32. St. Bede the Venerable, *Commentaires sur saint Luc*, L, 4:49, in H. Tissot, *Les Pères vous parlent de l'Evangile*, vol. 2 (Bruges: Apostolat liturgique—Paris: Société liturgique, 1955) 726.

33. See Eucharistic Prayer IV.

34. Commission Francophone Cistercienne, *Sur la trace de Dieu*, 105; *Hymnaire de La Liturgie des Heures* (Paris: Cerf—Chalet—Levain, 1989) 297 (Fiche de chant V 116-1).

THE ASSUMPTION: GLORY AND PRAISE TO GOD FOR MARY—Pages 213–222

1. There are good reasons for these scattered references of Scripture in the liturgy. Verse 19 makes the transition between the preceding eight chapters (Rev 4:1–11:9), which end with the Last Judgment, and the visions that follow (Rev 12:1–16:21). It was kept, with the omissions of "flashings of lightning and peals of thunder, an earthquake," which refer to the preceding vision. In verse 6b, it is said that the Woman is "taken care of" for 'twelve hundred and sixty days." The mention of this symbolic number, whose exact meaning is not known, was of no interest in a liturgical celebration. Verses 7-9 tell of the victorious battle of St. Michael and his angels against the dragon. These were omitted in order that attention might be taken away from the "grandiose vision" of the Woman, which concluded in verse 10 (without the repeated reference to the defeat of the dragon by Michael: 10c).

2. The Temple built by Herod the Great (37 B.C.–A.D. 4), the one that Jesus knew and frequented, had been destroyed by the Romans in A.D. 70, before the date of composition of the Book of Revelation.

3. Ps 132:7; 1 Chr 28:2.

4. According to Jeremiah (Jer 3:16; 31:31-34), the ark was the sign and the promise of the definitive covenant yet to come.

5. So, for example Isa 60:1; Bar 5:1.

6. The verb in Greek is in the present, the tense used for an action that lasts.

7. This adage has many variations, such as: *Paris ne s'est pas fait en un jour* ("Paris wasn't built in a day").

8. The fire-red color was that of a warrior.

9. These battles are reported in verses 7 to 9; see above, n. 1.

10. The general liturgical character of the Book of Revelation has been commented on, punctuated as it is with canticles and acclamations; also, there is a clear parallelism between the cult offered on earth and that which takes place in heaven before God and the Lamb: P. Prigent, " . . . Et le ciel s'ourit." *Apocalypse de saint Jean*, Lire la Bible 51 (Paris: Cerf, 1960).

11. Faith is a struggle, an onerous choosing between the "sign" of the Cross of Christ and that of the anti-Christ: F. Montagnini, "Le signe d'Ap 12 à la lumière de la christologie du Nouveau Testament," in *Nouvelle revue théologique* 89 (1967) 401-416, quoted in abridged form under the title "L'Eglise à la recherche du Christ (Ap 11:12)," in *Assemblée du Seigneur*, 2nd series, No. 66 (Paris: Publications de Saint-André—Cerf, 1973) 22-27.

On the possible contacts between these versions and those of pagan myths relative to the coming of a savior: A. Läpple, *L'Apocalypse de Jean*, Lire la Bible 24 (Paris: Cerf, 1966) 154–156.

12. G. Philips, "Marie et l'Eglise. Un thème théologique renouvelé," in *Marie. Etudes sur la Sainte Vierge*, under the direction of H. Du Manoir, vol. 7 (Paris: Beauchesne, 1964) 374.

13. See above, the second reading of the Mass of the Vigil. "Paul is not interested in the resurrection of non-Christians": L. Cerfaux, *Le Christ dans la théologie de saint Paul*, Lectio divina 6 (Paris: Cerf, 1954) 43.

14. See 1 Thess 4:13-18; 2 Thess 1:7-12; 2:3-12.

15. The *Bible de Jérusalem* and the *T.O.B.* translate more exactly: "Le Christ est ressuscité, *prémices* de ceux qui se sont endormis (qui sont morts)" i.e., "Christ was raised up again, *first fruits* of those who have gone to sleep (who have died)," which the Lectionary trans-

lates as: "Le Christ est ressuscité pour être parmi les morts le *premier* ressuscité" ("Christ was raised up again in order to be among you the *first* risen").

16. Exod 13:2; 23:16, 19; 34:22, 26; Lev 2:12, 14; 23:17, 20; Num 15:20; 18:12; Deut 18:4; 26:2, 10; etc.

Not too long ago, when we did not have as we do today the possibility of enjoying various fruits all year long, the first fruits of the year still had meaning. In Christian families of certain regions the sign of the cross was habitually made when one could finally, for the first time in that year, eat the fruits of the new season. It was an act of thanksgiving to God for the harvest of the year.

17. In this way St. Paul speaks of the "first payment" of the Spirit (2 Cor 1:22; 4:5), the "pledge of our inheritance" (Eph 1:14).

18. Eph 2:6; Col 2:12; 3:1.

19. 1 Cor 15:45-49.

20. In 1 Thess, St. Paul reacts against this wrong way of understanding this. Some thought that in order to join Christ when he returns, the living were at more of an advantage than those who had died a long time ago, and thought that the living would be ahead of them at the return of Christ. The Apostle writes that he had said nothing of the kind: " . . . the dead in Christ will rise first. Then we who are alive, who are left, will be caught up together with them in the clouds to meet the Lord in the air" (1 Thess 4:16-17). No one will have to wait for anyone else, and no one will be at either an advantage or at a disadvantage because of the time of his or her death. It is possible to say that someone died on such or such a date, before or after someone else, but in eternity there is no calendar: "Before" and "after" have no meaning there.

21. Here, too, we must be careful not to understand this in a material sense. Varying degrees of closeness to Christ are not to be measured by the yardstick that we use down here. " . . . [S]o that God may be all in all" (1 Cor 15:28b), and each one of us will be filled in whatever measure he may be able to be in communion with Christ.

22. John 1:1, 3, 14.

23. John 5:19, 30; 6:38; 7:16; 8:28, 42; 12:49; 14:10.

24. See P. Van Den Berghe, "Il faut qu'il règne," in *Assemblées du Seigneur*, 2nd series, No. 65 (Paris: Publications de Saint-André—Cerf, 1973) 10-16.

25. Canticle of Zechariah (*Benedictus*): Luke 1:68-79. See "Jean Baptiste, the Veilleur, l'Eveilleur," in *Days of the Lord* 1:131-136.

26. It is just the opposite on the Fourth Sunday of Advent, Year C, when we read the Gospel of the visitation, stopping just before Mary's canticle (Luke 1:39-45): *Days of the Lord* 1:158-160.

27. Gospel of the Fourth Sunday in Advent, Year B, and of the feast of the Annunciation: *Days of the Lord* 1:148-153; see above, pp. 140-141.

28. Commission Francophone Cistercienne, *La nuit, le jour* (Paris: Desclée, 1973) 138 (Fiche de chant V 250).

29. One has only to read for comparison what the angel says to Zechariah (Luke 1:13-17) and to Mary (Luke 1:30-35). In the first instance we have the announcement of the one who will bring back many of the sons of Israel to the Lord; and in the second we have the announcement of the one who "will be called the Son of the Most High," to whom "God will give the throne of David, his father," and whose "reign will be without end."

30. When she was pregnant, Rebekah had the impression that the "children jostled each other." Worried, "she went to consult the Lord," and it was said to her: "Two nations are in your womb, two peoples are quarrelling while still within you; but one shall surpass the other, and the older shall serve the younger." She gave birth to twins: Esau and Jacob (Gen 25:22-26).

31. 2 Sam 6:9 reports the words of David when the ark was being transferred to Jerusalem: "How can the ark of the Lord come to me?"

32. P. Claudel, *Corona benignitatis anni Dei*, "La Visitation," in *Oeuvre poétique*, La Pléïade 125, N.R.F. (Paris: Gallimard, 1967) 449. The quotation *Unde hoc mihi?* ("How is it that it should happen to me . . . ?") is taken from Luke 1:43.

33. Luke 11:28; Gospel of the Mass of the Evening.

34. On this formula of benediction, see above, p. 369, n. 26 (Gospel of the preceding Mass).

35. P. Grelot, *La Bible, Parole de dieu. Introduction théologique à l'étude de l'Ecriture sainte*, Bibliothèque de théologie, Théologie dogmatique, 1st series, vol. 5 (Paris: Desclée, 1965) 290.

36. See J. Dupont, "Le Magnificat comme discours sur Dieu," in *Nouvelle revue théologique* 102 (1980) 321–343; reprinted in *Etudes sur les Evangiles synoptiques*, vol. 2, Bibliotheca ephemeridum theologicarum lovaniensium, LXX-B (Leuven: University Press—Peeters, 1985) 953–975.

37. See "Marie et le Psautier," in *Days of the Lord* 1:176–180.

38. The similarity between the "Canticle of Mary" and the Beatitudes (Luke 6:20-26; Matt 11:25-26), "L'hymne de jubilation de Jésus" (Luke 10:21; Matt 11:25-26), and several parables, is particularly enlightening: J. Dupont, art. cit.

39. See, for example, Pss 11; 112; the "Canticle of Hannah," the mother of Samuel (1 Sam 2:1-10: in the *Psautier liturgique*, "Cantique de l'Ancien Testament" 3).

40. Deut 7:19; Ps 89:11; Isa 51:9; Sir 10:7-8.

41. This vocabulary is typical of the prayer of the "poor of the Lord": 1 Sam 2:4, 6-9; Pss 107:9, 36, 41; 113:7-9; 147:3-9.

42. J. Dupont, "Pour l'homélie de l'Assomption," in *Communautés et liturgies* 60 (1978) 367.

43. K. Rahner, *L'homme au miroir de l'année chrétienne* (Paris: Mame, 1966) 224.

44. D. Rimbaud, dans *Missel noté de l'assemblée* (Paris: Brepols—Cerf—Chalet—Levain, 1990) 338 (Fiche de chant V 289-1).

The Triumph of the Cross—Pages 223–225

1. St. Cyril of Jerusalem (ca. 315-386), *Catéchèses*, IV, 10; X, 19; XIII, 4, ed. J. Bouvet (Namur: Soleil levant, 1962) 88, 204, 262.

An inscription found near Sétif in Mauritania dating from 359 mentions, in a list of relics, a fragment of the true cross. Various witnesses from the fifth century speak of the desire of Christians to possess a piece of it; they often set them in gold and wore them around the neck and gave them as gifts to friends or to monasteries. In 569, St. Radegonde (ca. 520-587), the wife of Clotaire I, who had retired to a monastery, received from the emperor Justin II (566-578) a fragment of the relic of the cross preserved in Constantinople. From that day on her monastery, which had been called Notre-Dame, took the name of Sainte-Croix.

See, on the origins and history of the cult of the cross and its feast, the article "Croix" in *Catholicisme*, tome 3 (Paris: Letouzey et Ané, 1952) cols. 321–329; P. Jounel, "Le culte de la Croix dans la liturgie romaine," in *La Maison-Dieu* 75 (1963) 68–91; R. Bornert, "La célébration de la sainte Croix dans le rite byzantin," ibid., 92–108; I.-H. Dalmais, "La glorification de la sainte Croix dans l'Eglise copte," ibid., 109–118; A. G. Martimort, *The Church at Prayer: The Liturgy and Time* IV (Collegeville, Minn.: The Liturgical Press, 1986) 99–100; A. Adam, *La liturgie aujourd'hui. Précis de liturgie catholique*, Mysteria 1 (Paris: Brepols, 1989) 294.

2. See above, p. 342, n. 1.

3. Egeria, *Journal de voyage*, 48, in Sources chrétiennes 296 (Paris, 1982) 317. See *Days of the Lord* 2:270, n. 1.

4. The travel journal of Egeria recounts that the feast lasted eight days and was celebrated with as much solemnity as Easter. But her journal stops after the account of the procession which took place on the third day.

5. The tradition in the Latin Church that the cross was discovered by the mother of the emperor goes back to the fourth century (but must be taken with a grain of salt), but the same is not true for the transfer of the relic. St. Helena died at Nicomedia (present-day Izmit in Turkey) where she had joined her son after the end of her voyage to the Holy Land.

6. It was nevertheless not unknown to the Roman Church because the Greek and Oriental colonies in Rome observed it. It is sometimes difficult to imagine the diversity within the same city of so many different communities, each with their own traditions, churches, and liturgical calendars. On September 14 Roman liturgy celebrated, from the fourth to the seventh century, St. Cornelius, pope, and St. Cyprian, bishop of Carthage, who had been friends. The first died in exile in June 253, and the second was martyred in Carthage September 14, 258. In our present-day calendar, the feast is September 16.

7. Historical veracity would have had May 3 as the feast of the "Exaltation of the Cross," and September 14 for the "Discovery."

8. A commission established in 1741 by Pope Benedict XIV (1740-1758) had already suggested that the feast of May 3 be suppressed.

9. Until 1960 the feast of May 3 was considered more important ("double of the 2nd class") than that of September 14 ("major double").

10. Entrance antiphon (based on Gal 6:14).

THE CROSS OF CHRIST, OUR PRIDE AND OUR HOPE—Pages 226-235

1. Gen 3:1.
2. Gen 3:14.
3. A. De St. Exupéry, *Le Petit Prince* (Paris: Gallimard, 1946) 62.
4. Gen 3:1-24.
5. R. Cook, *L'arbre de vie, image du cosmos* (Paris: Seuil, 1975) 113.
6. A story from the Acts of the Apostles illustrates this. The boat that was carrying Paul as a prisoner to Rome was shipwrecked off Malta. All the passengers arrived safe and sound on land. But when Paul was about to throw an armful of dry wood on the fire, a viper jumped out and clung to his hand. The witnesses cried out: " 'This man must certainly be a murderer, though he escaped the sea. Justice has not let him remain alive.' But he shook the snake off into the fire and suffered no harm. They were expecting him to swell up or suddenly to fall down dead but, after waiting a long time and seeing nothing unusual happen to him, they changed their minds and began to say that he was a god" (Acts 28:1-6).
7. It suffices to recall the taking of the Bastille on July 14, 1789, at least as regards modern French history. Every nation celebrates its national holiday on the anniversary of some event that has become symbolic of its existence as a people.
8. See the articles "Exode," in *Vocabulaire de théologie biblique* (Paris: Cerf, 1970) cols. 423-425, and in *Dictionnaire encyclopédique de la Bible* (Paris: Brepols, 1987) 454-458; D. Barsotti, *Spiritualité de l'Exode*, Cahiers de la Pierre-qui-Vire (Paris: Desclée de Brouwer, 1959); Y. Saout, *Le grand souffle de l'Exode*, Cahiers de la Pierre-qui-Vire (Paris: Fayard—Mame, 1977); G. Colas, *L'Exode*, Ouvrir la Bible (Paris: Mame, 1981); C. Wiener, "Le livre de l'Exode," in *Cahiers bibliques* 54 (1985).
9. Heb 3:7-4:13.
10. Exod 14:1-15:21; Num 11:1-20; 14:1-25; 16:1-17:28; 20:1-13; Deut 9:1-10:11.
11. Being forced to give up going by the direct northern route shut off to him by the Amalekites and the Canaanites, Moses wanted to go around the Dead Sea on the east. In

order to do so, he had to ask the king of Edom for permission to cross his territory. Even though he promised to cause no damage—"We will not cross any fields or vineyards, nor drink any well water, but we will go straight along the royal road without turning to the right or to the left"—the king refused, threatening to fight if they disregarded his refusal. So Moses had to go around the whole region, which lengthened the journey considerably (Num 20:14-21).

12. In the region of the Sea of Suph (the Sea of Reeds) and in the Gulf of Aqaba (to the north of the Red Sea) are found minerals that are used in the fabrication of bronze: *Bible et Terre sainte* 25 (1960) 4-10; 123 (1970) 6-14.

Two fine specimens of bronze serpents have been found, one in Susa, in front of a temple (that could be dated to the seventh or even eighth century B.C.); and the other in a ditch full of offerings in the middle of the sands of Saudi Arabia. For color reproductions, see *En ce temps-là, la Bible* 12 (1969) 283.

13. The Bible recounts that at Marah Moses threw a piece of wood into the water to sweeten it (Exod 15:22-25) and that Elisha used salt to sweeten an impure spring (2 Kgs 2:19-22).

14. It is told very clearly in the Book of Numbers. But the veneration of "miraculous" objects—even today—carries a risk of misplaced devotion. 2 Kgs 18:4 tells that Hezekiah (727/729-699 B.C.) destroyed the bronze serpent that was in the Temple, even though it was purportedly the one that Moses had had made. But incense was burned before it, which might have been considered a form of worship forbidden by the Law (Exod 20:4).

15. The author of the Book of Wisdom is firm on this point: One can truly speak of "punishment" only when some tribulation or scourge penalizes the hardening (of their hearts), their refusal to listen to the Lord. And he reminds us of what happened to the Egyptians. They were not delivered from the evils that afflicted them because they did not believe in the Lord and because they did not have a mediator with God like Moses (Wis 15:14-16:4).

16. See below, pp. 232-235.

17. *Epître de Barnabé* (end of 2nd c.) 12, 7, in Sources chrétiennes 172 (Paris: Cerf, 1971) 171.

St. Justin (ca. 100-165) is one of the first Christian writers to make the comparison. He claimed to have found in the Timaeus of Plato the proof that the great Greek philosopher had read the story of the bronze serpent, "But without understanding it. He did not see that this sign was a cross: He thought that it was the letter x, and he said that, after God, the first principle, the second virtue was written as an x upon the universe" (*Première apologie*, 60, in A. Hamman, *La philosophie passe au Christ. L'oeuvre de Justin: Apologie I et II. Dialogue avec Tryphon*, Ichtus, Littératures chrétiennes 3 [Paris: Editions de Paris, 1958] 87).

18. Painters, stained-glass artists, and sculptors have also read Scripture this way. They have often shown the bronze serpent in the same scene as the serpent who tempted Eve in paradise, or with Christ on the cross: L. Réau, *Iconographie de l'art chrétien*, tome 2: *Iconographie de la Bible. Ancient Testament* (Paris: Presses universitaires de France, 1956) 208-210; E. Urech, *Dictionnaire de symboles chrétiens* (Neuchâtel: Delachaux et Niestlé, 1972) 166-168.

19. This text has already been read at the Mass of Palm Sunday (*Days of the Lord* 2:222-224) and at the Mass of the Twenty-sixth Sunday, Year A (Ibid., 4:222-223).

See J. Gnilka, "La carrière du Christ, appel à l'union et à la charité," in *Assemblées du Seigneur*, 2nd series, No. 57, 12-19; J. Thomas, "L'hymne de l'Epître aux Philippiens," in *Christus* 22 (1975) 334-345.

The liturgical translation of this hymn has produced abundant literature: S. Légasse, "L'Epître aux Philippiens," in *Cahiers Evangile* 33 (1980) 22-25.

20. The only way to resolve the contradiction would be to say that Jesus was not truly God or, on the contrary, that as God, he had taken on only the appearance of a man. In the first case, his death would no longer be a problem. In the second case, the solution to the problem would be illusory because a certain number of insoluble or absurd questions would arise, in particular: What is meant by "the appearance" of a man? What—or

who—died on the cross? and finally, What is a man, what are we? Nevertheless, some heretics did not hesitate to go into these questions.

21. Possible translations: *Il ne retint pas jalousement le rang qui l'égalait à Dieu* (''He did not hold on jealously to the rank that made him equal to God'') (*Bible de Jerusalem*); *Il n'a pas considéré comme une proie à saisir d'être l'égal de Dieu* (''He did not consider it a prize to be seized to be the equal of God'') (*T.O.B.*).

22. St. Paul discusses in several places the antithetical parallelism between the two Adams: Rom 5:12-21; 1 Cor 15:21-22, 45-49. See J. Daniélou, *Sacramentum futuri. Etudes sur les origines de la typologie biblique*, Etudes de théologie historique (Paris: Beauchesne, 1950) 3–12 (''Adam et le Christ dans l'Ecriture sainte''); the articles ''Adam,'' in *Vocabulaire de théologie biblique*, cols. 18–19, and in *Dictionnaire encyclopédique de la Bible*, 15–16.

23. ''Anéanti'' (reduced to nothing) is the translation of the *Bible de Jérusalem*. ''Vidé'' (emptied) is the meaning of the Greek verb *kenoō*. This is why we speak of the ''kenosis'' (*kenosis*) of Christ to designate his lowering of himself to our humanity.

24. See above, n. 20.

25. This reminds us, as it might have reminded Paul, of the poem of the Book of Isaiah (Isa 52:13–53:12) on the Servant of God.

26. Gal 5:18; Rom 6:3-4. And also Gal 2:19-20; 6:14-15.

27. This is the exact meaning of the Greek word used here.

28. St. Gregory of Nyssa (ca. 335–395), *Sixième homélie sur le Cantique des cantiques*, quoted in O. Clément, *Sources. Les mystiques chrétiens des origines. Textes et commentaires* (Paris: Stock, 1982) 28. To say the name of God is legitimate and necessary, on condition of being conscious that none of the names we give him can express him fully or adequately. See above, pp. 8–9.

29. J. Dupont, ''L'Evangile de saint Matthieu: quelques clés de lecture,'' in *Communautés et liturgies* 57 (1975) 11–13.

30. Origen (ca. 185–253), *Commentaire sur l'Epître aux Romains*, quoted in A.-M. Besnard, *Le mystère du nom. ''Quiconque invoquera le nom du Seigneur sera sauvé,''* Lectio divina 35 (Paris: Cerf, 1962) 188. See idem, *Un certain Jésus* (Paris: Cerf, 1968).

31. S. Légasse, art. cit., (n. 19) 25. See also F. Varillon, *L'humilité de Dieu* (Paris: Centurion, 1974).

32. St. Irenaeus (ca. 135–202), *Démonstration de la prédication apostolique*, 34, in Sources chrétiennes 62 (Paris: Cerf, 1958) 87.

The entire discussion of St. Irenaeus takes its inspiration from Phil 2:6-11. We can also see in it the intuition of St. Justin who saw in the cross a sign of the power and primacy of Christ stretching out to all of creation (above, n. 17).

The cosmic dimension of ''the tree of the cross'' was admirably discussed in *Une homélie inspirée du Traité sur la Pâque d'Hippolyte* (4th c.) 50–51, in Sources chrétiennes 27 (Paris: Cerf, 1950) 176–178. (The most significant excerpt is in *Missel dominical de l'assemblée*, édition entièrement renouvelée [Paris: Brepols, 1981] 1419.)

33. John 2:14, 21, 24; 4:54; 5:18; 7:30, 39; 19:35-37; 20:30-31.

34. John 1:1-18 is read at the Mass of the Day on Christmas: *Days of the Lord* 1:216–219. This realism, particularly noticeable in the speech about the bread of life (John 6:26-65) is characteristic of John's Eucharistic teaching.

Intentionally or not, his Gospel takes a position against any Docetic interpretation of the incarnation. (The heresy that attributed only the appearance of humanity to Christ is known as Docetism. See above, n. 20.)

35. In John, the attribute ''Son of Man'' refers to the humanity of the ''Son of God'' made flesh.

36. Gospel of the Fifth Sunday of Easter, Year A: *Days of the Lord* 3:158–161.

37. The sages of Israel, avid to acquire enlightenment—wisdom—often said that it was

inaccessible for man because not one human had ever gone up to heaven to bring it back: Deut 30:12; Prov 30:4; Wis 9:16; Bar 3:29.

38. I AM is the divine name revealed to Moses (Exod 3:14): *Days of the Lord* 2 (Third Sunday in Lent, Year C) 163–165.

39. See *Days of the Lord* 2:217–218; 3:28–29.

40. St. Leo the Great (440–461), *Huitième sermon sur la Passion du Seigneur*, 46, 7, Sources chrétiennes 74bis (Paris: Cerf, 1976) 115–117.

41. 1 John 3:16; 4:9-10.

42. That would be the equivalent, actually, of thinking that Christ, knowing that he would rise again, did not really suffer, or at least not as much as it seemed. This leads us into a kind of Docetism. See above, n. 6.

43. O. Clément, op. cit. (n. 28) 37.

44. D. Rimaud, *Les arbres dans la mer* (Paris: Desclée, 1975) 128–129; *Hymnaire de La Liturgie des Heures* (Paris: Cerf—Chalet—Levain, 1990) 256–257 (Fiche de chant H 67-1).

All Saints—Pages 236–237

1. See the article "Toussaint et Trépassés," in *Dictionnaire d'archéologie chrétienne et de liturgie*, tome 15/2 (Paris: Letouzey et Ané, 1953) cols. 2677-2682; C. Vagaggini, *Initiation théologique à la liturgie*, vol. 1, adapted from the Italian by Ph. Rouillard (Bruges: Apostolat liturgique; Paris: Société liturgique, 1959) 230–233 ("Communion avec les saints du ciel"); Ph. Rouillard, "Le culte des saints au temps des Pères," in *Assemblées du Seigneur*, 1st series, No. 89 (Bruges: Publications de St. André, 1963) 72–85.

2. The term "confessors" (of the faith) was first used for saints who had been arrested or deported during the presecutions, but who had not spilled their blood. Later on the title was given to all the saints, often in conjunction with their other title: pope, bishop, etc. Today this is the only title used.

3. The oldest Martyrology dates to the sixth century: It is called the "Hieronymian" because it was (erroneously) attributed to St. Jerome. The principal martyrologies are those of Bede, Ado, and Usuard in the eighth and ninth centuries. To the name of each of these martyrs and saints they add a brief note. The Roman Martyrology was promulgated by Pope Gregory XIII in 1584: last "typical" (that is to say, official) edition in 1919, revised in 1921. Since the seventeenth century a group of Jesuits called the "Bollandists" (from the first of them, Jean Bolland [1596-1665]) devote themselves to a critical study of all the documents relative to the saints (they are located in Brussels). Among their publications are the *Acta sanctorum* ("Acts of the Saints") in the order of the Calendar.

4. The pope had numerous "relics" brought from the catacombs. In those times there was a tendency to consider that all those who had been buried in these Christian graves (the catacombs) had been martyred, which was not really the case. The church consecrated by Pope Boniface IV kept this name of "St. Mary-in-the-Martyrs," but it is more often called "Santa Maria Rotunda" because of its shape. Subsequently, several famous persons were buried there: Raphael (1483-1520), Annibale Carrache (1560-1609), the kings Victor Emmanuel II (1820-1878) and Humbert I (1844-1900), and the queen Marguerite (1851-1926).

5. This action on the part of the pope was motivated by a concern for unity: All the Churches did not yet celebrate this feast, and those that did celebrated it on different dates.

6. The distinction between the two feasts (All Saints and All Souls, which is celebrated the next day) is not clear to everyone, to say the least. This should not astonish us, given that originally the cult of the martyrs was a form of the cult of the dead. See A. G. Martimort, *The Church at Prayer: The Liturgy and Time* IV (Collegeville, Minn.: The Liturgical

Press, 1986) 109–110, and above. The similarity between the two remains deeply anchored in people's minds, and it cannot be considered simply as a sort of deviation. The Church confidently prays for all the dead whose degree of holiness is known only to God, after having made mention of all the redeemed (Eucharistic Prayer III). Moreover, Vespers of the Day of All Saints was, formerly, immediately followed by First Vespers of All Souls, after which in many parishes there was a procession to the cemetery for a liturgy that usually contained a blessing of the tombs and a sermon.

7. Opening prayer of the Mass. The solemn invocation of the saints is part of the great liturgies: the blessing of the baptismal water during the Paschal Vigil, ordinations, religious profession, and major supplications. See the text of the *Litanie des saints* in *Prières de toujours* (Paris: Brepols, 1979) 146–147; *Missel dominical de l'assemblée*, 368–369; *Livre de la prière* (Paris: Brepols, 1987) 558–561. After invoking the memory of each group of saints by name, the liturgy adds: "All you holy angels of God . . . holy patriarchs and prophets . . . holy disciples of the Lord," etc., and it concludes with "All you saints of God, pray for us."

8. C. Vagaggini, op. cit. (n. 1) 178–184 ("Liturgie céleste et liturgie terrestre").

9. See Ph. Rouillard, "Signification de la Toussaint," in *La vie spirituelle* (1962) 500–506.

10. Commission Francophone Cistercienne, *Tropaires des dimanches*, Le Livre d'Heures d'En-Calcat (Dourgne, 1980) 149 (Fiche de chant W 103).

PEOPLE OF GOD, PEOPLE OF SAINTS—Pages 238–251

1. Rev 1:1. Today the term apocalypse is often used to describe any catastrophic incident. Using it this way leads us to forget that it is derived from the Greek for "revelation" (*apocalypsis*).

2. There is a general discussion of the Book of Revelation and a useful bibliography in *Days of the Lord* 3:81–83 and appropriate notes. See also the introductions in the *Bible de Jérusalem*, 1779–1781, and the *T.O.B.*, 3023–3029.

3. In the Bible, salvation comes from the East: Ezek 43; Matt 2:2, 9; 24:27; Luke 1:78.

4. These four angels, guarding the four corners of the earth, hold back the winds that are ready to burst forth (Rev 7:1).

5. 2 Cor 1:22 speaks in a similar vein: " . . . the one who anointed us is God; he has also put his seal upon us and given the Spirit in our hearts as a first installment."

6. *Sphragis* in Greek, *sigillum* in Latin. The sacramental prayer has preserved this ancient term. When the celebrant traces the sign of the cross with consecrated oil on the forehead of the confirmand, he says: "Receive the seal of the Holy Spirit, the gift of God."

7. So the seal is not, as it is in the Book of Ezekiel (Ezek 9:4-5), a mark made on the forehead of the just to distinguish them from the impious and to protect them from divine punishment.

8. The people of God, those who bear his mark, are in opposition to those who belong to the Beast (Satan), and bear his sign (Rev 13:7, 19; 14:9, 11; 16:2).

9. 144,000 = 12 x 12 x 1,000. The people of God are in their perfected state when the twelve tribes are reunited. But they are disunited when one of the twelve secedes: This schism is intolerable because it goes against the plan of God. This is the origin of the importance of the number twelve for the group of the apostles: After the resurrection, Peter suggests to the assembly of the disciples to bring the number back up to twelve and replace Judas who had defected (Acts 1:15-26). The heavenly Jerusalem has twelve gates on which are inscribed the names of the twelve tribes (Rev 21:12) and twelve courses of foundation stones that bear the names of the twelve apostles (Rev 21:14). The Woman, who symbolizes new humanity, has a crown of twelve stars. As for the number one thousand, it evokes a countless number, beyond which it is no use even trying to count. See the article "Nombre" (II. Significations symboliques), in *Vocabulaire de théologie biblique*, cols. 834–837.

10. The division of Israel into twelve tribes had already long disappeared when St. John wrote the Book of Revelation. But it always evoked the original and ideal unity of the people who had sprung from the twelve sons of Jacob.

11. See R. Swaeles, "Rassemblement et pèlerinage des dispersés," in Assemblées du Seigneur, 1st series, No. 72 (Bruges: Publications de Saint-André, 1965) 37–61.

12. See Days of the Lord 3:357, notes 43 and 44.

13. See J. Comblin, "La fête des Tabernacles," in Assemblées du Seigneur, 1st series, No. 72 (Bruges: Publications de Saint-André, 1965) 53–67.

14. The Book of Zechariah is composed of two parts (1–8, 9–14). The second part was undoubtedly written between 330 and 300 B.C. See the introductions of the Bible de Jérusalem, 1089–1090, and of the T.O.B., 1285–1240; the article "Zacharie, Livre," in Dictionnaire encyclopédique de la Bible, 1358–1360.

Ps 118 also gives us an echo of the ambiance in which the feast of Booths was celebrated. Similar was the atmosphere surrounding Jesus' entry into Jerusalem on Passion (Palm) Sunday (Matt 21:1-11; Mark 11:1-11; Luke 19:28-40; John 12:12-16). The crowd acclaimed him, using phrases taken from Ps 118 (vv. 25-26). The authorities were worried by this popular manifestation precisely because of this messianic undercurrent.

15. John 1:5-9.

16. See, for instance, I. De La Potterie, "Le Paraclet," in Assemblées du Seigneur, 1st series, No. 47 (Bruges: Publications de Saint-André, 1963) 47–55.

17. See C. Vagaggini, Initiation théologique à la liturgie, 231–246 ("La liturgie et les anges").

18. Eucharistic Prayer IV.

19. The two first verses of this text (1 John 3:1-2) are read on the Fourth Sunday of Easter, Year B: Days of the Lord 3:142-143.

20. "Before he was given up to death, a death he freely accepted" (Eucharistic Prayer II); "On the night he was betrayed" (Eucharistic Prayer III); "He destroyed death and restored life . . . to complete his work on earth and bring us the fullness of grace" (Eucharistic Prayer IV).

21. In equivalent terms: Mark 9:50; Luke 14:34.

22. G. K. Chesterton, L'homme éternel (Paris: Plon, 1927) 23.

23. Mark 8:31-33; Luke 9:21.

24. Matt 24:30; 26:64; Mark 13:26; 14:62; Luke 21:27; Rev 1:7.

25. We call "parousia" this glorious return of Christ. In the Greco-Roman world, the Greek term parousia meant: presence, coming, arrival, and was used to designate the solemn and official visit of a prince making his entry into a city or some other locality.

26. See also Ps 17:15. On the desire to see God: Vocabulaire de théologie biblique, cols. 1377–1378.

27. The story of this revelation is read on the Nineteenth Sunday in Ordinary Time, Year A: Days of the Lord 4:149-150.

28. Pss 27:4; 63:3.

29. John emphasizes particularly the fact that the "signs" accomplished by Jesus make manifest his glory and allow us to see in him the Son of God: John 2:11 (the miracle at Cana); John 4:53-54 (the healing of the son of the royal officer at Capernaum); John 11:40 (the resurrection of Lazarus); John 12:37 (the incredulity despite the "signs"); John 20:30-31 (the "signs" reported in order to foster faith).

30. St. Augustine (354-430), in Les Jours du Seigneur (Paris: Editions du Témoignage chrétien, 1951) 864.

31. Matt 4:12-5:2.

32. See "Practical Plan of the Gospel of Matthew," in Days of the Lord 4:15-16.

33. This text is also read on the Fourth Sunday in Ordinary Time, Year A: Days of the Lord 4:40-45.

The Gospel according to Luke (Luke 6:20-26) has handed down a version quite different from the Beatitudes, placed in another context (in the heart of Jesus' ministry in Galilee) and in another setting ("the discourse on the plain"). See "Practical Scheme of the Gospel According to Luke," in *Days of the Lord* 6:2-6. This version is read on the Sixth Sunday in Ordinary Time, Year C: ibid., 44–51.

It is useful to compare these two versions in order to get a better understanding of the evangelical message of the Beatitudes. But the liturgy does not offer such a synoptic reading. See the monumental study of J. Dupont, *Les Béatitudes*, 3 vols. (Paris: Gabalda, 1969–1973); the essential parts were published in an abridged form in *Cahiers Evangile* 24 (1978).

34. Some have not hesitated to go to this scandalous extreme, affirming that as long as there are rich and poor, it is the will of God, and that to change this state of affairs amounts to destabilizing society and compromising its natural equilibrium.

35. The quotation is a sort of compilation composed of four texts from the Book of Isaiah: Isa 26:19 (the dead); Isa 29:18 (the deaf); Isa 35:5-6 (the blind, the lame, the poor); and Isa 61:1 (the good news brought to the poor).

St. Luke (Luke 4:18) recounts that when Jesus preached for the first time at the synagogue of Nazareth he read another oracle from the same prophetic book (Isa 61:1-2), which uses similar terms to express the mission that he had come to accomplish: "The spirit of the Lord God is upon me, because the Lord has anointed me; he has sent me to bring glad tidings to the lowly, to heal the brokenhearted, to proclaim liberty to the captives and to release the prisoners, to announce a year of favor from the Lord." See the Third Sunday in Ordinary Time, Year C: *Days of the Lord* 6:26-27.

36. The four Beatitudes reported by Luke (Luke 6:20-23) are expressed in direct language: "Blessed are you who are poor . . . blessed are you who are now hungry . . . blessed are you who are now weeping . . . blessed are you when people hate you, and when they exclude and insult you, and denounce your name as evil on account of the Son of Man." But this variation is not in opposition to that of Matthew. Luke writes for the Christian communities that did in fact have a majority of humble folk converted to Christ (1 Cor 1:26-31), and of faithful who were persecuted for their faith in various ways.

37. See A. Gelin, *Les pauvres de Yahvé*, 3rd edition, Témoins de Dieu 14 (Paris: Cerf, 1962); S. Légasse, *Les pauvres en esprit. Evangile et non-violence*, Lectio divina 78 (Paris: Cerf, 1974).

38. Eph 4:2; Col 3:12.

39. Acts 2:42-47; 4:32. This ideal is no innovation of apostolic times. Deuteronomy (Deut 15:4) already prescribed: " . . . There should be no one of you in need."

40. Matt 3:15; 5:6, 10, 20; 6:1, 33; 11:19; 21:32; 23:23.

41. See Rom 8:17; 2 Cor 1:5; 4:10, 17; 7:4; Gal 2:20; Phil 3:10; Heb 12:1-2.

42. Matt 5:34; Luke 7:50; 8:48.

43. Luke 24:36; John 20:19, 21, 26.

See the articles "Paix," in *Vocabulaire de théologie biblique*, cols. 878–884, and in *Dictionnaire encyclopédique de la Bible*, 950–951.

44. "Do not give a false sign of peace"; "Be reconciled before the sun goes down," says *The Rule of St. Benedict* (ch. 4: "The instruments of good works").

45. The greeting was a wish for peace, as it is even today among the Jews: "Shalom!" (Peace!). It has remained traditional in Christian liturgy and we exchange a fraternal sign of peace before Communion.

46. The same word is translated as "fidélité" (fidelity) in the *Lectionary* and the *T.O.B.*; and by "bonne foi" (good faith) in the *Bible de Jérusalem*.

47. See the articles "Coeur," in *Vocabulaire de théologie biblique*, cols. 176–179; and in *Dictionnaire encyclopédique de la Bible*, 288–289.

48. Rom 5:5; 2 Cor 1:22; Gal 4:6; Eph 3:17.

49. J. Dupont, "Le message des Béatitudes," in *Cahiers Evangile* 24 (1978) 41.

50. Eucharistic Prayer II.

51. See also Titus 3:7; Heb 9:15; 1 Pet 1:4.

52. Commission Francophone Cistercienne, *Toussaint, Office du Soir, antienne pour le Cantique de Marie* (Fiche de chant W LH 132).

53. J.-P. Caussade (1675–1751), *L'abandon à la Providence divine*, vol. 1 (Paris: Gabalda, 1909) 42.

54. Ch. Péguy, *Le mystère de la charité de Jeanne d'Arc*, in *Oeuvres poétiques complètes*, Bibliothèque de la Pléiade 60, N.R.F. (Paris: Gallimard, 1957) 390.

55. Rev 3:5; 13:8; 17:8; 20:12, 15; 21:27. See also Exod 32:32-33; Ps 69:29; Dan 12:1; Phil 4:3.

56. St. Augustine (354–430), *La cité de Dieu*, XXX, 5, in *Oeuvres de saint Augustin*, Bibliothèque augustinienne 37 (Paris: Desclée de Brouwer, 1960) 719.

All Souls—Pages 252–257

1. See above, pp. 161–162.

2. For many people, even among Christians—especially those who do not often participate in the liturgy—the cult of all the faithful departed is more important than that of All Saints. For them, November 1 becomes the "Day of the Dead": They feel a duty to put flowers on the graves of their loved ones and to go as if on a pilgrimage to the cemetery. As for the liturgy, it has always made a clear distinction between the two feasts. But until the liturgical reform of Vatican Council II, Vespers of All Saints was immediately followed by Vespers of All Souls, after which in many places there was a procession to the cemetery. Prayers for all the dead were often introduced by a sermon. Many people considered this feast the most important of the year.

3. See the article "Défunts (Commémoration des)," in *Dictionnaire d'archéologie chrétienne et de liturgie*, tome 4/1, cols. 427–456.

4. These feelings have deep roots in human psychology. Even today, many people are not content to have simply inscribed on the tombstone the names and dates of birth and death of their dead, along with the usual "R.I.P." (*Requiescat in pace*—May he [or she] rest in peace). So we see all sorts of *ex votos*, photographs of the dead, vows of "perpetual memory," etc.

5. See art. cit. (n. 3), cols. 435–455; C. Pieri, "La mort en Occident dans l'épigraphie chrétienne. 3e—6e siècles," in *La Maison-Dieu* 144 (1980) 25–48.

6. See the article "Apocryphes du Nouveau Testament," in *Dictionnaire encyclopédique de la Bible*, 117 (No. 43) and 115 (No. 26).

7. According to the legend, Thecla was a young girl of Iconium in Phrygia, who was converted by the preaching of St. Paul and who miraculously escaped martyrdom on two occasions.

See the article "Thècle," in *Dictionnaire d'archéologie chrétienne et de liturgie*, tome 5/1, cols. 226–233 ("La légende de Thècle").

8. This is in fact one way to tell that we are here dealing with legend, and it helps us to determine at least approximately the date of their composition.

9. *De anima*, chapitre 51, in J.-P. Migne, *Patrologie latine*, vol. 2, col. 757.

10. *De corona*, chapitre 3, ibid., col. 79.

11. *Lettres*, 667, 2, ibid., vol. 4, col. 399.

12. St. Cyril of Jerusalem (ca. 315–386), *Catéchèses mystagogiques*, V, 8–9, Sources chrétiennes 126 (Paris: Cerf, 1966) 157, 159.

13. Ibid., V, 10, 159–160.

14. Deposed in 403 due to the intrigues of Theophilus, the patriarch of Alexandria (385–412) who was excommunicated by Pope Innocent I (401–417), St. John Chrysostom died in exile in 407.

15. The term *refrigerium* (refreshment) is used for the eternal happiness, the "consolation" that one hopes to obtain for the dead, in part by taking part in a funerary meal on the occasion of the death of a loved one as well as on anniversary dates. These meals are reminiscent of similar pagan practices. In fact, they did sometimes lead to abuses. The Church made efforts to suppress the practice, but was only partially successful, especially in North Africa, where the custom was deeply entrenched. So an effort was made to give the practice another slant or to replace it with another, in particular with a meal in which the poor were fed when someone died. This custom was maintained in a number of monasteries: In the refectory, the place of the person who had died remained empty for thirty days, sometimes marked by the presence of a crucifix, and during this month the food he or she would have consumed was given to the poor.

See A. Hamman, *Vie liturgique et vie sociale*, Bibliothèque de théologie (Paris, Tournai, Rome, New York: Desclée, 1968) 201–208 ("Les repas en l'honneur des morts").

16. St. John Chrysostom (ca. 350–407), *Homélie 41 sur la Première lettre aux Corinthiens*, in A. Hamman, *Jean Chrysostome commente saint Paul*, Les Pères dans la foi (Paris: Desclée de Brouwer, 1988) 339.

17. St. Augustine (350–407), *Confessions*, livre 9, XI, 27, in *Oeuvres de saint Augustin*, 14, Bibliothèque augustinienne (Paris: Desclée de Brouwer, 1962) 123.

18. Ibid., XI, 29, 125.

19. Ibid., XII, 32, 129.

20. *Les Constitutions apostoliques*, livre VIII, 42, in Sources chrétiennes 336 (Paris: Cerf, 1987) 259–261. The *Roman Missal* still contains special prayers for the eighth and the thirtieth days after the death, and for the anniversary. The death of a pope is observed with a period of grieving of nine days—the *novendiales*—during which the Eucharist is celebrated every day. The conclave to elect the successor of the dead pope gathers at the end of these nine days.

21. See above, pp. 161–162.

22. See above, pp. 236–237.

23. Amalarius was the disciple of Alcuin (ca. 735–801), the adviser to Charlemagne, who was behind the Carolingian reform in education and liturgy. The work of Amalarius, essentially liturgical, is of great value for our knowledge of the practices of the Church in those times when a combination of Roman and Gallic elements led eventually to the emergence of the Roman liturgy of the Middle Ages.

24. During the abbacy of St. Odilo, the monastery of Cluny and its dependent houses grew from 37 to 65. At the death of St. Hugues, the successor of St. Odilo (1049–1109), the Order counted 1200 houses. The abbot of Cluny gave them a constitution that put them all under the direct jurisdiction of the motherhouse. This centralization allowed, among other things, a unification of their liturgical customs. It was also true that Cluny, through its wide extension in the whole world, its power and independence in relation to the lords of the time and the bishops, was the principal instrument in the reform of the eleventh century, without mentioning its preponderant role in the evolution of Romanesque art. In 1088 St. Hugues undertook the construction of the church of Cluny, which counted three steeples. It was the largest edifice of Christendom up until the construction of St. Peter's in Rome.

25. Excerpt from the decree of St. Odilo, in *Dictionnaire d'archéologie chrétienne et de liturgie*, tome 6/1, col. 454.

26. Preface of the feast of All Saints.

27. See above, n. 15.

28. Commission Francophone Cistercienne, *Prières aux quatre-temps. Des poèmes et des chants*, Vivante liturgie 101 (Paris: Publications de Saint-André—Centurion, 1986) 116.

IN THE HOPE OF RESURRECTION—Pages 258-279

1. That is, Sundays, solemnities, and feast days celebrated like a Sunday, or on Sunday if it so falls, which is the case for the Commemoration of All the Dead. All these liturgies are the subject of the various volumes of *Days of the Lord*.

2. 2 Macc 12:43-46; Job 19:1, 23-27a; Wis 3:1-9; 4:7-15; Isa 25:6a, 7-9; Lam 3:17-26; Dan 12:1-3.

3. Acts 10:34-43; Rev 14:13; 20:11–21:1; 21:1-5a, 6b-7; Rom 5:5-11, 17-21; 6:3-9; 8:14-23, 31b-35, 37-39; 14:7-9, 10c-12; 1 Cor 15:20-24a, 25-28, 51-57; 2 Cor 4:14–5:1; 5:1, 6-10; Phil 3:20-21; 1 Thess 4:13-18; 2 Tim 2:8-13; 1 John 3:1-2, 14-16.

4. Pss 23:1-6; 25:6-7bc, 17-18, 20-21; 27:1, 4, 7, 8b, 9a, 13-14; 42:2, 3, 5bcd; 43:3-5; 63:2, 3-6, 8-9; 103:8, 10, 13-18; 116:5-6, 10-11, 15-16ac; 122:1-2, 4-9; 130:1-6b, 7-8; 143:1-2, 5-7ab, 8ab, 10. The *Lectionnaire pour les pays de langue française* adds: Pss 4:2, 7, 9; 16:1-2, 5-6, 9-10; 31:2-3, 6, 11, 15-17, 23-25; 34:5-6, 18-20, 23; 86:1-2, 5-6, 7, 15-16.

5. Matt 11:25; 25:34; John 3:16; 6:39, 40, 51; 11:25a, 26; Phil 3:20; 2 Tim 2:11-12a; Rev 1:5a, 6b; 14:13.

6. Matt 5:1-12a; 11:25-30; 25:1-13, 31-46; Mark 15:33-39; 16:1-6; Luke 7:11-17; 12:35-40; 23:33, 39-43, 44-46, 50, 52-53; 24:1-6a, 13-35; John 5:24-29; 6:37-40, 51-58; 11:17-27, 32-45; 12:23-28; 14:1-6; 17:24-26; 19:17-18, 25-39.

As well as the forty-five readings from the Bible that are suggested for the universal Church, the *Lectionnaire pour les pays de langue française* (Paris: Desclée—Mame, 1982) adds thirteen more: Job 14:1-3, 10-15; Wis 2:1-4a, 22-23; 3:1-9; 2:23; 3:1-6, 9; Rom 8:14-17; 8:18-23; 1 Cor 15:1-5, 11; 15:12, 16-20; 1 Pet 1:3-8; 1 John 4:7-10; Mark 10:28-30; Luke 2:25-38; John 3:16-17; 10:14-16.

For the funeral of children there is a choice between: Job 14:1-3, 10-15; Wis 2:23; 3:1-6, 9; Isa 25:6a, 7-9; Lam 3:17-26; Rom 6:3-4, 8-9; 14:7-9; 1 Cor 15:2-23; Eph 1:3-5; 1 Thess 4:13-14, 18; 1 Pet 1:3-8; 1 John 4:7-10; Rev 7:9-10, 15-17; 21:1, 3-5a; Matt 11:25-29; 18:1-5, 20; Mark 14:32-36; John 6:37-40; 10:14-16; 11:32b-38, 40; 17:1-3, 24-26; 19:25-30. To these texts the *Lectionnaire pour les pays de langue française* adds: Job 14:1-3, 10-15; Wis 2:23; 3:1-9; 1 Pet 1:3-8; 1 John 4:7-10; Rev 7:9-10, 15-17; 21:1, 3-5a; 21:9-10, 15-17; Matt 18:1-5, 10; Mark 14:32-36; John 10:14-16; 17:1-3; 24-26.

7. This does not really create any problems. Exactly the same thing happens at funeral Masses. Nevertheless, the *Missel dominical de l'assemblée* (Paris: Brepols, 1981) suggests three groups of readings: Isa 25:6-10a; Rev 21:1-5a, 6b-7; Mark 15:33-46 / Wis 3:1-6, 9; Rom 8:31b-35, 37-39; Luke 24:13-26 / Wis 4:7-15; 1 Thess 4:13-18; John 11:17-27. The *Missel de l'assemblée pour la semaine* (Paris: Brepols, 1985) suggests yet a fourth group: Isa 25:6-9; Rom 14:7-9, 10b-12; Luke 12:35-40. But these are only suggestions from the authors of these missals. They were made in the hope of helping those who find themselves perplexed by the abundance of texts.

8. The Word is proclaimed in order to throw light on the mystery being celebrated, and not directly in view of catechesis, to illustrate a sermon or to act as its point of departure. This is not the case, however, in the setting of a prayer vigil or some other meeting of the kind which can very well be planned around a theme that would call for the selection of a text or texts for that very purpose.

9. See H.-M. Féret, ''La mort dans la tradition biblique,'' in *Le mystère de la mort et sa célébration*, Lex orandi 12 (Paris: Cerf, 1951) 15–133; R. Martin-Achard, *De la mort à la résurrection d'après l'Ancien Testament* (Neuchâtel—Paris, 1956); P. Grelot, ''La théologie de la mort dans l'Ecriture sainte,'' in *La vie spirituelle. Supplément 77* (1966) 143–193; R. Poelman, ''Mort, où est ta victoire?'' in *Assemblées du Seigneur*, 1st series, No. 96 (Paris: Publications

de Saint-André—Cerf, 1967) 49–62; D. Dufrasne, "Le Lectionnaire des défunts: notes exégétiques pour l'homélie," in *Paroisse et liturgie* 50 (1968) 336–353; Groupe de Gap, "Mort et résurrection dans l'Ancien Testament (plan de travail)," in *Foi et vie. Cahiers bibliques* 8 (1970) 84–88.

10. Gen 2:7; Isa 29:16; 45:9; 64:7; Jer 18:6; Job 10:8-9; Rom 9:20-21.

11. Ps 139:13-15; Job 10:11.

12. See above, p. 50; the articles "Homme," "Corps," and "Sang," in *Dictionnaire encyclopédique de la Bible*, 593–595, 305–306, 1168–1169.

13. See the articles "Coeur and "Reins" in *Vocabulaire de théologie biblique*, cols. 176–179, 1085–1086; the articles "Coeur" and "Corps" in *Dictionnaire encyclopédique de la Bible* (preceding note, 288–289).

14. Indeed it is not easy to avoid all dualism, more satisfying to the intelligence, which is better equipped to grasp distinctions than unified concepts: infusion of the soul in the body, the separation of the soul and the body at the moment of death, etc. Still, dualism presents its own difficulties: How are we to understand a soul separated from a body, a vital principle in the absence of the matter it is supposed to animate, etc.? Moreover, as an entire system of thought, dualism leads almost inevitably to an attitude of disdain toward the body, which comes to be considered as the prison of the soul and without importance, which, paradoxically, sometimes leads to sexual immorality. The doctrines of reincarnation are based on a dualistic concept of man. Only the soul possesses individual identity. It reincarnates again and again in a series of bodies, for it has no particular adherence to any single one of them. These reincarnations have no other purpose than the progressive purification of the soul, and it is only the soul that counts.

15. This ancient concept of man considered in his physical and psychical—or spiritual—unity is closer to modern anthropology than the concept of Greek philosophy.

16. See the introductions of the *Bible de Jérusalem* (49–51) and of the *T.O.B.* (1463–1471); the article "Job, Livre," in *Dictionnaire encyclopédique de la Bible*, 673–674.

17. This poem in Job (ch. 19) follows the diatribe of one of his interlocutors (ch. 18).

18. Job 19:2-6; translation of the *T.O.B.*

19. It is composed of five poems corresponding to the five chapters of the present division of the Book. The first four are the poems called "alphabetical" because each verse begins with a letter of the Hebrew alphabet. This was a feature that made memorization easier; it also indicated that the subject had been treated thoroughly, as when we said that something has been gone through "from A to Z": see the *T.O.B.*, 1650.

20. See the introductions of the *Bible de Jérusalem* (2003–2008) and of the *T.O.B.* (581–583); the article "Maccabées, Livres," in *Dictionnaire encyclopédique de la Bible*, 763–765. The leader of this religious rebellion was called Judas Maccabeus, which gave the books their name. Since "Maccabeus" has the popular meaning of "macabre" [TRANSLATOR'S NOTE: *macchabée* in everyday French means "corpse"], it was recently decided to speak rather of "martyrs." In fact, this title is quite apt. For besides a good number of heroic acts, these books do tell of many martyrdoms, such as that of Eleazar (2 Macc 6:18-31) and that of the seven brothers (2 Macc 7:1-42) who preferred to die rather than to offend God.

21. Opening prayer.

22. Prayer over the Gifts.

23. See the introductions of the *Bible de Jérusalem* (961–962) and of the *T.O.B.* (2097–2101); the article "Sagesse, Livre," in *Dictionnaire encyclopédique de la Bible*, 1155–1157.

24. Burned down in 47 as a result of the war between Pompey (ca. 106–48 B.C.) and Caesar (ca. 101–44 B.C.) and partly reconstituted (200,000 vols.) by Anthony (ca. 83–30 B.C.) in the temple of Serapis, this prestigious library disappeared for good in A.D. 389 when the emperor of Byzantium, Theodosius I (379–395), had the temple closed.

25. Philo, the famous Jewish author (born between 15 and 10 B.C.), belonged to this com-

munity. Apollos, whom the Acts of the Apostles calls "an eloquent man" and "well-versed in the Scriptures," was a Jew of Alexandria who had converted to Christianity. See the article "Alexandrie," in *Dictionnaire encyclopédique de la Bible*, 32–34.

26. The *Lectionnaire pour la liturgie des défunts* suggests two passages taken out of this group of texts: Wis 1:4a, 22–23; 3:1-9; 2:33; 3:1-6, 9.

27. See P. Drijvers, *Les psaumes, genres littéraires et thèmes doctrinaux*, Lectio divina 21 (Paris: Cerf, 1958); D. Rimaud—J. Gelineau, *Guide du Psautier de la Bible de Jérusalem* (Paris: Cerf, 1962); A. George, *Prier les psaumes*, Foi vivante 15 (Paris: Cerf, 1967); R. Martin-Achard, *Approche des psaumes*, Cahiers bibliques (Neuchâtel—Paris: Delachaux and Niestlé, 1969); M. Mannati, "Pour prier avec les psaumes," in *Cahiers Evangile* 13 (1975); M. Gourges, "Les psaumes et Jésus—Jésus et les psaumes," in *Cahiers Evangile* 25 (1978); L. Monloubou, *L'imaginaire des psalmistes: Psaumes et symboles*, Lectio divina 101 (Paris: Cerf, 1979); P. Beauchamp, *Psaumes nuit et jour* (Paris: Seuil, 1980); P.-E. Bonnard, *Psaumes pour vivre*, Cahiers de l'Institut catholique de Lyon 4 (Lyon: Profac, 1981); J.-N. Aletti—J. Trublet, *Approche poétique et théologique des psaumes*, Initiations (Paris: Cerf, 1983); L. Sabourin, *Le Livre des psaumes traduit et interpreté*, Recherches (Paris: Bellarmin—Cerf, 1988); "Les psaumes: paroles sur Dieu, cris vers Dieu," in *Foi et vie, Cahier biblique* 27 (1988); L. Bouyer, *La Bible et l'Evangile*, Lectio divina 8 (Paris: Cerf, 1957) 227–243 ("Les psaumes, prières du peuple de Dieu").

28. For a list of psalms suggested by the *Lectionnaire pour la liturgie des défunts*, see above, n. 4.

29. Other factors came into play, as is the case any time someone begins to write: the degree and kind of personal culture, the use of language, style, etc.

30. This is so in particular for the Book of Qoheleth (Ecclesiastes).

31. *See Days of the Lord* 4:40–44.

32. Ibid., 116–118, and above, pp. 74–75.

33. Ibid., 3:143–146.

34. Ibid., 158–161.

35. Ibid., 2:149.

36. Ibid., 6:80–82.

37. Ibid., 2:129–132.

38. G. Bernanos, *La joie* (Paris: Plon, 1929) 237.

39. *Days of the Lord* 3:111–114.

40. Ibid., 4:247–248.

41. Ibid., 5:185–187; and above, pp. 45–48.

42. Ibid., 4:265–266.

43. Ibid., 3:331, n. 2.

44. Ibid., 3:68–69.

45. Ibid., 6:36–37.

46. Ibid., 4:245–246.

47. Ibid., 6:43–44.

48. Ibid., 6:62.

49. Ibid., 6:252–253.

50. Ibid., 3:142–143.

51. Ibid., 3:56–58.

52. Ibid., 4:194–195.

53. See above, pp. 19–22.

54. See above, pp. 71–73.

55. *Days of the Lord* 4:122–123.

56. Ibid., 3:172–173.

57. Ibid., 3:94–96.

58. Eucharistic Prayer IV.

59. Matt 27:46; Mark 15:34.

60. Pss 22:2; 31:6.

61. G. Marcel, *La Mort de Demain*, quoted in R. Troisfontaines, *De l'existence à l'être. La philosophie de Gabriel Marcel*, tome 2, Bibliothèque de la Faculté de philosophie et lettres de Namur 17 (Louvain: E. Nauwelaerts—Paris: J. Vrin, 1953) 151.

62. Eucharistic Prayer IV.

63. D. Rimaud, *Les arbres dans la mer* (Paris: Desclée, 1975) 66.

64. Commission Francophone Cistercienne, *La nuit, le jour . . . Hymnes et tropaires* (Paris: Desclée—Cerf, 1973) 169–170 (Fiche de chant S 77).

Dedication of the Basilica of the Lateran—Pages 280–281

1. Confiscated in 65 by Nero, the palace of the Lateran returned to the family of the Laterani in the second century; it was then taken over and made part of the imperial domain during the third century. See the articles "Latran," in the *Dictionnaire d'archéologie chrétienne et de liturgie*, tome 8/2, cols. 1529–1887; "Basilique," in *Catholicisme. Hier Aujourd-'hui, demain*, tome 1 (Paris: Letouzey et Ané, 1948) cols. 1295–1296; J. Maury—R. Percheron, *Itinéraires romains*, 3rd edition (Paris: Téqui, 1975) 256–264.

2. See the article "Constantin Ier," in *Dictionnaire encyclopédique du christianisme ancien*, vol. 1 (Paris: Cerf, 1990) 546–547.

3. From the sixth century on, there was built on the domain of the Lateran "an enormous complex of chapels, monasteries, hospices, and lodgings, all naturally fortified and contributing to the breaking up of Rome into enemy citadels. Logically, the life of the Church was centered here, as it was around the Vatican after the fifteenth century and in the vicinity of the Quirinal in the eighteenth century. The Lateran was the place where works that had survived from antiquity tended to be kept, such as the statue of Marcus Aurelius (121–180) and the she-wolf of the Capitol. Before it was pillaged by the Vandals it was here, too, that were kept the cult objects from the Temple of Jerusalem brought back by Titus" [translation by this book's translator] (J. Maury—R. Percheron, op. cit., 256).

4. Avignon was the residence of seven popes: Clement V (1305–1314), John XXII (1316–1334), Benedict XII (1334–1342), Clement VI (1342–1352), Innocent VI (1352–1362), Blessed Urban V (1362–1370), Gregory XI (1370–1378). It was Gregory XI who brought the papacy back to Rome in 1377, at the urgings of St. Catherine of Sienna (ca. 1347–1380).

5. Besides many regional councils, the 9th, 10th, 11th, 12th, and 18th ecumenical councils took place in the basilica and the palace of the Lateran: March 18–April 6, 1123; April 4, 1139; March 5–19 or 20, 1179; November 11–30, 1215; May 2, 1512–March 16, 1517. Vatican II (October 11, 1962–December 7, 1965) was the 21st ecumenical council. It was also at the palace of the Lateran that the agreements putting an end to the "Roman question," that had been an issue since 1871, were signed on February 11, 1929.

6. Every parish also celebrates as a solemn feast the anniversary of its own dedication. This celebration is fixed on October 25 or on the last Sunday of that month (in certain places in Belgium and France, from October 22 to November 6 respectively) for those churches whose date of consecration is unknown.

7. One should not forget that the word "cathedral" comes from Latin *cathedra*, which means "bishop's chair."

8. It is for this same reason that every Eucharist, the sacrament of unity par excellence, is celebrated in communion with the pope, the bishop of the diocese, and the entire college of bishops.

9. Opening prayer.

THE DWELLING PLACES WHERE GOD GATHERS HIS PEOPLE—
Pages 282–292

1. See L. Monloubou, *Un prêtre devient prophète: Ezéchiel,* Lectio divina 73 (Paris: Cerf, 1972) 153–180; the article "Ezéchiel," in *Dictionnaire encyclopédique de la Bible,* 463–464.
2. Ezek 8:1–11:25; 16:60-63.
3. Ezek 33:36.
4. Ezek 37:1-14: the vision of the dry bones.
5. Ezek 37:15-28; 47:13–48:34.
6. Ezek 40:1–47:23. This part of the Book of Ezekiel is full of ritual prescriptions. This is why the *Bible de Jérusalem* gives the title of "La torah d'Ezéchiel" (The torah of Ezekiel) to the eight last chapters of the book. See J. Asurmendi, "Le prophète Ezéchiel" in *Cahiers Evangile* 38 (1981); D. Ellul, "Ezéchiel 40:1–41:4: le nouveau Temple. Un complément confus de prescriptions sacerdotales ou l'épure prophétique d'une création sanctifiée?" in *Cahier biblique de Foi et vie* 25 (1986) 9–17.

This temple was never built according to the description of Ezekiel, but it is possible that Herod's architects may have drawn inspiration from this description for the plans of the "Third Temple" (as historians and archaeologists call it), which was built starting in 20–19 B.C. In fact, this building, which was essentially finished about ten years later, was built as an extension of the preceding temple, which was built after the Exile, completed in 515 B.C. This is why Jewish theologians call it the "Second Temple." It was the "Temple of Herod" that was destroyed in 70 by the armies of Titus. See the article "Temple," in *Dictionnaire encyclopédique de la Bible,* 1245–1246.

7. The text of the Book of Ezekiel, in particular chapters 40-48, has had a rocky history. See W. Zimmerli, "Le message du prophète Ezéchiel," in *Cahier biblique de Foi et vie* 11 (1972) 3–26.
8. This would be in September or October of 573 B.C., since the Jewish year begins in the fall.
9. From the outside wall of the holy of holies, the most sacred space of the sanctuary that could be reached only by passing through a whole succession of separations, one goes from the most profane area to more and more sacred ones. This is an image that evokes the successive purifications that the people of God must go through in preparing to meet God. These ten measurements have been compared to the ten words with which God organized the universe at the time of the creation (Gen 1): D. Ellul, art. cit., 16.
10. An interdict is a canonical punishment according to which the religious authorities forbid the celebration of the cult in a given church. This very heavy sentence, which is rarely laid, has as its purpose to make a religious community or a parish aware of its scandal-giving conduct, which is incompatible with the celebration of the cult and in particular the Eucharist.
11. Listening to the Word and observing the Law replaced the worship of the Temple: The liturgy of the synagogue began to evolve during this period. The old traditions and ancient fundamental texts were given a second look; a new language was elaborated. As it happened, the time of the Exile was one of intense theological and literary activity: the Book of Ezekiel, the second part of the Book of Isaiah, the Holiness Code (Lev 17–26), a part of the Pentateuch, the final redaction of Deuteronomy, and the revision of the earlier prophetic books. A whole new process had begun that was to continue right into the following period. See the article "Exil," in *Vocabulaire de théologie biblique,* cols. 420–421; in *Dictionnaire encyclopédique de la Bible,* 454.
12. For the description: 1 Kgs 7:23-26. See also 2 Chr 4:2-10; 2 Kgs 16:17-18. When the Babylonians took Jerusalem in 587 B.C., they tore it down and carried off the bronze (2 Kgs 25:13).

13. This oracle is read during the Easter Vigil: *Days of the Lord* 3:55–56.

14. St. Ephraem of Nisibis, deacon of Edessa (ca. 306–373), *Hymnes sur le Paradis,* II, 8–9, in Sources chrétiennes 137 (Paris: Cerf, 1968) 48–49.

15. Every period of drought is considered a catastrophe, even in temperate climates. Any prolonged lack of water makes us suddenly aware of the pricelessness of this gift of the heavens. All pollution is an ecological disaster to be very much feared.

See the article "Eau," in *Vocabulaire de théologie biblique,* cols. 303–309, and in *Dictionnaire encyclopédique de la Bible,* 268–269.

16. John 4:13-14; 7:37; 19:34; 1 Cor 10:4.

17. John 2:19, 21-22; Rev 22:1-17.

18. John 3:5; Acts 22:16; 1 Cor 6:11; Eph 5:26; Titus 3:5; Heb 10:22.

19. "Building" is often associated with "planting": Jdt 16:14; Isa 61:3; Jer 1:10; 2:21; 11:17; 12:14-17; 24:6; 31:28; 32:41; 42:10; 45:4.

20. See M.-A. Chevallier, "La construction de la communauté sur le fondement du Christ (1 Cor 3:5-17)," in *Paolo a una chiesa divisa (1 Cor 1–4),* Serie monografica di "Benedictina," Sezione Biblica-ecumenica 5 (Rome: Abbazia S. Paolo-fuori-le-mure, 1980) 107–129. (This volume, prepared by M. De Lorenzi, contains the lectures given during the fifth colloquium of exegetes that takes place regularly at the Roman abbey of St. Paul-Outside-the-Walls.

21. 2 Cor 10:8; 13:10.

22. See J. Dupont, *Le discours de Milet. Testament pastoral de saint Paul (Acts 20:18-36),* Lectio divina 32 (Paris: Cerf, 1962).

23. The election of Matthias (Acts 1:15-26); the setting apart of Barnabas and Saul who are sent on a mission (Acts 13:1-3).

24. 1 Cor 12:1-4. The Book of Acts speaks of Christians who were "prophets": 11:27-28; 13:1; 15:32; 19:6; 21:9-14. See also 1 Cor 11:5; 14:33-35.

25. This is the origin of the religious orders and congregations. Founded by charismatic men and women, these institutions have been created and adapted continuously through the centuries to respond to the needs of the times and the Church. Totally new forms of religious life are sometimes created, especially in our times.

26. The various ordained ministries also have their history. Recently, in the Latin Church, not only were the so-called "minor orders" suppressed, but also the subdiaconate. On the other hand, the order of "permanent deacons" was established, as well as new, non-ordained ministries, such as lay chaplains, both men and women, for hospitals, prisons, and schools; both men and women also have charge of some parishes. See A. Turck, "Des ministères pour quelle Eglise?" in *Communautés et liturgies* 58 (1976) 31–37 ("Au Zaïre: des paroisses officiellement confiées à des laïcs").

27. Vatican II published (November 18, 1965) a Decree on the Apostolate of the Laity (*Apostolicam actuositatem*), in *The Documents of Vatican II,* 489ff.

28. Certain members of the Christian community of Corinth forgot this. Some of them said, "I belong to Paul," and others, "I belong to Apollos," and still others, "I belong to Peter." The apostle objects strenuously to such a way of thinking and talking: "Is Christ divided? Was Paul crucified for you? Or were you baptized in the name of Paul?" (1 Cor 1:10-13). This text is read on the Third Sunday in Ordinary Time, Year A: *Days of the Lord* 4:31-33.

29. This text is read on the Eighteenth Sunday in Ordinary Time, Year C: *Days of the Lord* 6:150-151.

30. 1 Cor 3:18-19a, 21-23.

31. Matt 21:12-17; Mark 11:15-19; Luke 19:45-48.

32. After the homage Jesus accepted from the crowds, which made plain just how enthusiastic the populace was about him and his message, his actions in the Temple seemed to bespeak even greater pretensions. They were the talk of the city. The authorities must

have wondered just how far he was planning to go if they let things go on like that; there must be some way that they could show him to everyone as an imposter. This is why they asked him, "By what authority are you doing these things? And who gave you this authority?" (Matt 21:23; Mark 11:28; Luke 20:2).

33. John 2:1-11.

34. Ibid., 3:1-21.

35. See X. Léon-Dufour, *Lecture de l'Evangile selon saint Jean*, vol. 1, Parole de Dieu (Paris: Seuil, 1988) 246-275. The pages that follow owe much to this commentary.

36. From the scene at Bethany where the Baptist pays homage to Jesus (John 1:28) to the "sign" at Cana, the beginning of the John's Gospel reports what happened during the first week of the ministry of the Lord. Now it is said that the "first sign" produced by Jesus "made manifest his glory" and inspired faith in his disciples: the seventh day, like the resurrection. Similarly, right after telling the story of what happened in the Temple, the evangelist introduces Nicodemus, who intervened in Jesus' favor when a first attempt was made to arrest him (John 7:48-52) and who played an active role at the time when Jesus was being buried (John 20:39).

37. We sometimes tend to forget that the Gospels are not just the story of the sayings and actions of Jesus throughout his life. They are the proclamation of the good news and were preached to the Christian community for a long time before they were ever set down on paper. The very way they are presented points to this fact, and this can be seen especially clearly in the case of the Gospel of John. See *Days of the Lord* 3: 310, n. 19; 6:348, n. 43.

38. These were the animals that the faithful had to buy for offering sacrifice; the money-changers offered for sale the only coins that were authorized for offerings. So even though all this activity was required for the cult, it nevertheless brought a marketplace atmosphere into a whole section of the sacred enclosure, as merchants and money-changers undoubtedly took advantage of the situation to turn a tidy profit. This is still a problem today in places of pilgrimage. The pilgrims quite legitimately want to buy candles to burn in the sanctuary, and sometimes souvenirs as well. All that the Church authorities can do is to forbid the presence of such shops within the area over which it has jurisdiction and to make sure that nothing becomes commercialized that should not be, such as water from the grotto at Lourdes. As regards all the rest—the taste or lack thereof in the choice of objects of piety, the use of holy pictures on any sort of object whatever, the exploitation of the naive or superstition-tainted faith of some of the pilgrims—the battle is much more difficult and uncertain. One would have to convince both the merchants and the buyers of the inappropriateness of all that. As it is, what we hear from the merchants is: "That's what people want! If they don't find it in my shop, they'll go looking for it somewhere else; they don't even see the better-quality objects that I have for sale."

38. *Le Psautier. Version oeucuménique. Texte liturgique* translates: "L'amour de ta maison m'a perdu" (the love of your house has caused my ruin).

The New Testament quotes Ps 69, applying several verses to Christ: Matt 27:34, 48; John 15:25; Rom 15:3.

The Synoptic Gospels here refer to Isa 56:7 to explain the actions of Jesus. In those times, Christians may have had certain collections of quotations from the Bible, called *Testimonia* (witnessings) that they would study, searching for explanations of the teachings of Jesus that would be useful in catechesis. On this "Bible of the early Church" see C. H. Dodd, *Conformément aux Ecritures* (Paris: Seuil, 1968).

40. Matt 26:61; Mark 14:58.

41. This is explicit in the Synoptics. When he was asked by whose authority he did these things, Jesus answered with another question: "Where was John's baptism from? Was it of heavenly or human origin?" When they did not answer him, he, too, refused to answer their questions: (Matt 21:23-27; Mark 11:27-33; Luke 20:1-8).

42. The evangelist uses three different terms, each with its own precise meaning. First, he speaks of the *oikos* ("house") of the Father, then of the *hieron* ("temple"), a term that was used for the entire building where the faithful gathered, and lastly, *naos* ("sanctuary"), which designated the place of the divine presence deep within the temple precincts. We should recall that most Greco-Roman temples were rather small and were not places of assembly for crowds of the faithful, but were essentially sanctuaries of the divinity, represented by a statue. The altar used for sacrifices was located outside the temple, on the stairs that led up to the sanctuary. Many of the ancient temples that are still standing exhibit the bases of these altars at that spot on the steps.

43. The temple built by Herod the Great (37 B.C.–A.D. 4) had been destroyed in 70 by the armies of the Roman general Titus.

44. Matt 4:5-7; Luke 4:9-12.

45. John 2:11; 20:30-31; Matt 12:38; 16:1-4; Mark 8:11-12; Luke 11:16, 29.

46. Tob 13:16-18; 14:5-6; Sir 36:18-19; Isa 60:7, 13; Ezek 40–44 (see the first reading); Hag 2:7-9.

47. X. Léon-Dufour, op. cit. (n. 35) 270–271.

48. St. Caesarius of Arles (ca. 470–543), *Homélie pour l'anniversaire de la dédicace d'une église,* in *La Liturgie des Heures,* vol. 4 (Paris: Cerf—Desclée—Desclée de Brouwer—Mame, 1980) 1123–1124.

49. Originally, a church was officially dedicated primarily by the celebration of the Eucharist, with the bishop presiding, surrounded by the entire body of clergy and the faithful. Later on this rite was expanded to include the translation of the relics of saints and the lustration of the building with holy water. Still later this celebration became one of the most ostentatious and pompous of all the liturgy. With the Pontifical of the thirteenth century still in use even as late as 1961, after the celebrations of the night before, it still took several hours to carry out all the rites provided for this circumstance. In 1961 Pope John XXIII (1958–1963) had work begun on a simplification of this ritual, which was completely revised by the Pontifical published in 1977 by Paul VI (1963–1978). The celebration of the Eucharist again occupies the place of honor as the principal rite of the liturgy of the dedication of a church. See A. G. Martimort, *The Church at Prayer: Principles of the Liturgy,* I (Collegeville, Minn.: The Liturgical Press, 1987).

50. See R. Gantoy, "L'assemblée dans l'économie du salut," in *Assemblées du Seigneur,* 1st series, No. 1 (Bruges: Publications de Saint-André, 1962) 55–80. It is symptomatic that in order to ensure better cohesion in the assembly which then appears more as the subject of the liturgy, many celebrations take place outdoors on the esplanade in front of the church or basilica, for instance, rather than inside the church. This is done particularly in Rome for the major liturgies where the pope presides and for the funeral of a pope. The reason for holding these liturgies outdoors is not always a lack of room, as, for instance, in St. Peter's, which is sometimes ample for the participating crowds.

51. Translation of the Latin hymn *Urbs Jerusalem beata* from the former Office of a Dedication, in *La Liturgie des Heures,* vol. 4, 1203; the Latin text alone and the Gregorian melody are found in *Hymnaire de La Liturgie des Heures* (Paris: Cerf—Chalet—Levain, 1990) 290.

The Immaculate Conception of the Virgin Mary— Pages 293–297

1. After the invasion of Italy by Alaric I, king of the Visigoths (395–410), Pelagius took refuge in North Africa in 410, where he remained for some time before leaving for Pales-

tine. His teachings were systematized by Julian, the bishop of Eclanum in Apulia, near Beneventum (d. ca. 454).

2. Pelagianism was condemned by several African Councils, in particular the Council of Carthage (summer of 416 and May 1, 418), and the Council of Ephesus in 431.

3. St. Augustine often has recourse to the argument of the practice of the Church, to which those who contradicted him also referred for their viewpoint.

St. Augustine does not stop at the necessity of baptism. He developed a whole doctrine of grace, without which humans cannot accomplish a single good work, even when they have been "reborn of water and the Spirit." His positions on the absolute gratuitousness of grace were somewhat hardened by certain of his disciples, and towards the end of his life (and especially after his death), they led to virulent reactions on the part of certain monks, such as Cassian (d. ca. 435), Vincent of Lérins (d. a little before 450), and Faustus, monk and then abbot of Lérins before becoming bishop of Riez in Provence (d. before 500), all of whom accused the bishop of Hippo of innovation. The term "semi-pelagianism" has been used in the context of this affair. But this term is totally inappropriate. This is not a case of watered-down Pelagianism. What we have here is a perfectly understandable reaction on the part of the monks, in itself admirable enough, as are also some of the writings of Pelagius, which are of a deeply spiritual nature. For these religious, the somewhat rigid "augustinianism" of certain of his disciples seemed to deny the necessity for effort on the part of human beings, and therefore the value of any ascesis.

4. This apocryphal writing tells the life of Mary, whose birth was granted by God to Joachim and Anne, despite their advanced age. It has exercised considerable influence on Christian piety and on the liturgy: Joachim and Anne, the nativity of Mary, and her presentation in the Temple have become part of the liturgical calendar, and have been the subject of many works of art and literature. See the article "Apocryphes du Nouveau Testament," in *Dictionnaire encyclopédique de la Bible*, 115.

5. Canterbury and the monasteries were in frequent contact, further maintained when new monks were regularly sent. Under these conditions, it is only normal that the liturgical practices of the monasteries were largely adopted in England.

6. Letter 174, in J.-P. Migne, *Patrologie latine*, vol. 172, col. 356.

7. This individual, professor at Salamanca and canon of Toledo, Valencia, and Segovia, played an important role in the Council of Basel. He was part of a minority that remained where they were. A fervent partisan of the anti-pope Felix V and then reconciled through the actions of the legitimate pope Nicholas V, he wrote a precious history of the Council of Basel.

8. Convoked by Pope Martin V (1417–1431) shortly before his death, this council undertook the reform of the Church. But it came into conflict with the following pope, Eugene IV (1431–1447), who in 1433 did finally acknowledge its legitimacy. In 1438 the assembly was transported to Ferrara and then to Florence. But a minority of its members remained in Basel, and after having elected an anti-pope in 1439—Felix V, who submitted to Nicholas V (1447–1455) in 1449—they continued to hold their own irregular council until 1448.

9. Constitution *Cum praeexcelsa* of February 28, 1476, in G. Dumeige, *La foi catholique. Textes doctrinaux du Magistère de l'Eglise* (Paris: Orante, 1961) 233.

10. Constitution *Gravis nimis* of September 4, 1483, in G. Dumeige, op. cit., 234.

11. In G. Dumeige, op. cit., 234–235.

12. The use of three liturgical compositions at once could lead to some confusion, but it represented a real enrichment. The choice of St. Pius V was not particularly fortunate, for the composition of Leonard of Nogarolis was of great poetical beauty. He had drawn abundantly on the Song of Songs. A few religious orders such as the Franciscans and a few countries such as Spain were authorized to keep it.

13. Bull *Sollicitudo omnium Ecclesiarum*, in G. Dumeige, op. cit., 236–237.

14. We have here a particularly interesting example of what has often been found to have happened in the history of the Church. While the magisterium of the Church enjoys a guarantee of infallibility, this infallibility is shared to a degree with the entire Christian people; at the very least, the magisterium's privilege does not operate in isolation from the people. The Christian people cannot be in error when as a whole they believe in a given truth. It has often happened that the people have been ahead of the declarations of the magisterium. Personal piety is the usual way in which the faith of the Church, "the people of God," finds expression.

15. He received 604 responses: only 56 or 57 bishops were in opposition to such a definition; but of these, 24 were against the timing of it alone, while only 4 or 5 were opposed to it on the basis of dogma.

16. On the history of this doctrine, see J. Galot, "L'immaculée conception," in *Maria. Etudes sur la Sainte Vierge* under the direction of H. Du Manoir, vol. 7 (Paris: Beauchesne, 1964) 9–116; P. Tena, "La fête de l'Immaculée conception dans l'histoire et dans le dogme," in *Assemblées du Seigneur*, 1st series, No. 80 (Bruges: Publications de Saint-André, 1966) 7–18.

17. Bull *Ineffabilis Deus*, in G. Dumeige, op. cit., 238.

It was four years later, between February 11 and July 16, 1858, that the Virgin Mary appeared at Lourdes to Bernadette Soubirous (1844–1879), calling herself "the Immaculate Conception."

18. Prov 8:22-31 is now read at the Mass of Holy Trinity and also at the Mass of the Presentation of the Virgin Mary.

19. Preface.

20. G. Martelet, *L'Au-delà retrouvé. Christologie et fine dernières* (Paris: Desclée, 1974) 152.

MARY: FULL OF GRACE, NEW EVE, MOTHER OF THE LIVING—
Pages 298–306

1. See the article "Péché," in *Vocabulaire de théologie biblique*, cols. 932–935; the article "Chute de l'homme," in *Dictionnaire encyclopédique de la Bible*, 275–277.

2. See the articles "Genèse, Livre" and "Pentateuque," in *Dictionnaire encyclopédique de la Bible*, 523–525, 1002–1003.

Gen 3:9-15 is read on the Tenth Sunday in Ordinary Time, Year B: *Days of the Lord* 5:90-92.

3. See the article "Nudité," in *Dictionnaire encyclopédique de la Bible*, 909–910.

4. See the article "Serpent du paradis," in *Dictionnaire encyclopédique de la Bible*, 1193–1194, and above, p. 226.

5. Genesis says as explicitly as possible that "the serpent" is a creature of God, which had gone astray (Gen 3:1). It in no way provides any basis for dualistic thinking, according to which there would exist two equal and antagonistic powers, one at the origin of all evil, and the other, of all good.

6. See A. Vanneste, "Le Protévangile: Gen 3:9-15," in *Assemblées du Seigneur*, 2nd series, No. 41 (Paris: Publications de Saint-André—Cerf, 1971) 26–32.

7. In the collective sense: "Abram continued: 'See, you have given me no offspring' " (Gen 15:3); God says to him: "Look up at the sky and count the stars, if you can. Just so," he added, "shall your descendants be" (Gen 15:5); "It is through Isaac that descendants shall bear your name" (Gen 21:12).

In the individual sense: After the birth of Seth, Eve says: "God has granted me more offspring because of Abel . . . because Cain slew him" (Gen 4:25).

8. A. Vanneste, art. cit. (n. 6), p. 28.

9. This translation is called the "Vulgate" (from "popular," "widespread"). Even though other Biblical versions were always consulted—the Hebrew, the Greek, and a number of ancient translations—the "Vulgate," declared "authentic" by the Council of Trent (4th session, April 8, 1546) has always been the official translation for the liturgy in Latin (G.

Dumeige, *La foi catholique. Textes doctrinaux du Magistère de l'Eglise*, 99–100). In our day, completely new translations for the liturgy have been made in the vernacular of all the modern languages, using the different versions—Hebrew, Greek, and Latin.

The fact that, for French speakers, there are three different translations—the *Bible de Jérusalem*, the *T.O.B.*, and the *Bible de Maredsous*—has been particularly enriching. It is interesting and profitable to consult all three when studying a particular text. Moreover, the notes in each of the three explain the justification for a given translation, and they mention other possible ways to translate the passage.

10. Women play an important role in the history of the promise: Sarah (Gen 21:1-20), Rebekah (Gen 25:19-21; 30:1-8, 22-24), and in the announcements of the Messiah (the prophecy of the Emmanuel: Isa 7:14).

11. St. Justin (ca. 100–165), *Dialogue avec le Juif Tryphon*, 9, in A. Hamman, *La philosophie passe au Christ*, Littératures chrétiennes 3 (Paris: Editions de Paris, 1958) 290.

12. See the articles "Adam" and "Péché," in *Vocabulaire de théologie biblique*, cols. 16–19, 932–935; *Dictionnaire encyclopédique de la Bible*, 15–16, 994–997.

13. On the Letter to the Ephesians, see the introductions of the *Bible de Jérusalem* (1621–1622) and of the *T.O.B.* (édition intégrale 1988, 2815–2819); the article "Ephésiens, Epître," in *Dictionnaire encyclopédique de la Bible*, 416–418; J. Cambier, *Vie chrétienne en Eglise. L'épître aux Ephésiens, lue aux Chrétiens d'aujourd'hui* (Paris: Desclée, 1966); M. Zerwick, *La lettre aux Ephésiens, Parole et prière* (Paris: Desclée, 1967); R. Baulès, *L'insondable richesse du Christ. Etude des thèmes de l'épître aux Ephésiens*, Lectio divina 66 (Paris: Cerf, 1971).

14. Eph 1:3-14. This act of thanksgiving is read in its entirety on the Fifteenth Sunday in Ordinary Time, Year B: *Days of the Lord* 5:139–141. See also the Second Sunday after Christmas: ibid., 1:250.

15. In the Greek, verses 3-14 are one sentence.

16. This Trinitarian and Christological schema of the unfolding of grace is reflected also in the liturgy. See C. Vagaggini, *Initiation théologique à la liturgie*, vol. 1, 135–174 ("La liturgie et la dialectique christologique et trinitaire du salut. *A Patre per Christum in Spiritu ad Patrem*").

17. The *Bible de Jérusalem* translates: "C'est en lui que nous avons été mis à part" (It is in him that we have been made separate), and the *T.O.B.*: "En lui nous avons reçu notre part" (In him we have received our portion).

18. In everyday speech, choice implies a sorting out of what is acceptable and what is not: We leave some items aside, we exclude what we do not want. But this is not the case with God when he is said to choose. He excludes no one from his love. But he gives to each his or her place, vocation, and function within the perspective of his plan for the salvation of all.

19. The Litanies of the Blessed Virgin (called the Litanies of Loretto), in *Prières de toujours*, 137–138.

20. This is why it is read at the Mass of the Fourth Sunday in Advent, Year B: *Days of the Lord* 1:148–154.

21. See above, pp. 140–142.

22. To be exact, this same Gospel is read on August 22 (Holy Mary the Queen) and on October 7 (Our Lady of the Rosary). It is also suggested, among other passages of the Gospel, for the Masses of the Common of the Virgin Mary and for the Mass of the Rite of the Consecration of a Virgin.

23. See P. Claudel, "Les maternités miraculeuses," in *Assemblées du Seigneur*, 1st series, No. 6 (Bruges: Publications de Saint-André, 1965) 58–73.

24. Isa 6:1-13; Jer 1:4-10; Ezek 2:1-3:27.

25. Before the Council, the Missal called it the Annunciation of the Virgin Mary.

26. First reading of the Third Sunday in Advent, Year C: *Days of the Lord* 1:116.

27. First reading of the Fourteenth Sunday in Ordinary Time, Year A: *Days of the Lord* 4:114–115.

28. See the Fourth Sunday in Advent, Year A: *Days of the Lord* 1:139–140, and the feast of the Annunciation of the Lord.

29. "Full of grace" is one compound word in Greek: *kecharitomene.* This is why hyphens are used [in the French translation]. In the early Church the newly baptized were called the "re-born."

30. The psalms refer to this divine protection as the "shadow" of the Lord, coming from his hand or his wings: Pss 91:1; 17:8; 57:2; 63:8; 121:5. This image reminds one of the experience of Exodus (Exod 40:35; Wis 19:7) and the wonders God will accomplish at the end of days (Isa 4:5-6; Bar 5:7-8). "The shadow," like "the cloud," is the place where God's presence is made manifest. When the Temple was consecrated, "the cloud" filled the holy of holies, and Solomon cried out in amazement: "The Lord intends to dwell in the dark cloud" (1 Kgs 8:12). And lastly, the Beloved of the Song of Songs says: "I delight to rest in his shadow" (Cant 2:3).

31. "How can this be, since I have no relations with a man?" does not mean that Mary had taken a vow of virginity; she was in fact engaged to be married to Joseph. For that matter, this question is of little interest in the theological context of this page of the Gospel. What Luke wants to emphasize is the virgin birth of Jesus.

32. G. Martelet, *L'au-delà retrouvé. Christologie des fins dernières,* 152.

33. G. Bernanos, *Journal d'un curé de campagne,* 259.

34. Ch. Péguy, *Le porche du mystère de la deuxième vertu,* in *Oeuvres poétiques complètes* (Paris, La Pléiade 60, N.R.F.: Gallimard, 1957) 577.

35. Commission Francophone Cistercienne, *La nuit, le jour* (Paris: Desclée—Cerf, 1973) 134; *La Liturgie des Heures,* vol. 1, 1293–1294; *Missel noté de l'assemblée,* 346.

In the Margins of a Travel Diary Pages 307-317

1. Three texts of the Old Testament and eight of the New Testament occur twice; the story of the annunciation is read three times.

2. See *Days of the Lord* 1:13–16, 4:4–7.

3. One can sometimes omit a paragraph or even a whole page without really losing the benefits of this usual way of reading a book. This is what we do for the Gospels in Ordinary Time, even though we speak of "continuous reading."

On the other hand, in the case of a collection of poems or novellas we do not need to read them in any particular order or in their entirety. And the Bible, which is in reality a collection—or even a whole library—of works of all kinds of literary genres, contains, as well, a collection of poems, the psalms, that we do not necessarily read in order or in their entirety. But we can also read them "seriously," in order to gain a better appreciation of them.

4. For introductions to the reading of the Bible, besides those found in the *Bible de Jérusalem,* the *T.O.B.,* and other modern translations, see W. Harrington, *Nouvelle introduction à la Bible* (Paris: Seuil, 1971); E. Charpentier, "Pour une première lecture de la Bible," in *Cahiers Evangile* 10 (1974); *A la découverte de la Bible,* vol. 1: *Chemin d'un peuple, histoire d'un livre: L'Ancien Testament;* vol. 2: *Un seul Jésus Christ, une foule de témoins: Le Nouveau Testament* (Paris: Editions ouvrières, 1980); "Une première approche de la Bible," in *Cahiers Evangile* 35 (1981); P. Bagot—J.-Cl. Duss, *Pour lire la Bible* (Paris: Les bergers et les mages, 1983); *Aujourd'hui la Bible* (Paris: Editions de Paris, 1985); R. Poelman, *Ouvrons la Bible* (Paris—Fribourg: Editions Saint Paul, 1990).

For each book, refer to the introductions of the *Bible de Jérusalem* and the *T.O.B.* (édition intégrale 1988) or other modern translations of the Bible. *Days of the Lord* gives a bibliography for each book as it occurs for the first time in the Lectionary for Sundays in Ordinary Time.

5. All the modern Bibles contain notes, some more extensive than others, and they also give in the margin references to parallel passages in Scripture that may be useful to look up, and borrowings (exact or implicit quotations) from other books.

6. Origen (ca. 185–243) did an enormous amount of work in this area. He set out in six columns—whence the name "Hexapla"—the text of the entire Old Testament: the Hebrew, its phonetic transcription, four Greek translations (the one of Aquila, second century B.C.; the one of Symmachus, ca. 200; the Septuagint, second–first centuries B.C. that is quoted in the New Testament; and the one of Theodotian, A.D. first century). See the article "Versions anciennes de la Bible," in *Dictionnaire encyclopédique de la Bible*, 1302–1308.

7. In other words, "Before finding out what a text of the Bible means to *me*, I should find out what *it* says first." For reading the Bible is not the same as listening to a musical composition or looking at a work of art or even appreciating a poem. Of course, it is of value to know the intention and the attitude of the composer, the artist, or the poet, the "message" that he or she wishes to express. But there is no reason why one should not look for what is personally appealing in a work of art, to be primarily interested in the feelings that it evokes. We can decide we don't like it because "it says nothing to me," because we don't find any meaning in it, even if our opinion is totally different from that of critics and connoisseurs.

8. The work of the exegetes who do not share our faith is of great interest and value, depending on their degree of competence. Whether or not they are believers, they all share the same methods for establishing a text with a view to determining its precise objective meaning. We can all benefit from sharing the fruit of our experiences, particularly for the refinement of our methods of work, and for learning new ones.

A special place should be accorded ancient and modern Jewish exegesis. The Bible is our common heritage, and Christians owe what we call the Old Testament to the Jews. The major Greek translations (see above, n. 6) that Christians continue to consult were established by Jewish scholars. However, we should not forget that while the Bible is not the private property of anyone, we receive it from the Church and we read it within the Church, even when we read it in private. Because of its ministry, the Church can intervene to "define" the meaning of a particular text. What actually happens most often is that it intervenes to invalidate one particular suggested meaning; but such interventions calling on its infallible doctrinal authority are rare. One instance that comes to mind is the "Galileo affair" (1564–1642). It is of course regrettable that it condemned a theory which at the time seemed presumptuous even scientifically, and which seemed in contradiction with the Bible story of creation. The Church recognized its error when Galileo's theory could no longer be in question, and above all when a better understanding of the Bible and of the literary genres of the first chapters of Genesis allowed a fresh look at the doctrine of creation.

In modern times, certain interventions on the part of the "Pontifical Commission for Biblical Studies" (more commonly referred to as the "Biblical Commission"), created October 30, 1902, by Pope Leo XIII (1878–1903), have sometimes slowed down research or even stopped it altogether. But its decisions, which have the same value as those of the other "Roman Congregations" are not irreversible: history has borne this out.

9. In fact, in monasteries where *lectio divina* holds a place of great importance as one of the sources of spiritual life, it traditionally consists of the study of Scripture, the Fathers of the Church, and the major spiritual authors.

10. The bibliography relative to *lectio divina* is considerable, but not always very accessible, because a number of particularly interesting and well-documented articles have ap-

peared in periodicals of fairly small readership, in particular monasteries or other religious houses. See, among others, J. Leclercq, "La lecture divine," in *La Maison-Dieu* 5 (1946) 21–33, published also in *La liturgie et les paradoxes chrétiens* (Paris: Cerf, 1963) 243–257; A. Louf, "Exégèse scientifique ou *lectio* monastique," in *Collectanea cisterciensia* 22 (1960) 225–247; P.-Y. Emery, "L'Ecriture méditée. Quatre degrés: lecture, méditation, prière, contemplation," in *Lumen vitae* 20 (1965) 619–631; the article "Lectio divina et lecture spirituelle," in *Dictionnaire de spiritualité*, tome 9 (Paris: Beauchesne, 1976) cols. 470–487; E. Bianchi, *Une introduction à la "lectio divina,"* Vie monastique 15, Spiritualité orientale et vie monastique (Abbaye de Bellefontaine, 1983).

11. On Sundays in Eastertide the first reading is taken not from the Old Testament, but from the Acts of the Apostles.

During the week, there are only two readings: The first is taken from the Old Testament or from the apostolic writings. See "Plan des lectures bibliques en semaine," for example in *Missel de l'assemblée pour la semaine* (Paris: Brepols, 1985) 14–15. What we have here is "semi-continuous" reading (the excerpts are taken in the order in which they appear in the book) for the first reading, and "continuous" reading (in order, and without "skipping" anything, or almost nothing) for the Gospel.

All these texts are presented in N. Berthier—R. Gantoy, *Chaque jour ta Parole. Le Lectionnaire de semaine: notes de lecture, textes pour la prière*, 7 vols. (Paris: Publications de Saint-André—Cerf, 1979–1980).

12. See above, n. 3.

13. See above, n. 1.

14. The spiritual writers used imagery in order to express the individual character of each reading and the progression from one to the other. See Guigue II Le Chartreux (d. 1188): "Reading is the attentive study of Scripture, practiced by the studious mind. Meditation is one of the functions of the intelligence, which departs from the religious opening of the heart to God in order to push away all evil and obtain the good. Contemplation is a certain raising of the soul up to God, leaving itself behind, and tasting the joys of eternal sweetness. Having then described the four steps, we have now to examine how they affect us. Reading seeks the sweetness of a blessed life, meditations find this sweetness, prayer asks for it, and contemplation savors it. If we may be permitted to express ourself in such terms, reading brings solid nourishment to our mouths, meditation chews on this food, prayer obtains the right to taste it, and contemplation is the sweetness itself that rejoices us and renews us. Reading lies in the outer skin, meditation in the marrow, prayer in the expression of desire, and contemplation in the enjoyment of the sweetness obtained" (*Lettre sur la vie contemplative.* [*L'échelle des moines*], II–III, Sources chrétiennes 163 (Paris: Cerf, 1970) 85–87.

15. See *Days of the Lord* 6:362, n. 8.

16. Ibid., 3:111–114.

17. This is the tendency of what is called "allegorizing" exegesis, which uses a kind of symbolism that is sometimes a little artificial and not very convincing to the modern mind.

18. *Days of the Lord* has tried to make a contribution to the understanding of what we hear and do during the liturgy. See vol. 1, 17–19.

19. Mark 4:10; 7:17; 10:10; 13:3; John 16:19 (Jesus anticipates the question that the disciples do not dare ask him).

20. 1 Cor 3:11; 1 Pet 2:4, 7.

21. It met at three different periods: 1545–1549, 1551–1552, and 1562–1563.

22. This desire for deeper reform was not due to some sort of prejudice of the reforming party. The very year it was created, the Congregation for the Rites started an inquiry into the need for a reform of the liturgical books. In the seventeenth and eighteenth centuries the discovery of ancient Sacramentaries—the ancestors of the Missal—gave new vigor to

the idea: Shouldn't the faithful be allowed to benefit from these treasures from the prayer of bygone centuries? But immobility and resistance won out. Still, there was real reform in the liturgies of the dioceses of France. For a discussion of this affair, see A. G. Martimort, *The Church at Prayer: Principles of the Liturgy*, I (Collegeville, Minn.: The Liturgical Press, 1987) 23–76.

23. *Missale romanum ex decreto concilii tridentini restitutum, S. Pie V pontificis maximi jussu editum, aliorum pontificum cura recognitum, a Pio X reformatum et Benedicti XV auctoritate vulgatum.*

24. The new *Lectionary for the Mass* was promulgated May 25, 1969. A second edition, with modifications and additions, was promulgated January 21, 1981.

25. *Ecclesia semper reformanda.* See Y. Congar, *Vraie et fausse réforme dans l'Eglise,* Unam Sanctam 20 (Paris: Cerf, 1950) 461–462; ''Comment l'Eglise sainte doit se revouveler sans cesse,'' in *Irénikon* 34 (1961) 17.

26. Vatican II, *Constitution on the Sacred Liturgy (Sacrosanctum Concilium),* preamble (No. 1), in *The Documents of Vatican II,* 137.

27. The most typical instances are the solemnites of the Holy Trinity, the Body and Blood of Christ, and the Sacred Heart of Jesus; the Presentation of Jesus in the Temple; the feast of Christ the King. See above, pp. 5–7, 38–40, 66–68, 103–105; 4:256–264.

28. *Constitution sur la liturgie,* Nos. 9 and 10, op. cit. (n. 25), 155.

29. At the opening of the Council, in *Vatican II,* op. cit. (n. 25), 5.

30. At the end of the Council, ibid., 638 (the quotation is from St. Augustine).

31. Nicetas of Remesiana (seventh century), *Te Deum,* in *La Liturgie des Heures,* vol. 1, 805–806; vol. 3, 479; vol. 4, 381 (Fiche de chant L 62); *Missel noté de l'assemblée,* 458–459.